19

The Dominican Republic Reader

THE

DOMINICAN

REPUBLIC

READER

HISTORY, CULTURE, POLITICS

Eric Paul Roorda, Lauren Derby, and Raymundo González, editors

DUKE UNIVERSITY PRESS   *Durham and London*   2014

Printed in the United States of America on acid-free paper ∞
Typeset in Monotype Dante by BW&A Books, Inc.

Library of Congress Cataloging-in-Publication Data
The Dominican Republic reader : history, culture, politics /
Eric Paul Roorda, Lauren Derby, and Raymundo González, editors.
pages cm—(The Latin America readers)
Includes bibliographical references and index.
ISBN 978-0-8223-5688-2 (cloth : alk. paper)
ISBN 978-0-8223-5700-1 (pbk. : alk. paper)
1. Dominican Republic—Civilization. 2. Dominican Republic—History.
3. Dominican Republic—Social life and customs. I. Roorda, Eric.
II. Derby, Lauren Hutchinson. III. González, Raymundo. IV. Series: Latin
America readers.
F1935.D66 2014
972.93—dc23
2013047598

For A. E., Alida, and Frances: graces, muses, and companions.

For Julian, Alec, and James, fellow travelers who have swum in the Artibonite, relished *pollo criollo*, and been blessed by the *misterios*.

A mi madre.

Contents

III   *Revolutions*   91

IV   *Caudillos and Empires*   141

V   *The Idea of the Nation: Order and Progress*   191

IX   *Religious Practices*   387

X   *Popular Culture*   417

Acknowledgments

This anthology results from the help, cooperation, patience, and encouragement of many people. We thank all of them, but limitations of space and memory prevent us from acknowledging them all by name here.

Among the scholars who contributed to the book's conceptualization and content were Martha Arguello, Michiel Baud, Judith Bettelheim, Ginetta Candelario, Martha Ellen Davis, Elizabeth Deloughrey, Irwin Gellman, Luis Guarnizo, Jay Kaufman, Melissa Madera, Ryan Mann-Hamilton, April Mayes, Alan McPherson, Richard Price, Dixa Ramírez, Rob Ruck, Giovanni Savino, Cyrus Veeser, and Neici Zeller.

Research for the book depended on the guidance of the expert staffs at the Library of Congress (in particular the Hispanics Branch), National Archives II in College Park, Maryland, the National Archives of the United Kingdom in Kew, England, the David Nicholls Archive at Regents Park College, Oxford University, and the General Archive of the Nation in Santo Domingo. Juan Gadiel Acosta provided the technical expertise to reproduce the images from the latter's Photography Collection.

We are honored that Milly Quezada, Arianna Puello, and Joel Rosario, among others, graciously agreed to be interviewed.

Those who eased the permissions process included Ruth Nolasco, Naya Despradel, and Dulce María Núñez de Taveras, who teamed up to make the work of Flérida de Nolasco available; Marisol Mancebo of the Newark YMCA and her friend Johnny Ventura; Ruben Farje of the Organization of American States; Stephen Plotkin at the John F. Kennedy Presidential Library; Lara Hall at the Lyndon B. Johnson Presidential Library; Louisa Watrous at Mystic Seaport Museum; John Minichiello and Leslie Tobias-Olsen at the John Carter Brown Library; Kia Campbell and Margaret Kiechefer at the Library of Congress; Frank Arre at the Naval Historical Foundation; Christina Spearman at ESPN; Thomas Wells at the University of Tennessee Press; Lief Miliken at the University of Nebraska Press; Peter Froehlich at Indiana University Press; Lawrence Yates and Kendall Gott of the Combat Studies Institute at Fort Leavenworth; Evan O'Neill and Matt Peterson of the *Policy Innovations* website; Xavier Francisco Totti at Hunter College; and Ron Anderson, agent for Joel Rosario.

At Bellarmine University, numerous people gave their support in many ways over the years. Thanks go to the Bellarmine College of Arts and Sciences, the International Program, and the Faculty Development Fellowships for research and travel support. The members of the History Department, in particular Margaret H. Mahoney and Timothy K. Welliver, merit praise for their encouragement and good humor. Student assistant Maggie Harper contributed to preparing the manuscript. Jacen Beck of Armstrong Atlantic State University provided key assistance during two trips to the Dominican Republic, in 2000 and 2012. The National Endowment for the Humanities provided additional financial support.

At the University of California, Los Angeles, a group of graduate student assistants provided assistance to the project: Ann Fain, Victor Rodríguez, and Sara Moraga. Alex Huezo deserves a special mention for his assistance in excerpting and translating several entries, drafting introductions, and conducting two original interviews with contemporary Dominican musicians. Josefina Wallace also helped to edit translations. Cassia Roth helped with the index. Thanks go to the UCLA International Institute, the Latin American Institute, the Center for Women's Studies, the Academic Senate, and the History Department for research and travel support that facilitated the book's preparation, as well as the American Council of Learned Societies and the Huntington Library. The University of Utrecht also provided collegiality and support. Other people who contributed feedback, support, and vision were César Zapata, José Frias, the late Neil Whitehead, and Francisco Beras.

The General Archive of the Nation and the Dominican Academy of History work to preserve the historical record of the country and to promote research into the Dominican past, and we wish to gratefully acknowledge their support, as well as that of the organizations' leaders, AGN General Director Roberto Cassá, and ADH Administrative Director Verónica Cassá, as well as Frank Moya Pons, President of the Dominican Academy of History. In addition, through the Fundación Cultural Dominicana, Bernardo Vega has done a tremendous service to Dominican historiography by making US records, among other official documents, available on the island; we are very grateful for his support over the years.

Bill Nelson designed the map for the book.

The three outside readers provided extremely useful reviews of two previous drafts.

We are deeply indebted to Duke University Press for making this project possible, and for providing countless forms of assistance along the way. We deeply appreciate the generous support of The Hanes Fund for producing the volume. We are grateful to the Latin America Readers series editors, and to many talented DUP staff members for their help, such as Nicole Downing, Mitch Fraas, Alex Greenberg, China Medel, Lorien Olive, Alexandra Patterson, and Isabel Rios Torres, for tackling the toughest permissions, and especially Miriam Angress, for patiently shepherding us toward our goal. Our sincere thanks to senior editor Valerie Millholland for her unwavering support and patience.

A. E. Doyle and Andrew Apter both deserve special commendation for being unfailing bulwarks of support.

We would like to memorialize here three *dominicanista* colleagues, whose pathbreaking careers contributed in important ways to the study of Dominican society: Helen Safa, Isis Duarte, and the pioneering Patricia Pessar.

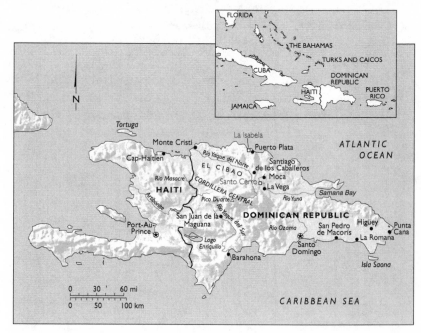

La República Dominicana, the Dominican Republic.

Introduction

The Dominican Republic is home to the oldest of the Old World societies planted in the New World. The blending of all things indigenous, European, and African, which is largely the history of the Americas, began with this Caribbean nation. The early history of Santo Domingo, as it was called, foreshadowed the way the Spanish Empire developed, and at the beginning of that process, no place in the hemisphere was more important.

Despite its historical significance in the drama "Old World meets New World," the Dominican Republic is familiar to most non-Dominicans only through a few elements of its history and culture. Many people are aware that it shares an island called Hispaniola with Haiti and that it was the place where Christopher Columbus chose to build a colony. Some people know that the country produces top major league baseball players and popular musicians. Other people have learned that it is a great option for an all-inclusive beach vacation. But not much else about the place is common knowledge outside its borders. People who visit the Dominican Republic but limit their experience to a week at a seaside resort gain little understanding of the country beyond the tourist enclave.

The relative obscurity of the Dominican Republic results partly from the fact that it has not received the academic attention in English that it deserves. It is more difficult to delve into the Dominican past and present than it is for most other Latin American nations. This Reader seeks to change that. It provides an introduction to the history, politics, and culture of the Dominican Republic, from precolonial history to current trends, combining primary sources such as essays, songs, poems, legal documents, and oral testimonies translated from Spanish, with excerpts from academic scholarship, to present the dramatic story of Dominican life since the country's founding.

By many measures, the Dominican Republic is a land of extremes. It has the highest mountain in the Caribbean archipelago, Pico Duarte in the Central Range, at more than 10,000 feet above sea level, as well as the lowest point, Lago Enriquillo, a saltwater lake 150 feet below sea level, which has doubled in size in recent years for mysterious reasons. It has the largest metropolis in the Caribbean, Santo Domingo, with a population of 2.2 million, which is also the oldest city in the hemisphere, founded more than 500 years ago, and one of the fastest growing, having tripled in size in the last four decades. Santo Domingo also has the newest subway system in the world. Beyond the capital city, the nation as a whole is also expanding rapidly, more than doubling in population since the 1970s, and increasing elevenfold in just the last ninety years; it is about as densely populated as Pakistan.

The Dominican Republic is a country in transition in many ways, with its burgeoning population, rapid urbanization, ongoing emigrant diaspora, democratic political development, and economic transformation. This anthology reflects these contemporary changes and traces their deep roots.

The collection begins with the indigenous Taíno people, who numbered some 1 million in the late fifteenth century, according to estimates going back to the first Spanish census in 1496. Considering this large native population, the arrival of Christopher Columbus on the island they called "Hayti" was less a discovery than an encounter, one characterized by deep misunderstanding on both sides. European contact brought famine and disease, which drastically reduced the numbers of indigenous people in the first decades of settlement, with only a few courageous priests to speak out against their abuse, to little effect. Spanish efforts to create a mining and plantation economy by dividing up the indigenous people and forcing them to work met first with the baffled incomprehension of the Taínos, who could not fathom the Spanish lust for gold, and then with their fierce resistance, as Indian communities held out militarily against the Spanish for decades, though in most cases they were unable to withstand their far better armed and supplied opponents. Traces of the indigenous population can be found today in scattered historical forms such as the paintings and carvings left on cave walls, words still embedded in Dominican Spanish, and foods such as *casabe*, a manioc flat bread that accompanies a proper lunch in the Cibao. Inaccurate versions of this early period are all that many outsiders have heard about the history of the Dominican Republic. For this reason, part I of this Reader offers a selection of sources that together represent the complexity of what took place more accurately than mainstream accounts, which underrepresent the size and relatively advanced state of the island's indigenous society and minimize the intense violence and massive scale of the Spanish assault on it.

The epochal watershed of Columbus's arrival in 1492 (and even more so, his return with a much larger fleet in 1493) initiated the first Spanish colony, but Santo Domingo's course of development soon diverged from that of subsequent colonies planted in the region, whether Spanish, French, or British. His return set in motion three related processes that defined the Dominican Republic as unique, even by Caribbean standards: first, the early arrival of enslaved Africans and then the early end to the importation of enslaved people; second, the preponderance of freedpeople over enslaved people early on; and last, the fact that the economy was based on cattle ranching, logging, and contraband rather than plantation agriculture. These factors combined to give rise to a far less hierarchical social order than elsewhere in Latin America, where enslavement exerted more influence on the economies, societies, and plantation cultures. As Sidney Mintz has said about the Caribbean as a whole, the region is intrinsically modern because it was populated by immigrants, it lacked an indigenous presence, and it was defined by the protoindustrial rhythms of plantation agriculture.[1] Yet the Dominican Republic departs from this model in certain key respects, which we have sought to highlight here.

In much of the Antilles peasant society only existed at the margins of plantation monoculture, but the underdevelopment of the colony of Santo Domingo enabled far more rural autonomy there than elsewhere. Though the Spanish imported and enslaved tens of thousands of Africans during the sixteenth century to mine gold and grow sugar and tobacco, once colonial attention shifted to the more profitable mainland, with its highly successful silver mining in Mexico and Bolivia, the Spanish colony of Santo Domingo foundered. The low demographic density and poverty of the colonists made it impossible to establish the capital-intensive forms of production found elsewhere.

Dominican history laments this period of poverty and neglect, since it failed to enable the affluence acquired by neighboring colonies, yet it did succeed in giving rise to a flourishing popular Creole culture rooted in a free peasantry in the mountainous highlands, locally termed *monteros*—the Dominican version of the *jíbaro* of Puerto Rico. Official neglect, a small, scattered population, and lax social control enabled a burgeoning "protopeasant" subsistence economy to emerge, of shifting agricultural settlements largely populated by people who had escaped from slavery, people who had been manumitted, and their progeny. They supplied smoked meat and tobacco to a thriving contraband economy based on neighboring La Tortuga Island and extending to Santiago de Cuba and Port Royal, Jamaica. This system of illicit ports and maritime links, transnational in scope, defied neat colonial boundaries. The importance of smoked meat to the ships' crews was the basis of this population of *buccaneers*, who took their name from the Taíno Arawak term *buccan*, a technique for smoking meat over an open fire.

This contraband economy of black "masterless men" was so successful that Spanish authorities resorted to draconian measures to contain it. The best known example was "the Devastations" of 1606, when Governor Domingo de Osorio burned northern settlements to the ground in a futile effort to curb contraband by forcing rural inhabitants closer to Santo Domingo. The fact that many of the wealthiest pirates in this pan-Antillean maritime community had formerly been enslaved probably doubly galled the Crown. This flourishing, illicit economy linking the sea with the interior helped to establish resilient individualism, informality, and rule-bending as enduring elements of Dominican cultural identity.

Colonial poverty and the fact that imports of enslaved people ceased in the sixteenth century also gave rise to another feature distinctive to the Dominican Republic: a far more familial and paternalistic form of slavery than elsewhere. The fact that most farms were small and slave owners had only a few slaves, who worked alongside family labor, fostered far more intimate relations between masters and slaves than in the larger-scale plantation model. Freedpeople were more numerous than enslaved people in the Dominican Republic as early as the seventeenth century, a fact that itself helped shape a very different culture of race and status-marking than elsewhere. If the constant lament of Dominican elites into the twentieth century was the stubborn "idleness of the island," this was testimony to the effectiveness of peasant resistance, as the peasantry perceived no need to withdraw from a secure subsistence base to enter the labor market. The lawless environment of colonial Santo Domingo dominates part II.

Tobacco and meat smuggling began to diminish in importance once a third of the western portion of the island was given to the French in 1697 and the French colony of Saint Domingue was born. As the neighboring French colony grew into the jewel in the crown of the French empire, providing more wealth to France than all the other colonies combined by the mid-eighteenth century, the Spanish side of the island also benefited indirectly, becoming a net purveyor of cattle, fine woods, and foodstuffs to the west, while serving as an important refuge for people escaping from the harsh treatment they suffered while enslaved within the plantation regime of colonial Haiti. While the two colonies developed distinct identities, trade alliances and population movement forged bonds among individuals across the frontier.

Traditional Dominican historiography vilifies Haiti, highlighting ethnic and cultural differences between the former French and Spanish colonies and assuming them to be primordial, constant, and unchanging across time and space. Indeed, François-Dominique Toussaint-Louverture conquered the Spanish side during the Haitian Revolution (1790–1804), Emperor Jean-Jacques Dessalines sacked Santiago and the Cibao Valley in 1805, and in 1822, owing to fears of further foreign intervention from the east, the newly unified Republic of Haiti occupied the even newer Dominican Republic, which had declared itself free from Spain just months before. The Dominicans finally gained their independence in 1844, not from Spain but from Haiti. While we cover this period in part III, we also strive to portray Haitian-Dominican relations even during this period as more complex than the traditional portrayal presumes. For instance, it is important to remember that there was some Dominican support for Haitian intervention, not least from people who were freed from slavery by the Haitian regime. We have also included selections in other sections on popular music and religious practices that demonstrate cultural continuities across the border, even when ideas of national difference blind observers to recognizing these forms.

One feature distinctive to the Dominican colony and the nation that grew from it was that blackness was not at all segregated, marginal, or univocally associated with menial work. As a result, many African-descended Dominicans rose to become prominent intellectuals, priests, and statesmen. Their voices are represented throughout this anthology, including that of Salomé Ureña de Henríquez, the national poet, first lady, and feminist. Dominican history includes many prominent men and women of color who played important roles in public life, even if they saw themselves as creoles, not black, and thus have not been included in the annals of African American history.

Another distinguishing feature of the Dominican Republic is that it has suffered far more foreign intervention than other Latin American countries. Part IV deals with the politics of the mid- to late nineteenth century, dominated by three strongmen, or *caudillos*, who often abetted the intrusions: Pedro Santana, Buenaventura Baez, and Ulíses "Lilís" Heureaux. This period included the Spanish recolonization effort of the 1860s and the US attempt to annex the Dominican Republic in the 1870s. The selections in this part of the Reader document the causes and results of those imperial episodes.

Part V presents the conversation about national identity that caudillo rule and foreign intervention sparked. How was the new nation to deal with the "northern colossus"? In this part, we seek to characterize the range of fears and dreams that pervaded the debates over this question, both between liberals and conservatives and within the community of late nineteenth-century liberal thinkers. For example, we hear from Pedro Francisco Bonó, who saw the essence of national identity as located in the tobacco cultivators of the Cibao Valley in the 1870s; Rafael Damirón, who chronicled a certain way of being Dominican called *dominicanidad* (dominicanity) via the mores and fashions of the cosmopolitan elite of the capital city, Santo Domingo; and finally critics of the savage capitalism of the foreign-owned sugar industry, which they saw as the ruin of the nation. A key contribution of this Reader is that it presents these primary Spanish sources in translation, since virtually none of them, unlike those of Cuba or Puerto Rico, have been translated or known outside the island before now. There are some interesting surprises, such as the fact that the renowned black abolitionist Frederick Douglass, alongside some prominent Dominicans, was a proponent of annexation to the United States.

Part VI returns to the subject of intervention, this time the US Marine occupation of 1916–1924, presenting documentation of both the brutality of this little-known war, including the use of waterboarding on suspected insurgents, and the depth of Dominican resistance to it.

The US occupation built the foundation for the long-lived dictatorship known as "The Era of Trujillo." Rafael Trujillo got his start as a Marine trainee, seized power in 1930, and kept it for three decades. During that time he simultaneously modernized the nation's economy and infrastructure and traumatized much of its citizenry. This collection of documents on the period is meant to reflect Trujillo's compelling personal amalgam of energy, efficiency, ambition, depravity, and megalomania.

Another key topic this Reader documents is Dominican state formation and political identity, from the caudillos of the nineteenth century to the two authoritarian leaders of the twentieth, Rafael Trujillo and the man who succeeded him in power, his intellectual enabler and protégé Joaquín Balaguer. Part VIII follows the nation's political misfortunes from the collapse of the Trujillo dictatorship through the power struggles of the early 1960s; the rise and fall of the populists Juan Bosch and José Francisco Peña Gómez; the revolution of 1965 and subsequent US invasion and occupation; the making, unmaking, and remaking of the Balaguer administration; the advent of relatively fair elections; and finally the rise of the three-time centrist president Leonel Fernández. These readings bring these events and personalities to life through materials such as the prize-winning poem that launched the young Balaguer's career, a story and interview by Juan Bosch, US Senate testimony from the general who ousted him, a radio address by Peña Gómez, and revelatory US intelligence reports on the post-Trujillo political climate and the notorious "Twelve Years" dictatorship orchestrated by Balaguer, among other items.

The last three parts delve deeper into everyday life in the Dominican Republic through an examination of religious beliefs, popular culture, and transnational migration. Part IX represents the broad range of overlapping Dominican belief systems, including Roman Catholicism, Protestant evangelicalism, and hybrid genres such as Vodú, Espiritismo, and the southwestern regional healing cult of Liborismo. Part X takes on the rich and complicated subject of popular culture, in particular notions of race, modes of masculinity and femininity, styles of music, and forms of magic. Dominican music has had an inordinate impact on the world and is best known through the current global boom of *bachata* and merengue. Three important but lesser known Dominican purveyors of Latin rhythms to the global music market are represented here: the operatic baritone singer Eduardo Brito, who rose from shoeshine boy to perform at the Waldorf Astoria in New York in the 1930s; the merengue star Johnny Ventura, who was so popular he was elected mayor of Santo Domingo; and Milly Quezada, one of the few women to achieve prominence in Dominican music. This part concludes with an account of the magical significance of names and some handy charms to use for obtaining a US visa.

The border-crossing theme continues in part XI, which explores the flow of Dominican emigration and immigration to gauge how they have changed the contours of everyday life there. In recent decades, hundreds of thousands of Dominicans have left the island permanently or for considerable periods of their lives, many of them going to New York City, which today has become a second Dominican capital. They are part of an enormous transnational community of individuals who might be seen as both Dominican and American, or as neither, because they represent a new hybrid of the two nations. In Dominican neighborhoods in the United States, youths have adapted African American forms such as hip-hop into the new styles of merenhouse and dembow, which have proven wildly popular. Dominicans have also made their mark on the production end of *regguetón*, since the Dominican duo Luny Tunes helped give rise to the genre, and the music producer and songwriter El Cata (Eduardo Bello Pou) from Barahona has collaborated with contemporary global music sensations Shakira and Pitbull. In addition, the best-selling immigrant writers Julia Alvarez and Junot Díaz have described the wrenching challenges of life in the United States to readers who otherwise would be blind to Dominican reality, and they portray Dominican domestic struggles in both countries as alternately explosive and joyous.

But the most visible of all the Dominicans in the United States play baseball for a living. More than 10 percent of all players in the major leagues, including many of its biggest stars, have come from the Dominican Republic or Dominican neighborhoods in the United States. The spectacular rise of Dominican baseball began in 1956 with the virtually forgotten Osvaldo "Ozzie" Virgil, an immigrant as a boy, who is featured in part XI. The appeal of emigration is powerful for poor Dominicans, many of whom attempt to reach Puerto Rico by sea and perish in the attempt, a fact that the merengue star Wilfrido Vargas lamented in the 1980s hit song "La Yola" (The Little Boat). The collection concludes with a glossary of Dominican American jokes and expressions.

An anthology of this size cannot be comprehensive.[2] Nonetheless, in one volume this Reader brings together translated materials by Dominicans about their challenges and excerpted selections of outstanding scholarship on the Dominican Republic by outsiders. It provides lesser known perspectives on topics such as the indigenous populations and their religious beliefs, the violence of the Spanish and the native resistance to them, the buccaneers and the world of the pirates, and the communities of maroon fugitives from slavery. The nineteenth and twentieth centuries saw decades of the destruction of war, which we see through the eyes of eyewitnesses and participants. We have collected the voices of army generals, peasant women, CIA operatives, popular healers, and many others so that *The Dominican Republic Reader* could extend as it does across ideologies and categories of age and gender. It provides insights into the reasons for the country's struggles for democracy, when and why political openings emerged, and why they were shut down. It offers a social, political, and cultural history, one that brings together perspectives from all sides—academic scholarship, journalism, religion, photography, testimonial literature, poetry, short stories, and several original interviews that were conducted especially for this Reader. Most of all, it offers a deeper understanding of the history of a country whose people, through a tumultuous past profoundly shaped by the United States, have faced adversity with courage, honor, wit, and poetry. We hope to inspire you to learn more about this compelling country.

All notes in the selections are the editors' unless otherwise indicated.

Notes

1. Sidney Mintz, *Caribbean Transformations* (Baltimore: Johns Hopkins University Press, 1974).
2. For those looking for an excellent overview of Dominican history, there is Frank Moya Pons, *Dominican Republic: A National History* (Princeton, NJ: Marcus Wiener, 2010).

I

European Encounters

Humans reached the shores of what was to become the Dominican Republic about 6,000 years ago, when the Casimiroid People came from the Yucatán Peninsula via Cuba. They made stone tools to fish and hunt manatees and sloths, driving the sloths to extinction. Around AD 250, waves of Amerindian newcomers began to arrive on the island, having moved up the archipelago of the Lesser Antilles from the coast of what is now Venezuela. They cultivated crops, made elaborately decorated pottery, cooked bread on ceramic griddles, and traveled in canoes made of whole trees. The word "canoe" is one of only a few words that survive of the languages spoken by their descendants, people known collectively as the Taíno. Other words with Taíno origins, including "hurricane," "hammock," "tobacco," and "barbecue," reflect other important aspects of their lives.

They were divided into several different chiefdoms whose regional variations have their contemporary parallel in differences that continue to define Dominicans' regional identities. It is an ongoing debate in the Dominican Republic whether one's allegiance is stronger to the nation or to one's home region, or *patria chica*.

The Spanish invasion introduced dozens of devastating new maladies, including influenza, cholera, smallpox, and many other infectious pathogens, which assailed the Taínos' unprepared immune systems, destroying entire towns at a time. Their harsh lives, spent working in the conquerors' mines and plantations or hiding in the mountains beyond the conquerors' control, often ended prematurely. Adding to the toll, Spanish military campaigns to suppress native resistance sometimes culminated in genocidal reprisals carried out on horseback with the aid of guns, steel swords, vicious mastiff dogs, and the gallows. Between epidemics and abuse, the "pre-Columbian" population dwindled rapidly.

The People Who Greeted Columbus

Irving Rouse

The classic secondary source on the indigenous people of the Dominican Republic is the archaeologist Irving Rouse, who began digging at Taíno sites in Puerto Rico in the 1930s. The introduction to his book The Taínos: Rise and Decline of the People Who Greeted Columbus *summarizes the culture of the Classic Taínos, which was more complex than the societies of Western and Eastern Taínos and Caribs on the neighboring islands.*

Columbus encountered large, permanent villages in Hispaniola and Puerto Rico, each governed by a chief, or cacique. They contained an average of one thousand to two thousand people and ranged in size from a single building to twenty to fifty houses, all made of wood and thatch. Several related families lived together in the same house.

The houses were irregularly arranged around a central plaza. The chief's home, larger and better made than the rest, was situated on the plaza. Round, conically roofed dwellings called *caney* predominated. They were accompanied, at least during colonial time, by rectangular *bohíos* [houses]. The houses had dirt floors, and there were no partitions between families. Although some chiefs slept on wooden platforms, most people used hammocks made of cordage. Goods were stored in baskets hung from the roof and walls. The chiefs and other persons of high rank received guests while sitting on carved wooden stools, or *duho*, which reminded the Spaniards of the thrones they knew in Europe.

The villages were loosely organized into district chiefdoms, each ruled by one of the village chiefs in the district, and the chiefdoms were in turn grouped into regional chiefdoms, each headed by the most prominent district chief. The villagers were divided into two classes (*nitaíno* and *naboria*), which the chroniclers equated with their own nobility and commoners. They searched in vain for a still lower class, comparable to their own slaves.

Columbus took special notice of the Taínos' goldwork because it offered him an opportunity to repay his debt to his patrons, the king and queen of Spain. The Taínos mined nuggets of gold locally and beat them into small plates. Archaeological research has shown that they were used interchangeably with cut shell to inlay wooden objects and to overlay clothing and ornaments. The Taínos could not cast the metal, but their caciques did wear *guanín*, ornaments made of a copper and gold alloy, that they obtained through trade with South America.

The local artisans were also experienced woodworkers, potters, weavers of cotton, and carvers of wood, stone, bone, and shell. Some may have specialized in different crafts, but the Taínos do not seem to have developed any craft into a full-time occupation. They made fire with a wooden drill.

The men went naked or covered their genitalia with cotton loincloths. Unmarried women wore headbands; wives wore short skirts (*nagua*), the length of which indicated the wearer's rank. Both sexes painted themselves before participating in ceremonies, the men also before going to war. Red was the favorite color; this may have given rise to the misconception that Native Americans have red skins.

It was fashionable to flatten the forehead by binding a hard object against it in childhood, before the skull was fully formed. Ears and nasal septa were pierced for the insertion of feathers, plugs, and other ornaments; and waists and necks were decorated with belts and necklaces. The Spaniards reported that the chiefs were distinguished by headdresses adorned with gold and feathers. Pendants in the form of carved human masks, called *guaíza*, were also worn as a sign of rank.

The Classic Taínos had a sophisticated form of agriculture. Instead of simply slashing and burning the forest to make a temporary clearing, as is common in the tropics, they heaped up mounds of earth in more permanent fields to cultivate root crops in the soft alluvial soil. The mounded fields were called *conuco*. The mounds, three feet high and some nine feet in circumference, were arranged in regular rows. They retarded erosion, improved the drainage, and thus permitted more lengthy storage of the mature tubers in the ground. They also made it easier to weed and to harvest the crops. The inhabitants of the dry southwestern part of Hispaniola are said to have constructed extensive irrigation systems.

Cassava was the principal root crop, followed by the sweet potato. Cassava thrived in a broad range of local conditions, from wet to dry. It could be grown over a period of ten to twelve months and kept in the ground for up to three years. The men used digging sticks to plant cassava cuttings. Women grated its starchy roots and squeezed out its often-poisonous juice in a basketry tube to obtain flour, from which they baked bread on a clay griddle. The bread, too, could be preserved for long periods of time. Sweet potato was eaten as a vegetable.

Indian corn (*maiz*) was less important, as is evidenced by the fact that it played no role in the Taínos' religion. It was grown on the forest floor by the slash-and-burn technique, and its kernels were eaten off the cob instead of being ground into flour and made into bread, as on the mainland. According to Gonzalo Fernández de Oviedo y Valdés, corn bread was inferior to cassava bread because it could not be stored in the high tropical humidity of the islands; it soon became moldy.

Other crops grown from seed included squash, beans, peppers, and peanuts. They were boiled with meat, fish, and cassava juice, a procedure that detoxified the juice. "Pepper pots" containing these ingredients were kept on the fire to provide food as needed. Alternatively, meat and fish were roasted on spits.

Fruits, calabashes, cotton, and tobacco were grown around the houses. The pineapple was cultivated, but not the peach palm and cacao, which were limited to the mainland and to Trinidad. Calabashes served as water containers. Tobacco was smoked in the form of cigars (*tabaco*), apparently for pleasure. Unlike the mainland ethnic groups, the Classic Taínos did not indulge in beer fermented from cassava or corn, nor did they chew coca. They collected a variety of wild fruits and vegetables, such as palms nuts, guava berries, and guáyiga roots, whose remains have been found archaeologically.

The chroniclers tell us that the Taínos caught fish in nets, speared them, and used hooks and lines. They also stupefied them with poison, trapped them in weirs, and stored both fish and turtles in weirs until they were ready to eat them. They drove hutias [a species of small rodent] into corrals by burning the prairies or chasing them with dogs and torches and kept them penned there until needed. They plucked iguanas off trees and decoyed wild parrots with tame birds. In the absence of large land mammals, they augmented their supply of protein by spearing manatees in the mouths of the rivers and by eating dogs. They may also have had guinea pigs, but the evidence for this is inconclusive. . . .

The Classic Taínos also played ball on the central plaza and elsewhere. Their ancestors appear to have used nonstructured areas, which may be termed ball grounds. They themselves often constructed specially designed ball courts, applying the term *batey* to both the game and the court where it was played. The court is said to have been rectangular. Ordinary spectators sat on its stones or embankments, the caciques and nobles on their stools.

Dugout canoes made from entire trees transported native peoples as they populated the Americas. The method of constructing them, which involved felling and burning out the enormous trunks, could produce vessels large enough to carry scores of people, as Columbus noted in his journal. Such canoes were still in use into the twentieth century, as shown on this postcard titled "Peasants' Canoe." Photographer unknown, black-and-white postcard, c. 1911. Courtesy of the Roorda/Doyle Collection.

The courts within the villages were for intramural games; other courts, in the countryside, were for games between villages.

Both men and women participated, always separately. The teams, each with ten to thirty players, occupied opposite ends of the court, as in tennis, and alternated in serving the ball. Players attempted to keep it in motion by bouncing it back and forth from their bodies to the ground inside the limits of the court. They were not allowed to touch it with their hands or feet. Its elasticity amazed the Spaniards, who had never seen rubber, the substance of which it was made.

Courts are said to have been in constant use. Wagers were made by the players and, in the case of inter-village games, by their caciques, who also offered small prizes—food, for example. The game was occasionally played before public decisions were made. . . .

Unlike the present inhabitants of the West Indies, the natives traveled by sea whenever possible. They used canoes (*canoa*), which they hollowed out of logs by alternately charring and chopping them with petaloid stone axes, known [to archaeologists] as celts. Spade-shaped paddles were the only means of propulsion until the Spaniards introduced sails. The largest canoes belonged to the chiefs. They were carved, painted, and kept in special boathouses reminiscent of those in Polynesia. Columbus reported that they could hold up to 150 people. On land, the chiefs traveled in litters and the ordinary people by foot. The latter carried burdens suspended from balance poles.

Both men and women were eligible to serve as chiefs and, as such, to live in specially built houses, sit on thronelike stools, have special forms of transportation, and wear insignia of their rank. Each cacique presided over the village in which he or she lived. They organized the daily activities and were responsible for the storage of surplus commodities, which they kept in buildings constructed for the purpose and redistributed among the villagers as needed. They acted as hosts when the village received visitors, and had charge of the political relations with other villages. The caciques owned the most powerful statues of gods (*zemis*) and supervised their worship. They organized the public feasts and dances and, having learned the songs by heart, directed the singing. Because their canoes were the largest in the village, they were responsible for public forms of transportation.

Village chiefs reportedly had the power of life or death over their subjects. The district and regional chiefs did not exercise this kind of control but could requisition food and military service. Their ability to do so depended upon their personalities and political relations. . . .

Individuals traced their descent through their mothers rather than their fathers. Goods, class status, and the office of chief were also inherited matrilineally. A man resided in the village of his mother's lineage. If he chose a wife from another village, he brought her to his own.

Polygyny was prevalent. Most men probably obtained wives in or near their own villages, but chiefs sometimes arranged long-distance marriages for political purposes. A commoner had to temporarily serve his prospective bride's family to compensate it for her loss; a chief could instead make a payment of goods. Only a chief could afford to have many wives.

Trade was widespread. Parties or single persons undertook long sea voyages for the purpose. Some districts excelled in making particular products. . . . Residents of eastern Hispaniola and western Puerto Rico are said to have exchanged daily visits across the Mona Passage. Such interaction was facilitated by a common language.

The Classic Taínos fought among themselves to avenge murders, to resolve disputes over hunting and fishing rights, or to force a chief who had received a bride price to deliver the woman purchased. They did not themselves obtain additional wives by raiding other communities and had difficulty fending off the Island-Caribs, who did.

Only the chiefs and nobles attended meetings at which war was declared. A chief was elected to lead the attack; the nobles served as his or her bodyguard. Before going into battle they painted their bodies red, hung small images of *zemis* on their foreheads, and danced. They fought with clubs (*macana*), with spears propelled by throwing sticks, and, in the eastern part of their territory, with bows and arrows. The Ciguayan and Borinquen Taínos, of northeastern Hispaniola and Puerto Rico, respectively, are said to have been the most warlike, probably because they were forced to defend themselves against Island-Carib raids. . . .

Because few women came to the original Spanish colony during the first twelve years of its existence, when it was being governed by Christopher Columbus and Bobadilla, we may reasonably assume that the custom of intermarriage between Spaniards and Taínos began at that time. Intermarriage continued through the terms of Ovando and Diego Columbus; the census of 1514 found that 40 percent of the officially recognized wives of Spanish men were Indian. Consequently, a large proportion of the modern population of the Dominican Republic, Puerto Rico, and Cuba is able to claim partial descent from the Taínos.

Religion of the Taíno People

Ramón Pané

Only a handful of accounts of Taíno culture were ever recorded by their conquerors. The best of these sources was also the first book ever written in the Americas, An Account of the Antiquities of the Indians, *by Fray Ramón Pané, a monk from Catalonia. Brother Ramón, of the Order of Saint Jerome, was present at the convent near Barcelona when King Ferdinand and Queen Isabella received Christopher Columbus there in 1493, after the admiral's first voyage to the "New World." Pané accompanied Columbus on his return voyage later that year. After their arrival, the admiral ordered the friar to go live with the native people, learn their language, gather information about them, and report back. Brother Ramón lived among the native people from 1494 to 1497, first learning the Macorís language spoken by the people near the north coast of the island and then moving in with a different group who taught him the dominant idiom of the Arawak language spoken on the island. He probably composed his text in 1498, from notes he took during the years he spent with the indigenous people.*

Fray Ramón Pané's original manuscript has been lost, but his account survived by a circuitous route. First it was transcribed by Columbus's son Fernando, whose copy was also lost, but not before being translated into the Venetian dialect of Italian by Alfonso de Ulloa. Peter Martyr and Bartolomé de Las Casas, the best known sources on the Taíno people, also summarized Pané's account in their narratives. Pané's book begins with a collection of Taíno beliefs about human origins, women, the sea, ghosts, and gods, sampled here.

Chapter 1: Where the Indians came from, and how

The island of Hispaniola has a province called Caonao, in which there is a mountain by the name of Canta, which has two caves called Cacibayagua and Amayauba. Most of the people who populated the island emerged from Cacibayagua. While they were living in that cave, they kept watch during the night, a job they entrusted to one named Marocael. He was late in getting to the door one day, they say, and because of that, the sun carried him

According to the creation story of the native Taíno people, human beings emerged from an enormous cave. There are many huge caverns in the Dominican Republic, such as this one near Santo Domingo. Engraving by unknown artist, from *Illustrated Home Book of the World's Great Nations*, edited by Thomas Powell (Chicago: People's Publishing Co., 1888). Courtesy of the Roorda/Doyle Collection.

away. Seeing that the sun had taken him away for his dereliction of duty, they closed the door to him, and he was turned to stone near the entrance. They also say that others, having left to go fishing, were caught by the sun and turned into *jobo* trees, also known as Mirobalanos.[1] The reason why Marocael was looking out and standing guard was to see which areas to send the people to and to distribute them, and it only seems that he showed up late, to his great regret.

Chapter 2: How the Men were Separated from the women

It happened that one called Guaguyona told another by the name of Yadruvava to go out to gather an herb called *digo*,[2] which they clean their bodies with when they bathe. Yadruvava went out ahead, but the sun came up and caught him on the road, and turned him into a kind of bird that sings in the morning, like a nightingale, called Yahuva Bayael. Guaguyona, seeing that the one he sent to gather the digo was not coming back, decided to leave the cave.

Chapter 3

Guaguyona . . . said to the women, leave your husbands, and let's go to other lands, and we'll bring lots of digo. Leave your children, because we'll come back for them later, and we'll bring nothing but the herb with us.

Chapter 4

Guaguyona left with all the women, and went looking for other lands. He arrived at Matanino, where after a brief stay he left the women behind, and went to another region, called Guanín.[3]

They had left the little children beside an *arroyo*. Later, when hunger started to bother the children . . . they cried and called for their mothers, who had left. The fathers could not comfort their children, because they cried from hunger for their mothers, saying "mama," demanding, no doubt, to be nursed. Crying that way begging for the breast, saying *"too, too,"* like someone asking for something they really, passionately want, they turned into little animals like the frogs called *tona*, because of the way they cried to be fed. And that's how the men were left without women. . . .

Chapter 6: How Guaguyona returned . . .

They say that when Guaguyona was away . . . he saw that he had left one woman in the sea, which made him very happy. He immediately started taking baths to clean himself, because he was full of those ulcers we call the "French disease."[4] Then the woman put him in a *guanara*, which means a place set off by itself, and being there cured his sores.[5] Afterward he asked her permission to continue on his way, and she consented. . . .

Chapter 7: How women came back to the island of Haiti, now called Hispaniola

It's said that one day the men went to take a bath; standing in the pouring rain, they became aroused for women. Often when it rained, they would go searching for the footprints of the women, but they had never been able to find any trace of them. But that day, while they were bathing . . . they saw coming down from some trees, through the branches, some kind of people who were neither men, nor women, because they had neither male nor female sex organs. The men tried to catch them, but they slipped away like eels. Two or three men were then selected by the chief to find out how many of the creatures there were, in order to get the same number of men afflicted with *caracaracol*, because they have rough hands, and could hang on to [the creatures] more tightly. [The scouts] told the chief that there were four of them, and so they got four men with caracaracol, which is an illness like mange that makes the skin rough, and they seized the creatures. Then the men discussed how they could turn the four creatures into women, since they were neither male nor female.

Chapter 8: How they found a way to make them into women

They searched to find a bird called *inriri cahuvayal* that lives in the trees, which we call a woodpecker. They tied the feet and hands of those people without the sex of either a male or a female, then took the bird and tied it to their bodies. The woodpecker, thinking they were wood, began his usual work, pecking and poking a hole in the spot where the "nature" of women is ordinarily located. And that's how the Indians say they got women, as told by the elders. . . .

Chapter 9: How they recount how the sea was made

There was a man referred to as Yaya [spirit essence], whose real name they do not know; his son was called Yayael, which means son of Yaya. Yayael wanted to kill his father, so he was sent into exile for four months. Then his father killed him, and put his bones into a hollowed-out gourd, which he hung from the roof of his house, where it remained suspended for some time. One day, Yaya felt the desire to see his son, so he said to his wife, "I want to see our son Yayael." She was happy to hear that, and taking down the gourd, she turned it over to see the bones of her son. Many fish, large and small, came out of it, and seeing that the bones had turned to fish, they decided to eat them.

They say that one day, Yaya having gone to his *conucos*, meaning possessions, which were his inheritance, four sons of a woman named Itiba Yauvava arrived. They were all from the same womb, and all twins, but their mother died in childbirth, and they had to open her up and take out the four sons. One had a case of caracaracol, and so his name became Caracaracol; the other three had no names.

Chapter 10: How the four twin sons of Itiba Yauvava, who died in childbirth, together came to get Yaya's gourd, where his son Yayael was, who had been turned into fish, and no one dared to take it except Caracaracol, who took it down and everyone filled up on fish

While they were eating, they heard Yaya returning from his conucos, and hurrying to hang up the gourd again quickly, they did not hang it well, and it fell to the ground and broke. They say that so much water came out of that gourd that it filled the whole world . . . and that is the origin of the sea. . . .

Chapter 13: About the appearance they say the dead have

They say that during the day the dead hide; at night they go have fun and eat a certain fruit called guava. . . . They change into fruit, have their recreation, and go about among the living.

They have this way of recognizing the dead: they touch the belly with their hand, and if they don't find a navel, they say that one is . . . dead, because they say the dead don't have belly buttons; and that's how they're fooled sometimes, because not taking note of that, they lie with some woman from the Realm of the Dead, and when they think they are embracing her, they have nothing, because she suddenly disappears. That's what they believe down to the present. . . . The dead do not appear to them during the day, but always at night, and because of that, no Indian goes out alone at night without great fear. . . .

Chapter 15: About the observations of these Indian medicine men; how they profess medicine, teach the Indians, and are often mistaken in their medicinal cures

All or most of the Indians of the island of Hispaniola have many *zemis* of different kinds. Some where they keep the bones of their father, of their mother, of their relatives and of other ancestors, which are made of stone or of wood; they possess many of both sorts; there are some that talk; others that cause edible things to sprout; others that bring rain, and others that make the wind blow. . . .

Chapter 19: How they make and look after the zemis of wood and of stone

Those of wood they make in the following manner: when someone goes out and it seems to them that a tree moves its roots, that man stops in fright and asks who it is; the tree responds, "Bring a medicine man here, he will tell you who I am." That Indian, having arrived at the doctor, tells him what he has seen. The wizard or witch doctor then goes to see the tree that the other told him about, sits next to it and prepares *cohoba*.[6] . . . Having done

The Taíno people worshipped a broad pantheon of deities represented by small statues called *zemis*. Individuals possessed their own personal zemis that they kept in their houses, while other zemis were objects of veneration for the entire community and "lived" in their own temple-like dwellings. "Taíno Shell Amulet." Haiti or Dominican Republic. Taíno, AD 700–1500. Carved shell. #055.00.01. Jay I. Kislak Collection, Rare Book and Special Collections Division, Library of Congress. Courtesy of the Kislak Collection of the Rare Book Division of the Library of Congress.

the cohoba, he rises and addresses the tree using all of its titles, as if they were those of a great lord, and says to him, "Tell me who you are, what you're doing here, what you want of me, and why you have had me called; tell me if you want to be chopped down, or if you want to come with me, and how you want to be taken; I will build you a house with an estate." Then, that tree or *zemi*, ready-made idol or devil, responds, saying in what form he wants to be made. The witch doctor cuts it down and fashions it in the way he has been ordered, constructs for it a house with grounds, and many times every year he prepares cohoba for it, which is to offer prayers to it, to satisfy it, to learn various good and bad things from the zemi, and also to ask for wealth. When they want to know if they will attain victory against their enemies, they enter a house where no one except the top men can go; their chief is the first to do the cohoba and play a musical instrument. While he does the cohoba, none of those who are in his entourage talk until he is finished. After his speech ends, he remains for a while with his head bowed, and his arms on his knees; then he raises his head looking to the sky and speaks. Then they all answer together out loud, and when they all have spoken to give him thanks, he recounts to them the vision he had while hallucinating on the cohoba that he inhaled and which went to his head; they say he conversed with the zemis, and that the Indians would attain victory; that their enemies will flee; that there will be many casualties, wars, famines and other such things, whatever the drunken one wants to say. . . . This cohoba isn't done only for the stone and wooden zemis, but also for the corpses of the dead. . . .

Chapter 22: About another zemi called Opiyelguoviran . . .

They say the zemi Opiyelguoviran has four feet like a dog; it's wooden; many times, it left the house at night and hid in the jungle, where they went to look for it, and returned to the house with it tied up with ropes, but it returned to the forest. They say that when the Christians arrived on the island of Hispaniola it fled and went to a lake; that they followed its tracks, but they never saw it again, and don't know anything about what happened to it. . . .

Chapter 23: About another zemi called Guabancex

The zemi Guabancex was in the country of one of the great chiefs, who was named Aumatex; this zemi is a woman, and they say there are two in her company: the one is the announcer, and the other is the gatherer and governor of the waters. When Guabancex gets mad, they say she makes the winds and waves rise, and causes everything on the land to fly around, and uproots trees; they say that zemi is a woman, and is made of the stone of that region; the other two zemis in her company are Guatauva, the town-crier and herald, who at Guabancex's command orders the other zemis of that province to help the wind blow and the rain fall. The other is called Coatrisquie, and of that one they say that he gathers the waters in the valleys between the mountains, and then lets them go to destroy the country. They are convinced of this. . . .

Chapter 25: Concerning what the two main chiefs told them . . .

The great Lord who they say dwells in the sky . . . ordered [chief] Cacivaquel to conduct the kind of fast that they all commonly observe, in which they remain secluded for five or six days without eating anything at all, except juices made of the same kind of herbs they use to wash. In the time they go without eating, due to the weakness they felt in the body and the head, they say that they have seen various things, perhaps that they had longed for, therefore all of them fast in honor of the zemis they have, in order to know if they will achieve victory over their enemies, to acquire riches, or whatever other thing they desire. They say that this chief affirmed that he spoke with the Yucca God, who announced to them that however many of them outlived the chief after his death, they would little enjoy his dominion, because there would arrive in the country a people wearing clothes who would dominate and kill them, and they would die of hunger. But they thought he was talking about the cannibal Caribs; later, considering that the Caribs do nothing but rob and go away, they believed it must be another people that the zemi talked about. Now they believe it was the Admiral and the men who arrived with him.

Translated by Eric Paul Roorda.

Notes

For a scrupulously researched reconstruction of the text, see Fray Ramón Pané and José Juan Arrom, *An Account of the Antiquities of the Indians: A New Edition, with an Introductory Study, Notes, & Appendixes*, translated by Susan C. Griswold (Durham, NC: Duke University Press, 1999).

1. Called hog plum tree in English, the species is nearly extinct in the Dominican Republic.
2. It is uncertain which plant the Taínos called *digo*. Las Casas wrote that the native people chewed coca but did not record their word for it. As Pané recorded later in his book, the Taínos took part in weeklong religious fasts, during which they subsisted entirely by chewing the herb they called *digo* and bathed in its juice, as the friar mentions.
3. Columbus referred to an island the Taínos called Guaní, which a chief told him was the source of the "metal jewel" he wore on a necklace. Matanino may also be the name for a neighboring Caribbean island.
4. This reference supports the argument that syphilis predated the arrival of Europeans in the Americas.
5. *Guanöru* means "disease" in Guajiro, a related Arawak language; perhaps a *guanara* was a kind of infirmary.
6. Cohoba trees, also called *yopo, jopo, nopo,* and *mopo,* of the genus *Anadenanthera* in the legume family, produce powerfully hallucinogenic beans. During religious ceremonies the Taíno ground them up and inhaled the powder from ritual vessels and then interpreted their hallucinations as religious experiences.

First Descriptions of the Land, First Violence against Its People

Christopher Columbus

During December 1492 and January 1493, on his first voyage to the Americas, Christopher Columbus (1451–1506) sailed along the north coast of the island shared today by the Dominican Republic and Haiti. Nearly two months before, at his first landfall in the Bahamas, he had taken seven native people captive; they spoke a language similar to this island's language. The admiral anchored the three Spanish ships at the most promising harbors and sent parties of men ashore to approach the inhabitants, who called where they lived Quisqueya. Columbus renamed it La Isla Española ("The Spanish Island"), which became "Hispaniola."

The part of the island the Spanish had come across was Marién, one of five major cacicazgos, areas ruled by major chiefs, like kingdoms. Marién occupied the northwest portion of the island. After a series of amicable exchanges with the people living there, the final encounter between the Spanish and the Taíno ended in misunderstanding and violence. That violent incident, occurring just before Columbus began his return voyage to Spain, set the precedent for the bloody conquest of the island he initiated on his return.

Columbus recorded his dazzled first impressions of the island in his journal, which was copied, paraphrased, and summarized before being lost. The following excerpt from the surviving version of the journal alternates between verbatim first person quotations from the admiral's own words and third person encapsulations of his narrative.

Thursday, December 6, 1492

All the island appeared to be more rocky than any that had been discovered. The trees are smaller. . . . It is a very high country, all open and clear, with a very fine air, and no such cold has been met with as elsewhere . . . there is a beautiful valley watered by a river; and in that district there must be many inhabitants, judging from the number of large canoes, like galleys, with fifteen benches.[1] All the natives fled as soon as they saw the ships. . . .

Friday, December 7

The Admiral discovered an opening, through which he could see a very large valley, covered with crops like barley, and he therefore judged that it must sustain a large population. Behind there was a high range of mountains. . . . He landed near a small river at the point of the harbor, flowing from valleys and plains, the beauty of which was a marvel to behold. Walking a short distance inland, the Admiral found much land under cultivation, and heard the singing of nightingales and other birds of Castile. Five men were seen, but they would not stop, running away. . . .

Sunday, December 9

He believed that the villages must be at a distance from the sea, whither they went when the ships arrived; for they all took to flight, taking everything with them, and they made smoke-signals, like a people at war. [This is] the most beautiful country, almost like the lands of Spain: these even have the advantage; for which reasons the Admiral gave the name of the said island *La Española*.

Tuesday, December 11

[The Indians from the Bahamas on board] have reason in saying the inhabitants are a clever race, for all the people of these islands are in great fear of those of Cariba. So the Admiral repeats, what he has said before, that the Cariba is nothing else but the Grand Khan, who ought now be very near. He sends ships to capture the islanders; and as they do not return, their countrymen believe that they have been eaten. Every day we understand better what these Indians say, and they us, so that very often we are intelligible to each other. . . .

Wednesday, December 12

The Admiral . . . set up a great cross on the west side of the [harbor], on a very picturesque height, "in sign," he says, "that your Highnesses hold this land for your own, but chiefly as a sign of our Lord Jesus Christ." This being done, three sailors strolled into the woods to see the trees and bushes.

Suddenly they came upon a crowd of people, all naked. [The sailors] called to them, and went towards them, but they ran away. At last they caught a woman; for I had ordered that some should be caught, that they might be treated well, and made to lose their fear. So they took the woman, who was very young and beautiful, to the ship, where she talked to the Indians on board, for they all speak the same language. The admiral caused her to be dressed, and gave her glass beads, hawks' bells, and brass ornaments; then sent her back to the shore very courteously, according to his custom. He sent three of the crew with her, and three of the Indians he had on board, that they might open communications with her people. . . .

Thursday, December 13

The three men who had been sent by the Admiral with the woman returned at 3 o'clock in the morning, not having gone with her to the village, because the distance appeared to be long, or because they were afraid. . . . The Admiral, with the desire of ascertaining whether there were any profitable commodities in that land, being so beautiful and fertile, and of having some speech with the people, and being desirous of serving the Sovereigns, determined to send again to the village, trusting in the news brought by the woman that the Christians were good people. For this service he selected nine men, well armed and suited for such an enterprise, with whom an Indian went from those who were on board. The men reached the village, which is four and a half leagues[2] to the southeast, and found that it was situated in a very large and open valley. As soon as the inhabitants saw the Christians coming they all fled inland, leaving their goods behind them. The village consisted of a thousand houses, with more than three thousand inhabitants. The Indian whom the Christians had brought with them ran after the fugitives, saying that they should have no fear, for the Christians did not come from Cariba, but were from heaven, and that they gave many beautiful things to all the people they met. They were so impressed with what he said, that upwards of two thousand came close up to the Christians, putting their hands on their heads, which was a sign of great reverence and friendship; and they were all trembling until they were reassured. The Christians related that, as soon as the natives had cast off their fear, they all went to the houses, and each one of them brought what he had to eat, consisting of yams, which are roots like large radishes, which they sow and cultivate in all their lands, and it is their staple food.[3] They make bread of it and roast it. The yam has the smell of a chestnut, and anyone would think he was eating chestnuts. They gave their guests bread and fish, and all they had. As the Indians who came in the ship had understood that the Admiral wanted to have some parrots, one of those who accompanied the Spaniards mentioned this, and the natives brought out parrots, and gave as many as they wanted, without asking anything for them. The natives asked the Spaniards not to go that night, and that they would give them many other things that they had in the mountains. While all those people were with the Spaniards, a great multitude was seen to come, with the husband of the woman whom the Admiral had honored and sent away. They brought her, riding on their shoulders, and they came to give thanks to the Christians for the honor the Admiral had done them, and for the gifts. The Christians reported to the Admiral that this was a handsomer and finer people than any that had hitherto been met with. . . . As regards beauty, the Christians said there was no comparison, both for men or women, and that their skins are whiter than the others. They saw two girls whose skins were as white as any that could be seen in Spain. They also said, concerning the beauty of the lands which they saw, that the best land in Castile could not be compared with it. And the Admiral also, comparing the lands they had visited before with these, said that there was no comparison between them, nor did the plain of Cordoba come near them, the difference being as great as night and day. They said that all these lands were cultivated, and that a very wide and large river passed through the center of the valley, and could irrigate all the fields. All the trees were green and full of fruit, and the plants tall and covered with flowers. The roads very broad and good. The climate was like April in Castile; the nightingale and other birds sang as they do in Spain during that month, and it was the most pleasant place in the world. Some birds sing sweetly at night. The crickets and frogs are heard a good deal. The fish are like those of Spain. They saw much aloe and mastic, and cotton-fields. They found no gold. . . .

Tuesday, December 25, Christmas Day

It pleased Our Lord that, at twelve o'clock at night, when the Admiral had retired to rest, and when all had fallen asleep, seeing that it was a dead calm and the sea like glass, the tiller being in the hands of a boy, the current carried the ship [*Santa María*] on one of the sand-banks. If it had not been night the bank could have been seen, and the surf on it heard for a good league. But the ship ran upon it so gently that it could scarcely be felt. The boy, who felt the rudder ground and heard the rush of the sea, cried out. The Admiral at once came up, and so quickly that no one had yet realized the ship was aground. . . . He ordered the masts to be cut away and the ship lightened as much as possible, to see if she would come off. But, as the water continued to recede, nothing more could be done. She turned broadside to the sea, although there was little or no sea running. Then the seams opened, and ship was lost. The Admiral sent a boat. . . . to inform the king [Guacanagarí], who had invited the ships to come on the previous Saturday. His town was about a league and a half away from the sandbank. They reported that he wept when he heard the news, and sent all his people with large canoes to unload the ship. This was done, and they landed all there was between decks in a very short time. Such was the great promptitude and diligence shown by that king. He himself, with brothers and relations, were actively assisting as well in the ship as in the care of the property when it was landed, that all might be properly guarded. Now and then he sent one of his relations weeping to the Admiral, to console him, saying that he must not feel sorrow or annoyance, for he would supply him all that was needed. The Admiral assured the Sovereigns that there could not have been such good watch kept in any part of Castile, for that there was not even a needle missing. He ordered that all the property should be placed by some houses which the king placed at his disposal, until they were emptied, when everything would be stowed and guarded in them. Armed men were placed round the stores to watch all night. "The king and all his people wept. They are a loving people, without covetousness, and fit for anything; and I assure Your Highnesses that there is no better land nor people. They love their neighbors as themselves, and their voices are the sweetest and gentlest in the world, and they are always smiling."

Wednesday, December 26

. . . The king dined on board the caravel with the Admiral and afterwards went on shore, where he received the Admiral with much honor. He gave him a repast of two or three kinds of yams, with shellfish and game, and other foods they have, besides the bread which they call *cacabi*.[4] He then took the Admiral to see some groves of trees near the houses, and they were accompanied by at least a thousand people, all naked. The king had on a shirt and a pair of gloves, given to him by the Admiral, and he was more delighted with the gloves than with anything else. In his manner of eating, both by his high-bred air and his exquisite cleanliness, he showed his nobility. After he had eaten, he remained some time at the table, and they brought him certain herbs, with which he rubbed his hands. The Admiral thought this was done to make them soft, and they also gave him water for his hands. . . .

Estatua de Colón,
Ciudad Trujillo, R. D.

Dominican popular belief holds that Columbus left a curse on the
island that he invaded in 1493. To avoid the curse (*fukú* in Dominican Spanish), many Dominicans avoid saying his name, instead
referring to him as "the Admiral." This perspective contrasts with
the tradition of trumpeting the Spanish heritage of the Dominican
Republic as "The Land Columbus Loved." The statue of Columbus in front of the cathedral in Santo Domingo was erected in
1886, when the four-hundredth anniversary of his first voyage was
approaching and such commemorations, which depicted him as
an agent of progress, were becoming popular. "Estatua de Colón,
Ciudad Trujillo, R.D.," photographer unknown, black-and-white
postcard, c. 1930s. Courtesy of the Roorda/Doyle Collection.

Wednesday, January 9

. . . The day before, when the Admiral went to the *Rio del Oro*, he said that he saw three mermaids, who rose well out of the sea, but they are not as beautiful as they are depicted.[5] . . .

Sunday, January 13

The Admiral . . . sent the boat to land at a beautiful beach to obtain yams to eat. They found some men with bows and arrows, with whom they stopped to speak, buying two bows and many arrows from them. They asked one of them to come on board the caravel and see the Admiral; who says that he was very wanting in reverence, more so than any native he had yet seen. His face was all stained with charcoal. . . . He wore his hair very long, brought together and fastened behind, and put into a small net of parrots' feathers. He was naked, like all the others. The Admiral supposed he belonged to the Caribs, who eat men.[6] . . . The Admiral ordered that the Indian should be fed, and given pieces of green and red cloth, and glass beads, which they like very much, and then sent on shore. He was told to bring gold if he had any, and it was believed that he had, from certain small ornaments that he was wearing. When the boat reached the shore, there were quite fifty-five men behind the trees, naked, with very long hair, as the women wear it in Castile. Behind the head they wore plumes of parrot feathers and feathers of other birds, and each man carried a bow. The Indian landed, and signed to the others to put down their bows and arrows. . . . As soon as they came to the boat the crew landed, and began to buy the bows and arrows and other arms, in accordance with an order of the Admiral. Having sold two bows, they did not want to give more, but began to attack the Spaniards, and to take hold of them. They were running back to pick up their bows and arrows where they had laid them aside, and took cords in their hands to bind the boat's crew. Seeing them rushing down, and being prepared—for the Admiral always warned them to be on their guard—the Christians attacked the Indians, and gave one a stab with a knife in the buttocks, wounding another in the breast with an arrow. Seeing that they could gain little, although the Christians were only seven and they numbered over fifty, they fled, so that none remained, throwing bows and arrows away. The Christians would have killed many, if the pilot, who was in command, had not prevented them. The Spaniards presently returned to the caravel with the boat. The Admiral regretted the affair for one reason, and was pleased for another. They would have fear of the Christians, and they were no doubt an ill-conditioned people, probably Caribs, who eat men. But the Admiral felt alarm lest they should do some harm to the 39 men left in the fortress and town in *Navidad*, in the event of their coming here in their boat. Even if they are not Caribs, they are a neighboring people, with similar habits, and fearless, and armed. The Admiral says all this, and adds that he would have liked to have captured some of them. He says that they lighted many smoke signals, as is the custom in this island of Española.

Notes

1. Mediterranean galleys were rowed by four crewmen per bench, so the native craft had a crew of some sixty oarsmen.

2. A Spanish league equaled approximately 2.6 miles or 4.2 kilometers.

3. The name is similar to the tubers called *ñames* today, but the description better fits the versatile yucca, which can be made into nutritious cassava bread.

4. *Cacabi* may be a reference to cassava bread.

5. Columbus probably saw three manatees.

6. They actually were Ciguayos, a group living in the northeast region of Hispaniola, who were vulnerable to Carib raids and so were more warlike than the Taínos and held out against the Spanish for a longer time.

Death of the Spanish at Navidad

Diego Álvarez Chanca

After the wreck of the Santa María, *there was not enough room on board the two remaining vessels to fit the crew of the lost flagship, so a group of them remained behind when the rest of the Spanish sailed away. They lived near the Taíno town, in a fort constructed partly from the timbers of the wrecked ship. Columbus gave this first Spanish settlement in the Americas the name Navidad, or Christmas, for the day of the shipwreck. Columbus returned to Navidad on his second voyage in 1493, in command of more than a thousand men aboard seventeen ships, to renew the Spanish invasion of Hispaniola. In the following letter, his ship's surgeon, Dr. Diego Álvarez Chanca, narrated what the Spanish found when they got there.*

As we went on making observations of . . . the neighboring land, some of our people discovered the bodies of two dead men in the grass by the river bank, one with a rope around his neck and the other with his feet bound. This was on the first day of our landing there. On the following day they found two other corpses farther on along the river, and it was noticed that one of them had been heavily bearded. This was regarded as a very suspicious circumstance by many of us, because, as I have already said, all these Indians are beardless.

This harbor is twelve leagues from the place where the Christians had been left by the admiral on his return to Spain from the first voyage, and under the protection of Guacamarí [called Guacanagarí in the journal of Columbus, and hereafter], a king of these Indians who I suppose is one of the principal sovereigns of this island. After we anchored at said spot, the admiral ordered two lombards [muskets] to be fired in order to see if there was any response from the Christians, who would fire in return, as a salute, for they also had lombards with them; but we received no reply, nor did we see on the seashore any body, or any signs of houses whatever. Our people then became very much chagrined, and began to realize what the circumstances naturally suggested. . . .

Next morning some of our men landed by order of the admiral, and went to the spot where the Christians had been housed. They found the building, which had been fortified to a certain degree by a palisade surrounding it, all burned up and leveled with the ground.

They found also some rags and stuffs which the Indians had brought to set the fort and the houses in the environs on fire. They observed, too, that the few Indians seen going about in that neighborhood were shy, and dared not approach, but, on the contrary, when called, fled.

This did not look well to us, for the admiral had said that on arriving at that place, so many of their canoes would come alongside the ships to see us that we should not be able to keep them off, and that so it had been on the other voyage, and as we saw now that they were suspicious of our men, it did not seem well to us.

. . . In those houses [some distance away] we found many belongings of the Christians, which it could not be believed that they should have bartered, such as a very handsome Moorish mantle, which had not been unfolded since they brought it from Castile, and stockings and pieces of cloth, and an anchor of the ship which the admiral had lost there on the previous voyage, and other things, from which our opinion was the more confirmed. . . .

We found that they had shown where eleven dead Christians were, already covered by the grass which had grown over them. All with one voice said that Caonabo and Mayreni [the cacique of Maguana and his brother] had killed them. But with all this they began to complain that the Christians had taken one, three, another four women, from which we came to believe that the evil which had fallen on them was the result of jealousy. . . .

And that evening [Guacanagarí] came with the admiral to the ships, and the horses and what we had there were shown to him. At this he was very astonished as being something unknown to him. He took supper on the ship, and this evening returned to his house. The admiral told him that he wished to settle there with him and wished to build houses, and he answered that it pleased him, but that the place was unhealthy, because it was very damp, and such was in fact the case. All this passed, there acting as interpreters two Indians of those who on the previous voyage had gone to Castile and who had remained alive of the seven whom we embarked in the port, for five of them died on the voyage and the others escaped by a hair's breadth. . . .

In the ship there were ten women of those whom we had taken in the islands of the Caribs; most of them were from Borinquen [Puerto Rico]. That brother of Guacanagarí talked with them; as we believe, he told them to do that which they did immediately on this night. And it was that, in the first watch, they threw themselves very quietly into the water and made their way ashore, so that by the time that they were missed, they had gone such a distance that with the boats they were unable to take more than four, whom they took as they were coming out of the water. They swam more than a full half league. On the morning of the next day, the admiral sent to Guacanagarí to tell him that he should send to him those women who had fled the night before and that he should command immediate search to be made for them. When they arrived, they found the village abandoned by its inhabitants, so that there was not a soul in it.

The First Christian Converts—and Martyrs—in the New World

Ramón Pané

After finding the fort at Navidad destroyed, the Spanish constructed a new settlement near present-day Puerto Plata. Columbus named it La Isabela for the queen of Spain. There he established his capital and set about the conquest of the island and the creation of the first European colony in the Americas. He sent the missionary priest Ramón Pané to begin converting the local people to Christianity.

In An Account of the Antiquities of the Indians, *the first book written in the New World, the "poor friar," as Pané called himself, recounted the fate of his first converts. These unfortunate Taínos became not only the first indigenous Christians but also the first martyrs in the New World. They apparently died as the result of a cultural misunderstanding concerning buried icons. The Taíno would sometimes "plant" zemi figurines representing agricultural deities in the fields to encourage a successful crop, "watering" the buried icon with their urine. But when neighbors of the Taíno Christians did the same thing with images of Christ and the Virgin Mary, Pané interpreted the action as a sacrilegious desecration, not an expression of reverence for the new gods he had introduced to them. Columbus's brother Bartholomew, left in charge when Christopher returned to Spain, agreed, ordering the brutal execution of the Indians accused of the blasphemous crime. Their relatives took revenge on the Taíno Christians.*

While . . . under the orders of Governor Don Cristóbal Colón [Christopher Columbus], God wished to illuminate with the light of the Holy Catholic Faith, everyone in the leading household in Magdalena in the province called Macorís, and the head of the house named Guavaoconel, which means son of Guavaenequin.

In said house there lived his servants and favorites, who are called *yahu naboriu* and there were a total of sixteen members of his family, among whom were five brothers. Of them, one died, and the other four received the water of holy baptism. I believe that they died as martyrs, because of what was seen of their perseverance and their death. The first that received death . . . was the Indian named Guaticava, who had received the name Juan Mateo. That was the first Christian who suffered cruel death, and I am certain that it made him a martyr, because, according to what I heard from some who were there when he died, he said: "Dios naboria daca, Dios naboria daca," which means: "I am a servant of God." That's also how his brother Antonio died, and with him, another, saying the same thing. . . .

Then the Lord Admiral told me that the language of Macorís . . . was not spoken all over the island; for that reason I went to live with another leading chief [Guarionex, ruler of the region of Maguá], a lord who ruled many vassals, because his language was understood through the whole country. . . . At first he showed us goodwill, and gave us hope that he would do what we would wish him to do, and to be a Christian, because he asked us to teach him the Lord's Prayer, the Hail Mary, and the Creed and all of the other prayers and other things appropriate to a Christian. He learned the Lord's Prayer, the Hail Mary and the Creed; many in his household did the same; he would say his prayers every morning and make everyone else in the house say them twice. But then he became angry and abandoned his good intention, which was the fault of other chiefs in that area, who reprimanded him because he obeyed the Christian law, being that the Christians were cruel and had taken over their lands by force. For that reason they advised him no longer to occupy himself with Christian things, but rather to come to terms with them and conspire to kill the Christians, because the latter could never be satisfied, and so they had resolved not to follow Christian customs in any way. For that reason he distanced himself from his previous goodwill, and we, seeing that he was detaching himself and renouncing that which we had taught him, decided to take our leave and go where one might harvest more fruit, teaching the Indians and indoctrinating them into things having to do with the holy faith. So, we went to another head chief, a man who was called Maviatúe, who demonstrated his goodwill to us, saying he would like to be Christian.

The day after we set forth from the village and dwelling of Guarionex, to go to another chief named Maviatúe, Guarionex's people built a house next to the house of prayer; in the latter we had left some images, before which the catechumens kneeled and prayed; they were the mother, the brothers and the relatives of the aforementioned Juan Mateo, the first Christian, . . . all members of whose household became Christians, and persevered in their good intention according to our faith; and so it was that the entire family was left to guard the chapel and some fields that I had tilled or had told others to till.[1] . . . The second day after we went to Maviatúe, six men arrived at the house of prayer that the said catechumens, seven in number, had under their custody, and by mandate of Guarionex, told them to take those images that I had left in the power of the catechumens, and break them and destroy them, because Fray Ramón and his companions had gone away and would not come to know the authors of the deed. The six servants of Guarionex who went there, encountered the six boys who guarded the house of prayer, fearing what happened next; the boys, warned, opposed their entrance, but they entered by force, took the images and carried them off.

Chapter 26: About what happened to the images, and the miracle that God worked to demonstrate his power

The Indians left the house of prayer, threw the images to the ground, covered them with earth and urinated on them saying: "Now your fruit will be good and big"; that is what they said because they buried them in a tilled field, meaning that whatever was planted there would bear good fruit; all of that, as vituperation. When the boys who were guarding the chapel . . . saw that, they ran to their elders, who were in the fields, and told them that Guarionex's people had destroyed and ridiculed the images. As soon as the elders learned what had happened, they ran yelling to tell it to Don Bartholomew Columbus, who was in charge of the government for the Admiral, his brother, when he went to Castile. Don Bartholomew, as deputy of the Viceroy and Governor of the islands, put the wrongdoers on trial, and, the truth revealed, had them burned in public. In spite of this, Guarionex and his vassals did not renounce the wicked aim they harbored to kill the Christians on a certain day designated for the Indians to deliver the tribute that they pay in gold. But the conspiracy was discovered, and the plotters were captured on the same day that they proposed to put it into effect. Nevertheless, continuing their perverse design, they carried it out, and killed four men and Juan Mateo, the leader, and his brother Antonio, who had received the holy baptism; then they ran to where the images were hidden, and threw away the pieces. Some days passed, and the owner of that field went to harvest *ajes*, which have certain roots resembling turnips, and others that look like radishes; in the place where the images were buried, two or three *ajes* had grown, as if they had been placed with one in the middle of the other, in the form of a cross.

Translated by Eric Paul Roorda.

Note

1. The indigenous people's agricultural technique was to build up soil into mounds in garden plots called *conucos*, rather than plowing the soil, as Europeans did. The priest's order to till their fields must have been difficult for them to understand.

Founding Santo Domingo

Antonio de Herrera y Tordesillas

Bartholomew Columbus relocated the Spanish capital from La Isabela to the south coast of Hispaniola in 1496, founding Santo Domingo, the oldest European city in the Western Hemisphere and the capital of the Dominican Republic. The location had many advantages, but there was some confusion about what the name of the new settlement would be. The following version of these events comes from General History of the Deeds of the Castilians in the Islands and Mainland of the Ocean Sea, *written by Antonio de Herrera y Tordesillas (1559–1625) between 1601 and 1615 and published in Madrid.*

[Christopher Columbus] wrote from Cádiz to his brother Don Bartholomew, to go to the southern part of the island, and look for some port; and it being comfortable and convenient, to move everything from Isabela, and depopulate it. And Don Bartholomew, leaving in his place his nephew Don Diego, departed with the healthiest men to the mines of San Cristóbal; and asking which was the closest to the sea, he made port at Río de Ozama, as the Indians called it, a very gracious river, and populated on both sides. He reconnoitered it, did soundings, and found that ships of three hundred tons and more could enter, and he determined to begin building a fortress of adobe on the top of the riverbank bluff, above the mouth of the river, and on the east side. He sent to call the people from La Isabela, to begin the settlement, and he gave it for a name, Santo Domingo, for having arrived on the feast day of Santo Domingo [de Guzmán], or on Sunday [Domingo], or because his father was named Domingo, even though the Admiral always called it La Isabela Nueva [New Isabela]. They left the old La Isabela, the officers who commanded two caravels, and some men; and beginning the work, he decided to get to know the King of Bohechio, called Jaragua, about whose state, and policies, and of his sister Anacaona, he had heard great things.

Translated by Eric Paul Roorda.

Begun in 1502, the oldest European structure in the hemisphere is the Torre del Homenaje, the Tower of Homage, named for the bastions of medieval castles where feudal lords received their vassals. The tower stands inside Fortaleza Ozama on the bluff above the Ozama River and has been known as "The Jail of Columbus" because Governor Tomás Bobadilla was said to have imprisoned his predecessor there prior to sending him to Spain to face corruption charges. Photograph by Frank T. Arms, 1899. Frank T. Arms Collection, Photography Collection, #1947/1835/57. © Mystic Seaport Museum.

The Indian Monarchs

Luis Joseph Peguero

Only two months after founding Santo Domingo, Bartholomew Columbus set out to find the most powerful monarchs on the island, the caciques of Jaragua, one of the five major realms on the island, occupying the southwest quadrant of Hispaniola. The expedition to the mountainous west set in motion a familiar sequence of events; a small band of heavily armed, mounted Spanish warriors penetrated a well-populated but vulnerable empire and unleashed havoc. The same basic scenario was repeated again and again, in Cuba, Mexico, Peru, and beyond, during the Spanish Conquest. In the Dominican version of this bloody narrative, three native Taíno leaders have emerged as resistance figures, becoming iconic in Dominican culture: Anacaona, Cotubanamá, and Enriquillo.

Queen Anacaona of Jaragua evokes the dignity, beauty, and grace of the native people and represents their collective brutalization at the hands of the Spanish conquerors. Her brother Bohechio ruled Jaragua, and her husband, Caonabo, ruled the region of Maguana, to the east. Caonabo resisted Spanish domination but was tricked by Columbus into being captured and died while en route to Spain. The Spanish accused Bohechio of conspiring to kill the men at Navidad. They captured and condemned him, leaving his widowed sister Anacaona as ruler. But not for long. Governor Nicolás de Ovando, pretending to come in peace, asked her to convene the Taíno leaders and then had the hall where they had assembled set on fire. Anacaona herself was seized, taken to Santo Domingo, and hanged, despite her eloquent appeal for justice and understanding.

Luis Joseph Peguero, a rancher, poet, historian, moralist, fervent Catholic, and founder of the town of Baní, narrated her fate differently 260 years later in his book History of the Conquest of the Spanish Island of Santo Domingo *(1762). Supposedly a translation of* General History of the Deeds of the Castilians in the Islands and Mainland of the Ocean Sea *(1601–1615), by Antonio de Herrera y Tordesillas, Peguero's version departs from that chronicle and from the much earlier one left by Bartolomé de Las Casas, as well as from the Anacaona narrative accepted today. In Peguero's 1762 retelling, which was the first book written in vernacular Dominican Spanish, she was the sister of Caonabo and the wife of Bohechio, not the other way around, and she perished in the flames along with her chiefs rather than going to the gallows. In other ways, though, Peguero's Anacaona, described in the first selection here, is very recognizable as the woman contemporary Dominicans revere.*

Cotubanamá, the subject of the second selection, was the ruler of the easternmost region of the island, called Higüey. He held out against the Spanish after they had conquered the other four realms of the major caciques. The standard version of his demise parallels that of Anacaona: he was captured by a Spanish expedition, taken to Santo Domingo, and hanged. Peguero's account has him die in an ambush; Peguero's description of the legendary chief presages modern Dominican notions of masculinity.

Enriquillo, described in the third selection, is said to have been the nephew of Anacaona and the son of one of the chiefs of Jaragua who were burned alive by the Spanish. In 1519 Enriquillo sparked the most famous Indian uprising against the Spanish in Dominican history, which lasted fifteen years. During that time, he defeated several Spanish expeditions sent to root him out of his mountainous base of operations and established a kind of independent state in the vicinity of the large saltwater lake now known as Lago Enriquillo, near the present-day border with Haiti. The region is a forbidding place, the habitat of only the prickliest life forms: crocodiles, scorpions, cacti, and at that time Taíno guerrilla fighters. The rebel chief finally made peace in 1533 on terms that granted freedom for his followers in an autonomous area, and he died peacefully the following year in the city of Santo Domingo. From innumerable retellings of his exploits, Enriquillo has become the quintessential Dominican hero, to the extent that the highest rank in the Dominican Boy Scouts is called the Enriquillo Scout. In the selection here, Peguero describes the beginning of Enriquillo's long struggle with authority.

Peguero's portrayals of Anacaona, Cotubanamá, and Enriquillo anticipate the exalted status the Indian nobility now occupy in Dominican popular culture and national identity.

Queen Anacaona

Governor Don Bartholomew Columbus . . . left from the city of Santo Domingo (as it would be called, although the town had no name yet) and walking to the west, found the mouth of a large river, where he had the fortune to find many Indians in canoes engaged in fishing; the fifty Spanish crossed, with the horses swimming; they passed through the lands of many powerful chiefs, who courted them with pleasure, and after a march of thirty leagues from Santo Domingo found the mighty Neyba River (as it is called by the Indians), on the west bank of which stood an army of twenty thousand Indians, ready for battle. . . . But because the Governor spoke and understood their language well, he told them he meant them no harm, but came only to visit their King Bohechio and make friends with him on behalf of his own King of Castile. . . . They went another thirty leagues and came to the court of Jaragua, which was a beautiful town . . . with little order to the streets, but lovely, spacious plazas bordered by trees planted to divert the heat. . . .

The entire nobility of the kingdom turned out to receive them, twenty-two chiefs accompanied by their King Bohechio, and his wife, Anacaona, a woman of commanding presence who, though slightly adorned, impressed the Castilians with her gravity. . . . Thirty virgins, completely nude except for a little skirt of fine cotton covering their secret parts, came in before the royalty, with bouquets of flowers in their hands, doing a dance with their maracas and drums, arriving five at a time, and they placed their little bouquets of flowers at the feet of Governor Don Bartholomew, singing and jumping. . . . The chiefs showed their reverence to the Governor, touching the ground with their right hand, then touching their lips, in a ceremony the chiefs reserve solely for their king.

The Spanish lodged in the palace, which had room for many more than they numbered, [and] were served a simple but abundant dinner of fish, yams, cassava, cornbread, and a variety of beverages. . . .

All of them were given hammock beds, enfolded by an arc of rattan covered with linen, to close off the area around the head from mosquitoes, because there was a great multitude of that plague of mosquitoes in the whole province. The following morning they gave them a breakfast as big as the dinner the night before; and then, the king and queen and chiefs being present in the plaza, two squadrons of warriors appeared, armed with bows and arrows, and showy crests made of feathers of various colors, and naked bodies. They began a kind of skirmish and ridiculous ceremonies, and then they joined in a battle as bitter as if they were mortal enemies, and in a short time there were five or six dead, and many wounded, all with much rejoicing without doing anything for the dead and wounded, and many more would have been in that game, if Don Bartholomew and the King had not commanded that such pitiful brutality cease.

Anacaona was Queen of Jaragua, wife of King Bohechio, and sister of King Caonabo of Maguana; she was a gracious, courtly, affable, respectable woman, who had a masculine spirit for war; because she was known for her understanding, for the deference of her chiefs, and for the ease with which she understood the Castilian tongue; she came to know God and was baptized after she came to terms with the Castilians, of whom she was very

One of the most widely admired figures in Dominican history is the Taíno queen Anacaona. Like the other native monarchs, she won praise from the Spanish invaders for her personal attributes but met a violent death at their hands. "Reception from Anacaona, called the Golden Flower, on Hispaniola for Bartholomew Columbus, Hermano del Almirante," from *Cristobal Colon*, by Conde Roselly de Lorgues (Barcelona: D. Jaime Seix, 1878). Courtesy of the Roorda/Doyle Collection.

fond: we cannot resist this aside, to repair the damage done by the scant uniformity of the historians in this case. . . . In his natural history, Gonzalo Fernández de Oviedo, discussing the dissolution and lasciviousness of the Indian women, says Anacaona was very dissolute, and compared her to a hen, vain and cruel; and said she was concubine not only to the chiefs but also to the Spanish; and further he said of her, that when her husband was taken she stopped governing her court, and because the chiefs did not want to obey the Catholic monarchy, she returned to Maguana, and did not return to Jaragua until they had agreed to be obedient; that she was a fallen woman. . . . These implications have made us doubt the faith of the author; a mistake will be from the pen; and from that preternatural hatred that the Spanish have toward the Indians; when toward Indian women there is an intimate love for what they produce with their affections; and the tendency belonging to nature, is to despise that which is craved.

When the brutal entertainment of the fight had ended, Governor don Bartholomew said to King Bohechio and his chiefs, that his brother the Admiral had gone to see the powerful King and Queen of Castile, his masters; among whose tributaries were many of the gentlemen on the island; and because they pay tribute to the monarchs, they would recognize the good friendship that is there, and solicit the same from all of the gentlemen chiefs on the south coast: Bohechio responded, that they could not pay tribute, because in their territory there is no gold; that they had looked for it, and they could not go outside their realm to get it, just as they do not want others to come and fish in their lagoons. . . . [So] the Indians of Jaragua paid tribute in cotton, cassava and fish.

. . . After the death of King Bohechio, his wife, Queen Anacaona, governed the Court and Province of Jaragua, a woman of complete authority, and respected and loved by all of the men of the Province, of which there were many, and in policy and language, and many other qualities, she exceeded all of the Indians of the island, and the Spanish gentlemen were fond of her.

The Indians felt put-upon, because some rebellious Spanish were living with them . . . who on occasion persecuted them. . . . Sebastian de Biloria wrote a letter to the Commander [Nicolas de Ovando], in which he said that in that Province there were great rumors of war . . . ; the Commander did not want to assign the business to anyone else, so he agreed to go in person, to visit that province, which was the westernmost on the island, the most remote, because it was seventy leagues from Santo Domingo; and without delay he set out with three hundred infantry and seventy cavalry, who moved with great haste.

Knowing that the Commander was coming to Jaragua, Anacaona called her Chiefs and gentlemen of the province to come and show reverence as a sign of their vassalage . . . each with more than five hundred servants; all without Arms [but] with many of their musical instruments, dancers, and singers; and from the shore of the pretty lake of Asuey [present-day Lake Enriquillo], they carried the chiefs and gentlemen on their shoulders to the Court of Anacaona, where they were lodged according to custom in a big wooden house, and all of the soldiers in others adjoining.

Sebastian de Biloria approached the Commander, and told him not to trust these Indians who wanted to kill him, and for that reason to always keep in sight twenty-five soldiers with weapons in hand; but then, the Chiefs arrived giving obeisance according to their custom, making three bows, and on the last one they removed their Crowns, and put their heads at the feet of the Commander; and they passed by making room for the next, one by one; and Anacaona, who did not speak the Castilian language poorly, announced the province and lordship of each one. And then they served a splendid feast, with diverse dishes and beverages.

Never before had the Count seen such celebrations; repeated and different dances; the Areitos from Maguá;[1] games and diversions that the Indians played over two days. Anacaona, eating with the Commander one day, and it was the last of her life, asked two questions . . . : "Commander, when will you make me a Christian? Because that grandeur is all that my Crown lacks; . . . I would like to know what I will be called when I am Christian." The Commander told her *Ana*, without the *Caona*, [and] she turned her face to her vassals, and told them, "From now on, no one call me anything but Ana of Castille and Jaragua."

The second question was why the soldiers remained armed all day, being that all of them were vassals of the same King, and there was no reason to distrust her people, that if some neglected something in their treatment of the Governor, it was because no one had informed her, in order to punish them: or if the Governor or other Gentlemen had found poor hospitality in her Court. The Commander responded that the most appropriate dress for Spanish soldiers is the adornment of arms, and that it was not good discipline to be without them. [He said] that that afternoon the Spanish wanted to play a game of sticks,[2] and they would invite all of her Chiefs; and when they rose from the table, he gave the order to the horsemen to mount up and for the soldiers to be in sight with their weapons, saying to the Chiefs that he would put his hand on his chest as a sign of solidarity to all of them with their Queen:

He did it this way, when the Chiefs entered [the palace], he gave the sign of solidarity to all of them, which was the same signal to set fire to Anacaona and the rest, and they burned in the palace with pitiful howls, and because the houses were all made of wood. . . . more than half the population burned.

. . . Pitiful spectacle! Unheard-of evil! Contrary to the laws of good hospitality, which are so considerable in Castilian politeness . . . [was] the unjust death of Anacaona, and without baptism.

Cotubanamá

The Spanish pursued the Indians through the mountains, and every day there were big, bloody fights; and they went to give it to the town of Chief Cotubanamá . . . who had a large body, well formed, and of excessive might, so that he was able to manage a thicker bow than that of the other Indians, and he ran like a hare, and screamed like a goat: he kept his chest covered with a breastplate made of two pieces of fabric and turtle shells, with which he repelled arrows and spears; and such was his skill with the bow, he could shoot arrows and dodge the lances they threw at the same time; he was warmly praised by the Castilians: and they wanted to find him; moreover in that population Captain [Juan de] Esquival had information that with his wife and children [Cotubanamá] had crossed to the island of Saona; and he [Esquival] determined to go there, because he was certain that until he caught [Cotubanamá], there would be no end to that war, which had already lasted two months.

A caravel arrived on the coast of Higüey sent by Commander Ovando, with provisions and munitions for the army, and Esquival ordered that the same night, the caravel would cross to Saona with one hundred men, before Cotubanamá's spies could detect them, and cross over with their canoes to warn him; leaving the rest of the men in command of Captain Juan Ponce de Leon, to stay on the coast, where the caravel could return to pick them up in case they were needed on Saona.

They embarked, and crossed the two leagues of sea that are in that little gulf, to get from Hispaniola to Saona; and they arrived at dawn, because of the calm night; and going ashore with their arms, and supplies, they climbed a high promontory, and discovered a town; they rushed on it and caught them off guard and killed the valiant Cotubanamá.

Enriquillo

A Spanish youth named Valenzuela inherited a *repartimiento* of Indians [an allotment of men forced to labor for a Spanish master] from his father, who was given it because he was the first conquistador and founder of the town of San Juan Bautista de la Maguana, and on his *encomienda* [a tract of land, with its inhabitants, granted to a Spanish colonist] served a chief who was called Enriquillo, who had been raised since he was a boy in the monastery of the Fathers of Saint Francis . . . located in the Province of Jaragua, in which was located the court of King Bohechio, one of the five Kings who dominated the island; he was instructed by a friar named Brother Remigio, who taught him to read and write, and instructed him well, with Christian politeness and good morals, and Enriquillo had a good body, well proportioned, because he was born when the Indians had lost the custom of making their children artificially ugly at birth (as it is said) and emerging from adolescence, he married a noble Indian girl, christened as Doña Mencía Bahoruco, because that was the name of the province of her cacique father, Bahoruco, in the mountains on the southern coast fifty-five leagues from the port of Santo Domingo and in the Province of Jaragua. Enriquillo showed gravity and severity with the Indians on his work gang [*cuadrilla*] serving Valenzuela, and among his possessions he had a strong, tame chestnut mare, which Valenzuela wanted to buy, and he not wanting to sell her, [Valenzuela] took her by force; and not contented with that he stole [Enriquillo's] wife, and took her (with bold recklessness) as his concubine. . . .

Enriquillo suffered these injuries with patience and dissimulation, and the three-month term of service ended, which the gangs of Indians work every three months, and then they leave (and go to their villages to tend to their work and fisheries . . .). He determined to go to his land in Bahoruco and no longer obey any Spaniard and defend himself from them until the last breath of his life, and gathering his Indians he left with them and some others who joined them.

The time came for the break to end, and because Enriquillo and his work gang did not come back, Valenzuela thought he was angry about what had occurred, and decided to go look for him with eleven men, and find him, tie him up, and whip him well . . . armed with lances and some machetes, while the Indians brought their arrows and many rocks; and they went out to the encounter with Enriquillo leading them and he said to Valenzuela, "we very well could leave, Valenzuela, and listen, we were born as free as you were, and with even more nobility than you, and if we have served you it was to give pleasure to our beloved King, and your grandeur does not mandate that you treat us how you treat us, if you want slaves you can buy those negroes that have been brought, because we do not have to go with you even if we lose our lives." . . . Valenzuela called him dog, and thief, and closed with him and the Indians, but they fought with such spirit that in a short time they killed three of the Spanish, and wounded eight, and Valenzuela took two arrow wounds that he died of in San Juan.

Translated by Eric Paul Roorda.

Notes

1. "Areitos" were Taíno ritual dances and songs; Maguá was the north coast region ruled by the cacique Guarionex.
2. This may refer to bohordos or bofordar, a sixteenth-century equestrian game played with reed-spears filled at the bottom with sand. Participants usually dressed as Moors while playing the game. Many thanks to Teofilo Ruiz for this clarification.

Criminals as Kings

Bartolomé de Las Casas

The Spanish colonizers systematically enslaved and brutalized the Taíno people. The invaders divided the indigenous population among themselves to extract labor and tribute from them, called the encomienda system. *Bartolomé de Las Casas (1484–1566) decried the abuses of the Spanish masters, called* encomenderos, *in extensive writing and debating, earning the sobriquet "Defender of the Indians." In his* History of the Indies, *begun in 1526, he recounted the atrocious behavior he had witnessed; first as one of the* encomenderos *himself, then as a repentant monk who argued for mercy for the natives. Among many other abuses, he described the rampant sexual exploitation of the Taíno women by Spanish men. The demographic disaster triggered in 1492, which devastated the Taíno culture to such an extent that within a century there were no recognizable "Indians" remaining to be seen, has led to the myth of their utter extinction. Yet their mixed-race children carried the DNA of the pre-Columbian population forward, and cultural traces remained in ritual and myth, even as their numbers plummeted in the years following the conquest.*

Along with the other privileges and favors that Governor Bobadilla[1] granted to these three hundred settlers [the *encomenderos*], he made them pay the Crown only one-eleventh of the gold they collected, and so that they would not have to wórry about going to dig the gold themselves, they asked him to give them Indians to extract the gold and plant grain fields to provide their bread. He ordered or advised them to join together in groups of two, forming partnerships in their enterprises and splitting the profits they might earn; and to each of these partnerships he assigned the people of a certain cacique or lord, thus giving them great satisfaction and pleasure. Thus you could see men of mean estate, who had been whipped and had their ears cut off in Castile, and been banished here as murderers, and against whom criminal proceedings were still pending for their crimes, holding kings and natural lords [the Taíno nobility] as their vassals and servants.

These lords and caciques had daughters, sisters, or other close female relatives who were immediately taken as concubines, either by force or willingly. Thus all of these three hundred gentlemen were for some years living in mortal sin with their Indian mistresses, not counting the great sins they daily and hourly committed as oppressors and tyrants over these people. These ladies, whom they kept as concubines, were called their *criadas* [servants]. Thus they would refer in each other's presence to my *criada* so and so or to the *criada* of such a person as if they were saying my wife or the wife of such a person.

Note

1. Francisco de Bobadilla succeeded Christopher Columbus as governor of the Indies in 1500. He died in a shipwreck on his return voyage to Spain in 1502.

A Voice in the Wilderness:
Brother Antonio Montesino

Bartolomé de Las Casas

Even before the more famous Bartolomé de Las Casas protested the harsh exploita-
tion of the Taíno people, Antonio Montesino, one of the first three Dominican friars
to arrive on the island, spoke out against the abuse directly to the abusers them-
selves. In December 1511, Brother Antonio delivered two sermons denouncing those
who victimized the local people and refused to offer them communion. Las Casas,
who heard Montesino and was moved by his message, told of the outcry the priest
provoked in the new city of Santo Domingo.

The Dominican friars at that time had already noticed that the island Indians
were dying because of the miserable life and harsh captivity they endured.
For a long time the friars witnessed, on the one hand, Spanish brutality,
Spanish indifference to the material and spiritual well-being of the Indians
and on the other, the innocence, the docility, and the extraordinary patience
of the Indians themselves. As spiritual and God-fearing men they began to
contrast reality with justice and to discuss among themselves these hideous
and unheard of wrongs. "Are these not men?" they asked. Finally, after long
and serious discussion, they decided to preach publicly in the pulpits, to
proclaim the state in which those of our sinners were, who held and ill-used
these people, and warn them of where they would go, should they die in
that state, to receive the reward of their inhumanity and greed.

The Father Vicar, invoking due obedience, entrusted the task of preaching to the most noted preacher among them, after the Father Vicar himself.
He was Father Fray Anton Montesino, the second of the three friars who
brought the Order to the island. . . . This Father Anton Montesino was a
gifted preacher, severe in condemning vices, very emphatic, almost passionate in his sermons and his speech, so that his sermons had great effect, or
so it was believed. To this man, as to a brave leader, they committed the

first sermon on this subject, so new to the Spaniards of this island. Its novelty consisted in declaring that killing these people was a greater sin than squashing bedbugs.

Since it was the season of Advent, they agreed that the sermon should be preached on the fourth Sunday, on which they sing the Gospel where St. John the Evangelist says ". . . the Jews sent priests and Levites from Jerusalem to ask him, Who art thou? . . . he said, I am the voice of one crying in the wilderness . . ." To ensure that the whole of Santo Domingo should hear the sermon and no one, at least of the principal people, should be absent, they sent word to the second Admiral, who was then governing the island, and to the royal officials and the judges, each at his own house, informing them that on Sunday there would be a special sermon in the principal church, on a topic that concerned them all; and begging them all to attend and hear it . . .

Sunday came, and at the hour for preaching Father Fray Anton Montesino mounted the pulpit with his sermon, written out and signed by the others, and announced his text, "I am the voice of one crying out in the wilderness." He said something by way of introduction about the significance of the Advent season. Next he began to describe the barrenness of the desert of the consciences of the Spaniards of this island; the blindness in which they lived; the danger they incurred of condemnation, for the deadly sins in which they were constantly immersed and in which they would die. Then he returned to his text, and said, "It is to warn you of these sins that I stand here, I who am the voice of Christ crying in the wilderness of this island; and it is vital that you hear me, not with divided attention, but with all your heart and with all your mind. The message you are about to hear will be the most disturbing you have ever heard, the hardest and harshest and most dreadful you ever thought to hear." He expanded this theme for some time with terrible stinging words that made them tremble and fancy that they were already before the judgment seat. He declared to them in majestic tones the nature and the content of his message: "The message," he cried, "that you are all in mortal sin, that you live in it and will die in it, because of the cruelty and oppression with which you treat these innocent people. Tell me, by what right do you hold these Indians in such cruel and horrible servitude? By what authority did you make unprovoked war on these people, living in peace and quiet on their land, and with unheard-of savagery kill and consume so great a number of them? Why do you keep them worn-out and downtrodden, without feeding them or tending their illnesses, so that they die—or rather you kill them—by reason of the heavy

The first person to speak out for the victimized native people was Friar Antonio Montesino, who lambasted his compatriots from the pulpit for their extreme cruelty. This forty-five-foot statue of the brave monk has loomed over the Santo Domingo waterfront since 1982. Photograph by Eric Paul Roorda, June 2012.

labor you lay upon them, to get gold every day? What care do you take to have them taught to know their God and Maker, to be baptized, to hear Mass and keep their Sundays and their holy days?

"Are they not men? Have they no soul? No reason? Are you not required to love them as you love yourselves? Do you not understand this? Do you not feel it? How can you be sunk so deep in unfeeling sleep? Be sure that you have no more hope of salvation, in the state you are in, than Turks or Moors who lack and reject the faith of Jesus Christ." So, in his peroration, he explained the message that he had earlier emphasized. He left them aghast, some as if they could not believe their ears, some more obdurate than ever, some a little stricken in conscience, but—as I heard afterward—none converted.

His sermon over, he left the pulpit with his head held high, for he was not a man to show fear; nor was he afraid, nor did he greatly care if he shocked his hearers by doing and saying what God commanded. He returned with his companion to their straw hut, where they had nothing to eat but some cabbage soup without oil; but this was often their lot. When he had gone, the church was full of mutterings, so that they could hardly finish the Mass.

After dinner, which probably no one much enjoyed, the whole city assembled at the house of the Admiral, the second to hold that office and title,

Don Diego Colon, son of the first Admiral, the discoverer of these Indies. There were present, in particular, the royal officials: treasurer, accountant, factor, and overseer. They decided to go and reprimand the preacher and give him a fright, if not actually punish him, as a breaker of the peace and an advocate of revolution. . . .

They knocked at the convent gate, and when the porter opened, they told him to fetch the Vicar and the friar who had preached the scandalous sermon. The Vicar, the venerable Father Fray Pedro de Cordoba, came to the gate alone. They told him, with more arrogance than humility, that he should call the preacher. He replied, most prudently, that there was no need for that; . . . Eventually the Admiral and his companions, seeing that the Father Vicar was not to be intimidated by their authority, changed their tone, and asked him with due humility to their tone, to send for [Montesino]. . . . The holy man, seeing that they were taking a different approach and speaking less heatedly than when they arrived, called the Father Fray Anton Montesino, who came, with what inward fears may be imagined. They all sat down, and the Admiral, on behalf of all, stated his complaint. He said that the Father had made bold to preach doctrines prejudicial to the King's authority and damaging to the public interest. He had said Spanish settlers had no right to hold Indians, although the King, who was Lord of all the Indies, had conferred that right upon them, in recognition of their labors in conquering these islands and subjugating the heathen who lived there. The sermon had been so disrespectful to the King and so prejudicial to the settlers' rights that they were resolved to insist that the friar should take back all that he had said. If he would not, they would know what further steps to take.

The Father Vicar replied that the friar's sermon represented the opinion and the wishes of himself and all the others. They had agreed to it after long and mature deliberation. They had decided that it should be preached as evangelical truth, necessary for all the Spaniards of the island, and for the Indians, whom they saw dying day by day without paying more attention than they would to animals. They were compelled to this by Divine command and by the profession they made at baptism, first as Christians and then as friars and preachers of the truth. They intended no disservice to the King, who had sent them here to preach as they thought necessary for the salvation of souls. They were wholly loyal to His service, and were sure that when His Highness was fully informed of what was happening here and of what they had preached about it, He would deem Himself well served and would thank them.

This speech, with the arguments the holy man adduced in justification

Cathedral of Santo Domingo, Built in 1512. In its Crypt are Enshrined the Mortal Remains of Christopher Columbus in Fulfillment of his Dying Wishes, Ciudad Trujillo, Dominican Republic

Construction of the first cathedral in the hemisphere began in 1512, when the Montesino controversy was at its height, and continued for almost three decades. "Catedral de Santo Domingo, Construido en 1512," photographer unknown, color linen postcard, c. 1930s. Courtesy of the Roorda/Doyle Collection.

of the sermon, gave them very little pleasure. . . . If their Indians were taken from them, all their hopes and ambitions would be frustrated; so all of them, especially the leaders, became more extreme in their demands. They all insisted that the Father should retract on the following Sunday what he had said in his sermon, and went so far in their blindness as to say that if this were not done the friars should pack their bags to return to Spain; to which the Father Vicar replied, "That, gentlemen, would give us little trouble." This was true, for their possessions consisted of no more than the habits of coarse frieze that they wore, and some blankets of the same material to cover them at night . . . the utensils of the Mass, and a few books, all of which could have fitted into two chests.

When they saw that the servants of God were unmoved by these threats, they again tried a soft approach. They besought the friars to reconsider and, after due thought, to preach another sermon modifying what had been said in the first, in order to calm the populace, who had been roused and were in a state of dangerous excitement. They laid great stress on the importance of calming the people by a more moderate sermon, and eventually the fathers, to get rid of them and put an end to frivolous importunities, agreed that at the appropriate hour on the following Sunday Father Fray Anton Montesino would preach a second sermon on the same topic as the first. . . . They at once announced that they had reached agreement with the Vicar and that on the following Sunday the friar would retract all that he had said. There was no need to invite people to attend this second sermon, for the whole city was there, everyone urging his neighbor to come along and hear a friar take back all that he had said a week before.

The hour of the sermon arrived and the friar mounted the pulpit and gave out the text that was from the Book of Job, in Chap. 36: "I will fetch my knowledge from afar, and will ascribe righteousness to my Maker, for truly my words are not false . . ." "I refer again to the basis of the knowledge and truth that I preached to you last Sunday, and I will prove to you that my words, that so offend you, are true." Once they heard the text, the more intelligent among the congregation saw at once where it would lead him, and they could hardly bear to let him continue. He began . . . by recapitulating all he had said . . . against the injustice and tyranny in which they held those oppressed and worn-out people. He repeated his conviction that they could not, in their present state, hope for salvation. In the hope that they might in time mend their ways, he told them that [the friars] would not shrive [give communion to] any man among them, any more than they would an unrepentant robber. His hearers could publish this abroad, and write about it to whom they chose in Castile; for he was sure that they were serving God and doing no small service to the King.

The sermon ended, he returned to his house, leaving the people in the church dismayed, muttering, and more than ever enraged against the friars. . . .

They all came out of church seething with rage and went off to their dinners; to them, a bitter feast. They paid no more attention to the friars, for talking to them was clearly a waste of time. They decided instead to write to the King by the next ships, informing Him that these friars had come to the island and were threatening the foundations of their society by preaching revolutionary doctrines in defiance of His Highness's commands; that they had consigned everyone to Hell for holding Indians and employing them in the mines and other necessary work; and that their preaching amounted to nothing less than robbing His Highness of sovereignty and revenue.

These letters, when they reached the Court, caused great consternation.

The Royal Response

Ferdinand I

Christopher Columbus's son Diego Columbus (1474?–1526), who became the fourth governor of the Indies in 1509, joined the outraged colonists in complaining about Montesino to King Ferdinand I (1503–1564) of Spain. In the royal response to the controversy, the king commanded Montesino to be silent on the subject or else be sent back to Spain to be punished for his actions. Montesino did return to Spain and was able to help persuade King Ferdinand to promulgate the "Laws of Burgos" to protect the Indians in December 1512. These and other later royal decrees, however, did little to prevent the continued abuse of the indigenous people.

I [King Ferdinand] also saw the sermon that you say was preached by a Dominican friar named Fray Antonio Montesino, and although he has always been given to indiscreet preaching, I was greatly amazed he could say what he did, because all the lawyers say there is no basis either in theology or in canon or civil law for it; and I am sure they are right, because when I and My Wife the Queen, Who is in heaven, issued a decree commanding that the Indians be compelled to serve the Christians as they do now, We ordered all the members of Our council and many other civil and canon lawyers and theologians assembled to discuss the matter, and considering the donation that Our Most Holy Father [Pope] Alexander VI made to Us of all the islands and mainland discovered and to be discovered in those regions, an authorized copy of which will be sent with the present letter, as well as the other written opinions, both in law and philosophy, that existed on the subject, they decided in the presence and with the advice of the present Archbishop of Seville that the Indians should be assigned to work for the Spaniards, and that this was in accord both with human and divine law. And since it is clear by logic that even laymen can comprehend how necessary it is for this business of the servitude of the Indians to the Spaniards to be handled as it is, I am even more amazed at those friars who refuse to absolve the settlers, who go to confession, until they free their Indians, when these Indians were given to them by My orders, so that even if there was a burden of conscience to be borne in this matter, which there is not, it would be on My part or on that of the people who advised Us that these things should be arranged as they are, rather than on the part of the settlers who have the Indians. Thus you were certainly right to take the action you did with regard to the preacher and the others who in their obstinacy refused to grant absolution [to the *encomenderos*] because of the magnitude of their error, because the populace had be calmed down and the Indians prevented from believing that the things they were saying were right, and because this business is so prejudicial to the welfare of those regions. And seeing that the preacher was not alone in the said error, but was joined in it by others among the Dominican friars living on that island, all the members of the council were of the opinion that they should send an order to you to put all of them in a ship and send them back here to their superior to explain what induced them to do such a thing so unheard of and lacking in any foundation, so that he could punish them as they deserved.

II

Pirates, Governors, and Slaves

When there were no more Taínos left to dominate, the conquerors turned to a new source of unpaid labor and sex, importing unwilling immigrants from Africa. The first enslaved Africans arrived in Santo Domingo soon after its founding. With the early intermingling of Amerindian, European, and African blood, an increasingly diverse human population took shape on the island. Along with gradations of free and unfree status came new social and racial complexities.

When in the 1500s the Spanish Crown shifted its attention to the mainland, where the mining economies of Mexico and Peru began to produce great wealth for the Crown, the city of Santo Domingo lost its status as capital, and the colony declined. Although there was little European immigration and planters were too poor to purchase many slaves to augment production, a surprisingly affluent if illicit economy developed in the shadows of colonial control, one that afforded an impressive amount of upward mobility for former slaves. This smuggling economy became the basis of an emergent creole culture that incorporated both the backwoods monteros and people who had escaped enslavement, who lived a nomadic lifestyle that did not include settled cultivation and instead relied on hunting wild pigs and cattle and gathering tuber crops. The monteros operated in symbiosis with their maritime counterparts, the pirates, corsairs, and buccaneers who traded and formed part of a community of "masterless men" operating between La Tortuga off the coast of northern Hispaniola, Puerto Rico, Port Royal in Jamaica, and Santiago de Cuba.

The countryside has never been easy to control from the city. The history of the Dominican Republic offers many examples of that tenet, among them the independence of the monteros in the hinterland and the outlaw buccaneers who ranged along the craggy coastline of Hispaniola and its neighboring islands. The Spanish policy of strict trade control led to the "devastations" of outlying towns in 1606, when the colonial authorities torched settlements and forcibly relocated their inhabitants to areas closer to Santo Domingo rather than allow them to trade freely with anyone they met. Despite these drastic measures, groups of people and livestock remained beyond the practical jurisdiction of the metropolis on the Ozama River. The freely roaming cattlemen and woodcutters of the interior and labyrinthine coastline proved impossible to restrict. The monteros helped to establish resilient individualism as an enduring element of Dominican cultural identity. The pioneer families who trickled back after the "devastations" to hew out a life in the bountiful interior might have felt like renegade Taínos, as they called their subsistence farms *conucos* and their cabins *bohíos*. The tradition of rural autonomy embodied by these colonial Dominicans came into contention with the ongoing exertion of power from the center of officialdom, Santo Domingo. Eventually, as growing populations concentrated in the valleys and in port towns along the coast, strong allegiances developed between the residents and their home areas. That three-way tension between central control, regional loyalty, and spirited individualism has characterized much of the Dominican national experience.

Spanish naval forces also conducted periodic raids against the coast-hugging buccaneers, who engaged in smuggling with foreign traders and preyed on Spanish shipping. Despite occasional successes, the Spanish failed to dislodge the pirate communities entirely from their favorite gathering places, most of them in the western wilds of Hispaniola and the nearby island of Tortuga. Not until Spain gave that region (approximately a third of the island's territory) to France in 1697 were the unallied freebooters eradicated. In their place, the two western peninsulas and the land between them became a French colony that was soon inhabited mainly by Africans. The advent of Saint Domingue, later Haiti, multiplied the diversity of peoples and languages on the island. It also eventually led to a great deal of conflict between the French and the Spanish sides.

Las Casas Blamed for the African Slave Trade

Augustus Francis MacNutt

After many years of arguing the case for mercy for the Indians, in writing and in public debates, Bartolomé de Las Casas gained the ear of the king of Spain, who directed him to draft a proposal for their protection. His biographer, Augustus Francis MacNutt, defended the "Defender of the Indians" from charges that the Dominican monk's response to Ferdinand I initiated the African slave trade. This passage begins with Las Casas pondering what to propose to the king.

It is indicative of the priority of importance which Las Casas habitually gave to spiritual over temporal aids, that he first had recourse to the priors of the religious orders, asking them to have their communities pray unceasingly and with special earnestness, that his mind might be illumined by divine grace to perceive what course he must follow. He next drew up his plan, but perhaps in no act of his long career is there less evidence of the action of divine guidance, for, in framing his project, he committed an error which he himself sincerely and frankly deplored with touching humility, and which has served all his detractors ever since as ground on which to bring a grave charge against him. . . . Las Casas acceded to the request of certain of the colonists in Santo Domingo to ask the King's consent to the importation of negro slaves to replace the Indians who should be freed. This recommendation cost Las Casas dearly enough and later exposed his reputation to unjustifiable attacks, some of which even represented him as having *introduced* negro slavery into America; others as having been betrayed by blind zeal in favour of the Indians into promoting the slave-trade at the expense of the Africans. No one more sincerely deplored his course in this matter than he himself when he realised the significance of what he had done, and the sincerity and humility of his compunction should have sufficed to disarm his detractors. . . . The moral aspect of the question of slavery was not under consideration and the recommendation of Las Casas is seen upon examination to reduce itself to this: he advised that Spanish colonists in America should be allowed the privilege, common in Spain and Portugal, of employing negro slave labour on their properties. Since Spaniards might hold African slaves in Spain, it implied no approval of slavery as an institution, to permit them to do the same in the colonies. Las Casas was engaged in defending a hitherto free people from the curse of a peculiarly cruel form of slavery, but had he regarded the institution as justifiable in itself, he would have modified the ardour of his opposition to its extension.

The Slave Problem in Santo Domingo

Álvaro de Castro

The danger of insurrections and the problem of runaway slaves arose for the Spanish colonizers soon after their king allowed the introduction of captives from Africa. Governor Diego Columbus himself was the first Spanish slaveholder to face an uprising when one broke out on his sugar plantation on the day after Christmas in 1522. After a desperate defense, the rebel slaves capitulated. Columbus Jr. ordered most of the survivors to be hanged, setting the precedent for harsh treatment of rebellious slaves, whether they rose up or ran away. Less than two decades later, the archbishop of Santo Domingo estimated the number of slaves on the island and outlined some of the problems they posed to their putative masters, addressing his observations to the supervisory Council of the Indies in Seville, Spain.

There were more than 25,000 or 30,000 Negroes there compared to no more than 1,200 settlers on the plantations or at the mines; . . . there were over two or three thousand runaway slaves hiding on the Cape of San Nicolás,[1] among the Ciguayos, on the Samaná Peninsula, and on the Cape of Higüey. . . . There is much trading going on among them, based on articles stolen from farms and ranches which they raid. We have reached a point where every Negro, regardless of how new he is to the territory, steals something every day, sometimes even gold. Some do this so that they may pay the daily fee that they owe their masters [for the privilege of hiring themselves out]; others, to give it to their women or to buy clothes. This stolen property finds its way into the hands of the two or three hundred female Negroes called *ganadoras* [the earners] who walk the streets of this city earning money with which to pay their masters' daily, monthly or yearly fees, but keeping whatever is left over for themselves. They travel all over the island stealing, transporting and secreting their merchandise. These Negroes are so richly dressed and decorated with gold that, in my opinion, they have more freedom than we have.

Note

1. Cape San Nicolás is on the northwest tip of the island.

Lemba and the Maroons of Hispaniola

Alonso López de Cerrato

Alonso López de Cerrato, a lawyer, became the twelfth governor of the colony of Santo Domingo in 1543, when the communities of maroons, or runaway slaves, were growing in number and size. He led the campaign to eradicate the maroons, succeeding in killing one of their leaders, Diego de Guzmán, and suborning another, Diego de Ocampo, who then helped the governor track down other fugitives. But soon after Cerrato left for a new government post in Guatemala, the most famous slave rebellion in Dominican history broke out, led by Sebastian Lemba. The African-born Lemba eluded Spanish expeditions sent against him and raided settlements using guerrilla tactics, until he was finally killed in 1548. Cerrato wrote this report on the maroon wars for Emperor Charles V (1500–1558) of Spain.

There was a group of 200 to 300 male and female Negroes in the Baoruco region . . . there was a similar one in Vega made up of 40–50 individuals. They had spears which they had made themselves as well as some weapons which they had stolen from fallen Spaniards, whose bodies they had covered with bullhide. They were so dangerous that no one dared to venture out unless he was in a group of fifteen or twenty people. And since there were 12,000 Negroes on the island who could revolt at any time, it seemed best to try to deal with this dangerous evil head on. The situation worsened with the flight of quite a few Negroes from San Juan de la Maguana. These individuals joined a group led by a Negro captain and rebel called Diego de Guzmán, and raided the town, burned part of a neighboring sugar mill, and engaged the Spaniards in battle. One of the Spaniards and two of the Negro captains were killed in the confrontation. Such being the situation, a military officer was sent out with thirty men. They found the Negroes in Baoruco, killed Captain Guzmán as well as another rebel who was even worse than he, plus another seventeen Negroes. Of the Spaniards, one was killed and sixteen were wounded, including their leader. Consequently, two other captains accompanied by the infantry and the cavalry were ordered to exterminate the maroon Negroes throughout the island, and were told they could not return to the city until this was accomplished.

Ten years had passed since the Negro Diego de Campo had made himself leader of the maroons. A handful of men was sent out to attack him in his base of operations at la Vega. He fled from there to San Juan de la Maguana, destroying property on two sugar plantations along the way and taking about 100 Negroes with him from those plantations and from Azúa. They then went to Baoruco, then to San Juan, burning parts of the sugar refineries, and damaging their property. The Admiral Governor then set out with 150 infantry and cavalrymen to go against the maroons himself. But he reached a peaceful agreement with them and returned to the city. The Negroes, however, disregarded the agreement, returned to San Juan and Azúa, burned down refineries, stole Negro men and women, and killed 3 mestizos. Once again, new forces were sent after them, killing and capturing many of the maroons. Those captured were either exiled, hanged, burned, or tortured, or had their feet cut off. The severity of these punishments reveals the harshness and cruelty with which the rebellious slaves were typically treated during that period.

There were two bands—that of Captain Lemba, made up of 140 Negroes, and another one which had been discovered at the beginning of May in the Province of Higüey, and which had existed unnoticed for more than 15 years in the mountains by the sea. An expedition was sent to defeat the first band. Most of the fugitives were either captured, killed, or brought to justice, so that Lemba was left with fewer than 20 men. However, despite the reduction of his forces, he continued his highwayman tactics. He was finally killed in September. Only 6 or 7 of his men escaped, and these probably joined the 15 who had just rebelled in la Vega.

Francis Drake's Sacking of Santo Domingo

Walter Bigges

Among the first and most famous of the mariners who harassed the Spanish Empire in the New World was Sir Francis Drake (1540–1596), who made his first voyage to the Caribbean with John Hawkins (1532–1595) in 1563. In the years that followed, Drake carried out the policy of covert aggression that Queen Elizabeth I (1533–1603) directed against her erstwhile brother-in-law King Phillip II (1527–1598). English "sea dogs" were free to prey on Spain's overseas possessions, while the queen denied having anything to do with their depredations. Drake circumnavigated the globe attacking Spanish ships and ports and returned to be knighted by Queen Elizabeth. In 1585, when open war broke out between Spain and England, Drake returned to the Caribbean once more, steering to the city of Santo Domingo. The following narrative, written by one of Drake's officers, begins with the English landing on New Year's Day, 1586, and recounts their systematic sacking of the colonial capital, including the Alcázar de Colón, built by Diego Columbus, the oldest palace in the Americas.

It was advised and resolved, with the consent of the Lieutenant General, the Vice Admiral, and all the rest of the Captains to proceed to the great island of Hispaniola . . . allured thereunto, by the glorious fame of the city of Santo Domingo, being the ancientest and chief inhabited place in all that tract of country thereabouts. And so proceeding in this determination, by the way we met with a small frigate, bound for the same place, the which the Vice Admiral took, and having duly examined the men that were in her, there was one found by whom we were advertised, the harbor to be a barred harbor, and the shore or land to be well fortified, having a castle thereupon furnished with great store of artillery, without the danger whereof, was no convenient landing place within ten miles of the city, to which the said pilot took on him to conduct us.

All things being thus considered on, the whole forces were commanded in the evening to embark themselves into pinnaces, boats, and other small barks appointed for this service. Our soldiers being thus embarked . . . all this night we lay on the sea, bearing small sail until our arrival to the land-

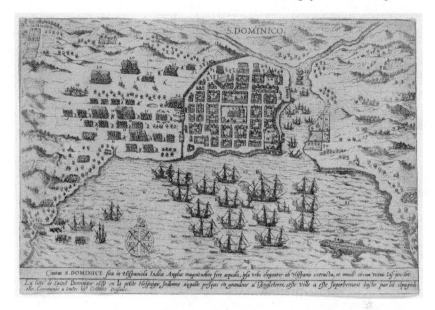

This map from 1588 shows three stages in Francis Drake's capture of Santo Domingo simultaneously: his fleet at anchor off the Caribbean coast, the English troops landing at the mouth of the Haina River to the west, and the army drawn up outside the walls, preparing to attack, occupy, and loot the city. Map by Giovanni Battista Boazio, from *A Summarie and True Discourse of Sir Frances Drakes West Indian Voyage*, by Captain Walter Bigges (London: Richard Field, 1589). Kraus Collection of Drake, Library of Congress, Prints and Photographs Division.

ing place [at the mouth of the Haina River], which was about the break of day, and so we landed, nine or ten miles to the westward of the brave city of Santo Domingo: for at that time not yet is known to us, any landing place, where the sea surge doth not threaten to overset a pinnace or boat . . . about eight of the clock, we began to march, and about noon time, or towards one of the clock we approached the town, where the gentlemen and those of the better sort, being some hundred and fifty brave horses or rather more, began to present themselves, but our small musket shot played upon them . . . they were driven to give us leave to proceed towards the gates of the town, which were the next to the seaward. They had manned them both and planted their ordinance for that present and sudden alarm without the gates, and also some troops of small shot in ambuscade upon the highway side. We divided our whole force, being some thousand or twelve hundred men, into two parts, to enterprise both the gates at one instant, the Lieutenant General [Drake] having openly vowed to Captain Powell (who led the troop that entered by the other gate) that with God's good favor he would not rest until meeting in the marketplace.

Their ordinance had no sooner discharged upon our near approach, and made some execution among us, though not much, but the Lieutenant General began forthwith to advance both his voice of encouragement and pace of marching, the first man that was slain with the ordinance being very near unto himself, and thereupon hasted all that he might to keep them from recharging of the ordinance. And not withstanding the ambuscades, we marched or rather ran so roundly into them, as pell-mell we entered the gates with them, and gave them more care every man to save himself by flight, than reason to stand any longer to their broken fight, we forthwith repaired to the marketplace, but to be truly understood a place of very fair spacious square ground before the great Church, whither also came as had been agreed, Captain Powell with the other troop, which place with some part next unto it we strengthened with barricades, and there as the most convenient place assured ourselves, the city being far too spacious for so small and weary a troop to undertake to guard. Somewhat after midnight they who had the guard of the Castle, hearing us busy about the gates of the said Castle, abandoned the same, some being taken prisoners, and some flying away by the help of boats, to the other side of the harbor, and so into the country.

The next day we quartered a little more at large, but not in the half part of the town, and so making substantial trenches, and planting all the ordinance, that each part was correspondent to other, we held this town the space of one month.

In the which time happened some accidents more than are well remembered for the present, but amongst other things it chanced that the General sent on his message to the Spaniards a negro boy with a flag of white, signifying truce as is the Spaniards' ordinary manner to do there, when they approach to speak to us, which boy unhappily was first met withal, by some of those who had been belonging as officers for the king in the Spanish galley, which with the town was lately fallen into our hands, who without all order or reason, and contrary to that good usage wherewith we had entertained their messengers, furiously stroked the boy through the body with one of their horsemen's staves, with which wound the boy returned to the General, and after he had declared the manner of this wrongful cruelty, died forthwith in his presence, wherewith the General being greatly passioned, commanded the Provost Marshall, to cause a couple of Friars, then prisoners, to be carried to the same place where the boy was stroken, accompanied with sufficient guard of our soldiers, and there presently to be hanged, dispatch-

Diego Columbus (1479–1526) served for fifteen years as governor and viceroy of the colony his father founded, beginning in 1509. Soon after his arrival he ordered the construction of an official residence reminiscent of the royal palace in Seville, Spain, which became known as the Alcázar de Colón. Sacked by the forces of Francis Drake, the building fell into ruin, as seen here in 1915. But its 1952 restoration was the center-piece of the Columbus-oriented tourism campaign in Santo Domingo. Forty years later, the government built a cruise ship terminal directly across the Ozama River, but vessels rarely call there. Nonetheless, the Alcázar is the most visited museum in the Dominican Republic. "Santo Domingo (R.D.) Ruinas del Alcazar de Colón," photographer unknown, black-and-white postcard c. 1915. Courtesy of the Roorda/Doyle Collection.

ing at the same instant another poor prisoner, with this reason wherefore this execution was done, and with this message further, that until the party who had thus murdered the General's messenger, were delivered into our hands, to receive condign punishment, there should no day pass, wherein there should not two prisoners be hanged, until they were all consumed which were in our hands.

Whereupon the day following, he that had been Captain of the King's galley, brought the offender to the town's end, offering to deliver him into our hands, but it was thought more honorable revenge, to make them there in our sight, to perform the execution themselves, which was done accordingly.

In this time also passed many treaties between their commissioners and us, for ransom of their city, but upon disagreements, we still spent the early mornings in firing the outmost houses: but they being built very magnificently of stone, with high lofts, gave us no small travail to ruin them. And albeit for divers days together, we ordained each morning by daybreak, until the heat began at nine of the clock, that two hundred mariners did naught else but labor to fire and burn the said houses without our trenches, whilst the soldiers in a like proportion stood forth for their guard: yet did we not or could not in this time consume so much as one third part of the town. And so in the end, what wearied with firing, and what hastened by other respects, we were content to accept of five and twenty thousand Ducats for the ransom of the rest of the town.

Amongst other things which happened and were found at *St. Domingo,* I may not omit to let the world know one very notable mark and token of the unsatiable ambition of the Spanish king and his nation, which was found in the king's house, wherein the chief governor of that city and country is appointed always to lodge, which was this. In the coming to the hall or other rooms of this house, you must first ascend up by a fair large pair of stairs, at the head of which stairs is a handsome spacious place to walk in, somewhat like unto a gallery. Wherein, upon one of the walls, right over against you as you enter the said place, so as your eye cannot escape the sight of it, there is described and painted in a very large [e]scutcheon the arms of the King of *Spain;* and in the lower part of the said [e]scutcheon [there] is likewise described a globe, containing in it the whole circuit of the sea and the earth, whereupon is a horse standing on his hinder part within the globe, and the other forepart without the globe, lifted up as it were to leap, with a scroll painted in his mouth, wherein was written these words in Latin, NON SUF-FICIT ORBIS, which is as much to say as, *The world sufficeth not.* . . .

Colonial Delinquency

Carlos Esteban Deive

The Bad Life: Delinquency and Roguery in the Spanish Colony of Santo Domingo *(1988), by Carlos Esteban Deive, is a compendium of sixteenth- and seventeenth-century court cases revealing the seamy side of colonial life. The first selection describes the nexus of prostitution and sorcery-for-hire dominated by women who doubled as madams and witches. The practices detailed in the piece, especially mixing potions from herbs, powders, and other ingredients, are still common in Dominican culture. This fact accounts for the abundance of botánicas, stores that stock everything required for such practices, found in every Dominican community, on the island or abroad. The second selection from Deive's book concerns the importance of individual reputations across the social spectrum and the virulence of slander in the mid-1600s. The Dominican rumor mill has continued to spin through the country's history down to the present day, ruining reputations, influencing elections, and provoking panics.*

To Curdle the Sea

Love and hate, the two great levers of humanity, foretold from ancient times the birth of venal magic, reserved almost exclusively for women. An amalgam of adultery, neurosis, jealousy, sexual dissatisfaction, rancor, and anxiety liberally fed the crudest superstitions and the purses of the trot-between-monasteries [*trotaconventos*] and the in-and-out women [*correderas*].

The abundance of procuresses with their reputation as sorceresses demonstrated that doing the work of the madam had come to be a lucrative profession, such that as Cervantes said, it was indispensable "to all well organized republics." Many old and middle-aged women, but also young women, took up procuring like a calling, such that sometimes they resembled in their dress more respectable ones, such as vendors, hair stylists, and midwives.

All of these go-betweens practiced their arts in very different matters. Virgins made use of them to lose their virginity. Others—who had ceased to be virgins—received artificial concoctions to mend the signs of lost virginity. Some had to resort to love potions to attract shy men. Others preferred a charm to keep a husband or get revenge on him.

Procuring is, in large measure, the office of the specialists in the confection of love potions that serve equally to destroy an engagement or to bring about a wedding through trickery. . . .

The most heterogeneous ingredients went into the preparation of love potions. More than the stimulating or aphrodisiacal effects of the extracts and plants, the clients of the procuresses believed blindly in the power of the occult forces. . . .

In 1559 there took place in Santo Domingo one of those rare court cases against various madams practicing sorcery. All of them were experts in potions, spells, prayers, and enchantments of a venal character.

Vitoria Ruiz, twenty-five years old, inhabitant of the houses adjacent to the Hospital of San Andrés, wanted to free herself from her husband, Iñigo López, with whom she was getting along badly. This friction had been the result of the ruin of the only farm that the husband administered and from which he scarcely drew daily sustenance. Vitoria intended to keep her spouse from returning to the house, and the best way to do that was sending him to Spain.

One night, the woman entered the corral and, with the help of a slave, dug a hole near a papaya tree, where she buried a colored container with four round and polished stones, which she had previously sprinkled with vinegar. The operation concluded, she recited a psalm and sent away the slave.

Vitoria was not a sorceress with great knowledge of either the dark sciences or that strange ceremony called the *buca beca*—as she testified in court—which she could not have performed without the work of another person, a crippled woman of an uncertain age, who apparently lived on alms, called Beatriz Dávalos. There were many prestigious citizens of the city who visited the miserable hut of Dávalos, native of Ubeda, in Andalucía, simply to ask her to pray to God for them, because moreover she had the reputation of a saint.

Vitoria's intentions went beyond the desire to separate from her husband. She foolishly fell in love with the merchant Luis Pérez de Calatrava, and to attract him to her arms she sought the counsel of Jertu Corona, an Andalusian gypsy who, according to what was said, knew how to attract men until they were crazy with jealousy. Jertu Corona mastered other powers. If she wanted to she was capable of causing a ship that was sixty leagues out to sea to return to port. She dressed sloppily and when the moon rose above the tops of the palm trees she doffed her hat and saluted it solemnly.

Vitoria Ruiz entered, therefore, into dealings with Jertu Corona and, after much effort, obtained, in the absence of a shirt—considered essential for any love spell—one of the merchant's handkerchiefs.

"Place it folded over a fig tree," the gypsy explained to her.

The woman followed all of the madam's instructions to the letter and after a few days, she returned the handkerchief to the wardrobe where Luis Pérez kept his clothes, not very certain of success, because Corona had warned her there was nothing as effective as a shirt. The service cost Vitoria two hundred pesos.

Jertu Corona had as a partner Catalina Barba, a pimp's lover. In the house of the former could be seen, neatly lined up in bottles, various species of herbs: lavender, rosemary, etc. . . . The most abundant of them were some stinking plants that Vitoria could not identify.

When the gypsy and Catalina set about to perform a work, they walled themselves into a secret chamber and performed strange rituals and offered sacrifices. In the center of the room stood an iron brazier, around which they danced and beat the floor with their feet, all in a state of silence impressive to those who waited expectantly outside. Occasionally Catalina fell into a trance and had to be revived with cloths soaked in vinegar.

During the trial they proceeded to reveal the names and activities of other sorceresses, all of them residents of the city. One of them, the prostitute Catalina Méndez, specialized in counter-spells and telling fortunes with cards. . . .

The cousin of Catalina Méndez was Cristóbal Camacho, who not only had a close friendship with the sorceresses mentioned, but also practiced the same profession. The most common ingredients in his preparations were powders and corn kernels. He also performed a kind of sleight-of-hand called *masecoral* with enviable ability.

Camacho emphatically denied before the judges that he took part in such activities and to ingratiate himself with them he offered new facts about the procuresses. Of Beatriz Dávalos, for example, he knew that "she curdled the sea" when she took a fancy to, and that Luisa Hernández, the widow of Jorge León who made buttons, asked her for a slip of paper with a spell on it to put into the vestment of a clergyman of some authority, with whom she fell in love. The talisman worked so well, according to Camacho, that the button-maker gave birth to a child. To tie herself well to the priest, Dávalos furthermore recommended that she pour the blood of a chicken into a pot, so that in a short time many little piglets would be born. Camacho testified, fully convinced, that in that regard Luisa treated her lover splendidly well.

For her part, Dávalos energetically protested being attacked as a sorceress. In her opinion, all of the women who pursued that profession ought to be burned in the public square. Camacho, she said, was the worst witch doctor in the city, because he had a demon bewitched and in chains in a cave, with whom he talked very often.

A Reputation Lost among Slaves

Slander was a social plague that was so widespread in Spain and the Indies that, to believe Sánchez Melo, a slave trader of that epoch, all of the punishments sent from Heaven could be attributed to the poison of that serpent. In actual fact, the hand of God could scarcely be seen in this plague, which was more the manifestation of class conflict.

The most despicable woman in a cloak, she who occupied the lowest rung on the social ladder, found in the discrediting of someone else's reputation a favorable opportunity to avenge the humiliations and abuses suffered for a long time. It was enough to circulate a rumor, a calumnious accusation, to ruin the reputation of a woman and set in motion a tragedy.

A victim of that state of affairs was the Portuguese soldier Silvestre Cuello, whose vile and scurrilous murder served to slake the thirst for vengeance of some black slaves annoyed by the poor treatment they had received from the woman who was mistress to them all. Silvestre Cuello had come to Santo Domingo from Brazil, as many other Portuguese had, in search of better fortune. . . . Since the mid-seventeenth century, many of these Portuguese who resided in Santo Domingo had replaced the Spanish and the Creoles as soldiers in the garrison of the presidio and the fort of the city. It is possible that Cuello had been one of those who occupied a place in the island's military and for unknown reasons, left it for other more lucrative pursuits.

What is certain is that, in 1641, Cuello had taken up life as a farmer on the Piedra ranch, property of Luis Jubel y Brusquete. There he met his compatriot Rodrigo Landrove Figueroa, native of Lisbon and friend of Jubel and his wife Doña Isabel del Castillo.

Doña Isabel lived on the ranch, where she endured long and tedious periods of time while her husband, in the company of his brother-in-law Damián del Castillo, was engaged in capturing fugitive blacks in the mountains of the island. Of a strong and decisive character, Doña Isabel managed the affairs of the ranch with an iron hand and inflicted whippings for punishment without any fuss.

The lady's outrages made the slaves rebellious. Closed in their huts, or while assembled on the land, they conspired in low voices and contrived sinister plots to free themselves from their mistress. Soon a rumor began to spread around the ranch that Doña Isabel was having illicit relations with Cuello in the absence of her husband. By word of mouth, the blacks spread it around the slave quarter, the gullies, and the watering troughs.

As was to be expected, the calumny reached the ears of Doña Isabel, who from time to time commented on it to Landrove with remorse.

"Does it seem to you, Rodrigo, that my reputation has been lost among the blacks?"

Landrove tried to make light of the rumor and advised Doña Isabel to pay it no mind. Even so, he began to keep watch around the big house, the woman's dwelling, to ascertain if Cuello was involved in the rumors. Seeing nothing, he deduced that the malicious story was the work of the slaves, upset by the mistreatment from their mistress.

One night, while Cuello was relaxing in the kitchen house of the ranch conversing with the freedman Juan Quijado, the slaves Pedro—mulatto—and Melchor Luis, overseer, violently burst in, stabbing with a lance the Portuguese, who with great difficulty succeeded in getting out of the kitchen and took refuge in Quijado's room.

Such a strange racket had to be heard by Doña Isabel, because, approaching the place, she asked the free black what had happened. He answered rudely and Doña Isabel, alarmed at such seeming insolence, severely reprimanded him. Then Pedro intervened and, with an air even more shameless, told her to be quiet, saying what had occurred was by order of her husband.

Staggering, with his hand in his wound to stop the blood that flowed from him, Cuello left the house and went to ask a priest to take his confession. With him were Pedro, Melchor Luis, Juana de Chávez—his wife—, Quijada, the bricklayer Jerónimo, and Landrove. The last two withdrew, afraid after what had happened. They then called four blacks and ordered them to dig a grave.

Believing him to be dead, Juana de Chávez moored herself to Cuello by hand and foot. Precisely at midnight, they placed the body on a board and carried it, lighting the way with torches, to the shrubs at the foot of which the hole had been dug. At that moment, the Portuguese opened his eyes, pricked himself up and, with a trembling voice, whispered:

"Pedro, tell my master Don Luis . . ."

Angered, the slave replied that Jubel was no longer his master and "with a knife he carried stabbed him in the back of the head." Quijada intervened to plead that, for the love of God, Cuello should be permitted to finish what he was saying, but as he could see that Cuello was in agony, he offered him a crucifix that he carried in a little pouch. Cuello kissed it softly and, turning his eyes, already going dim, toward Pedro, he said he forgave him. The slave, by way of reply, stabbed him again.

Old Quilengo, another ranch slave, arrived at that time, and finished him off with a machete blow. Once he was buried, they returned to the cabins. Doña Isabel waited for them tearfully and Pedro threatened her if she did not declare that she had sent them to kill the Portuguese for having gone too far with her.

News of the brutal murder reached Santo Domingo and the judge Juan de Retuerta was put in charge of the investigation. . . .

The Council ordered the imprisonment of Jubel and the ranch slaves. Some of the blacks had fled and gone into the mountains. Diego de los Reyes—expert hunter of fugitive slaves—was commissioned to pursue them. . . .

Jubel protested his innocence and asserted that before the crime had been committed and before he had gone to the mountains with his brother-in-law to hunt fugitives, he had fired the Portuguese. Nevertheless, he accused Damián del Castillo of being guilty of everything that had happened for trying to induce his sister to file for divorce with the aim of getting away with the dowry Jubel had received from Doña Isabel.

The rancher's explanation did not convince Judge Retuerta, above all after Landrove, having told Jubel what had happened, heard him say:

"If I were she not only would I kill him, I would make mincemeat out of him."

The sentence handed down on June 26, 1642, condemned Pedro, Quilengo, and Melchor Luis to death on the gibbet; six years of exile for Jerónimo; and permanent exile and the loss of his estate for Jubel, who appealed. The case rose to the Council of the Indies, which confirmed it a year later and recommended that Judge Retuerta be sanctioned with a fine for having violated the provision of the law that said in criminal cases it is not permitted to name married women, which had not been followed during the trial when the slaves were questioned about Doña Isabel.

Translated by Eric Paul Roorda.

The Bulls

Flérida de Nolasco

Bullfighting was all the rage in colonial Santo Domingo. This was probably due in part to the fact that the country turned toward cattle ranching in the eighteenth century to provide meat products to the French colony of Saint Domingue before the Haitian Revolution, a cattle trade that involved the entire nation from Higüey to Pedernales. Cattle ranching remains important in the northeast and elsewhere, and the religious society, or cofradia of Bayaguana holds two major pilgrimages in which they round up bulls for the church tithe. But there is no trace of bullfighting in the Dominican Republic now, whereas it used to generate both enormous popular enthusiasm and deep official concern, as the following description from Flérida de Nolasco shows. Today, the passion of the people for sporting diversions is mainly focused on cockfighting and baseball.

And what will we say about the bulls? It is enough to record that no festival, sacred or profane, was held that was not crowned by the essential element of the bullfight; that everyone wanted to take part in them; that there was no scarcity of those who, bragging that they weren't worried and rising above the tremendous affront of excommunication, presented themselves in the square in front of the Dominican Convent to assist in the recital of the nine-day prayer of the Virgin of the Rosary. Bulls were never lacking. . . .

All in all, the craze for the bulls was something excessively scandalous, as well as when they galloped back and forth mounted on horses, "with hats tucked under arms and lassos in hand, with serious disregard for authority."

The lack of authority of [Governor] Alonso de Mendoza [president of the Royal Court in 1552] was ridiculed for good reason (the verses of Lázaro Bejarano spreading by word of mouth) and he made a stand to punish the nonsense, unsuitability, and foolishness. But the irrepressible enthusiasm for the bulls, who could break that?

Where they labored so little, where work and ordinary duties began to seem damaging to one's name and reputation, it was inescapable that they would fill the abundance of free time on their hands (because the idleness of this Island was the greatest in the world), with vain diversions. And so we see how the delirium for bullfights continued unabated throughout the colonial period.

It was in the year 1677 when the Archbishop Fernández de Navarrete wrote to the King, and he told him:

"Sir . . . The number of bulls that have been played this year crossed the line and went too far."

Translated by Eric Paul Roorda.

The Buccaneers of Hispaniola

Alexander O. Exquemelin

The Buccaneers of America (1678), by Alexander O. Exquemelin (1645–1707), is the best firsthand account of the pirates of the Caribbean. Beginning in 1666, Exquemelin spent three years working for the French West Indies Company on the island of Tortuga, the most famous pirate haven in the region, and then accompanied the famous English pirate Captain Henry Morgan for five years as his ship's surgeon. Settling in Holland after returning from the Caribbean in 1675, Exquemelin recorded his experiences and described the places he had been in great detail and with stylistic flair. His book, translated into English in 1684, became the inspiration for much of the art and fiction of piracy that has been produced since then. In this passage he describes the economy of the male buccaneer (from the Taíno word for barbecue, buccan, by way of the French boucanier), based on contraband hunting and curing meat for ship provisions, which thrived in the sixteenth century due to the extensive herds of feral cattle and boars, descendants of those Columbus had brought from the Canary Islands on his ships. Plebeian European indentured servants, fugitives from slavery, and freedpeople worked side by side in this illicit meat market, based at La Tortuga island off the coast of Haiti.

The hunters are subdivided into two sorts; for some of these only hunt wild bulls and cows, others only wild boars. The first of these are called bucaniers, and not long ago were about six hundred on this island, but now they are reckoned about three hundred. The cause has been the great decrease of wild cattle, which has been such, that, far from getting rich, they now are but poor in their trade. When the bucaniers go into the woods to hunt for wild bulls and cows, they commonly remain there a twelvemonth or two years, without returning home. After the hunt is over, and the spoil divided, they commonly sail to Tortuga, to provide themselves with guns, powder, and shot, and other necessaries for another expedition; the rest of their gains they spend prodigally, giving themselves to all manner of vices and debauchery, particularly to drunkenness, which they practice mostly with brandy: this they drink as liberally as the Spaniards do water. Some-

Buccaneer comes from a Taíno word for a technique for smoking meat, as depicted in this illustration from a 1744 edition of Alexandre Olivier Exquemelin's *History of the Filibusters of the Indies*, published in Trevoux, France. "Pirate Smoking a Pipe," engraving by Alexandre Olivier Exquemelin, from *Histoire des avanturiers flibustiers, qui sont signalez dans les Indes, etc.* (Trevoux, France: Par la Compagnie, 1744), vol. 1. Courtesy of the John Carter Brown Library at Brown University.

times they buy together a pipe of wine; this they stave at one end, and never cease drinking till it is out. Thus sottishly they live till they have no money left, and as freely gratify their lusts; for which they find more women than they can use; for all the tavern-keepers and strumpets wait for these lewd bucaniers just as they do at Amsterdam for the arrival of the East India fleet.

The said bucaniers are very cruel and tyrannical to their servants, so that commonly they had rather be galley-slaves, or saw Brazil wood in the rasp-houses of Holland, than serve such barbarous masters.

The second sort hunt nothing but wild boars; the flesh of these they salt, and sell it so to the planters. These hunters have the same vicious customs, and are as much addicted to debauchery as the former; but their manner of hunting is different from that in Europe; for these bucaniers have certain places designed for hunting, where they live for three or four months, and sometimes a whole year. Such places are called deza boulan; and in these, with only the company of five or six friends, they continue all the said time in mutual friendship. The first bucaniers many times agree with planters to furnish them with meat all the year at a certain price: the payment hereof is often made with two or three hundredweight of tobacco in the leaf; but the planters commonly into the bargain furnish them with a servant, whom they send to help. To the servant they afford sufficient necessaries for the purpose, especially of powder and shot to hunt withal.

The planters here have but very few slaves; for want of which, themselves and their servants are constrained to do all the drudgery. These servants commonly bind themselves to their masters for three years; but their masters, having no consciences, often traffic with their bodies, as with horses at a fair, selling them to other masters as they sell negroes. Yea, to advance this trade, some persons go purposely into France (and likewise to England, and other countries) to pick up young men or boys, whom they inveigle and transport; and having once got them into these islands, they work them like horses, the toil imposed on them being much harder than what they enjoin the negroes, their slaves; for these they endeavour to preserve, being their perpetual bondmen: but for their white servants, they care not whether they live or die, seeing they are to serve them no longer than three years. These miserable kidnapped people are frequently subject to a disease, which in these parts is called coma, being a total privation of their senses. This distemper is judged to proceed from their hard usage, and the change of their native climate; and there being often among these some of good quality, tender education, and soft constitutions, they are more easily seized with this disease, and others of those countries, than those of harder bodies, and laborious lives. Beside the hard usage in their diet, apparel, and rest, many times they beat them so cruelly, that they fall down dead under the hands of their cruel masters.

Business Deals with the Buccaneers

Jean-Baptiste Labat

The "Pirate Priest" Jean-Baptiste Labat (1663–1738) spent twelve years in the Carib-bean, arriving in Martinique as a missionary of the Dominican Order in 1694. In 1701 he visited Hispaniola on an inspection tour of the settlements on the western end of the island. The Spanish had recently formally ceded the region to the French after decades of fighting the buccaneers, in hopes that King Louis XIV (1638–1715) would suppress their incessant attacks on the Spanish colony to the east. Father Labat traveled from one French outpost to the next, checking in on other clerics who were attempting to bring religion to the unruly frontier. On one leg of his voyage, a storm battered Labat's vessel and swept its kitchen overboard, forcing the captain to seek shelter along the coast. The ship attracted the attention of the local buc-caneers, who offered to trade their famous smoked meat for guns and ammunition. The French priest took charge of supervising the transaction. His detailed account of what he saw, which is the first selection here, is perhaps the most vivid of all the eyewitness accounts we have of buccaneer culture and cuisine.

The various French vessels that transported Labat during his visit to Hispaniola in 1701 were engaged in illicit trade with the Spanish colonists. This trade prolifer-ated with the collusion of the Spanish authorities in the port towns, as described in his memoir. But the smuggling, while lucrative, was not without risk, because Span-ish coast guard ships seized foreign traders whenever possible. The coast guard's incentive was "prize money" earned for capturing violators of colonial trade laws and selling their vessels and illegal cargoes, whereas officials on land sought to profit from bribes and kickbacks from those violators.

Labat found out about the danger of capture personally when a Spanish patrol apprehended his vessel for smuggling. He was fortunate that King Louis XIV had just placed his Bourbon relative Philip of Anjou (1683–1746) on the throne of Spain—which was news to the priest—making the French and Spanish allies and saving the ship and its cargo from confiscation. In the end, the Spanish crewmen themselves purchased the French contraband on the sly, and Labat's companions "at length parted from the Spaniards very good friends, leaving them all our old shirts, half-rotten thread, and other oddments, while we went off with their good piastres."

The second selection here is Labat's description of the ins and outs of the smuggling business.

Our barque had two cannons but only one cannon ball, and this round could not be fired, as it was used to crush the mustard we used with our *cochon boucanné* [barbecued pork] . . . we saw some men making signals who we took to be hunters. But as it is unsafe to run risks on this coast, and they might prove to be anything but honest folks and try to seize the barque, we loaded the muskets with ball and the cannons with grape shot. I then went ashore with a couple of men to ascertain if there was anything to fear, and returned with two hunters, who gave us fresh pork and *cochon boucanné* while we regaled them with wine and brandy. We made a bargain with these hunters to supply us with 1,800 pounds of smoked meat, and 300 pounds of *mantegne*, or pig's fat. This *mantegne* is eaten by the Spaniards during Lent in virtue of the Pope's bull of the Crusade which allows them many privileges and, among others, to eat the extremities of animals such as the feet and head. They therefore cut off these extremities so that there is but little left of the animal.

We were to pay for the meat and the *mantegne* in powder, shot, and cloth, etc., and the hunters asked us to send some men to help them bring the meat to the ship. We gave them six men, and I went to choose the meat and took my boy with me to carry my hammock.

The clothes of these buccaneers simply consisted of a pair of trousers with a shirt worn over them fastened at the waist by a belt of bull's hide. A sheath containing three or four long knives and a *gargoussier* [cartridge bag] are fastened to this belt. They wore a small hat with a brim about four inches wide cut to a point above the eyes. Their shoes are made out of one piece of hide, and have no seams.

The guns we use in the Islands are called *boucaniers* after the buccaneers, and the best guns are made in Nantes and Bordeaux. The barrel is four feet long and they fire a bullet weighing one ounce. The *gargoussier* is a leather bag, ten inches long and six inches deep, and is used to carry cartridges. . . .

We arrived rather late at the hunter's *boucan*. They had plenty of meat dried or being dried, and two or three pigs which they had killed that day, so we made a very hearty supper.

The meat is cured as follows. As soon as a pig is killed, it is cleaned and the meat cut into as long strips as possible. These strips, which are about one and a half inches thick, are then powdered with salt, and left for twenty-four hours. After this the salt is brushed off, and the strips are laid flat on shelves made of lathes in the *boucan*. This *boucan* is a little dome-shaped hut, or *ajoupa* made of leaves. A fire is lighted on the floor of the *boucan*, on which is thrown the skin and bones of the animal. These make a thick pungent smoke that penetrates the meat, which eventually becomes so dry that it is as hard as a board.

The strips are then taken out and tied up in bundles of 100 pounds each. In former days a bundle was worth three pieces of eight, or three piastres, or Spanish écus, which are called pieces of eight because each piece is worth eight reals. But while I was in San Domingo the price had risen, as pigs were not plentiful, and a bundle containing 100 pounds was worth as much as six pieces of eight.

After staying two days at the *boucan* we returned to the barque and set sail as soon as we had settled our account with the hunters and given them drink. . . .

Now according to their law no nation is allowed to trade with the Spaniards under any pretext whatever. Any ship they find within a certain distance of their coasts is confiscated if they catch her, for it is taken for granted that she is only there for trading; and to condemn her, it is considered sufficient proof if Spanish money or articles manufactured in their countries be found on board.

This is their law, but it is easily evaded.

For instance, if you wish to enter one of their ports to trade, you say that you are short of water, fuel, or victuals, or that you have a split mast, or a leak which cannot be plugged without removing the cargo. An officer is sent to explain all these things to the Governor, and, by giving him a good present, makes him believe what you wish him to believe. His officers can be made blind in the same way if necessary, and then permission is granted to enter the port and unload the ship in order to repair her. All formalities are carefully observed. A seal is placed on the door of the warehouse by which the cargo is brought in, but equal care is taken that there is another door left unsealed by which it is taken out at night, and replaced by cases of indigo, cochenille, vanilla, cacao, tobacco, etc., etc., and silver in bars and specie. As soon as this has been done one finds the mast repaired, the leak plugged, and the ship ready to sail.

Means must now be found to enable the purchasers to sell their merchandise. To do this you go again to the Governor, and explain that you have not sufficient money to pay for provisions, or the repairs which have been done, and ask him to allow you to sell enough cargo to pay for these things. The Governor and his Council will pull the long faces they consider necessary for the occasion, and permission is given to sell a few cases. A few cases are sold, in fact the whole cargo is sold publicly, and in all probability to the agents of the Governor and his officers. No one can complain, for each purchaser pretends that his share is the portion of the cargo which had to be sold to defray the cost of the repairs, etc. In this way the largest cargoes are disposed of.

With regard, however, to the smaller cargoes which are more frequently carried by the English, French, and Dutch ships, they are generally disposed of at places some distance from the towns.

A few cannons are fired to warn the Spanish settlers in the neighborhood of the arrival of the ship and they come in their canoes to buy what they require. This trade is mostly done at night, and the captain must be careful never to allow more people to come on the ship than his crew can tackle. The word "Credit" is never mentioned in this business, which is called trading *a la Pique*, and nothing is accepted in payment but cash, or produce actually delivered on board the ship.

A table and barricade are generally placed under the poop to serve as a counter on which samples of the cargo are displayed. The merchant and a few men, all well armed, stand behind this counter, and are guarded by armed members of the crew on the poop. The captain and the rest of the crew, all armed to the teeth, remain on deck to welcome the visitors, give them drinks, and see them politely in their canoes as soon as they have made their purchases. A few cannons are fired to salute people of distinction or persons who have made large purchases when they leave the ship. This compliment pleases them very much, and certainly nothing is lost by it.

But above all it is necessary to be on your guard, and also to be always the stronger; for if the Spaniards see a chance of seizing the ship it is very seldom that they fail to do so. They will then first pillage her, and then send her to the bottom with all the crew, so that no one can complain of their treachery; for if a case of the kind should be reported to the Governor or the King's officers they would insist on complete reparation, not as one might imagine to the owners of the ship, but to themselves.

What I have just related is not fancy, but the common practice on the coasts of Hispaniola, Caracas and Cartagena, and has been the sad fate of many French, Dutch, and English sailors. . . .

The Idea of Value on Hispaniola

Antonio Sánchez Valverde

Antonio Sánchez Valverde (1729–1790) is considered to be the greatest Dominican author and intellectual of his time. A mulatto priest, he became belligerent when his career advancement was hindered by his race, and he developed a critical perspective on Spanish authority. In several works he sought to vindicate metropolitan discourses against the purported ills of creole societies, including the environmental determinist view of the Americas—that its inhabitants were as retrograde as the climate. In this text he takes on Cornelius De Pauw (1739–1799), a French writer with a highly jaundiced view of the New World. Sánchez Valverde defended creole society, including Afro-descended freebooters (such as Lorencín, see below), from its detractors at a moment of extreme poverty, when many urban whites had left and a full two years could pass without Spanish ships stopping at local ports. He defended slavery as a key motor for the development that the Spanish colony needed so badly, and the pirates who, in his view, became chief engines of economic growth, since they provided the labor the country so desperately needed. Sánchez Valverde offers an unusually proto-populist defense of the economy, which was almost entirely dependent on contraband trade with Saint-Domingue, the richest of all French imperial possessions by the 1780s. This extract is from The Idea of Value in the Island of Española, *his greatest work, which was published in Spain in 1785 during his third and last stay there.*

As the *French* have grown in number, they needed us for their provisions and subsistence since they lacked pastures and Cattle Herders, and for every Sugar Mill that they have established, they needed livestock to power them and to transport the final product. What we had in excess on the *Island* was livestock and horses that were of no use to us without major effort. We had neither the trade to warrant their domestication nor settlers to buy the product. Consequently, a very useful door was opened, to take what was superfluous and turn it into something useful for our Neighbors. We exchanged our animals for the tools and utensils that we lacked and *Slaves* which we sorely needed. The same commerce was occurring on the Coasts

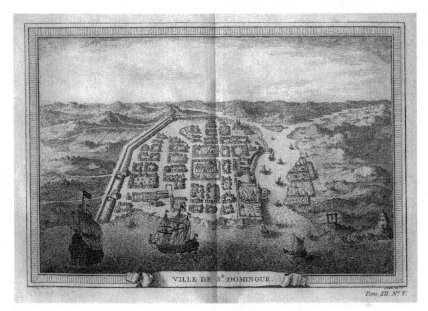

This map by the French geographer and philosophe Jacques-Nicolas Bellin (1703–1772) shows in detail the many religious buildings and fortifications of Santo Domingo in 1754. "Ville de St. Domingue," from *Histoire general des voyages*, by Abbè Prevost (Paris: Didot, 1754). Courtesy of the Roorda/Doyle Collection.

with the *Dutch* and with the *English*, who looked to trade with the adjacent islands. By this stroke of luck we slowly equipped ourselves with slaves and tools. We began to cultivate the land and to build our own Sugar Mills and Machines for refining.

Although necessary and very useful, these activities were deceitful; and they ensured that we were impeded from licensing Privateers to blockade the coastal smugglers, and thus we discovered another Gold Mine. Nothing is more courageous than poverty and that destiny excited all of the Citizens [*Vecinos*] of the Capital to commence open warfare in their boats and canoes, which were stocked with twenty or thirty well-armed yet exposed men. They would sack a Smuggler Boat, seize it and split the profits. They grew in number and arms and in that way many Citizens became wealthy and made themselves famous Corsairs and the Talk of all the Gulf of Mexico.

Dominicans who were skilled and eager to participate in this trade became involved in the War that we referred to as *Italy* in the 1740s, which was so lucrative for them that they increased their investment in these forays, enabling them to reach enemy Ports. They sought out and protected the trading ships which were most often raided—that of the *Continent* with

New York and that of *England*—seizing many Ships of considerable cargo and finances, and ended up cutting off their trade with the *Islands*. Among the most distinguished of the Corsair Captains of that period were Josef Antonio, Domingo Guerrero, Don Francisco Valencia and Olave, and above all, Don Francisco Gallardo, who made more and larger captures than anyone. Some rigs mounted elsewhere even traveled to *Santo Domingo* in search of crew since they highly respected the locals (*Naturales*) for their vigor and their Nautical skills.

When the war was finished, the Contrabandists' smuggling continued along the Coast with the same benefits as that of the *Island*. Among other cargo that they seized, Captain Don Domingo Sánchez and others captured a number of *Slave Men* and *Slave Women*. This continued until the breach of 1761 with the *English*. Privateering was then more profitable than ever. Since this Nation was not separated from the Americans because those that today we call *Realists* were the enemy, the bounty of our Corsairs was immense. Captain Lorenzo Daniel, known by the people as *Lorencín*, who had previously been the terror of the Contrabandists, became the scourge of the *English*, from whom he proceeded to plunder sixty *Trading Ships* as well as *Warships*. He traveled in a Sloop at the Rearguard of those same enemy Squadrons, mocking the War Frigates and taking prisoners from their Hulls.

You can already see how the input of so many ships and their goods helped relieve the suffering of our miserable *Island*, as well as foreigners in the Capital, and *Neighbors* from other *Spanish* Colonies, who came in search of these same goods to take to their respective *Islands* or Provinces. Above all, the *Slaves* were the most useful and valuable commodity. Besides those slaves, there has been a continual influx of fugitive slaves from the *French* border, other slaves that the *French* have brought for sale; and other slaves that the *Spanish* have bought in exchange for livestock and cattle.

Translated by Lauren Derby.

III

Revolutions

During the eighteenth century, eastern Hispaniola declined in every way; the population dwindled and the economy stagnated under Spanish rule. At the same time, the French colony of Saint-Domingue blossomed with cotton, sugar, tobacco, coffee, indigo, and cacao. Africans captured by the slave trade arrived by the thousands annually to cultivate the fertile valleys and hillsides on the western side of the island. While the French extracted a fortune in cash crops from the soil of Sainte-Domingue, the Spanish neglected Santo Domingo. Increasingly, the Dominican people living in the hinterland looked west for trade opportunities, finding on the French side of the island a healthy market for their livestock and an abundant supply of commodities that the Spanish could not furnish. The cross-border commerce depended on personal relationships that blurred the line between Spanish Santo Domingo and French Saint-Domingue. Business alliances and marital unions defied the state's efforts to impose the political separation of the respective colonies, building instead a transnational identity for the frontier region of the island.

The mountainous borderlands also harbored communities of escaped slaves and their descendants, called maroons, mostly from the French side, who successfully resisted all efforts by the authorities on the Spanish side to bring them under control. This section contains two different accounts of maroon society in the late eighteenth and early nineteenth centuries. The backcountry monteros, like the maroons, subsisted largely outside the sphere of market exchange and became iconic figures in Dominican history and culture. A portrait of the montero is the first selection here. In breaking out of slavery, the maroons anticipated the uprising led by the fugitive slave Boukman (?–1791) in 1790, which signaled the beginning of the Haitian Revolution. When a slave insurrection broke out at the largest and one of the oldest sugar plantations on the Spanish side in 1796, however, it did not have much in common with the Haitian rebellion, either in terms of its motivation or in its outcome. That event, called the Boca Nigua Revolt, is recounted here.

The Haitian Revolution, which continued until 1804, had an enormous impact on the eastern side of Hispaniola. Armies of French, Spanish, British, and Haitian troops fought for control of the Dominican portion of the island, with efforts to retake the French colony launched from Spanish territory. This section also includes accounts from the tumultuous period lasting from 1800, when Toussaint-Louverture (1743–1803) invaded and occupied Santo Domingo, to 1844, when the Dominican Republic gained its independence from Haiti.

The Monteros and the Guerreros

Manuel Vicente Hernández González

While the period of the late eighteenth and early nineteenth centuries was one of both foreign intervention and war, it also saw the consolidation of a creole type of backwoods peasant that is typically Dominican, the montero, who resembled the Puerto Rican jíbaro—a type Sidney Mintz has called a "protopeasant" and that is a byproduct of the affluence of the interior contraband economy and the lack of effective control of the mountainous rural hinterlands. One distinctive feature of the Dominican Republic is that by the seventeenth century, freedpeople were more numerous than enslaved people, a feature some travelers noted with a degree of shock and dismay. The freedpeople majority is also a reason why Dominicans constantly complained about the laziness of Dominican labor: the labor force consisted early on of predominantly peasant cultivators who steadfastly refused to engage in wage labor.

These two selections, from A Study of the Dominican South *by Manuel Vicente Hernández González, concern Higüey in the 1780s. The first reflects the long struggle of Dominican elites against the hunting economy of the interior. Due to the small population and the heavily forested interior, a form of mountain peasantry based on hunting and slash-and-burn agriculture survived well into the twentieth century, especially in certain more isolated zones. Hunting for feral cattle and boar that had come to the island with Columbus and developed into extensive herds over time became a central protein source and way of life for much of the rural poor population. These monteros first provided meat products for the buccaneers and pirates who dominated the island in the seventeenth century. Hunting from the large portions of untilled mountain or state lands provided a secure protein source for peasants, eventually becoming the centerpiece of creole cuisine in beloved dishes such as sancocho, a stew that combines poultry, beef, and pork with tuber crops such as ñame, yucca, and batata, which were gathered from the bush.*

National officials struggled over the preponderance of this contraband economy, complaining about it vociferously since it did not augment the national coffers. While revolution was emerging in the western French colony, bringing with it foreign intervention, the Spanish colony was abandoned by the metropolis, with only two ships bringing provisions in five years. Without this central outlet for commerce, contraband expanded, until even the easternmost tip of the island was drawn into provisioning beef and wood to the French colony. Concerns that citizens seemed to prefer hunting and gathering to artisanal trades or cultivation, and laments over their purported laziness and thievery, became a constant refrain on the part of elites, until the state grew strong enough under the Trujillo regime to effectively transform them into settled cultivators. Monteros were also cast as a threat to ranching, which emerged in the mid-eighteenth century as the central core of the economy. Even ranchers in eastern Higüey drove cattle to the border to sell it in Port-au-Prince, until the revolutionary war there temporarily put a stop to this trade.

One of the oldest ruling families in Higüey was the Guerreros. Their wills from the eighteenth century, sampled in the second selection, reveal the poverty and isolation of the Dominican social elite during this period. From the preponderance of illiteracy, even among provincial governors and mayors, to the small number of slaves (from two to eight per household), it is clear that there was limited social distance between master and slave—a characteristic of free-range cattle-ranching economies in which there were few slaves—and that they were treated relatively well, as they were entrusted with driving the herd over large distances and being on the road for weeks at a time, frequently alongside the owner. In one passage the mayor frees his two elderly slaves on his death. The property lists reveal a world in which patriarchy was symbolized by male arms such as lances and machetes but women were important purveyors of property in their own right, channeling wealth into their marriages and independently conveying it to their children. Clearly the conventional emblems of honor were not important determinants of social criteria, since even elites chose partners born out of wedlock, and formal marriage was uncommon even among this sector of the rural ruling class. Land tenancy was held in shares (here pesos) that enabled access to land held in common, a system that made livestock the most important property, with tools and slaves a distant second. These wills also demonstrate the paucity of material culture in the rural interior, where one set of clothes and a single silver spoon or plate served as emblems of social distinction. The Higüey Cathedral is the location of the national patron saint, the Virgin of Altagracia, and thus it is not surprising that all testaments request burial adjacent to a shrine.

The area cultivated was small and as a consequence there was a scarcity of comestible fruits and vegetables. That scarcity was attributed "to the slight application of those inhabitants to work." To remedy it, it was ordered in 1773 that all of those who did not have as their "own profession such as that of carpentry, blacksmithing, or shoemaking had to work to cultivate all crops according to their abilities and inclinations so that in this way not only to bring about an abundance of produce but also to avoid the idleness and the related unfruitful occupation of the montero to which the people who live there are dedicated, with the resulting damage to animal husbandry, because with the licentious life of the mountains, which now goes beyond that which traditionally belonged to the mountain life, they take other people's belongings and they kill not only wild pigs, but with this pretext, also kill cattle, usually when they are found without their owner's brand, because, though they know whose cattle they are, the malice of the ill-bred toward domestic livestock does not impede them from taking those that belong to other people."

Among the traditional elite, the Guerreros were one of the oldest lineages in the dominant class of Higüey. One of the most significant members, the Governor of Arms José Guerrero, who did not know how to sign his last will in 1763, had seven children from his marriage to María Ignacio Garrido, and was the owner of the ranch of San José with its facilities, hunting grounds, and cattle, recorded as having a value of 560 pesos in principal, fifty head of cattle within the compound of the ranch house, and eight slaves. He asked to be interred in front of the altar of Las Ánimas.

Another member of the lineage who survived him was Luis Guerrero de Puente, judge-mayor on various occasions, who at least knew how to sign his name, who gave his last will in 1762. He asked to be buried in front of the Altar of the Holy Spirit. He married twice, the first time with María de los Santos, with whom he had six children, of which four reached adulthood, and the second time with María de la Rosa, without descendants; his estate was recorded with 300 pesos bequeathed to the Hospital of San Nicolás de Bari in the capital and 50 to the major local sacristy. His assets were summarized as two slaves, one male and the other female, she already old, half of whose value belonged to his wife, and who were freed with the condition that the male gave two masses for the days of his life and the female one; a large bowl, two drinking troughs, a table, a knife-sharpening wheel, two small planted plots, 250 pesos of land in Mata Chalupa, where his chaplaincy was located, and 200 given in payment of a debt in the area of Asuy, in the jurisdiction of El Seibo.

Luis Guerrero contracted nuptials with Ana Facunda, who could not sign her name, with whom he had eight offspring. The property of the marriage consisted of their clothes, a silver pitcher and plate, nine cups made of coconuts, a small cauldron for making chocolate, a large copper cooking vessel, six pieces of porcelain, little earthenware plates, a gold cross, three cigar

Ruinas de la Iglesia Católica de San Nicolás, la más antigua de América, Ciudad Trujillo—República Dominicana. Construida en 1503

Ruins of the Catholic Church of Saint Nicholas, the Oldest in America, Built in 1503, Ciudad Trujillo, Dominican Republic

San Nicolas Barí, the oldest church in the Western Hemisphere, supported a hospital as well. The prominent (if not prosperous) Guerrero family helped to support the institution with bequests in their wills. "Ruinas de la Iglesia Católica de San Nicolás," photographer unknown, color linen postcard, c. 1930s. Courtesy of the Roorda/Doyle Collection.

cases made of alloy, twelve little mahogany tables, two grills, two stools, a saddle and a bit, a house in the town and another with a kitchen and a pig-sty on the ranch, a few pigs, eight large earthenware jugs, five stallions, six mares, a filly, and a sword. They were the owners of 375 pesos of land with a stockade and hunting grounds with ninety head of cattle.

Another Guerrero who also served in public offices, Juan Martín, who asked to be buried in the Altar of the Most Holy Christ, married Mariana Sánchez and had four children, and he knew how to sign his name. He prepared his will in 1778 on the ranch of Guanito. He brought to the marriage five stallions, two mares, and 50 head of cattle, a plot planted in plantains and sugarcane, six pesos of land in the mountains, a machete, a knife, an axe, a hoe, a coat, taffeta trousers, shoes, stockings, silver buckle and epaulet, cloak and hat, a little bar of gold alloy, a pair of storage trunks, an old shotgun, nine large earthenware jars, six coconut palm trees, and a wooden writing desk. His property was recorded as including a 100-peso donation to the chaplaincy of the major sacristy. He was the owner of 65 pesos of land on the ranch of Mana, inherited from his mother, to which he added eight more from his father and 100 purchased from Juan de las Nieves, another five on the Guanito ranch, and two in the hunting land of Quiabón, inherited from his father, and five he acquired, seventeen in the farmlands of Manrique, and another four *reales* of land in Los Cerritos.

Some of those who went to the public offices, such as Felipe Santiago, did so to contract nuptials with women who were illegitimate. This he did with Nicolasa de Altagracia, daughter of Francisca Guerrero, with whom he had a son, Gabriel. His property was three horses, three pairs of gold buttons, a silver spoon, three small cups, a small pot, a saddle with its bit, five and a half pesos of land in Baigua, seven and a half in La Campiña, jurisdiction of El Seibo, seven and a half inherited from his parents, half of the plantain plantation of Anamoya, six cacao trees, a small lance, a broken axe, and a small mortar made of lignum vitae wood. His wife, who died before he did, brought to the conjugal union 115 pesos in dishware, land, and animals, among which were seven horses, a small cup, some golden earrings, a silver spoon, a little gold cross and some enameled pieces, a gold rosary, six dogs, a woman's side-saddle, one large earthenware jug and two regular-sized ones, five cows, formal clothing, seven pesos of land in the hunting grounds of Guaraqueibana, a lance, a machete, and a knife.

Translated by Eric Paul Roorda.

The Border Maroons of Le Maniel

Médéric Louis Élie Moreau de Saint-Méry

Straddling the mountainous border between French Saint-Domingue and Spanish Santo Domingo, Le Maniel was the most famous maroon community in the history of Hispaniola. The fugitives living in remote Le Maniel were almost all slaves who had escaped from French plantations or their descendants, so it was mainly the French authorities who pursued them. But the pursuit was unsuccessful, because the Spanish authorities saw the advantage of having Le Maniel as a buffer between them and the French, and Dominican monteros kept the maroons supplied in a lucrative trade relationship between mountain neighbors. When French slave-hunting expeditions approached, the monteros warned the maroons of their approach, allowing them to escape into Spanish territory. While professing to assist the French, the Spanish colonial government refused to allow French forces to pursue maroons across the border. Instead, any French slaves captured by the Spanish became the property of the king of Spain. As a result, the maroon community of Le Maniel survived into the nineteenth century, eschewing a formal treaty recognizing their sovereignty but agreeing to a de facto settlement with the French colonial government in 1786. In return for being left alone, the maroons of Le Maniel promised to return any newly escaped slaves who came into their territory to their masters rather than giving them sanctuary. As part of the deal, the government paid the maroons a generous cash bounty for each fugitive they sent west back to slavery, money the maroons could then use to buy what they needed from the monteros to their east.

Médéric Louis Élie Moreau de Saint-Méry (1750–1819) was a wealthy planter and lawyer born in Martinique who took a seat in the French Parliament in 1771. Five years later he moved to Saint-Domingue, where he served on the Superior Council in Cap Français, now Cap Haitien. When the French Revolution broke out he was in Paris, where he gave out the keys to the Bastille in July 1789. He was close to the French planters, who were avidly defending their rights at the time in Paris, and he took part in the revolutionary Constitutional Assembly in 1789 as a deputy representing Martinique and guided the National Assembly of the new Republic of France to its vote to condone slavery in May 1791. He eventually was forced to flee to Philadelphia, Pennsylvania. His work Laws and Constitutions of the French

Colonies of the Leeward Islands in America *(1784–1790) described slavery and the inferior status of free people of color in six volumes, dividing the population of the French colonies into 128 different racial categories in a "hierarchy of pigment" that placed whites at the top.*

That pyramid of race on the French side of Hispaniola came crashing down in 1791 while he was away in revolutionary Paris trying to preserve it. In August, the Jamaican-born maroon leader Boukman triggered the slave revolt that became the Haitian Revolution. But the original maroon community at Le Maniel distanced itself from this revolution. Having secured their undisputed independence five years before, it was not their fight. The history of Le Maniel was first related in Moreau de Saint-Méry's Topographical, Physical, Civil, Political and Historical Description of the French Part of the Island of St. Dominic, *originally published in 1797.*

For over eighty-five years, maroon Negroes lived in the mountains of Bahoruco or Béate and the surrounding areas, which they regarded as their own territory and which formed the theater for their terrible brigandage. . . .

The Negroes continued their disorders in 1779, 1780, and 1781. A detachment from Jacmel was even sent out against them at the end of March 1781, but unsuccessfully, for it had to return for lack of water at Anses-à-Pitre. In the month of October, new crimes caused a sergeant and ten men to be sent from Port-au-Prince to Grands-Bois, and as many men again to Fond-Verrettes, and finally twenty cooperative colored men, paid thirty sous a day, to land belonging to Mme. de Lilancour.

Finally, in 1782, M. de Saint-Larry, a former surveyor and lieutenant of the militia, who since 1779 had been living at Anses-à-Pitre, where he was constantly required to be on his guard, being far away from any French settlement and near the badly policed Spaniards, made an attempt to get to know those Spaniards who were in contact with the maroon Negroes. He succeeded in winning their allegiance, and confided to Diego Félis, a free Spanish quadroon, his plan to convince the Negroes to surrender and form a community sanctioned by the government. . . .

The Negroes gave a favorable response. . . . M. de Saint-Larry had Diego Félis deliver them some gifts, and ask that a dozen of them present themselves on the plain of Trou-Jacob, which was five leagues from his home; he himself intended to go alone, by sea.

On the appointed day, fourteen Negroes, covered only by a *tanga* [loincloth], wearing a leather pouch at the waist, and sporting firearms and machetes, came from one direction, accompanied by Diego Félis; M. de Saint-Larry, attired in uniform, came from the other, along with Messieurs López and Silvère. The maroon leaders were Santiago, a Spanish Creole

Negro captured by the maroons forty-five years earlier, and Philippe, who had been born in the forest. They announced that they were willing to withdraw to the parish of Neybes, where they would be governed by three or four Spaniards, and to be baptized there a year later, and that they would go after that to the place assigned them. Santiago gave 137 grains of corn to demonstrate the number of Negroes involved; and M. de Saint-Larry, after distributing some gifts of cloth and handkerchiefs among them, promised to return in two months' time. . . .

The Chamber of Agriculture of Port-au-Prince, being thus consulted, as I said above, decided, on the third of May, 1783, that these Negroes should be granted their freedom and made welcome, on condition that they settle in the French colony. . . .

The Negroes numbered 130, of whom 125 were either French or the descendants of French Negroes. It was agreed that Santiago, their leader, even though he was Spanish, would settle with the 125 in French territory, and that all the homes of these Negroes would be demolished. The Negroes promised to pursue and capture all [future] maroon Negroes of the two nations for a bounty of twelve gourdes, as agreed by the treaty of the third of June, 1777, between France and Spain.

On the twelfth of June, the two administrators of the colony approved in common all that had been arranged, pardoned and freed these Negroes by official decree, and allowed them enough provisions for the eight months, until the land they were given would be sufficiently productive. . . .

Since then, the Negroes have strictly made good their promise not to make any more incursions; but their proximity still keeps settlers away, and the mounted-police posts have been re-established.

Such is the true information on these individuals who sometimes devastated great expanses of land, and among whom may be found men sixty years old who never lived anywhere but in these forests where they were born. The particular characteristic of these latter men is disquiet, and it is painted all over their faces; fear works on them all. One could fill a whole volume with all that has been said about their numbers and their way of life. Fear has counted up to eighteen hundred of them. Their real abode is near Nisao, in the mountains that are north of Azua, and this was their place of retreat when they were forced to flee from the mountains of Bahoruco, where they plotted their raids and found a ready sustenance from wild animals. As outposts, they use huts manned by two watchmen who retreat to another post, and so on from post to post until all have rejoined the main body of troops. Their sentries are dogs, of which they have a great many, and the Spaniards buy for them, even in the French sector, arms and munitions.

When they pillaged they would set out and await, for a long time if necessary, the propitious moment. Cruel if they wanted to intimidate or get revenge, they abducted other Negroes and made them their slaves. They only accepted those who came to them voluntarily, and only after making sure that they were not spies; on the least suspicion, they would put them to death. The only example of someone escaping from their colony is the mulatto woman belonging to M. Fouquet, a settler in the mountains at Cul-de-Sac.

These Negroes, after the expedition of M. de Saint-Vilmé, wandered about for fear of being surprised, and were sometimes obliged to live off of tree leaves and wild fruits. The acute dysentery that resulted, and the smallpox that struck them after that, killed off a great number of them. They even contemplated surrender, but Santiago, who had been living among them for some fifty years, dissuaded them from this course. Taking advantage of their superstitiousness, he leads them by exercising among them the role of priest. He taught them how to pray in Spanish, and a tiny cross and a rosary are, in his hands, two weapons with which he soon overwhelms their feeble powers of reason.

Who could assure that this influence will not continue to be exercised, as it has been for so long? Who would dare affirm that whoever Santiago's successor might be will not be even more formidable than he? In that eventuality, the governor should resolve to destroy this community forever. But in that case, it will be necessary to recall that their numbers have increased, during the period that they have been free from pursuit. But a troop whose supplies and munitions are renewed, pursuing another that lacks these advantages and whose wounded are as much as condemned to death by the climate, is sure to triumph if confidence does not abandon it.

The "People-Eater"

Raymundo González

As the Haitian Revolution gained strength in the neighboring French colony in the early 1790s and an army of thousands rose up to force the hand of the French settlers on the issue of abolition, these events were sure to touch the lives of those who lived next door, especially as French, Spanish, and British troops were deployed to the island, which spread the war to its eastern portion. Yet what transpired on the Spanish side of the island was not a parallel call for revolution but a far more inchoate form of social banditry, to use Eric Hobsbawm's concept, in which one or more individuals wreaked social havoc on colonial society and property. A series of murderous attacks commenced in 1790 against Spanish colonists, leaving twenty-nine people dead and nearly as many wounded in a three-year span. The assaults, which also included the killing of livestock and destruction of crops, created a panic over what colonists imagined was a single perpetrator, an individual popularly named the Comegente, or "People-eater." The "People-eater" has been a subject of interest for Dominican essayists ever since. In this selection, Raymundo González describes this series of events and the popular and official responses and interprets them as a struggle between the country and the city, in a context in which the lifestyle and mores of rural and urban dwellers were worlds apart.

Between the years 1790 and 1793 the population of the adjacent cities and haciendas of the Spanish part of the island followed carefully the news of a dangerous criminal who seemed to strike with impunity in the areas around settlements. For more than three years, daily life in towns and cities was deeply disturbed by these events. The government and the municipalities issued edicts so that slaves were not sent alone on the interior roads of the colony; and days were established when washerwomen were permitted to go to the rivers to do their household chores, among other measures that the authorities experimented with as a means to keep watch over men's and women's activities in the nearby countryside.

The town councils also armed teams of hunters to catch the offender, while many landowners offered a bounty to catch him dead or alive. Contemporary sources speak of more than two thousand people with firearms and dogs crossing the forests and mountains searching for traces of the perpetrator, although without success. The "People-eater," the popular name given to this criminal, or "unknown Black" to the authorities, escaped the most tenacious efforts at entrapment, as if he vanished into thin air.

Little by little this personage came to acquire in popular culture an air of mystery as if he had some form of magical luck protecting him from the authorities. . . . To give an idea of the scale of terror engendered by the Comegente's depredations, one need only examine the testimony of the Archbishop of Santo Domingo in his visit to the city of Santiago, in which he mentions that the men "would not dare walk alone day or night" and that he saw women yelling for answers, and screaming and sobbing in the church. Also in Santiago the town council even formally requested that the Archbishopric "send a solemn prayer so that God protects them and imprisons this Black man," which the prelate had to oppose.

The misdeeds attributed to the "People-eater" commenced in March 1790; they ended between May and June 1793. During that time the "People-eater" acted within a wide area made up of the most populated regions of the Spanish colony. The jurisdictions of the parishes of Santiago, La Vega, and Cotuí appear to have been most affected, but the deaths extended as far as the haciendas close to the city of Santo Domingo.

The action of the "People-eater" was linked to the countryside. This was his theater and hiding place. But we are not referring to the countryside in terms of how it was viewed by the city—large farms with slaves that produced wealth for their masters—but rather the countryside as the site of thousands of dispersed and anonymous freed blacks and mulattos who were living in the mountains a life of autonomous subsistence in the wilderness. The "People-eater" was assumed to live within the protection of the impenetrable forests and marshes. He belonged to that alternate rural world that was not dominated by colonial authorities; subjection that was, in colonial ideology, the prerequisite for its existence.

Both Antonio Sánchez Valverde and M. L. E. Moreau de Saint-Méry alike pointed out that the Spanish colony contained many dispersed rural communities. These communities were numerous, especially around Santo Domingo, Santiago, La Vega, and Cotuí. Sánchez Valverde speaks of a "considerable number of poor who only had their huts in the countryside and their pig corrals . . ." with reference to the poor residents between the Áminas and Macorís Rivers around Cotuí. And he adds that "among the Populations of La Vega and Cotuí one can and should count at least three thousand people in that condition, who in fact are very useful for their livestock rearing, although this group also contains many lazy people who should be pursued by Justice."

This dispersed population and the elites' negative view of it—set in motion by the Haitian Revolution—were dominant features of rural life in the Spanish part of the island at the end of the eighteenth century. These two aspects are very important to take into account when explaining the geographical distribution of the "People-eater."

The victims were usually women, although there were a significant number of men, especially among the wounded. It would seem that the "People-eater" acted in an indiscriminate manner, with a preference for weaker victims (the elderly, women, children), as is suggested by contemporary accounts; but from another angle, a very interesting feature can be observed. Many of the victims of the violence especially those who were anonymous, were slaves. One can thus interpret these actions as an attack on property. This reading also links violence against slaves with other acts attributed to the "People-eater," who was said to have caused "the destruction of harvests and deaths of every kind of animal." The fact that these were acts against property explains why the plantation owners came together and placed a reward on the perpetrator's head.

On the other hand, the victims who appear with complete names, or who are simply listed by their nicknames, appear to have been people from within the towns and cities, and when this was not the case, they were linked to plantations that were an extension of the towns and cities in the countryside. It is certain that if the victims were anonymous, it means they lived in one of the dispersed and anonymous villages that fell within the category of the subsistence peasantry of freedmen.

The geographical distribution of the victims of the "People-eater" suggests that, more than the horrible crimes that were attributed to this person, he symbolized, in some way, the contrast between the autonomy of the rural freedmen and the city's domination of the colony. This was the case in a double sense: to inspire dread, insecurity, anxiety, and fear in the inhabitants of towns and cities . . . the "People-eater," as a phenomenon, asserted the autonomy of the subsistence peasantry. Conversely, the figure of the "People-eater" represented the city's contempt and its refusal to accept forms of rural life that were not subjected to planter control, forms that the city could not comprehend except within the exclusive lens of the barbarism and vices that were seen as inherent to the culture of the freed peasantry.

Until 1793, the authorities of the Spanish colony of Santo Domingo warned that the "People-eater" menace was making the level of fear in the countryside intolerable. Rural militias which were summoned to the frontier due to the revolutionary events unfolding in the neighboring French colony, were rerouted to search for him, and they resisted abandoning their towns and cities until their own families were better protected, since they feared leaving them defenseless. Meanwhile, the ministers, the Court, the governor, Joaquín García, and the Archbishop, for their part, impatiently watched the turn of events in the French territory that they feared foretold catastrophe for the Spanish colony. For them, the increase in cattle theft by the insurgents in the frontier zone and the inability of the black rebel forces loyal to Spain, led by Jean François, to combat the revolutionary insurgents, among other things, were indications of a great danger that they feared they could not contain. And so they petitioned the king to dispatch more troops that would at least be able to control the army of the insurgent slaves that these officials thought would cross the mountains to the Spanish side, extending social unrest and disorder to the whole island.

It was in this context that the deaths of several slaves near Santo Domingo added a new ingredient to the situation that had been creating a panic among the urban population of the Spanish colony for more than three years. A Committee of Plantation Owners formally solicited the government to capture the "unknown black" and formed its own squadron of hunters for this purpose. Soon the Royal Court of the island intervened and in April of 1793 it named a commission under the direction of one of its ministers, with broad powers, accompanied by some 200 men between the troops and the militia, to put an end to a state of affairs that if prolonged, they surmised would have grave consequences.

The Court of Santo Domingo named Don Pedro Catani, the most senior among the judges of that tribunal, to direct this commission, and certainly the choice could not have been better. Catani not only counted to his credit the mediation that had been carried out in New Granada on the occasion of another rural revolt known as the Revolt of the Comuneros;[1] but he also had a deep understanding of the agrarian problems of the country, as he demonstrated in a report he wrote in 1788 on the development of the colony.

The beginning of operations in April 1793 was not very different from previous pursuits of the "People-eater." Everywhere the lack of tracks or clear signs appeared to submerge the operation in confusion. As Catani wrote, "it was not possible to discover the perpetrators because there were no eyewitnesses, nor anyone who could provide news of the case, nor a trace of the suspect." The authorities sent two groups of horsemen with lances to search the mountains and places in the vicinity so as to arrest any suspect person, and they too returned with nothing. "The lancers returned the next day from the tasks they were charged with without having found anyone in those mountains, nor any suspects in the places visited."

With these results, Catani came up with a plan to widen his men's radius of action by creating several centers of action for different companies of militias, which were assigned different areas to patrol. They radiated out from the plantations where the prisoners were also gathered. The judge would pass review on these prisoners so as to authorize the militias to clean them up and transfer them to the capital.

During the 31 days the committee was in operation, the Main Judge of Santo Domingo interrogated residents of the countryside who were suspect only because they lived in the mountainous interior and were not formally employed. Of these only 24 were charged to be sent to prison, but after returning to the capital, the authorities continued operating the ambulatory patrols to trap "suspects." In this way, hundreds of prisoners arrived in the capital after Catani's commission went into effect. After this battering of the countryside, the "People-eater" vanished. Catani himself explains this fact:

"I remitted 24 defendants to the jurisdiction of the Royal Court with their corresponding indictments, including idlers, thieves, runaway slaves, escaped convicts, and other criminals, not long after my return and by my orders and dispositions, they were arrested and taken into custody, and among others one Luis Ferrer, as I had planned, against whom I am filing lawsuits and who could be culprits of very serious crimes. . . . With these rulings the bloodthirsty black, which the common people called 'People-eater,' disappeared, not because he was what they called him, rather because there were many People-eaters, who carried out their wicked acts under the cover that they were committed by one, who did not exist, of which this Royal Court has certain proofs." . . .

In the report that Judge Catani presented in May 1793 to the High Court of Santo Domingo regarding the capture of the "Unknown Black" or "People-eater," he returned to the issue of the rural free peasantry. Confirming the image of the dangerous countryside teeming with unruly freedmen, he asserted that the rural zones of the Spanish part of the island were experiencing a wave of social criminality. . . .

This report presents an analysis of rural society, and proposes some remedies:

There are three classes of people in the countryside: slaves, destined to serve the sugar mills and landed estates of their owners; other paid slaves or day laborers, who provide a daily amount to their masters; and other free blacks, who reside wherever they wish, working for themselves, or for another if it suits them. . . . The freedmen are the worst . . . they are not subjugated; they are located mostly in the mountains; they live as they wish with total liberty and independence; they go around half naked and are the cause and origin of all the damage that can occur on the Island. These blacks are for the most part idlers, vagrants, fornicators, drunks, and thieves; you can find only 10 percent who don't have these vices, and who are really industrious. The freedmen are the ones who assist, protect and foment the runaway slaves and their thievery. If the slaves steal from their owners, they find in them a recipient for the stolen goods; if they flee, they are in close contact; the freedmen hide and shelter them, and provide reconnaisance to augment their fortune. They also make it extremely difficult to apprehend runaways, and contributing to this are the dense and vast and tangled forests and mountains, which they know intimately.

Catani's arguments not only reveal the slave society's perspective on freedmen, but also allow us a glimpse of the extent to which the phenomenon of rural dispersion was a form of resistance for those who opposed slave society once they found their freedom. Freedom was clearly preferred to day labor on haciendas. When the direct relation of domination disappeared, the former slaves looked for ways to supplement their income, something they could not do while residing within slave society, where they were subject to a rigid subordination that in all practical terms did not differentiate between freedmen and slaves. They knew through the experience of their ancestors that the mountains were a space of freedom.

However, this was not apparent to colonial society, which could only see rural dispersion as a manifestation of the purported inherent vices of the freedmen. For this reason Catani found that "indolence and idleness is the origin and encouragement of all evil; from it are born theft, drunkenness, concubinage, wrath, revenge, carnage, lack of religion, and every kind of wickedness that could be imagined."

In order to avoid these problems and convert "this class into useful people and the public" he proposed a plan to convert them into peasants:

"They should create a kind of god father of all of them, and not allow them to relocate from their place of residence to the interior, but rather remain only in areas close to crown roads and principal footpaths, and oblige each to work according to his strength. . . . Every four or six months they could be visited by officials, or a commissioner, and those not found to be working the land indicated when examined would be sent to jail, and later expelled from the island. An obstinate evil requires a violent remedy."

And he continued with a series of proposed rules that would constrain their mobility. In reality, the system he proposed was a solution that had slavery as its premise. For this reason, the "problem" of the subsistence peasantry could not be resolved during the colonial period. Only with emancipation could this population have the opportunity to become integrated into global society. But the stigma that colonial slave society had forged for the freedman would remain for a long time to come.

Translated by Lauren Derby and Eric Paul Roorda.

Note

1. A 1781 peasant revolt in the viceroyalty of New Granada, around what is today Santander, Colombia, that demanded lower royal taxes and better economic treatment.

The Boca Nigua Revolt

David Patrick Geggus

In the midst of the revolution in neighboring Saint-Domingue, incidents of unrest among the slaves in Santo Domingo threatened to trigger a general uprising there, as well. A slave conspiracy in Hinche in 1793 unsettled the Spanish colonial authorities along the border. A much more serious revolt broke out in 1796 among the many slaves living on the Boca Nigua sugar plantation, the largest in the colony at the time, near Santo Domingo. Were these events truly revolutionary in nature, inspired by the French Revolution and the unfolding Haitian Revolution, seeking the abolition of slavery? When David Patrick Geggus analyzed these incidents, among others in Cuba and Puerto Rico, in his article "Slave Resistance in the Spanish Caribbean in the Mid-1790s," he found that what happened at Boca Nigua did not fit this pattern.

In October 1796 an uprising took place on the Boca Nigua sugar estate that was situated on the coast some fifteen miles west of Santo Domingo City. The plantation had about 200 slaves, of whom 110 to 120 were adult or adolescent males. By the standards of Jamaica or Saint Domingue, the plantation was of only average size, but it was considered the largest and best run in Santo Domingo. Its buildings were new, and it had probably been built up since the opening of the slave trade in 1786. Most of the adult slaves were no doubt Africans. Several of them had French names and may have been fugitives from Saint Domingue or, more likely, had been purchased there. French records show that the plantation manager did business in Cap Français.

Though the plantation belonged to the absentee Marqués de Yranda, it was managed by his nephew, Juan Bautista Oyarzábal, who acted as if it were his own. The work force was said to be well treated, "not like black slaves," and some of them supposedly acknowledged this fact. Because of the estate's exposed situation, the manager had provided it since the war's outbreak with an armory and two small cannon. As on isolated plantations on Saint Domingue's south coast, the slaves, it seems, were expected to defend the estate against foreign attacks. . . .

The accounts concur in that the plot began as an act of personal revenge by Francisco Sopó, the slave driver. Two or three months before the uprising, an African slave named Benito had committed suicide after being whipped, either for stealing or not performing a task. He hoped in death to return to his native land, "as not a few of those wretches believe," commented the investigating judge. Another slave died shortly afterward in the plantation hospital; the slaves blamed the estate doctor for his death. Both men were godsons of Francisco Sopó. According to the judge, Francisco was deeply fond of them. To the archbishop, Francisco was "overwhelmingly besotted and in love with" Benito. Whether it was ritual kinship or homosexual desire that stirred his passions, Francisco determined to take revenge on the white distiller who had punished Benito. He discussed his plan with Antonio the carter, who shared the same hut, and the plot began to snowball. As well as drowning the distiller in a barrel of rum, they decided to kill the white refiner (so they might be put in charge of the refinery, the judge speculated). Their ambitions aroused, they eventually planned to kill all the estate's white staff, including Oyarzábal, and to fortify the plantation, while raising the slaves of the surrounding area.

To learn how the slaves had rebelled in Saint Domingue, Francisco and Antonio contacted three former soldiers of Jean-François's black auxiliaries who were working on the nearby San Juan plantation. All five were Africans of the same ethnic group and regarded one another as "kin" (*parientes*). To gain the confidence of the three ex-soldiers, Francisco and Antonio paid them frequent visits at night, secretly using the plantation's horses, or during the day under the cover of selling pigs. They took them presents of rum and cane syrup. Nevertheless, the ex-soldiers refused to get involved in the plot, telling the slaves that they were well treated. They also refused to take them to Saint Domingue, saying it was too dangerous there.

Over several weeks the two conspirators recruited slaves on the Boca Nigua plantation, initially those of their own ethnic group, it was said, and then others. Tomás Congo Aguirre, a slave "of extremely bad habits" from the neighboring Buenavista estate, seems to have been the only outsider to have joined the plot. This perhaps suggests that the two leaders were "Congo" slaves as well. Bakongo from the Zaire River basin were the most numerous victims of the Atlantic slave trade in the late eighteenth century, and in Saint Domingue they formed by far the largest group of young African males. Other slaves at Boca Nigua who soon became involved in the plot were the elderly Papa Pier, Piti Juan, Christóval Cesar, and Antonio's wife, Ana María.

Ana María was a domestic slave who worked in the plantation house.

Like Francisco, she was said to have been favored by Oyarzábal, though according to the governor she was willing to murder him herself. The ambiguous position of these "elite" slaves is dramatically underscored by their actions during the week before the rebellion. Apparently having second thoughts, Ana María approached Francisco about informing the manager of the conspiracy. He dissuaded her, promising he would do so himself at an opportune moment. When on Friday, October 28, the conspirators set the date of the uprising for the following Sunday, Francisco revealed the plot that evening to the white distiller—the very person whom he wanted to kill in the first place. The archbishop later commented smugly that this would seem extraordinary to anyone who was not familiar with blacks. It may be that Francisco was seeking to cover himself in the event of failure or that he and Ana María had only reluctantly accepted the extension of the original plan for revenge. Or perhaps it was the refusal that day of the three ex-soldiers to join in the rebellion that caused the slave driver's confidence to desert him. . . .

Like many other slave conspirators in the Americas, those of Boca Nigua doubtless chose a Sunday evening for their rebellion so they would not have to fight after a full day's work in the fields. At sundown they gathered as usual to receive their weekly allotment of plantains, then suddenly attacked the plantation house armed with an assortment of weapons. These included not only lances, knives, machetes, and sticks fitted with nails, but also hunting rifles, blunderbusses, and pistols, which appear to have been their own. A volley from the house broke the slaves' charge, and they split up into small groups surrounding the building at a distance. Tomás Congo led a second attack but without success. Several slaves were wounded.

Apparently at this point, if not sooner, Francisco joined the whites in the plantation house. During the night he persuaded them to slip out of the house and try to escape through the canefields and winding mountain paths. Though Tomás Congo set fire to a canefield to light up the countryside and, as he truculently said later, to kill any whites hiding in it, all made good their escape. Francisco's behavior perplexed the judges. They were unsure if he had laid a trap for the fleeing whites or had genuinely fallen out with his co-conspirators, perhaps wishing to distinguish between Oyarzábal and his employees.

In the morning the rebels ransacked the plantation house, smashing the furniture and carrying off food and clothing to their huts. Ana María helped in the distribution and provided keys to locked doors. Antonio, her husband, was elected "general" in Francisco's absence, while a disappointed Tomás Congo had to accept second in command. The rebels also took mus-

A mural at the site of the Boca Nigua revolt depicts Ana María, one of the leaders of the uprising, striking the chains from the slaves' limbs. Photograph by Eric Paul Roorda, June 2012.

kets and ammunition. Supposedly unfamiliar with the use of screws, they tied together with cord the guns whose locks had not been attached. Artillerymen, guards, and pickets were named, and a cavalry was formed using the plantation animals. The insurgents loaded the estate's two cannon with scrap metal and nails and chose "cannon people" as their watchword, as a reply to "Who goes there?" An expedition led by Papa Pier then went into the nearby hills to recruit slaves on the Nigua estate, which overlooked the plantation. When they arrived, they found its slaves had fled.

The rebels planned to march farther inland the next day to burn the San Cristóbal plantation and raise its slaves. Thus reinforced they would return and surprise the small fort at Haina on the coast, halfway to Santo Domingo. Some insurgents added they were then to march on the much larger castle of San Gerónimo, which guarded the capital, to seize its weapons. Meanwhile, they decided to hold a feast to celebrate their success, and perhaps to attract more support. Antonio assured his followers he was working for them. He promised freedom to all who would take up arms, but said he would keep as his slaves those who did not. That evening, amid drumming and dancing, the insurgents feasted on the master's meat and wine. Ana

María presided over the festivities elaborately dressed and "seated beneath an awning where she received the treatment due to a queen, replying with kind words and expressions of generosity." According to the Audiencia's report, Ana María and her husband received the titles of queen and king.

The use by slaves of political titles mirroring state authority was common in American societies. Kings and other officials were elected by African slaves involved in conspiracies in Antigua (1736), Louisiana (1791), Trinidad (1805), Jamaica (1816), and Demerara (1823). At the beginning of the Saint Domingue slave revolt, as well, local kings were chosen, and the creole leader Jean François and his wife were supposedly feted as king and queen, though he soon took the title grand admiral. The Boca Nigua insurgents' strange mixture of caution and seeming complacency also might be traced to a ritualized approach to warfare learned in Africa, where dancing was an important part of martial preparation. There was possibly a religious dimension to their actions, too, that escaped the whites' notice. On the other hand, hunger and exhilaration at putting their oppressors to flight might provide a sufficient explanation why they, like slave rebels elsewhere, turned to premature celebration. In addition, one senses a naïve confidence stemming from the possession of the two cannon.

During this time, the administration in Santo Domingo had been alerted and preparations were taken to confront the rebels. Two slaves fled the estate during the revolt and early on Monday morning reached the capital, where they informed the plantation steward, Antonio Collar. Some hours later fifty troops of the Cantabrian and Santo Domingo regiments were dispatched together with Manuel Bravo, a judge of the Audiencia who had investigated the colony's two other slave conspiracies of recent years. They had to march about fifteen miles. On the way they learned that Oyarzábal had escaped, helped by the darkness and the local free population. Orders were given to mobilize local residents to cut off access to the region. At nightfall the small expedition reached the still-deserted Nigua plantation on the hill above the insurgents' estate. Down below they could hear the sounds of drumming and celebration, and at 9:00 P.M. the scene was suddenly lit up when a cannon shot set a canefield on fire.

Bravo, the judge, was anxious to kill the "poisonous Hydra" before the revolt spread, but he waited until dawn before crossing the Nigua River. Guided by locals, the soldiers attempted to attack the plantation simultaneously from four directions, but they were brusquely repelled by sustained and heavy fire from muskets and cannon. Falling back to the river with their wounded, they were pursued and a firefight began. After a quarter of an hour, however, the rebels suddenly withdrew and then abandoned the plantation, setting fire to some buildings but failing to burn the green canes. Some surrendered; most fled for the hills. A manhunt then began in the forests between Boca Nigua and Azua, seventy miles away. More troops arrived; but it was the local *monteros*, smallholders armed with lances and machetes, who proved most effective in pursuit. With Oyarzábal offering a reward for recaptured slaves, all but two were retaken within five days. Tomás Congo held out for three weeks. In the attack and following pursuit, six slaves were killed and ten wounded, of whom one later died. The soldiers lost one dead and six wounded. . . .

Sentences were carried out during the first days of December. Francisco Sopó, Antonio the carter, Ana María, Papa Pier, and Tomás Congo Aguirre were hanged, beheaded, and quartered. Two other leaders were hanged and beheaded. Four slaves were found innocent, but most of the rest received one hundred lashes. Another nineteen, including six women and two girls under age seventeen, were given either fifty or twenty-five lashes each. The three former soldiers of Jean-François were condemned to eight years' hard labor in different Spanish colonies. Most of the slaves who were whipped were additionally sentenced to work for ten years with irons on their legs or neck after their return to the plantation. After the executions, all had to pass under the gallows to witness the dangling corpses of their comrades.

The day of execution was extremely tense, according to Governor García. Afraid that the execution might produce disturbances worthy of the Saint Domingue Revolution, he stationed one hundred soldiers around the gallows, put the rest of the garrison on alert, and closed the city gates. The governor feared both the numerous slaves and free blacks in Santo Domingo and the growing number of French migrants from Saint Domingue, who outnumbered Spaniards on the city streets. Like the *regent* of the Audiencia, Joseph Antonio Urizar, he assumed that the latter included "Philanthropists," partisans of liberty and equality, though Manuel Bravo noted the French were only too pleased by the swift suppression of the uprising.

Hayti and San Domingo

James Franklin

The British merchant James Franklin made several business trips to the Republic of Haiti, spending time there during the period when it controlled the whole island. He published his views of the country in 1828, six years after Jean-Pierre Boyer (1776– 1850) invaded the fledgling Dominican Republic and annexed it to Haiti. Franklin entitled his work The Present State of Hayti (San Domingo) *and used the two place names interchangeably. His pejorative summary of the island's history up to that point included the following portrayal of its dual identity during the late colonial period and the first years of revolutionary turmoil, which engulfed both halves of the island but affected them differently.*

The Spanish division of Hayti is said to contain two-thirds of the whole, and is estimated at about three thousand one hundred and fifty square leagues, an extent of country capable of affording the means of subsistence to a population of at least seven millions of souls. In local advantages this part certainly exceeds the western division, from its soil being almost in a virgin state, and a very large proportion of its valleys and elevations never having been tilled. The indolence and inactivity inherent in the Spanish character have been displayed in all their colours in this part of St. Domingo; for although their district possessed all the natural means required to raise them to an equal pitch of splendour with their French neighbours, yet so powerful were their propensities for pleasure, and every species of amusement, that they devoted but little of their time to the improvement of their properties, and they obtained from them but little beyond a scanty supply for their own immediate wants. From every source of information that can be consulted, it appears that the Spaniards, from their earliest settlement down to the period when they finally quitted the country, depended more on their mines than on anything that possibly could be derived from either agriculture or commerce; consequently agriculture was in a backward state, and the culture of the soil made but a very slow progress: indeed, but a very small proportion of the country was in a state of tillage; the inhabitants merely paid a little attention to the natural pastures which abounded in all the plains of the east, and whose luxuriance and verdure continued throughout the whole year. In these they raised large herds of cattle, for which they found a market, not only among their neighbours the French, who required a considerable supply for their estates, but they exported very large quantities to Jamaica and Cuba. To the raising of cattle, therefore, and to the occasional cutting of wood—mahogany, cedar, and a variety of other timbers for ornamental work, as well as dye-woods—did the Spaniards devote their time, and hence did they contrive to satisfy their moderate and contracted wants, without having recourse to tillage. . . .

The wants of the French in cattle, mules, and horses, were exceedingly extensive, and offered to the Spaniards an opportunity of improving their properties, by providing a vent for the sale of their stock. It gave an impulse to industry, and the once inert and unconcerned Spanish planter became in time an active and enterprising agriculturist, shaking off that languor by which he had been previously characterized, and at length assuming a degree of animation and spirit, which enabled him to take advantage of those resources which nature had placed within his reach.

A mutual interchange and good understanding between the two powers of France and Spain having taken place, this intercourse, become more frequent and reciprocally beneficial, continued for a series of years. In 1790, however, this most important branch of their commerce was cut off by the convulsion into which the neighbouring province was thrown. All that part of the population who dwelt on the frontiers withdrew themselves into the interior, leaving behind them their cattle, which fell into the hands of their rapacious neighbours, whose inroads caused much consternation amongst the proprietors; but their slaves, from habit or from some other powerful cause, remained unmoved and attached to them, although they had before them such strong incentives to revolt. Every appeal made by these people (and it is said, that they made innumerable ones) to the cabinet of Spain for protection against the fatal example of the French division, met with a very cold reception, if not a positive rejection. In this state of suspense and continued fear and alarm the people remained, until the disgraceful Treaty of Basel [1795] gave Hispaniola to the republican government of France. . . .

Receiving no answer to their prayers or to their remonstrances, the people were left in a state bordering on despondency, with the only alternative of leaving their native land, or of swearing allegiance to a power in whom they could not confide, and which they had been taught to detest. Emigration therefore was determined on, and all orders of nuns, friars, clergy, and men of property and influence—with their families and their slaves, embarked for Cuba, Porto Rico, and the Spanish main, leaving behind them their possessions, to seek a shelter, and to find homes and occupations, in a country in which they might be protected by laws to which they had been accustomed, and submit to a government which they had been taught to respect. The extent of this emigration was considerable, and is said to have amounted to one third of the population; and it is evident from a subsequent census that this was not an exaggeration, and that so large a proportion of the people absolutely left the country, abandoning their abodes and much wealth rather than submit to a people whom they hated as the usurpers of their possessions. In the years 1789 and 1790, about which time the first disturbances among the slaves in the French part of the island commenced, it appears the Spanish division contained about one hundred and fifty thousand souls or upwards; but by a subsequent census taken immediately after the cession to the French, and after the spirit for emigration had in some measure subsided, there remained only about one hundred thousand of all descriptions, a very strong proof of the detestation in which the Spaniards held this treaty, which assigned them over as subjects of the republican government of France. . . .

Notwithstanding the enmity which always existed between the two colonies, a smuggling trade was carried on, which, although not very extensive, was exceedingly productive to the Spaniards, as it took off part of their horned cattle, mules, horses, etc., and in return for which they received the products and manufactures of Europe, and slaves, which they could not obtain by the regular course of importation, on any thing like the same moderate or favourable terms. It is stated, that the French purchased annually upwards of twenty-five thousand head of horned cattle and about two thousand five hundred mules and horses; and that the Spaniards also transmitted upwards of half a million of dollars in specie during the year, for the purchase of goods, implements of agriculture, and negroes. Large shipments of mahogany and dye-woods found their way to Spain and different parts of Europe, and the United States, and indirectly to England: and a considerable intercourse existed with the islands of Porto Rico, Cuba, and Jamaica, to which latter two islands cattle were exported, and mahogany and dye-woods found a market in Jamaica more advantageous than any that could be found in Europe, owing to their being able to procure their returns in a more direct way than through the mother-country or any of the European states. . . .

Toussaint's Conquest

Jonathan Brown

*The French Revolution and the Haitian Revolution unfolded simultaneously on op-
posite sides of the Atlantic. In the middle of all the changes was François-Dominique
Toussaint-Louverture, the charismatic former steward who became the leader of the
slave revolt. The armies deployed by the new Paris regime were victorious in the
War of the Pyrenees (1793–1795) against Spain, which ceded the colony of Santo Domingo to France as part of the peace settlement, the Treaty of Basel. The following
selection is from the pen of the New Hampshire doctor Jonathan Brown, who lived in
the Dominican Republic for more than a year, 1833–1834, while researching his book*
The History and Present Condition of St. Domingo *(1837). In this excerpt from
it he narrates Toussaint's clever course of action from 1795 to 1800, as he overcame
the Dominican refusal to be ceded without consent and proceeded to unify the island
under his rule.*

Toussaint conceived the design of seizing upon the Spanish territory, which
had already been ceded to France by the treaty of Bâsle, but from the inter-
position of other events had never been given up by the Spaniards to those
who had acquired it by treaty. But Toussaint could not at that time carry
his projected enterprise into execution, from the unsettled state of his own
power and the arrival of the new commissioners from France. Now, when
he had no longer a rival or an enemy to contend with in his own government, he applied himself to his old design against the Spanish territory. . . .

Toussaint now proceeded actively in his design, and he made his preparations with a caution and foresight to secure success, as he well knew
that success would be the surest guarantee of his own safety in an enterprise which might in its consequences bring on a renewal of hostilities between France and Spain. He made his arrangements in profound secrecy,
and when every thing was in readiness he wrote a letter to Don Joachim
Garcia, the Spanish governor at Santo Domingo, demanding, in respectful
language, some reparation for the insult lately offered to the French agent in
that city, and adding that his surprise was great that such a violation of the

laws of nations should have been perpetrated within his territory: but that he trusted not to remain long in suspense before ample satisfaction should be rendered for the injustice.

"Reasons of state," continued the letter, "have determined the agent of the French government in St. Domingo to take possession of the Spanish territory in virtue of the treaty of Bâsle, by which it was ceded to the French republic by His Catholic Majesty." . . .

This document, half letter and half manifesto, was dispatched at the same time that ten thousand troops commenced their march to invade the Spanish territory. The latter penetrated in two columns:—that of the North, under Gen. Moyse, marched upon Santiago de los Caballeros, and that of the South, under Toussaint in person, proceeded along the coast by way of Azua toward the city of Santo Domingo.

These operations had all been carried on so secretly that the Spanish governor had been kept in profound ignorance of the preparations against him; and it was at the same moment that he received tidings of the invasion and that these two distant columns of Toussaint's army had already affected a junction with each other and were in full march for Santo Domingo. . . .

The Spaniards made but little resistance to their invaders. A few ambuscades among the mountain defiles of Cibao, and a little skirmishing behind the rivers Guayavin and Amina, and in the department of the Ozama, behind the river Nisao, were all the efforts made to arrest the advance of the victorious blacks. They had no difficulty in driving the Spaniards from all these positions, as they overwhelmed them with numbers, and terror had already paralyzed all energy in the ranks of the enemy before Toussaint had come up. The black general-in-chief ordered detachments to disperse the resistance which was made: but when this had been effected he recalled his forces, to prevent as much as possible all bloodshed in his march. These orders, and the precipitate flight of the Spaniards, saved almost all effusion of blood, and not more than one hundred men were slain during the whole march.

The success of the campaign justified the expectations of Toussaint, for Don Garcia, the Spanish governor, seeing all his [military out]posts carried one after another, and the very seat of his government invaded, considered himself happy at last to be permitted to yield a peaceable submission to the demands of Toussaint, who took possession of the territory, assuring the inhabitants of oblivion of the past and protection in the future. After a series of negotiations which looked extremely like capitulation, though both sides were careful not to name the word, on the 27th of January, 1800, the flag of Spain was taken down at Santo Domingo, under a salute of twenty-one guns, and that of France was hoisted in its place under another salute of twenty-two. Just at this moment the officer bearing dispatches from Cap Francois arrived at Santo Domingo, and delivered orders from the consular government which countermanded the expedition against the Spanish territory. Toussaint affected great regret that he had not received sooner these commands of the French government, but added that it was now too late.

The army of blacks entered Santo Domingo in a sort of triumph. Their chief was met by the Spanish governor and the alcalde of the town, who, according to an ancient Spanish usage, invited him to make oath in the name of the Holy Trinity that he would govern with wisdom that part of the island of which he had just taken possession. Toussaint, whose tact and self-possession never forsook him, made his refusal as obliging as possible, assuring them that he was not required to govern as a Spanish officer who had come to relieve Don Garcia, but in the name and for the interests of the French republic; "but I swear," added he, "in the name of the God who now hears me, to forget all that is past, and to make it the aim of all my cares and exertions to render happy and contented the Spanish population who have now become French." After this assurance the Spanish governor was satisfied; and with a thousand protestations of fidelity he delivered up the keys of the city. Toussaint covered them with his hand, saying "I accept them in the name of the French republic," and then turning himself toward the crowd of people around him, he added, "let us now go and thank the Author of all things for having crowned with such success an enterprise founded on the faith of treaties and laws of the republic." Followed by the governor and all the Spanish authorities he entered the cathedral, where Te Deum was chanted in a manner the most pompous.

The whole island was now nominally under the French republic, but in reality governed absolutely by Toussaint. The dominion of Spain was at an end in St. Domingo, and almost all the large Spanish planters gathered together their effects and left the island. Great numbers sailed for Cuba—others for the Spanish colonies upon the continent of America,—and none of the ancient white population were soon after to be found in the Spanish territory, except the lower class of citizens in the towns and the herdsmen of the country. Don Joachim Garcia, finding his situation among the new authorities irksome and equivocal, soon departed for the Spanish Main, with a large retinue of Spanish colonists, among whom were great numbers of ecclesiastics. . . .

From the Bay of Samana to Cape Tiburon every thing was now under the dominion of Toussaint; and with nothing more to gain he now occupied his time in enjoying the triumphs of his success. He journeyed in state from town to town throughout the Spanish territory, and his approach was announced every where by the salutes of artillery and ringing of bells. The clergy came out barefoot to meet him, and received him in procession under the dais, while Toussaint, by treating them graciously and offering them his protection, added immensely to the firmness of his own power in that part of the island. The influence of the priesthood exerted in his favor among so bigoted a race, produced results which were immediate; and within a few days from the time when his power had been extended to that part of the island his control over the Spaniards was in all respects equal to that over the blacks.

The union of all parts of the island under the same government gave an increase to its prosperity, which manifested itself by immediate results. The cultivators of the French part were furnished with a ready supply of horses and mules for purposes of agriculture, and the Spaniards drew immense benefits from the greater extension of internal commerce and the easier and more profitable sale of horses and cattle. Extensive roads were opened, through the energy and activity of Toussaint's administration, as great thoroughfares of communication between the distant points of the island; and one of these, which extended from the city of Santo Domingo to Laxavon, was not less than two hundred forty miles in extent. The use of carriages had been hitherto unknown in most parts of the Spanish territory—and when introduced, as they were now, it was alone through the enterprise and luxury of negroes who but a few years before had been slaves. The invasion of the blacks, which had excited so much alarm among the Spaniards, and had been deemed a disaster to be prevented at every sacrifice, so far from having proved a calamity, seemed to have added immense benefits to the neglected lands and wandering population of that territory, and given every thing an impulse of prosperity which seemed about to revive the epoch of its ancient magnificence.

After the War, *Tertulias*

William Walton Jr.

War frequently swept the area that would eventually become the Dominican Republic, especially the strategic city of Santo Domingo. Several of these conflicts receive mention in the 1810 traveler's account below, which is a portrait of a war-torn nation. At the time when William Walton Jr. sailed along the coast of Hispaniola and traversed much of its interior, the Spanish side of the island was recovering from a particularly violent cycle in its history, beginning with its cession to France in 1795 and subsequent occupation by Haitian troops under the command of Toussaint-Louverture. Napoleon Bonaparte sent an army to suppress the Haitian Revolution, causing more war for the Spanish side of the island, where a French force remained even after Haitian independence was secured in 1804. The year after, the newly proclaimed emperor of Haiti, Jean-Jacques Dessalines (1758–1806), invaded the eastern half of the island and once again occupied Santo Domingo. A French fleet drove his army out of the city, but this army sacked Santiago on its retreat back westward through the Cibao. The waters off Santo Domingo then became the scene of the last naval fleet action fought during the Napoleonic Wars, when the Royal Navy command of Admiral Sir John Thomas Duckworth (1747–1817) defeated a French squadron at the Battle of San Domingo on February 6, 1806. Bringing seven "ships of the line" into action, the British captured or destroyed all five of the French ships of that class, including the 105-gun flagship Imperial, *one of two that ran aground and burned at Haina. Closer to the time of Walton's journey, in July 1809, the Spanish regained their colony from France after a destructive eight-month siege of Santo Domingo, another bloody event mentioned in his account, which dates from the following year.*

Despite the destruction caused by fifteen years of war, the poor Dominicans Walton observed in 1810 put a high priority on having a good time. The scandalized British visitor recorded what he saw at their tertulias *(balls), including their musical instruments, dances, and fashions, but he was mainly interested in Dominican women, noting their boldness and their immersion in their social calendars.*

Haina is a considerable bay . . . without an entrance into the large and beautiful river of that name, that falls into it, owing to an irregular bar of sand; but it is navigable some distance up, and is very convenient for floating of those woods with which it is lined. There is a ferry-canoe to cross, by swimming your horse, that is held by a halter on the side of the boat. This is the general mode also of crossing cattle, though to this day many rivers are crossed in a long frame, covered with bulls' hides, which the ferryman pushes over as he swims to the other side, and in which the passenger places himself horizontally. . . .

Here, in [1655], Admiral Penn landed 9,000 men under General Venables, to capture the city of Santo Domingo, where they were defeated by the armed peasantry, and compelled to embark in disgrace. They were however successful in Jamaica, though Cromwell on their return sent both commanders to the Tower, as a punishment for the failure of the first attempt. . . .

To the East of the capital, and leading to Seibo, are those immense plains pertinently called *Los Llanos,* where the eye wanders unobstructed over an extent of grassy surface, as level as the sea, but occasionally diversified by a natural clump of trees that seem planted by hand of man, to resemble a park. They are however nothing more than groups of small trees and shrubs that have grown spontaneously on the margin of a spring, or collection of water, formed by a small hollow, and round which they thrive to the extent fertilized by the oozing moisture of the pool. Here the ranging cattle seek shelter and refreshment from the mid-day heat, and to the bending boughs the weary and parched traveler suspends his hammock, which always forms part of his equipage.

This astonishing plains constitutes almost a sixth of the island, extending nearly to the East end, a distance of more than 90 miles on a width of about 30. On it, the cattle of more than a hundred owners pasture in herds, and are annually collected, counted, and the young branded, at the season when the calf cannot mistake its mother. The dexterity with which the herdsman on horseback, with a lance in his hand, separates one of his master's from the rest, is wonderful. In the dry season when the blade is long and rank, it is customary to burn all the grass on the plains, which serves as an annual manure, for in that season the cattle generally take to the forests in search of the herbage the sun has not had the power to parch. The operation of burning is performed by setting fire to the most eastern part of the tract, from whence the wind regularly blows; it spreads in long and succeeding volumes, frequently making the traveler recede. . . .

In general, the natives are agile, strong, healthy, and capable of bearing the greatest fatigue. With two plantains per day, and a small strip of jerked meat, they will travel and perform the hardest duty, and their wants scarcely exceed a hammock, sword-blade, or machete by their sides, with a little tobacco . . .

The appearance of the town [of Santo Domingo] is picturesque, but gloomy, from the massive piles of buildings, unadorned with steeples; and romantic, from being interspersed with gardens and verdure. The houses are generally very good, built in the old Spanish style, with flat roofs, and a yard or *patio* in the middle, with surrounding galleries inside, and balconies to the street. The lower windows are all iron grated, [and] many of the doors fold, and give entrance to a large vestibule or passage, where the porter sits. The water for drinking is collected into cisterns by spouts from the flat roofs. . . .

The cathedral contains the first cross which Columbus planted in the island, accompanied by the Royal standard of his sovereigns. By the common people, the former is esteemed highly miraculous, and is much revered. It stands in a silver case, richly inlaid, in a tabernacle with three locks, the keys of which are kept by three of the first dignitaries of the church. . . . The chapel where the sacrament is kept, has a small roof or dome painted in compartments, and is ornamented with large paintings of the twelve apostles, copied by Velasquez, a native painter now residing there whose talents, though unassisted by any schooling, are particularly great in taking likenesses, the strongest that can be imagined, though the blendings of color are coarse. . . . During the late siege, a bomb, shot from the Spanish batteries, fell on the roof of the church, where it lodged, but from the train being extinguished, did not explode or do any damage; a circumstance considered by the people miraculous, and it is now shewn as a curiosity. . . .

In the other parts of town are several convents and nunneries, whose inmates deserted them when the flag changed. They have been of late years in a state of decay; for the French turned them principally into barracks, hospitals, public stores, and one church into a playhouse. At present they are allotted as dwellings for the poor, whose wooden houses were burnt and destroyed during the siege, whilst the spacious courts, and damp aisles once trod by the vestal, are now choked with rubbish and moulder away, more from neglect, than from dilapidating hand of time. The different orders are, however, soon expected to return, and resume their respective properties.

The Dominican, Franciscan, and Merci convents are the principal religious establishments; they are large and spacious buildings, with each a well finished but pillaged church, and are comparable to many in Spain and Portugal. There is a college that formerly belonged to the Jesuits, in which

were once educated those young men who most shone at the bar of the audience, and the neighboring islands sent their children thither; but now the
church, which has an elegant dome, and the other apartments, are turned
by government into store houses. The nunneries of Santa Clara and Re-
gina, serve only to shelter the poor. There are besides two hospitals, one of
which, formerly destined to receive all the leprous persons, was called St.
Lazarus, besides several pretty parish churches, private chapels, oratorios,
&c. . . .

The lower order of the Spanish people of colour, accompany their grotesque dances with yells, and music created out of slips of hard sounding
wood, or a furrowed calabash, scraped quickly with a thin bone; the baujo,
rattles made by putting small pebbles into a calabash; the teeth fixed in the
jawbone of a horse, scraped with rapid motion; and the drum. The steps
are singular and obscene, the whole accompaniment and style appear to be
derived from the African Congos and Indian Din mixed, and is the usual
ceremony on the death of a relation, which they solemnize like the gypsies
in Spain, with dances and music. The greatest compliment the lover pays his
favourite in the dance for her graceful action, is to put his hat from his own,
on her head, to wear during the evening, and which she generally returns
by presenting him with a lighted cigar, from her own stock.

The dresses of the ladies at their balls or tertulias are fanciful, and generally consist of a muslin dress sometimes worked in colours, with handsome
fringe and tassels at the bottom. Over this they wear a close body or spencer
of coloured, often red taffeta, or velvet, embroidered with gold. Their slippers are of embroidered silk, their stockings are of the finest, and often with
gold clocks, or sandaled; and the well formed leg and foot, by the short-
ness of the petticoats, are displayed in luxuriant advantage to the admiring
partner. Their hair is generally braided with chains of pearls, or flowers,
which forms a contrast with the dark glossy dye, and is confined with several ornamental or gold combs. The women though not handsome have a
playful voluptuousness about them which cannot fail at first sight, to please
a European, accustomed to the more distant and demure manners, of the
society of his own clime, but though they thus attract, they seldom continue
to interest. The care of domestic convenience and comfort by no means en-
ters into their department, and they think of little else than dressing to go to
the church, or processions in a morning, and the assemblies of the evening.

Stupid Spain

Carlos Urrutia de Montoya

The period of España Boba, or "stupid Spain," lasted from 1809, when Spain regained control of its Dominican colony, until 1821, when it lost control again, this time to the Dominican independence movement. As the name implies, the colonial administration of those years was not a success, marked by arbitrary rules that offended local sensibilities. When King Ferdinand VII abrogated the liberal Spanish constitution in 1814, the trend toward oppressive government control worsened badly, as that action gave wider latitude to colonial administrators to clamp down on their jurisdictions even more tightly. On receiving word of the king's decision, the conservative captain-general of Santo Domingo, Carlos Urrutia de Montoya (1751–1825), issued his "Edict of Good Government." The decree imposed a wide range of new regulations covering many areas of daily life; in each case, the royal official's message to the people was to clean it up.

The Edict of Good Government (1814)

Do not dispose of dead animals, trash, or human waste in the streets or plazas. Violators must pay a fine of four pesos or serve an equal number of days in prison or public labor, depending on the social standing of the individuals, and must clean up that which they dirtied by any of these means.

The storm sewers in the street are for draining rainwater, not for disposing of human filth and the pestilence of interior functions, which muddy the streets and ferment there, prejudicing the public health. Violators must pay four pesos or serve four days, and must leave the storm sewer in a state of perfect dryness.

Removal of paving stones for the purpose of obtaining soil is prohibited. Citizens are responsible for filling any holes or ditches on their side of the street in front or on the sides of their houses, and not with trash or leaves. Any case of noncompliance will be punished with a fine of ten pesos, or a sentence of an equal number of days.

Do not allow pigs, horses, dogs, or other quadrupeds to roam the streets.

A fine of one peso will be imposed for the first offense, two for the second. Third offense will result in the loss of the animal.

Do not cut fruit trees or other trees deemed useful, which are under the care of the government, for party decorations or to decorate the streets for festivals, which leaves holes in the pavement.

Do not speak or sing dirty, obscene, or indecent words in any public place, by day or by night. Violators may be exiled from the city or imprisoned.

Brothels, prostitution, and pimping are prohibited. The mayors of the four districts of the city will be held personally responsible for transgressions that take place in their areas of control.

Dancing lessons at night behind closed doors involving both sexes are prohibited. The owners of any houses where such activities take place must pay a fine of four pesos or four days in jail or at public labor.

Begging by children is prohibited. They must learn a useful trade. If the parents of children who beg are found to be in legitimate need, the priests will be advised to elicit the charity of their parishioners to give aid to their fellow man.

No organized dances will be permitted in the streets or public plazas without prior written permission from the authorities.

No parties will be permitted to continue past 1 o'clock in the morning. Violators must pay a fine of four pesos or serve an equal number of days in prison or public labor.

No singing or playing music in the street after 10 o'clock at night, except during authorized civic or religious events. Violators must serve ten days in prison or public labor.

Anyone who is apprehended in a cloaked or disguised state on the corners, in the plazas, or inside any citizen's house, will be considered a suspicious person, and sentenced to a period in prison or public labor to be determined by the justices.

Cantinas, which provide haven to vagabonds, sharp operators, and other very disorderly types, are prohibited from hosting parties. The operators of such establishments found to be in violation must serve ten days in prison or public labor, and all food or drink found in the cantina will be confiscated.

All sales of all items by stores of all kinds are prohibited after 10 o'clock at night, except for a legitimate emergency. First offense will result in a fine of six pesos or a sentence of that many days; punishments will be doubled upon the second offense; three-time violators will be prohibited from operating a business.

Any gaming establishment allowing the entry of the sons of respectable families, married women, or slaves will be shut down immediately.

Translated by Eric Paul Roorda.

The Dominican Bolívar

José Núñez de Cáceres

The Dominican Republic followed a unique path to independence; or perhaps it is more accurate to say, several paths. First it broke free from Spain in 1821, then from Haiti in 1844, then from Spain again in 1865, and finally in 1924 from the United States. The first Dominican independence movement developed as part of the broader wars for Latin American independence led by Simón Bolívar (1783–1830). The "Liberator" and his allies expelled the Spanish in warfare that began around 1807 and lasted until 1824, by which time every Spanish colony other than Puerto Rico and Cuba, which remained in the empire, had gained independence. That is, every colony except Santo Domingo.

The first of all of the colonies of the Spanish New World empire, Santo Domingo had been the last to declare independence during these wars, not doing so until December 1821. As in other recently independent Latin American states, the leaders of the new Dominican Republic were economic, social, and political elites. Their aims were socially conservative, mainly being to preserve important aspects of the status quo, such as economic domination by an oligarchy of local families and the institution of slavery, while gaining more political power at the expense of metropolitan Spain.

José Núñez de Cáceres (1772–1846), the leader of the Dominican independence movement of 1821, was himself the top administrator of the Spanish colonial authorities, a position he had occupied for twelve years. He gained his inspiration from Bolívar and modeled his political agenda accordingly, subscribing to Bolívar's vision of a large, united, circum-Caribbean state to be called Gran Colombia, and appealing to the great general for his support and for entry into the new Pan-American republic. Núñez de Cáceres was not a military man himself but a gifted man of letters: a historian, journalist, essayist, and polemicist. Though he is best known as the leader of the independence movement and as drafter of the first Dominican Declaration of Independence, which eloquently set forth the reasons why the colony was parting ways with its mother country, his fables are also part of the Dominican literary canon.

Like other documents in its genre, the Dominican Declaration of Independence of 1821 was a jeremiad, and a bitter one. It denounced the 328 years of colonial history as one long disappointment for inhabitants of "the Spanish part of the Island of Haiti," especially after the "furious hurricane" of the cession to France after 1795. Dominicans got no credit for their sacrifice in the war to restore Spanish rule in 1809, the Declaration complained. Since then, it claimed, the first colony in the Spanish New World empire had become the last, in terms of progress, despite the long tradition of higher education in Santo Domingo. After a Lockean and Jeffersonian justification for the new government on the basis of the consent of the governed and the rights to life, liberty, and property, the goals of the nation were set forth, with emphasis on the virtues of home rule in law, education, agriculture, the arts, trade, and the national budget. "We will have everything at home and will not have to send for anything a distance of 1,300 leagues, where our necessities are not understood." Free of the "enslavement" of the Spanish mercantile system of colonial trade, "the good Dominican people" could decide their own affairs. In conclusion, the prospect of joining other new Latin American states under the leadership of Bolívar was welcomed: "Long live the Homeland, long live independence, long live the Union of Colombia!" With seven other like-minded colonists, Núñez de Cáceres signed the document, with the title "President" after his name, on December 1, 1821.

Just five weeks after he and his allies declared the independence of the Dominican Republic, the neighboring Republic of Haiti invaded, uniting the island while extinguishing Dominican autonomy. The Haitian Revolution of 1790–1804 had been a protracted and incredibly bloody affair that destroyed the status quo of white plantation oligarchy and black slavery, replacing it with the first truly revolutionary republic in world history. Jean-Pierre Boyer (1776–1850) abolished slavery in the new Dominican Republic as he had across his native land and combined the two countries into one. That arrangement lasted for twenty-two years until the next Dominican declaration of independence.

Núñez de Cáceres went into exile after the Haitian invasion, as did many of the elites who had supported the formation of a Dominican republic. Prior to the open break with Spain in 1821, he had expressed his patriotic political views in the veiled form of Aesopian fables, which he could publish with less risk of being punished by the Spanish royal authorities. This fable is one of his most prophetic; it warns against giving power to unqualified, uniform-loving military chiefs.

The Rabbit, the Sheep, and the Shepherd

Against those who attain elevated posts and wear grand uniforms without the necessary qualities:

We vary as a matter of record,
and we talk without consonants,
because a ridiculous story
is good to sing between the acts of a comedy.

Everyone knows that the Rabbit,
Why ignore the fact?
is a symbol of cowardice
among other irrationalities.

However, my Lord
gave him such guile and art,
that the Lion enlisted him
into his brave troops.

He got into full dress whites
with a plumed hat,
embroidery and braids,
and a long, curved cutlass.

Such a plump, pompous turkey,
to show off his personage
he went out to the pasture arm in arm
with his gossipy friend the Hare.

Chance would have it
that the Shepherd that afternoon
brought his flock of sheep
to that same pasture to graze them.

Upon seeing the strange figure
they believed, without looking closely,
that it was a Wolf in disguise,
and they ran every which way.

This unexpected turn of events
startled the Rabbit,
who started to flee from the sheep
as if they were hungry greyhounds.

Farewell, fine friend,
Farewell feathers, goodbye saber!
Leave them in peace this time,
because the important thing is to save yourself.

At the same time that the Shepherd
saw his flock scattering,
he came across the ridiculous creature
but did not recognize him in his getup.

He caught the Rabbit at his den
just as he was about to slip in,
and, firmly in hand,
made him a prisoner unable to escape.

A blow from the shepherd's crook
struck him on his flanks;
then the Rabbit screamed
and said "don't kill me."

"If I frightened your sheep,
this is a blameless act,
I confess to you that it was fear
of greyhounds that seized me."

To this the Shepherd answered back:
"Shame on you, infamous villain,
if indeed a few gentle animals
seem like greyhounds to you.

"How would they appear to you
if you were ever to get close
to real enemies
prepared for combat?

"And so that your fear
does not on some other occasion
bring harm to somebody else as it did to me:
die now for being a coward."

He who embraces a career
without having the qualities
and virtues that it requires,
will end up the same way.

Translated by Eric Paul Roorda.

Arrogant Bell Bottoms

César Nicolás Penson

Due to a lack of sources, we know little about everyday life during the Haitian oc-cupation (1822–1844). This fragment comes from Cosas Añejas *(Old Things), a book of legends from the period by César Nicolás Penson (1855–1901). An author, lawyer, and educator, Penson is considered the father of Dominican journalism because he founded the first Dominican newspaper and helped to establish the country's domi-nant press, Santo Domingo's* Listín Diario. *Born eleven years after the occupation ended, he grew up hearing stories about the period at a time when the Haitian civil service had been relocated to the capital city. This tale provides a glimpse of how Haitians were perceived by Dominicans then. Four young men are described as elegant, educated French dandies, sporting a combination of French styles with some creole touches such as bell-bottom pants, a style they introduced into the coun-try. This trouser style appeared in other corners of the transatlantic world at that time, including Cuba, where it became popular among freed dockworkers as part of a homegrown fashion that was probably inspired by US naval uniforms. Indeed, in Cuba these men, called* los negros curros *(lit. the "showy blacks," the expressive style of urban freedmen), were brazen and showy in their dramatic costume, call-ing attention to themselves in aggressive "displays of vanity"—to quote the Cuban ethnologist Fernando Ortiz—so as definitively to mark themselves as nonslaves.[1] This form of 1840s self-fashioning may well have been the precursor of the tíguere, an aggressively male urban underclass figure who scales the social ladder through illicit means and is typically attractive and stylish—a popular Dominican cultural stereotype that emerged during this period. Like the zoot-suiters of the United States in the 1940s, the tígueres were disdained by elites as poor men who called attention to themselves with their extravagant attire in a way that was inappropriate to their station in life; since they were bohemians who snubbed manual labor, preferring to acquire wealth illicitly. The young men described by Penson were sons of the Hai-tian civil service, and between the lines of the descriptions of their French education and style one can perceive clearly the intimidation Dominicans felt regarding their French-speaking and European-educated cosmopolitan neighbors.*

Desecration!

At eleven at night the moon shone over the palace of the council of elders, as they used to call the illustrious Cabildo (district council) and regiment of the old city.

It was February, 1840. Four men, walking slowly, joined at the arms and humming the Marseillaise, upset the silence of the desolate city. They walked through a street furrowed with potholes, enameled with little pools, with piles of dirt in places, and scattered with rough stones of different sizes.

A spectral clarity outlined the edges of the ancient houses, and once in a while a cool breeze came through from the north, sweeping up the usual cloud of dust which covers our streets during the dry season. The men marched in time with the sublime yet haughty stanzas of Roger, the island's composer.

The four men were young. Two were Haitian, the others were French. By order of age and hierarchy they were: Alcius Ponthieux, Altidor Ponthieux, Monsieur C., and Joseph Salvador.

Alcius Ponthieux was young and dashing; bright green eyes, light mestizo [mixed race] in color, with oval face, slight beard, of medium height. He was a man of indisputable talent, and something of a poet. Altidor was his brother. Altidor, a handsome young man, shared the oval face of his brother. A "native of the African coasts," as the Quisqueyan poet said, similar to the portrait of a woman, Altidor was beautiful as a man can be and a magnificent example of his race. His smooth skin the color of pure ebony, his chiseled nose, expressive eyes, with light down on his upper lip, and the same size as his brother; this was the more interesting figure of the younger of the Ponthieux.

The pair was congenial and popular, intelligent and learned. As every Haitian of means, they had been trained in France, and had an excellent library, which was left behind when they left the Dominican land free behind them.

The father of these young men was a *tutumpoten* [bigshot who acquires jobs for his clients], as is gracefully said here by the common people. He was the administrator general, and lived in a way that dwarfed the former governing families of old Española: Joaquín García, the Kindelán, and the Urrutia. Those under him were destined for public offices, such as Administration of Hacienda and others.

The third of the quartet was the elegant, young Frenchman, of the manly, handsome Caucasian type. His face almost round, with eyes black and determined, aquiline nose, fine mouth, black moustache and hair, rosy skin, and sound stature.

He had the rare privilege of giving his name to a style introduced in the country: slim pants with fluted base, which were tied with a struggle and a sweat more appropriate to a higher task, and for which their owners were frequently laughed at in church or in the street because of their owners' affectation. They were named in honor of their inventor.

The Ponthieux were elegant and vain, the *dandies* of that period. They dressed perfectly, with frock coats of the Parisian cut, flannel trousers with stirrups (Alcius had ones with rubber and was the first to introduce that here), a shirt with a high collar and ascot, with a colored tie with a little ribbon in the middle, covering Alcius's head with a *water-proof,* a tall hat that had the honor of carrying this name and that gets narrower at the top. They wore magnificent boots underneath their pants.

The fourth and most humble in the group was an artisan, a shoemaker, a person of the color that said nothing in particular, except that by contrast he was a very ugly *gringo* who wore quotidian white twill.

They arrived at the middle of Silversmith Street where it leads into San Francisco Street. . . .

"Allons enfants de la patrie . . ." [Let's go, children of the nation] they sang in arrogant chorus. Their vibrant voices echoed through the entire neighborhood, as far as the river, until they were muffled by the weightiness and shadow of the monastery.

Translated by Lauren Derby.

Note

1. Fernando Ortiz, "The Afro-Cuban Festival 'Day of the Kings,'" in *Cuban Festivals: A Century of Afro-Cuban Culture*, edited by Judith Bettelheim (Princeton, NJ: Markus Wiener, 2001), 43.

Dominicans Unite!

La Trinitaria

The second Dominican independence movement sought an end to the forced union with Haiti. At the movement's center was La Trinitaria, a conspiracy named after the central Christian metaphor of the Trinity and led by a trinity of activists: Juan Pablo Duarte (1813–1876), Francisco del Rosario Sánchez (1817–1861), and Ramón Mella (1816–1864). "Duarte, Sánchez y Mella" are the three most important patriotic figures in Dominican history, with the intellectual visionary Duarte first among them. His Spanish father had fled to Puerto Rico in 1802 after Toussaint-Louverture invaded Santo Domingo and then returned, along with Spanish rule, before Juan Pablo's birth in the colonial capital in 1813. He was nine years old when Haiti invaded, fifteen when his parents sent him to be educated in the United States, and twenty-five when, after his return, he founded La Trinitaria with a small group of patriotic collaborators. Getting wind of the insurgency, the Haitian government sent Duarte into exile in 1843. He went to Caracas, Venezuela, where he fell ill, and though he found ways to correspond with Sánchez and Mella and the other plotters, he was unable to join his compatriots except in spirit when they signed the second Dominican Declaration of Independence on January 16, 1844, the first selection here. As in the first Declaration of 1821, echoes of the United States version can be heard in this document. Its second section argues that the Haitian Constitution could not be applicable to the Dominican Republic, for "the Eastern part of the Island has more just claim on the Western half, going back to the time of the immortal Columbus."

The revolutionary conspiracy then launched the Dominican war for independence with an assault on the iconic Conde Gate in the city walls and the Ozama Fortress, the oldest structure in Santo Domingo, on February 27, 1844. February 27 is the date when Dominicans celebrate their Independence Day, and a weeklong patriotic carnival takes place in the capital at that time. At Independence Park, near the Conde Gate, the Altar of the Fatherland contains the tombs and larger-than-life statues of Duarte, Sánchez, and Mella; a color guard stands watch there around the clock, and an eternal flame burns in their memory.

*"Declaration of the Communities of the Eastern Part of the Island,
formerly Hispaniola or Santo Domingo, Concerning the Causes
of their Separation from the Haitian Republic"*

The decent attention and the respect that is owed to the opinion of all men
and to the civilized nations, demand that when a People that have been
united with another, would like to resume their rights in order to vindicate them, and to dissolve political bonds, it would declare with frankness
and good faith, the causes that move it to this separation, so that it is not
believed that it is ambition, or the spirit of newness that could move them.
We believe to have demonstrated with a heroic constancy, that the evils of
government have to be suffered, while they are bearable, which is much
better than to do justice by abolishing conventions; but when a long series
of injustices, violations, and vexations, continuing toward the same end,
reveal the plan to reduce everything to despotism and to the most absolute
tyranny, it collides with the sacred right of the people and its obligation, to
shake off the yoke of such government, and to provide new guarantees; assuring its stability, and its future prosperity. Because men in society united
with the sole aim to conspire for their preservation, which is the supreme
law, receive from nature the right to propose and to request the means to
obtain it: for that reason, such principles authorize them to be on guard
against whatever could deprive them of that right, when society finds itself
threatened.

Here is why the people of the Eastern Part of the Island formerly Hispaniola or of Santo Domingo, using that which is theirs, driven by twenty-two
years of oppression and hearing the clamors from all parts of the fatherland,
have made the firm resolution to separate themselves forever from the Haitian Republic, and to constitute themselves as a free and sovereign state.

[For] twenty-two years the Dominican People, because of one of those
fates of fortune, have been suffering the most ignominious oppression . . . a
yoke was imposed on them that was heavier and more degrading than that
of the old metropolis. [For] twenty-two years the communities have been
deprived of their rights, been deprived violently of those benefits they deserved, if they were considered to be aggregated parts of the Republic. And
little was needed to cause them to lose even the desire to liberate themselves from such humiliating slavery!!! . . .

When in February 1822, the eastern part of the Island, yielding only to
the power of circumstances, did not refuse to receive the army of General
Boyer, who as a friend crossed the border from one part to the other, the

Dominican Spanish did not think that he would break, with such under-handed perfidy, the promises that served as the pretext to occupy the towns, and without which he would have had to conquer immense difficulties and perhaps to march over our corpses, if luck had favored him.

No Dominican received him then, without giving signs of his desire to get along well with his new fellow citizens: the simplest class of the towns he was occupying, coming out to meet him, thought to find in him he who had just received in the North the title of peacemaker, and the protection that he had promised so hypocritically. A little later, seeing through the disguise that hid his sinister aims, everyone realized that they were in the hands of an oppressor, of a wild beast of a tyrant!

Upon entering the city of Santo Domingo, disorder and vice entered with him in a rush. Perfidy, division, calumny, violence, denunciation, usurpation, hatred, and the type of personalities up to then uncommon among those innocent People. His decrees and his disposition were the beginning of the discord and the harbinger of destruction. By means of his disruptive and Machiavellian system, he forced the leading and wealthiest families to emigrate, and with them went the talent, the riches, the commerce, and the agriculture: he sent away their counsel and the important employment they provided, the men who would be able to represent the rights of their fellow citizens, to petition for the remedy of wrongs, and to demonstrate the real requirements of the Fatherland. Scorning all principles of public justice and of nations, he reduced many families to indigence, taking their property to add to that of the Republic, or to give it to individuals from the Western part, or to sell it to them at the very lowest prices. He razed the countryside, plundered the churches of their riches, trampled on and spoiled with vilification the Ministers of Religion, took from them their rents and rights, and because of his abandonment let Public buildings fall into total ruin, so that his functionaries could profit from the spoils and thereby satisfy the greed they brought with them from the West.

Later, to give to his injustices an appearance of legality, he dictated a law, by which the State took over the property of those who were absent, whose siblings and close relatives existed even then, submerged in misery. His avarice still unsatisfied, with a sacrilegious hand he illegally set upon the lands of the sons of the East: he authorized the robbery and the fraud of the law of July 8 of 1824, in which he prohibited the sharing of communal lands, which by virtue of agreement and for the benefit and necessity of families, had been practiced since the discovery of the Island, in order that the State should profit from them, to complete the ruination of animal husbandry and to impoverish a multitude of fathers with families. Little did he care! To destroy everything, to ruin everything! This was the object of his insatiable greed . . . ![1]

Fertile in imagining evils by which he could complete the work of bringing about our ruin and reducing everything to nothing, he put in place a monetary system, that unfeelingly has been reducing by degrees, the families, the employees, the businessmen, and the general population, to deep misery. With such aims the Haitian Government propagated its corrupt principles. Through the influence of its infernal politics it unleashed passions, provoked divisions, concocted slanderous schemes, conducted espionage, and introduced vice and discord into the home. If a Spanish person spoke out against the tyranny and the oppression, he was denounced as suspicious, and thrown into prison, and some were forced to climb the gallows, in order to terrorize the others, so that the sentiments passed down from our fathers would expire all at once.

The embattled and persecuted Fatherland could not find safe refuge from this tyrannical rage, except in the hearts of an afflicted youth and among some pure souls who knew to hide their sacrosanct principles, in order to get the word out in more promising times and to energetically reanimate those who lay in a beaten, soporific state.

Twenty-two years of the perverted administration of Boyer have passed, during whose epoch, the inhabitants of the East have endured so many privations, that there are too many to count: he treated them worse than a people conquered by force; he squeezed the juice out of them, taking every benefit he could in order to satiate his greed and that of his followers; he made slaves of them in the name of liberty; he forced them to pay a debt that they had not contracted, as had those of the Western part, to take advantage of other people's property; on the contrary, they owe us for the riches that they have usurped or embezzled. . . .

DOMINICANS! (Comprising under this name all of the sons of the East and those who want to follow our destiny) the national interest summons us to union! With firm resolution let us demonstrate that we are dignified defenders of liberty: let us sacrifice hatred and personal interests before the altars of the fatherland: let the feeling of public interest be the motive that decides us in favor of the just cause of liberty and that of separation: with that, we do not diminish the happiness of the western Republic, we make our own.

Our cause is holy: we do not lack resources, beyond what we have in our own soil, because we will take advantage . . . if it becomes necessary, of what could be facilitated for us by foreigners.

The territory of the Dominican Republic is divided into four provinces, namely Santo Domingo, Santiago or Cibao, Azua to Ocoa, and Seybo, [and] the Government will be made up of a certain number of members from each of these so that they all participate in their sovereignty proportionally.

The Provisional Government will consist of an assembly composed of eleven elected members in the same proportional manner. This assembly will itself resume all powers until the constitution of the State is formed, and will determine the means that they judge most convenient, to maintain the acquired liberty, and for that purpose will call on one of the most distinguished patriots to be chief of the army, adding whatever staff are necessary in order to protect our borders.

Dominicans unite! Already the opportune moment is presented to us from Neiba to Samaná, from Azua to Monte Cristi, the opinions stand in agreement, and there is no Dominican who does not exclaim with enthusiasm: SEPARATION, GOD, FATHERLAND, and LIBERTY.

Translated by Eric Paul Roorda.

Note

1. All ellipses in the original, up to this point.

IV

Caudillos and Empires

In the 1844 war for independence from Haiti, the dominant military figure to emerge among the Dominican forces was an eastern rancher, Pedro Santana (1801–1864), who rose to the rank of general and then turned on the leaders of La Trinitaria, sending them into exile. He commanded the victorious Dominican forces at the Battle of Las Carreras, the climactic engagement of the conflict, fought April 21, 1849. Santana was the very picture of the Latin American caudillo, or local strongman. For thirty years, he and his Blue Party followers vied with Buenaventura Báez (1812–1884) and his Red Party for control of the capital and the reins (and purse strings) of power in the Dominican Republic. Santana and Báez alternated as president; Santana became the first, the fourth, and the eighth president of the country, while Báez was third, sixth, tenth, thirteenth, and sixteenth. Their rivalry as caudillo leaders is the subject of the first selection in this part. In 1861, to protect himself from the threat of domestic rivals, mounting national debt, and Haitian invasion, Santana invited Spain to retake the Dominican Republic with his collaboration. The Spanish recolonization effort collapsed in failure due to a Dominican uprising that became known as the War of the Restoration (1863–1865).

Although Dominicans united to fight the Spanish and regain control of their homeland, internecine power struggles began again soon after the Restoration (of independence). As during the antebellum period, the Blue and Red Parties continued to fight it out over the rather meager spoils of national office, and while Santana had died, Báez lived on. In 1870, Báez followed his rival Santana's example by inviting an outside power to come to his aid, this time by asking President Ulysses S. Grant (1822–1885) to annex the island to the United States. Grant put the proposal before the Senate, but it failed by a single vote. Arguments for and against the annexation treaty are included here; the loudest voice opposed to it was General Gregorio Luperón (1839–1897), hero of the War of the Restoration, who is one of the leading patriotic figures in Dominican national culture.

The dominant figure of the late nineteenth century was Ulíses Heureaux (1845–1899), a child of Haitians and erudite protégé of Luperón, who rose to power in the late 1880s and ruled as dictator throughout the 1890s. Known by his nickname, Lilís, he professed to accept much of the program urged by the positivist intellectuals of the 1880s and 1890s, including political free-dom, civic enhancements, and expanded secular education. An increasingly self-consumed autocrat, he imprisoned, murdered, or forced into exile those of his critics whom he could not co-opt or suborn, including some of the leading lights of the Dominican intelligentsia. His close surveillance of his enemies at home and abroad comes through in a letter included here. He borrowed heavily from foreign banks in order to carry out some of the same improvements that liberal voices were calling for around the republic and the region of Latin America, such as city lighting and landscaping, public health measures, and railroad construction. But at the same time he spent lavishly on sinecures and bribes to maintain the allegiance of his supporters, with special attention to the military, which had been the base of his power going back early in his career. Plunging the government deeply into debt, Lilís also exposed the country to a new kind of foreign domination, one that lasted longer than the Spanish recolonization of the 1860s: US intervention.

Pedro Santana

Miguel Ángel Monclús

Pedro Santana, the military hero of the 1844 war against Haiti, took control of the new Dominican Republic soon after his victories in the field assured its independence. He had been part of the conspiracy that had plotted the uprising, the Trinitaria movement, having been recruited to the cause by one of its founders, Tomás Bobadilla (1785–1871), an influential writer who became the first governor of the Dominican Republic in March 1844, one month after the outbreak of the revolution at El Conde Gate in Santo Domingo. Bobadilla was ousted three months later by two other Trinitaria founders, Francisco del Rosario Sánchez and Ramón Mella, whom Santana deposed in turn in November 1844.

Miguel Ángel Monclús (1873–1967), the author of this selection, was a writer and diplomat; his novel Cachón *(1958) evokes the mythical* ciguapa, *said to have originated with the Taíno, a creature with backward feet that camouflaged its tracks by walking backward. This selection from his book* Caudillismo en La República Dominicana *(1946) offers a brief sketch of the personality and political tactics of Santana, the first in a long line of strongmen in Dominican history. In the author's tone and language one can also see traces of the prejudice against the rural strongman that was characteristic of the urban intelligentsia.*

Pedro Santana was born in Hinche on 29 June 1801. He was the twin brother of Ramón and both received the names of the saints whose day it was on the religious calendar; our old custom, inherited from Spain. Nothing is known about the Santanas from that town in the West. What is known, is that because of the Haitian occupation of that area, the majority of the Hispanic population left, and among them was the Santana family. . . . Pedro Santana, the father of the twins, was a rancher, and bringing his herd, or part of it, he made his way to greener pastures, which he found in the East of the country. The family settled in Seybo. . . .

The offspring of Pedro Santana, Colonel of the Colonial Militia, Pedro and Ramón . . . both were heirs to the economic prestige, modest but influential for that time in Seybo, that their father had; they inherited as well, the ramifications of his participation in the Battle of Palo Hincado,[1] where Pedro Santana, senior, gained an intrepid reputation. With these assets, in that relatively unpopulated and poor area, those young men stood out early as influential people of the place. In addition, the material estate they had inherited was constantly growing, above all in the form of cattle, which were the real source of their wealth.

The memories there are of Pedro and Ramón portray their characters and temperaments differently. The first was impulsive from an early age; intense and surly in temperament, authoritarian, and of little intellectual achievement. He did have an instinctive intelligence that at least distinguished him among the creoles, a rudimentary intelligence that with time and commerce with people and things, in some ways came to seem like culture. The second, Ramón, was reflective, thoughtful, and more capable of understanding, and in a certain sense he functioned as a mentor to the first. Both possessed average instruction; little more than elementary school, all that was possible to obtain at that time in that place.

For the reasons previously explained, the Santana brothers assumed in Seybo, from the 1840s on, more or less the power of local representatives, like Bernabé Sandoval in Los Llanos and Matías Moreno in Monte Plata and Boyá: for that reason, the propagators of the separatist ideal fixed on them, because it was certain, they had in no sense compromised with the dominators, the Haitians; before long, they stood out as adversaries, such that Charles Gerard Ainé[2] tried to capture them and take them to Port-au-Prince, as suspicious individuals with tendencies contrary to the state . . . and the political unity of the Island under Haitian tutelage. A short while after, one person worked determinedly in the spirit of the Santanas to involve them in the movement that would crystallize in the work of 27 February 1844, who had long maintained contact with them and who deserved their full credit: Tomás Bobadilla. . . .

Pedro Santana was lifted from the ranch to the command of the army and from there to the Presidency of the Republic, by the same modes that were the sum of his temperament. The success of Dominican arms in the war, exploited in his favor in the legislature, developed through use into idolatry, exacerbating the authoritarian and despotic tendencies that he had. The work of the legislature assured his election, but in a short time that body became one assigned the role mainly of working as an office of pimps. It gave the first signs of that when it convened the Constitutional convention in San Cristóbal. . . .

From the outset of his period in power—as anointed President of the Republic, by virtue of being the visible head of important affairs of state, and in consequence of his observed participation with the February conspirators, of the barracks uprising of July 3, and of the gallows that soon were erected—a considerable sector of [public] opinion had already been declared as adverse. That adverse opinion was always swelling.

One event that is still not clear, but is of incalculable importance for what took place, gave an unmistakable sign of discontent. We allude to the Puello plot.[3] . . . The Puello conspiracy was an act of discontent and of anti-Santana reaction. . . . The antinationalists who later became the *baecistas*, then behaved like brothers with the *santanistas* and, grazing a pasture together, formed a Government. . . . It is certain that the Puellos in that spurious situation had become a destabilizing force, and it was necessary to eliminate them. The same had already happened to María Trinidad Sánchez,[4] and the same thing would be done with others. . . .

Translated by Eric Paul Roorda.

Notes

1. First major battle of the war to reconquer Santo Domingo for Spain, November 7, 1808; a force of 2,000 Dominican and Puerto Rican troops under Juan Sánchez Ramírez (1762–1811) defeated 600 Haitian troops; in December Sánchez Ramírez became the first captain general of the restored Spanish colony.
2. Better known as Rivière-Hérard (1787–1850), president of Haiti from April 1843 to May 1844, during which time the Dominican independence movement erupted.
3. The brothers Joaquín and Gabino Puello were members of the Trinitaria executed by Santana in 1847.
4. María Trinidad Sánchez (1784–1845), aunt of Francisco del Rosario Sánchez, was a Trinitaria conspirator and had smuggled cartridges in her skirt. She led a plot against Santana, who arrested her and ordered her execution by firing squad on the first anniversary of the El Conde Gate uprising, February 27, 1845.

The Caudillo of the South

Buenaventura Báez

The enduring caudillo Buenaventura Báez, the grandson of the author Antonio Sán-chez Valverde, came from Azua in the South. The son of a wealthy landowning father and a mulatto slave mother, Báez received his education in France. In 1846, he invited Napoleon III to absorb the Dominican nation, the first of several such invitations he extended to other powers over the years, all ending in the young republic escaping annexation by near misses. These selections from his pen represent three stages in his long career. The first, published in the Accusation, *a political periodical, soon after he began his second term as president, is an indictment of Pedro Santana. The second, a pronouncement from his next term as president, critically analyzes Dominican political instability in the immediate wake of the War of the Restoration; indeed, two months later, Báez was deposed again. In the last piece, written in 1876, two years after the end of his fourth period in office, and published in a Santo Domingo newspaper, he looks back on his periods in office and states his case for a return to power. In fact, "The Caudillo of the South" was back as president for his fifth and final time just ten days after this appeal appeared. Deposed one last time in 1878, Báez died in exile in Puerto Rico in 1884.*

A Question (1856)

Why does Santana still call himself general-in-chief of the armies of the Republic after the Senate has stripped him of that rank?

Can it be that deep down Santana believes he is the owner of the position, which he would take to the apogee of terrorism? We understand that it is very significant that this man still treats himself as general-in-chief, and could be considered rebellious if he continues claiming for himself a military rank that has already been stripped from him.

A Message from the President of the Republic (1866)

Our present state is a state of peace, but only of seeming peace . . . and we cannot allow ourselves thoughtlessly to rest on our laurels. This from the outside; from the inside, without concern for eliciting the criticism of those who think without comparative analysis that the application of the theory of democracy is in conflict with the armed forces, and that the latter can turn into an element of tyranny, I will say with the conscience of the man who wants to fulfill his duties with no other ambition than the salvation of the homeland: that in a country like ours in which bad passions are so little curbed by principles of order, opinion alone is insufficient to imprint character with the principle of authority; because the minorities, encouraged by the idea of a surprise victory, are constantly drilling, confident in their ability to win, it will be necessary to resort to seeking out the gathering of those of that opinion when they have already taken to the countryside; and in this way the continual cycle of anarchy [continues] between the victors and the vanquished, who will change their roles on the morning after we fight the last battle.

To His Fellow Citizens (1876)

Here in exile, alone with my memories, nourishing my understanding with the good doctrine of that loyal friend called science, I have dedicated myself to study in detail the short history of political events in Santo Domingo.

Here I have meditated, in the same way, over their [the Dominicans'] long and ongoing fratricidal struggles, and comparing their misfortunes in thirty-two years of independent life, with the tranquility and happiness that one enjoys in other countries, where citizens respect the institutions, I have come to understand that the remedy for our evils is liberty, only the practice of true liberty, which is nothing more than obedience to the law.

I have also examined the four periods of my mandate, and I confess frankly that if any error could be pointed out, it would be the product not of my will, but of the circumstances, being excusable not only because of the country lagging behind the times, but because of the lamentable conflict in which we have lived, having fought for our independence, then with internal enemies created sometimes by impatience, and sometimes by ignorance. . . .

I will not deny that during the last part of my time in office, I had weakness forced on me so that I did not impede the passage of severe laws. . . . I found myself in the midst of the difficult need of having to defend myself and I did. . . . Nevertheless I deplore, with all my soul, how much blood I have spilled. . . .

This abuse that has contributed in part to the ruin of Santo Domingo has to stop. . . . I only have to add that if the spontaneous will of the majority of my fellow citizens would designate me one more time as first magistrate of the nations, my administrative program will be in agreement with the instructions I have expressed here, pledging myself most of all to the development of public education, to the equitable and honorable disposition of the income of the state and the improvement of the means of communication and establishment and advancement of industry.

Translated by Eric Paul Roorda.

In the Army Camp at Bermejo

Pedro Francisco Bonó

Spain's bloody, failed campaign to bring its former colony of Santo Domingo back into the fold with Cuba and Puerto Rico ranks as one of the more bizarre episodes in Latin American history. The series of events began when the republic's general-president, Pedro Santana, extended an unprecedented invitation to Spain to resume its colonial control of the nation, with Santana serving as the first governor-general of Santo Domingo. The erstwhile mother country accepted the plan, which was made public in March 1861.

In an effort to prevent recolonization, Francisco del Rosario Sánchez, one of the founding fathers of the Dominican Republic, as a member of La Trinitaria in 1844 along with Duarte and Mella, soon led an invasion from Haiti, which failed, and Santana's forces apprehended him and carried out his execution on July 4, 1861. Subsequent Spanish regulations offended many Dominicans, whose anger soon found expression in armed opposition to foreign authority. Open rebellion broke out with a bold raid from Haiti led by a group of fourteen Dominicans, who raised a flag at Capotillo near the border. El Grito de Capotillo, the Capotillo call for revolution, took place on August 16, 1863. Since the war, the date of August 16 has been celebrated as a second day of independence and added to the Dominican calendar of national holidays. Known as Restoration Day, it is now also the date of presidential inaugurations every four years.

What follows is an unusually candid description of an encampment penned by a remarkable figure in Dominican letters, Pedro Francisco Bonó (1828–1906), a liberal statesman and politician who was minister of war during the Restoration War. He broke with the social conservatism of the day, to the extent that his populism and love for his compatriots make him sound more like a Fabian socialist than a liberal state-builder, a trait that colors his description here of the war's leadership, as well as his portrayal of the generosity of the local landowner. This excerpt offers a fine-grained portrayal of an army encampment, one that describes like a black-and-white photograph the conditions he finds there, down to the cannon's bandaged wheels and the shocking nakedness of the soldiers. While his contemporaries would surely decry the prevalence of montería *or hunting as a provision source for the troops due to its primitive connotations, Bonó explains in unflinching detail how the system of food provisioning operated in the encampment. One gets the sense that the style of nomadic peasantry characteristic of the Dominican interior may have trans-lated easily into army life, since the soldiers were carrying on a lifestyle, from the hammocks to the plantain and pork diet, with which they were intimately familiar.*

On the 5th of October of 1863 in my capacity as Minister of War I made a visit of inspection along the whole line of the East and at five in the af-ternoon after an extremely arduous journey and under a constant rain I arrived at the outposts of the army camp at Bermejo. On my approach of-ficers and soldiers came out to me, and surrounded by them I came to the headquarters of the command. The headquarters was the largest hut in the entire Camp, where everything was scattered about in God-knows-what or-der. The ammunition was eight or more boxes of munitions that were on top of a barbeque grill, and reclined on his side there was a soldier tranquilly smoking his pipe. Various hanging hammocks, some stacked rifles, two or three blunderbusses, a war chest, a piece of bacon, and around forty or fifty plantains was all there was. At the door of the headquarters was a cannon saved in the action of those days when the Dominican troops, under the command of Colonel Mota, were routed by the Spanish under the orders of General Santana. Said cannon was in such a lamentable condition that the wheels were fastened or held together with binding twine.

"Where is Santiago Mota?" I asked the artillery commander, Pedro Faus-tino Royer a Grullo.

"He left this morning for Yamasá to confer with Manzueta and he won't be much longer, because he told us he would return before nightfall."

"Fine, but in the meantime send to have a hut prepared for me to sleep tonight."

In fifteen minutes for fifty centavos four men built me a hut at once in which I could lodge myself. We put the saddle, the packs, and the guns in it, and the horses were put out in the savanna to eat, and I took to my ham-mock, which had previously been hung by one of my assistants.

Around the time of evening prayers a group of horsemen going by indi-cated to me that Santiago Mota had arrived. I got up out of my hammock and put my head outside. Santiago approached me and dismounted.

"We waited for you all day yesterday, Mr. Minister, and you don't know how sorry I am not to have been here for your arrival, but I was called to General Headquarters by the General President with all dispatch, as you already understand."

"Naturally, you had to respond, now that the enemy prepares to attack again today."

"They are not always in Guanuma, but we will attempt to attack them ourselves and that is why I was summoned."

"When? Tomorrow?"

"No, many more reinforcements are needed from Yamasá, which can't take long to get here."

"But are you ready?"

"As always and every day with greater desire to fight and finish kicking out those whites."

Santiago's eyes flashed as he spoke to me. His bearing and gestures exhibited courage and boldness, the impatience to fight that dominated him, as he said.

Santiago was one of the most outstanding heroes of that period we call Restoration. Young, passionate, resolute. His bravery and passion later made him undertake the very risky exploit of leading peasants in battle on the plains of Los Llanos against a disciplined force, double in number. The result was the death and the dispersal of all the people after being decimated, and the death of Santiago from a bullet wound in his chest.

But at the time he was talking to me, no one foresaw his impending death.

"Are you well accommodated?" he asked me. "If it rains the roof of your hut will not shelter you; if you stay here tomorrow I will have them cover it with royal palm fronds."

"Thank you."

"Let's go to the headquarters so you can rest and to allow your companions to rest. We can finish talking there."

We made our way to the headquarters, where I finished talking to Santiago about the reason for my visit.

It was nine P.M. when I returned to my lodging by the long and tortuous street of the huts of the camp. It had stopped raining in torrents, and the night had cleared sufficiently to see all objects at a distance. The camp produced a muffled roar like a human beehive. There were a multitude of soldiers stretched out reclined on the road in a particular way, a royal palm frond served them for a mattress and they covered themselves with another, in such a way so that even if it rained as it had just finished doing, the frond on top served as a roof and the one below like a kind of skiff, because the water flowed under it and did not make the men wet. In the picturesque language of that epoch the royal palm fronds were called the fabric of Moca.

In many huts the rosary of Mary was heard being recited loudly. Two or three candles around a saddlebag stood in for a votive image. Passing close by them I saw that one of them had earned six reales and another four reales and another had earned four filled pastries made with yucca flour.

Very near my hut I saw an individual walking by dressed gravely in a coat of black fabric, but under it, like the squire of Lazarillo de Tormes,[1] he had no shirt or other article of clothing that would prevent contact with the skin; this person only had some underpants.

I entered my hut, got myself into my hammock, and slept until the next day, on which, with the sun already high, I set out again. The whole camp was on their feet. They assembled for review. Hardly any of them were dressed. Rags were their clothes. The headquarters drummer was wearing only a woman's dress; it was laughable to see him bend over in his gown. The bugler was naked from the waist up. All were barefoot and had bare legs. I reviewed the troops and they numbered 280 men: from Macorís about one hundred, from Cotuí around forty, from Cevico sixteen; from La Vega about fifty; those from Monte Plata numbered seventy men, all of them, though half-naked, carried good rifles, though with arms and baggage that had passed from the ranks of the Spanish to ours. Their spacious hut accommodated all of them and was built down near the stream bed. I reviewed the arms of those from Cotuí, Macorís, and Cevico, they only had six blunderbusses, forty carbines, sixteen rifles; the cavalry only had two or three flintlock pistols, but all of them had sabers.

I reviewed the munitions: fourteen boxes of cartridges, with wet powder, containing four hundred packets of sixteen cartridges each; five cannon charges; twelve pots of shrapnel and ten cannonballs: and they faced an army of 8,000 men of regular and provisioned troops.

"And what do we eat here?" I asked Santiago.

"That is not a concern," he said, "each soldier is a montero, as you will have seen when you reviewed them."

The review ended and everyone dispersed: some took up gourds and went down to the stream for water, others peeled plantains and began to roast them.

And I inspected the huts in greater detail, none of which lacked a butcher block with one or two sides of bacon, and they each raised one or two pigs. The camp mainly lived on marauding, but that was easy for them because it was situated in the middle of a mountain hunting area.

"But this can't go on this way," I said to Santiago.

"Bah! And how to fix it?" he answered me.

"Easily. We will talk to old man Isidro, owner of the San Pedro ranch, so he gives us cattle in exchange for IOUs payable to the bearer that I will give him from the Government."

"Very well, by chance old man Isidro is coming right now, so we will talk to him."

A little old man about seventy years old approached us, of medium brown complexion [Moreno], completely stooped, but sharp and smart, though supported by a large walking stick.

[The following exchange is in Dominican dialect.]

"Mr. Isidro," Santiago said to him, "this is Mr. Minister of War."

"Very glad to meet you, Sir," the old man said to me.

"And I much more to see you and address you," I answered. "You are known to me, by reputation at least; on July 7 you gave considerable cattle to the revolution. I heard then that you were the richest rancher in these parts."

"You see, Sir, there were then enough cattle, more than two hundred tethered pairs, they paid me in Santiago in gold, Sir, all in gold and well paid."

"Well, then, would you like to make the same deal now?"

"Oh, now I can't, the enemy is at San Pedro and I can't use the pastures."

"Then you refuse?"

"I don't refuse, Sir, I will send word to gather cattle from my land, all you want, and we will fatten them up later."

"Good, thank you in the name of the nation."

"There's no reason for thanks, Sir. I can smell the reeking Spanish a league away."

Old man Isidro stayed for lunch. I had bought two rashers of bacon and a half bunch of plantains and I knew that my assistants had to eat. When we arrived at the hut one of them had already placed the cauldron over the fire for me. . . .

Translated by Eric Paul Roorda.

Note

1. In the anonymous picaresque Spanish novella *The Life of Lazarillo de Tormes and of His Fortunes and Adversities* (1554), the protagonist serves a series of masters, including the Squire, who parades around in fine clothing, acting noble, but is really poor.

The War of the Restoration

Carlos Vargas

The armed opposition to Spanish rule was strongest in the fertile Cibao Valley, which had a long tradition of local autonomy and opposition to the central power emanating from the distant capital. The city of Santiago de los Caballeros took the lead in the War of the Restoration. An irregular Dominican army numbering in the thousands mustered in the Cibao, but it was tenacious guerrilla tactics and a host of diseases that inflicted high mortality and low morale on the Spanish forces, under the command of the former president Pedro Santana.

By early 1864, with nearly 10,000 casualties from wounds or fevers, the Spanish military position was precarious. The colonial governor, Captain-General Carlos de Vargas, sent a plaintive report to his superior, part of which is reproduced here, quantifying the incredibly high rate of attrition experienced in his command. Like other generals who have been charged with winning unwinnable wars, Vargas presented this butcher's bill to the minister of war along with a request for several thousand fresh troops. By the time Vargas sent this letter to Madrid, the queen of Spain had proclaimed Pedro Santana the "Count of Las Carreras"; he died soon afterward, in June 1864.

"Private Dispatch to the Minister of War," February 29, 1864

. . . Although the army has been increased to 22,518 men, it only counts 9,431 in the active ranks; 7,005 wounded and sick have been sent to Puerto Rico and during the next to the last month the following number were sent to Cuba: 2,314 with 1,102 men listed in statement No. 2 as having been placed at the military hospital of this city [Santo Domingo], thus making 3,413 men, which will give Your Excellency an idea of the state of health of this vanishing army without any need of the enemy actually having to appear. [The Dominicans'] latest tactics have been interception of convoys.

To give Your Excellency a brief though exact idea of what is happening to our army it is sufficient to explain what has happened to Infantry Battalion No. 5. It landed on the 20th of December from Havana with 44 officers and

1,226 men; it spent exactly one month in operations and another on duty at this very garrison. Today it counts on two chiefs, nine officers, and 208 men; in other words, a casualty list of 35 officers and 1,018 soldiers. This, Excellency, may seem incredible at 1,500 miles distance, but this is accurate. . . .

It is to be regretted that a possible termination of the war would consist in our being trapped between Puerto Plata and Samaná, at this point with the menace of contagious diseases seizing us during the coming month of May, typhoid taking the monopoly of the territory, thus adding to the picture of desolation described by the Captain General of this island when he said that it was indispensable for reinforcements to be sent at once, since what could be accomplished in two months might prove impossible in four if a further lapse of time were permitted without giving the Monte Cristi Rebellion a death blow. The time, unfortunately, has lapsed, and with things having become worse the reinforcements required are now, of course, much greater. We are confined to only one plan now which is based on defensive tactics. . . .

Nevertheless, I have decided on Gándara's trip to Cuba so that you can confer with that worthy Captain General and decide if, in our critical circumstances it would be convenient for the 5,000 men scheduled to arrive in that Island within a brief period of time, to be sent here immediately to substitute at the different points of defense. . . .

Spanish Recolonization: A Postmortem

US Commission of Inquiry to Santo Domingo

As part of his own preparations for annexing the Dominican Republic, President Ulysses S. Grant convened a US government commission of inquiry to study the country. Their work included a succinct analysis of Spain's failures: civil, political, religious, and military.

The commissioners took especial pains, in all parts of the country, to examine into the causes of the failure that followed this annexation, as well as of the unpopularity and overthrow of the Spanish rule in the island. These have been generally stated to them as follows:

1. That contrary to the understanding between the Dominican and Spanish governments, the public offices of all sorts were unduly filled with Spaniards, to the exclusion of the Dominicans.

2. That the Spanish subordinate functionaries were not generally native Spaniards, but Spanish subjects drawn from Cuba and Porto Rico—colonies where blacks and men of color are held as slaves; and that the atmosphere in which these men had been brought up had filled them with a prejudice which unfitted them utterly for the administration of government in a country where the great majority of the population are colored and a considerable number are blacks.

3. That some of the superior officers and very many of the soldiery were brutal beyond endurance, and that very little effective redress could be obtained. It was stated to the commission by a venerable clergyman in charge of one of the most important parishes on the island—a man of acknowledged devotion to Christian duty, and entirely trustworthy—that the Spanish governor of that province had, to his certain knowledge, been concerned in the assassination of a mother to obtain control of the person of her daughter; that he had entered the clergyman's house, stick in hand, and threatened him with ignominious chastisement; and that in various ways the Span-

iards oppressed the people, treating them as conquered, and insulting their local authorities.

4. That the Spanish rulers showed a mania for regulating the details of ordinary life, in some cases resulting in positive indignities to the people.

5. That the ecclesiastical administration was at variance with their ideas. Practically, religious toleration had grown up in the republic. This fact the new archbishop under the Spaniards does not seem to have recognized. Protestant churches were shut and orders were issued to the clergy of the established church to enforce a multitude of vexatious regulations upon their flocks, involving spying upon families. To use the language of a venerable priest, "The archbishop was a worthy man, but he seemed to consider that he was living in the time of the Inquisition." To these may be added the fact that the Masonic fraternity, which possesses a very large and wide-spread membership among the best men of the island, was understood to be menaced.

6. That there were manifested on various occasions certain deep-seated political ideas. Of these may be mentioned opposition to the monarchy and to colonial subjection, and attachment to the name of the republic.

7. That there was aroused a popular apprehension, founded upon a knowledge of Spanish administration on the neighboring islands, that slavery would be reestablished, either by reducing the colored Dominican people to the condition of slaves, or by new importations.

Although these causes were not equally operative in all the parts of the country and the better class of Spanish officials mitigated them considerably in some districts, they were sufficient, when joined to uneasiness under the colonial yoke, to cause an insurrection, which soon became a revolution. The people revolted in all parts of the interior, and aided by greater knowledge of the country and greater familiarity with guerrilla warfare, resisted all attempts to put them down. They finally drove the Spaniards into the strongholds on the coast, where the soldiers died by wholesale of the malignant fevers engendered in close and filthy barracks devoid of all sanitary appliances. Of the Spanish losses no exact data could be obtained; the best opinion seemed to be that the Spaniards sent in all about 35,000 troops, of whom between six and eight thousand were lost by desertion and the causes above alluded to.

Making the Case for US Annexation

Ulysses S. Grant

The end of the Spanish effort to recolonize the country did not prevent further attempts to annex it. President Buenaventura Báez, back in power after the War of the Restoration, proposed annexation to the United States. The importance of naval power was starting to dominate strategic thinking in Washington, D.C., at the time, with the beginning of an expansionist movement to establish a network of naval bases around the world that US navy ships could employ. Acquiring Samaná Bay, a deepwater harbor on the northeast coast of the Dominican Republic, would contribute to that effort and was one of the main aspects of the Báez plan that appealed to President Ulysses S. Grant. He feared that some other aspiring world power would move in on Samaná if the United States did not. He elaborated on this concern, along with other reasons for Dominican annexation, in his second State of the Union address.

During the last session of Congress a treaty for the annexation of the Republic of San Domingo to the United States failed to receive the requisite two-thirds vote of the Senate. I was thoroughly convinced then that the best interests of this country, commercially and materially, demanded its ratification. Time has only confirmed me in this view. I now firmly believe that the moment it is known that the United States have entirely abandoned the project of accepting as a part of its territory the island of San Domingo a free port will be negotiated for by European nations in the Bay of Samaná. A large commercial city will spring up, to which we will be tributary without receiving corresponding benefits, and then will be seen the folly of our rejecting so great a prize. The Government of San Domingo has voluntarily sought this annexation. It is a weak power, numbering probably less than 120,000 souls, and yet possessing one of the richest territories under the sun, capable of supporting a population of ten million people in luxury. The people of San Domingo are not capable of maintaining themselves in their present condition, and must look for outside support. They yearn for the protection of our free institutions and laws, our progress and civilization. Shall we refuse them?

The acquisition of San Domingo is desirable because of its geographical position. It commands the entrance to the Caribbean Sea and the Isthmus transit of commerce. It possesses the richest soil, [the] best and most capacious harbors, [the] most salubrious climate, and the most valuable products of the forests, mines, and soil of any of the West India Islands. Its possession by us will in a few years build up a coastwise commerce of immense magnitude, which will go far toward restoring to us our lost merchant marine. It will give to us those articles which we consume so largely and do not produce, thus equalizing our exports and imports. In case of foreign war it will give us command of all the islands referred to, and thus prevent an enemy from ever again possessing himself of rendezvous upon our very coast. . . .

San Domingo, with a stable government, under which her immense resources can be developed, will give remunerative wages to tens of thousands of laborers not now upon the island. This labor will take advantage of every available means of transportation to abandon the adjacent islands and seek the blessings of freedom and its sequence—each inhabitant receiving the reward of his own labor. Porto Rico and Cuba will have to abolish slavery, as a measure of self-preservation, to retain their laborers.

San Domingo will become a large consumer of the products of Northern farms and manufactories. The cheap rate at which her citizens can be furnished with food, tools, and machinery will make it necessary that contiguous islands should have the same advantages in order to compete in the production of sugar, coffee, tobacco, tropical fruits, etc. This will open to us a still wider market for our products. The production of our own supply of these articles will cut off more than one hundred millions of our annual imports, besides largely increasing our exports. . . .

The acquisition of San Domingo is an adherence to the "Monroe doctrine"; it is a measure of national protection; it is asserting our just claim to a controlling influence over the great commercial traffic soon to flow from west to east by way of the Isthmus of Darien; it is to build up our merchant marine; it is to furnish new markets for the products of our farms, shops, and manufactories; it is to make slavery insupportable in Cuba and Porto Rico at once, and ultimately so in Brazil; it is to settle the unhappy condition of Cuba and end an exterminating conflict; it is to provide honest means of paying our honest debts without overtaxing the people; it is to furnish our citizens with the necessaries of everyday life at cheaper rates than ever before; and it is, in fine, a rapid stride toward that greatness which the intelligence, industry, and enterprise of the citizens of the United States entitle this country to assume among nations.

. . . So convinced am I of the advantages to flow from the acquisition of San Domingo, and of the great disadvantages—I might almost say calamities—to flow from non-acquisition, that I believe the subject has only to be investigated to be approved.

Dominican Support for Annexation

US Commission of Inquiry to Santo Domingo

Ulysses S. Grant appointed the great abolitionist, author, and orator Frederick Douglass (1818–1895) as Assistant Secretary to the Commission of Inquiry to Santo Domingo, which he formed to investigate the potential for annexation. Douglass traveled to the Dominican Republic in January 1871 and spent more than two months touring the country and interacting with its people. He determined that annexation to the United States would be in their best interest, a case he made in the favorable report of the commission, which he coauthored, published later that year. His stance on the issue put him at odds with his old friend and political ally Senator Charles Sumner of Massachusetts, who led the opposition to the treaty when Grant proposed it to the Senate. The highly positive impressions of Dominicans recorded by Douglass and the other members of the Commission of Inquiry contrasted with the derogatory characterizations made by some of those who were opposed to annexing the country's mixed-race population. Some of what Douglass and his colleagues wrote about the Dominicans' enthusiasm for annexation seems like wishful thinking; it could well have been the case that the people they asked were being polite to the visitors, saying what they wanted to hear about the Yankees taking over. It is easy to imagine the people who met the impressive foreigners deferring to them, avoiding disagreement with the great man by responding with a frequently heard Dominicanism, the side step "You are the one who knows." It is also likely that some Dominicans who were comfortable with the patron-client model felt that hitching themselves to a rich and powerful neighbor could bring protection, economic growth, and an end to the political strife of the past.

Desire for Annexation

Although bitterly disappointed in the results of the Spanish annexation, the people who were soon involved in new revolutions, ceased not to look abroad in the hope of relief.

To the surprise of the commission, in almost all parts of the country, even the remotest, the people were found to be familiar with the question of annexation to the United States, and to have discussed it among themselves with intelligence.

All classes in all parts of the republic were consulted—magistrates and ecclesiastics of every grade, officials, civil and military, citizens of all professions and occupations, in town and country—and everywhere there was a general agreement in the declaration that their only hope of permanent peace and prosperity is in annexation to and becoming part of the people of the United States. They generally declared their belief that the strong arm of this republic, taking them under protection as part of the nation, would at once end the efforts and hopes of every seditious revolutionary leader, and establish law, order, and prosperity . . .

American Colonists

The incorporation into public sentiment of a feeling strongly favorable to annexation to the United States in preference to any other power is partially due to the presence in various parts of the country of small colonies of colored people formerly from the United States. These persons, or their immediate ancestors, generally came into the country in the time of President Boyer. Their love of the country of their birth seems to have deepened with time, and they all look upon American institutions as the only means of rescuing the country from its present insecurity. Very touching expression of this met the commissioners at various points. These people live on the best of terms with their neighbors, speaking the language of the country and conforming in general to its customs, and they have formed in a greater or less degree centers from which respect for the United States has gone forth.

The Popular Disposition

When asked if they would not prefer to remain an independent nation, the people generally answered that they would be glad to preserve their independence if it were possible, but since experience had shown that the nation could not sustain itself, they were compelled to look abroad for support, and, if they must sink their nationality, they preferred the American Union, with free institutions, a friendly people, and common interests.

They seem to us to be more nearly unanimous upon this than we have ever before known a people to be upon any political question which they were called on to consider. It was only by diligent search that the exceedingly small proportion who opposed annexation could be found at all. The principal part of the opposition which does exist appears to be among certain trad-

The cover of the March 11, 1871, edition of *Harper's Weekly* featured the three principal members of the Commission of Inquiry to Santo Domingo, along with a Santo Domingo street scene showing the reputed "Altar That Columbus Built." Frederick Douglass served as assistant secretary of the Commission, which included as president Benjamin Franklin Wade (1800–1878), former Radical Republican senator from Ohio; Andrew Dickson White (1832–1918), cofounder and first president of Cornell University, later the first president of the American Historical Association; and Samuel Gridley Howe (1801–1876), physician, abolitionist, and advocate for the education of the blind. Cover of *Harper's Weekly*, March 11, 1871. Courtesy of the Roorda/Doyle Collection.

The artist James Taylor accompanied the Commission of Inquiry in 1871, recording their travels around the Dominican Republic in a series of watercolors he called "Views of Santo Domingo." This one, "Annexation Demonstration in Santo Domingo City," shows supporters gathered on the grounds of the Torre del Homenaje, the oldest fort in the hemisphere. Library of Congress, Prints and Photographs Division, Lot 9634, LC-USZ62-92837.

In another watercolor by Taylor, the details in this domestic tableau, titled "Group of Natives around a Well in Samaná City," represent many aspects of Dominican daily life: the mango tree, the pets, and the grandmother in a rocking chair smoking a cigar. Library of Congress, Prints and Photographs Division, Lot 9634, LC-USZ62-70939.

Taylor's "Superstitious Burial Ceremony in Capilla del Rosario" illustrates the elaborate funerary rites practiced in the Dominican Republic. The Chapel of the Rosary, on the east bank of the Ozama River across from Santo Domingo, is one of the oldest and most venerated places of worship in the country. Library of Congress, Prints and Photographs Division, Lot 9634, LC-USZ62-70943.

ers in the ports, some of whom, in case of annexation and competition with American enterprise, would lose control of branches of business of which in its present narrow channels they have a monopoly; others are but agents of houses abroad, and, in the event of these branch establishments being withdrawn, would be supplemented. To these should be added certain agents of houses in neighboring islands, who have made pecuniary advances to rebel leaders, though these would without a doubt favor annexation if it were consummated under the direction of those whom they support. Besides these, a small number scattered in various parts of the country oppose annexation for reasons peculiar to themselves—some from misunderstanding of the matter; some few from a liking for the turmoil which the present condition of things permits; some from opposition to the present administration. . . . The commissioners and their agents traversed the country in every direction without guards or weapons. They slept at night in open cabins, no watch of any sort being kept. The character of the country and condition of the roads obliged them to move slowly and separately through moun-

Taylor's watercolor "The Embarkadero, or Wharf of Santo Domingo, with Columbus Tree in the Background" portrays the bustling waterfront of the capital. The large *ceiba* tree was spuriously reputed to stand at the landing spot the Admiral had chosen when he first came ashore. Library of Congress, Prints and Photographs Division, Lot 9634, LC-USZ62-70945.

Taylor's watercolor "View of Samaná Bay, the U.S. Coaling Station and the Marciaq's Store" shows the part of the Dominican Republic that appeared most attractive from the strategic perspective of the Grant administration. Today it is perhaps the most attractive from the point of view of a tourist. Library of Congress, Prints and Photographs Division, Lot 9634, LC-USZ62-70941.

tain passes, ravines, forests, and thickets, in which a handful of resolute opponents could easily have destroyed them. Especially was this true in the Cibao, the district generally referred to in unfavorable reports, every important route of which they explored. When, as in two or three cases, members of the commission had for short distances an escort of honor, it was made up of citizens in citizen garb, unarmed, so far as could be seen, and with no military guard whatever. Neither commissioner nor attachés, so far as known, ever carried sword, dagger, or pistol. Their movements were easily foreknown. But they never encountered any shadow of a hostile demonstration; nothing but kindness met them in all quarters and among all classes; and this was not less marked in the Cibao than elsewhere. . . .

Condition of the People

The physical, mental, and moral condition of the inhabitants of Santo Domingo was found to be much more advanced than had been anticipated. The population is generally of mixed blood. The great majority, especially along the coast, are neither pure black nor pure white; they are mixed in every conceivable degree. In some parts of the interior considerable numbers of the pure white race are to be found, and generally in the mixed race the white blood predominates. The Dominican people differ widely in this particular from the Haytian, among whom the black race is in complete ascendency. The cultivated and educated, such as the president, members of his cabinet, senators, judges, and local magistrates, compare well with the same class in other countries; and the uneducated appear equal to the same class in any country with which we are acquainted. They seem to be practically destitute of prejudice of class, race, or color. In their intercourse with each other and with strangers they are courteous in manner, respectful and polite. In all their relations with them the commissioners found them kind and hospitable. The testimony shows them to be an honest and inoffensive people, among whom, in the rural districts, a person may travel alone and unarmed all over the country, with treasure, without danger. All of the numerous parties attached to the commissions, which traversed various parts of the country, bear the same testimony concerning the people. The judicial officers stated that high crimes, such as murder, arson, burglary, and the like, are nearly unknown among them. No pauper class exists, and beggary is almost unknown. They are a temperate people, and drunken men are rarely seen. Among the popular vices is that of petty gambling, which is indulged in openly and extensively, especially by the Spanish portion of the population.

They are all Roman Catholics, except the American emigrants sent out in 1824 and succeeding years, who, with their descendents, now form a number of settlements, and mount to several thousand persons. These are mostly Methodists and Baptists. They live among the Catholics in peace and harmony. No intolerance of religious persecution can be discovered among them.

The people are generally poor, living in cheap and humble dwellings, which, though well adapted to their country, might appear rude and uncomfortable to those accustomed to houses made for a more rigorous climate. In the country almost every family possess all the land they desire to cultivate, which is usually one small field, for an acre or two well tilled is sufficient, in this fertile land, to furnish a family with their food. The reason they universally assign for not cultivating more, is that amid constantly recurring revolutions, it is very uncertain who may reap the crop; besides, there is no market now for surplus produce.

The evidence taken shows that the Dominican people are not averse to work when certain of reasonable reward, but are good and faithful laborers. An abundance of labor can now be had at about ten dollars or less per month. Appearances make it probable that the elements necessary to physical persistency exist among the people especially in that large proportion in whom Spanish blood predominates. The decline of these people in numbers and in enterprise is sufficiently accounted for by social and political causes, without the gratuitous assumption that the race is dying out or effete.

Opposition to US Annexation

Justin S. Morrill

Senator Charles Sumner (1811–1874) of Massachusetts led the fight against Grant's proposed treaty of annexation. His acclaimed "Naboth's Vineyard" speech compared the president to the biblical King Ahab, who coveted and underhandedly acquired land that was not his by right and was punished by God. Senator Justin Morrill (1810–1898) of Vermont, best remembered for sponsoring the act to create land-grant colleges, also opposed the plan to annex the Dominican Republic. His reasons, delivered in a speech on April 7, 1871, were not as high-minded as Sumner's but represented sentiments that many racists in the United States shared. Arguments like Sumner's and Morrill's combined to narrowly defeat the annexation proposal in the Senate.

The annual message of the President brought into one golden sheaf the heads of a large number of arguments in behalf of Santo Domingo annexation, strong enough to stand while closely huddled together, but doomed to bend and fall one after another when standing alone and examined separately. . . . It is useless to disguise the fact that the people of a portion of our present territory have not become assimilated with the American people and American institutions, and the time when they will do so must be computed, not in years, but by generations. To say nothing of our newly acquired Siberia, commonly called Alaska, it must be conceded that Arizona, New Mexico, Utah, and the portion of Texas bordering upon Mexico are yet not only essentially un-American, but that they have no overwhelming attachment to our form of government nor to the Anglo-Saxon race. . . . One of the arguments in behalf of annexation is that we need the bay of Samaná as a harbor for the protection of our commerce. Why do we need it? . . . We are asked to buy the site, next to fortify and improve it, and then to occupy it with a naval fleet, with the vain idea that we might thus fire the languid brains and torpid muscles of the Dominicans to make sugar, grow coffee, and hack down the mahogany trees . . . all for the desperate purpose of establishing a permanent commerce and American institutions where nothing has been permanent but failures and revolutions, or for the even more desperate purpose of finding security for our Republic by making it fast to a tropical island, whose foundations have been often shaken by earthquakes, and which is scarred all over with the political as well as atmospherical hurricanes of previous centuries. . . . A people wholly without education, led in factions by unprincipled and desperate chiefs, destitute of all ambition which a high civilization inspires, reeking in filth and laziness, regardless of marriage or its binding power, who never invented anything nor comprehended the use of the inventions of others, whose virtue is indexed by a priesthood elevated by no scrap of learning and wretchedly debauched in morals, would prove a serious political and moral as well as financial incumbrance . . . one hundred and sixty thousand poor Dominican men and women, unaccustomed and unwilling to labor. . . . Its colored population, without thrift or fertility, steadily diminishes in number, and whites never go and stay there with any purpose to make it a family home. . . .

But were all other circumstances favorable to Dominican annexation as they are in fact repugnant to the scheme, there still remains one more vital consideration, namely, do the people of Santo Domingo really desire to sink their independent existence and be permanently stitched to the mere selvage of the United States? Decidedly no! The ruling passion of the people, mainly descendants of Indians and forty different African races, is a hatred of the white race. Smothered it may be for a time, but it is sooner or later to crop out.

Dominican Nationalism versus Annexation

Gregorio Luperón

Adding to the chorus against annexation were the Dominican nationalists, General Gregorio Luperón most prominent among them. In a letter of protest he wrote to Grant in late 1869 he summarized their opposition. Luperón was particularly angry that the US navy, charging piracy, sank the Telegraph, *a ship that was being used to ferry Dominican nationalist revolutionaries from Haiti in an attempt to topple Buenaventura Báez. Sentiments against foreign domination would be expressed again during the periods of US intervention that punctuated twentieth-century Dominican history.*

Today I again repeat our protest, not vacillating with doubt, but authorized by the commission of a violent act, and convinced that an evil legal intrigue wants to decide the fate of my Fatherland. . . . I and my numerous exiled compatriots also represent the interests of the Dominican Republic, and we have to address you frankly. Spain, in spite of its traditional quixotism, rejected the cowardly Báez's undignified petition and to our understanding, the Spanish Government's course of action was more honorable than yours. The American Government has entered an iniquitous combination; it has allied with the traitor Báez to persecute good citizens and annihilate Dominican independence. Your Excellency had the weakness to order, to authorize the destruction of *Telegraph,* accepting the immoral decree of Báez's mercenary Senate. Eternal ruin. . . .

Mr. President Grant: if we appeal to the impartial judgment of the civilized nations, and we ask which is the real pirate, between General Luperón, who embarked on the steamship *Telegraph,* seeking to save the territorial integrity of the land where he was born, or President Grant, who sent his steamships to protect Samaná, without previous authorization from the American Congress; the answer in my view would not be very difficult. Mr. President: Your Excellency has abused his power to protect the basest corruption. And if it is certain that it is humiliating for the Dominican people to have such traitorous leaders, it is no less shameful for the great American people that its government would consent to such ruinous intimidations. This fact is an affront to both nations.

In this degrading task, the traitors lose time, work, and honor; sooner or later the facts will be restored. Swindles of this type have no future, a Nation cannot be erased . . . like an imprint stamped on sand. The American Government notified the French in 1866, that for them to remain in Mexico was a threat to the Americas; the Dominican people thought the same, and our Congress recognized the victorious [Benito] Juárez with the title "Meritorious of America."[1] Now as well, will not the usurpations of your Government be a threat to [Latin] America? Ignorance and treason are the original causes of all of our problems; there are people who endlessly retreat, using their experience to add to their disgrace, constantly making things worse. The Dominican people owe Santana and Báez for this condition; why does Your Excellency want to take part in it? It is undignified of your people to have to be the moral protectors of our progress. The repeated Monroe Doctrine contains your faults and your ravings; we believe that [Latin] America has to remain on its own, removed from all European influence, to live as in the Old World, with its own wine,[2] local and independent; but we do not think that [Latin] America has to be yankee. . . . The Dominican Republic is a very small bit of ground, but great calamities have befallen the nations that have tried to usurp it.

Translated by Eric Paul Roorda.

Notes

1. The Austrian archduke Maximilian, with the support of Napoleon III and a French army, declared himself emperor of Mexico in 1862. The French withdrew after threats from the United States in 1866, and Benito Juárez defeated Maximilian the following year.
2. This line echoes a famous quotation by Simon Bolívar, roughly, "The wine may be bitter, but it is ours."

A Lesson in "Quiet Good-Breeding"

Samuel Hazard

One of the most vivid and detailed travelers' accounts of the nineteenth-century Do-
minican Republic was left by Samuel Hazard, an artist who traveled all around the
country both independently and with members of the US Commission of Inquiry
on Santo Domingo. In 1873 he published Santo Domingo Past and Present with
a Glance at Hayti, *an account of his journey. His observations, while obsessively*
concerned with Dominican racial peculiarities, nonetheless capture a broad swath
of the Dominican Republic during the presidency of Buenaventura Báez, when he
sought unsuccessfully to merge his nation's fortunes with those of the United States.
Hazard visited Puerto Plata and Santo Domingo by steamship and then traveled
overland on horseback through the Cibao Valley to Santiago and on to Monte Cristi.
This excerpt from Hazard's travelogue offers some idea of the panoramic view he had
of the Dominican Republic and documents how the north coast port of Puerto Plata
was the central port of European commerce, especially for the export of tobacco—the
most important creole crop—to Germany, until the shift to US trade dominance at
the turn of the twentieth century.

The harbour [of Puerto Plata] is one of the most picturesque in the island,
though not by any means one of the best; for the shore shelves so gradually
that vessels have to anchor at some distance, and even small boats cannot
land their passengers, who are compelled to mount upon the backs of the
stalwart negro boatmen and be carried ashore, a ludicrous sight indeed. . . .

The town of Puerto Plata, like the few towns still left in the Island of St
Domingo, is a very old town indeed, as far as its location is concerned, for
the buildings were utterly destroyed by the Spaniards when they evacuated the island in 1865. The town, however, has been rebuilt after a fashion,
with moderate-sized houses of wood, and in the outskirts with small cabins
made of strips of the palm and withes, and roofed with thatch. That it had
at one time been a place of very great importance and solid structures, is
evident from the ruins of many of the warehouses and buildings still stand-

ing, which are composed of stone and the material of the country known as "mamposteria"; a sort of concrete. . . .

The port of Puerto Plata is the most active one on the Island of St. Domingo; in fact, it constitutes, with the capital, the only places worthy of that name; and here is done the principal commerce of the island. This is almost exclusively confined to the foreign merchants, the majority of whom are Germans, who have the entire monopoly of the tobacco trade of the region of the "Vega Real"; which is almost the exclusive seat of its culture, having for the capital of the district the town of Santiago, the first in importance in the island. . . .

This business of tobacco gives rise and life to the entire trade of the town of Puerto Plata. Without it there would be nothing for the storekeepers, as there is in this vicinity no agriculture other than the growing of a few fruits in a shiftless sort of way. There is also the shipping of mahogany and other woods, the loading of which, however, generally takes place at the mouths of various creeks and or in the bays along the coast. . . .

The population of Puerto Plata is variously estimated at from two to three thousand inhabitants, mostly "people of colour"; which may mean jet-black African, mulatto, or not pure white. This name, however, is never bestowed on a Dominican if possible, as they are very "touchy" on this subject, all being equally citizens. . . . Of this population, the whites and mulattoes are the storekeepers and tradesmen in the town, and the blacks and mestizos are the labourers about warehouses, ships, &c. . . . Here in Puerto Plata there are a large number of negroes from the English islands Nassau, St Thomas, Jamaica, &c., most of them speaking English quite well: in fact, a large number of the coloured people speak some little of two or three languages.

I was struck by the free, frank, and manly way in which these men look and speak, evidently showing they feel their importance as freemen very different from the same class in Cuba. . . .

Thence we strolled to the outskirts of the town, and so on to the small river from which the carriers get the water with which the towns-folk are supplied. A sudden turn in the road displayed to the astonished gaze of most of our party forty or fifty women of various ages, in various positions in the river, washing clothes. Some were entirely nude, some with only a waist-cloth, but all industriously washing away and chattering like parrots. Our stopping to look was the occasion of much merriment and chaffing, increased by the vigorous screams of a nude old beldame of "Vaya, vaya" (go away), which we presently did.

Finding ourselves at a small "tienda mista" (notion store), with country garden attached, I engaged the proprietor in conversation, while he kindly took us through his place, knocked the wild, the sweet, and the bitter oranges from the trees for us; showed us the chayote, the mango, the caimito, breadfruit, yuca, from which cassava bread is made; the banana in its various forms, under the general name of platano; the shaddock; the calabash, from which they make their bowls and cups; the various kinds of palm, including the cocoa, and many other fruits and plants, all growing almost without culture in a little place of an acre or two; and, to use his expression, "It is their nature; they grow themselves."

Amidst mud and mire, in front of this place, stretched the "Camino Real" (royal road, in name only) that runs into the interior to the large town of Santiago in La Vega, one day's journey from Puerto Plata. Upon this road that day, I think, there must have passed at least two hundred mules and horses, each carrying two bales or *ceroons* of tobacco, of about one hundred and twenty-five pounds each; and as this was the beginning of the tobacco harvest, we were told it was a daily occurrence. . . .

Having finished up pretty well sight-seeing in the town and vicinity, we adjourned at twelve o clock precisely to the French hotel for breakfast, this being the regular hour for that meal, the habits of the people being adapted to the nature of the climate. They rise early, five or six o clock, have a cup of chocolate or coffee and a roll and some fruit, and then go about their affairs until twelve o clock, the breakfast hour, followed by the siesta until two; then business again from two till four; after which, at six o clock, is the dinner. It is the custom for those who have horses, at this hour of the day, to take their "paseo" on horseback, the evening hours being usually delightfully fresh for such exercise on their easy-going horses. I noticed that in many of the habitations the hammock is used in lieu of bed, being made either of grass or canvas. . . .

This being the first day of the carnival [in Santo Domingo], the streets all the afternoon were filled with maskers and mummers, who at this season have much liberty allowed them; but with it all, in the two or three days to which this privilege extends, we heard of no disorderly conduct whatever. It was in strong contrast, as we turned from one of these processions of merrymakers, to meet another making its way along the plaza; but it was a procession of a very different order; a funeral, which, with its four-wheeled canopy trimmed with white, and drawn by one horse, was carrying to its last resting-place the remains of an aged citizen, whose friends on foot formed the funeral cortege. . . .

Upon the quays, between the well and the city walls, we found large quantities of the woods of the country, such as lignum, fustic, ebony, ironwood, and mahogany, together with dye woods, being weighed in large scales preparatory to shipment; and it makes quite a busy and strange scene, with the background of wooden booths of the roughest description, where the workmen regale themselves with "san cocho " (a stew), bad rum, cakes, &c., the end of the quay being devoted to the sale (wholesale) of fruits and vegetables.

To these landings come the country people from far up the river Ozama, in their strange boats, a canoe dug out of huge trees, which, propelled by its one man occupant, probably comes forty or fifty miles to bring a couple of hundred plantains, not worth perhaps more than thirty or forty cents a hundred; or perhaps the "canotero" brings down a more valuable freight, in the shape of two or three bits of mahogany, the average size of which is about three feet long by two square, the value of each piece not exceeding $8 to $10 here. . . .

At last we arrived on the banks of the main river, the Yuna. . . . The river was quite wide and with a swift current, the shores low and gravelly, as was the bed of the river. . . . The negro boatmen were very skilful in getting over without loss our cargoes and horses. This was done by means of a cotton-wood canoe, a large ceiba-tree furnishing the material, the canoe being simply the trunk of one of these trees hollowed out by fire and axe.

In this a perfectly made negro stood with a long pole and pushed his way over; the horses, having their halter straps held by another negro, swam after the canoe, which was allowed to drift with the current of the stream, while the negro poled its head to the shore; an amusing as well as exciting scene. . . .

After many windings in the road, we came in sight of Santiago, high up on a plateau, its abrupt cliffs and walls giving it the appearance of a regularly fortified place, as at this point the town itself was not visible. . . . Descending to the river bank, and then mounting up a steep hill, we enter this queer, ancient, and historic city, bearing still about it, with its ruined walls and grass-grown streets, vestiges of its antiquity, relieved only by the fresh new houses of stone and plaster that have in later days been built. . . .

It is situated on the right bank of the Yaqui river . . . and from its frequent destructions, it possesses now no building worthy the attention particularly of the traveller. It is built, as usual, around a large plaza or square, in which is held the market, the largest and most busy one we had seen, where it was a most amusing and instructive sight to stroll and see the country people with their products of every variety for sale.

The streets are quite straight, and pretty generally run at right angles to

This undated photograph demonstrates the ancient method, dating to the early 1500s and still in use in the twentieth century, of ferrying horses across a river alongside a dugout canoe. "Don Paneho [Pancho?] Swimming Horses, Isabella River," photographer unknown, black-and-white photograph, c. 1905. Hanna-McCormick Family Collection, Library of Congress, Prints and Photographs Division, LC-USZ62-72428.

each other, the houses in the main part of the town being almost entirely constructed of stone, while in the outskirts they consist of frame-work or the usual palm-thatched houses of the country; and for this reason, seen from the hill at the back of the town, and looking across to the opposite bank of the river, the town presents a rather irregular appearance. . . .

The climate is undoubtedly the finest in the island, the place being noted for its salubrity, and it now possesses a population of about 8,000 inhabitants, largely composed of whites, the majority of whom are as intelligent and polished as can be met with anywhere . . .

Being situated in the heart of the tobacco region, Santiago is a place of active business, and controls this trade, many of the merchants being simply the agents of the foreign houses established at Puerto Plata; and this influence, principally German, controls this part of the traffic of the island. . . .

The tobacco raised in the vicinity seeks this place as its depot, where it is packed on the backs of mules or horses, and, in charge of the teamsters who specially follow this calling, is despatched to Puerto Plata, whence it is shipped to Hamburg. . . .

Night soon overtook me on my lonely road, and I was not sorry to join company with three wild-looking soldiers, as they informed me they were going the same road, two of whom were on foot, the third being mounted on a diminutive jackass, with the rations and arms of the party. . . . As I rode alongside the mounted one, the two footmen kept always ahead, singing at the top of their voices some Dominican refrain, which seemed to enliven their weary journey.

They gave me some amusing accounts of their fights with the Haytians, and seemed to hold them in great contempt, as they (the Dominicans) did not hesitate to attack with the odds against them of sometimes five to one. At the time I considered this as braggadocio, but I was credibly informed by a Haytian general that this was absolutely the fact, as the Haytian people were not fond of fighting, and they dreaded the machete of the Dominican soldiers, a sort of sword with which all Dominicans of the lower ranks are armed, whether they are soldiers or civilians. . . .

On entering the house, I found it to be a substantial wooden building in the usual fashion of the country, with several rooms, the main one being filled with quite a number of women of all ages, busying themselves by candlelight in shelling the native white and red bean, or "frijole" of the country. . . . I found all of these women kind, bright, and intelligent, with a natural dignity and refinement quite surprising in people of their habits and situation, and the younger people I found could read and write, while several books of poetry in Spanish, and one or two illustrated French magazines, showed some disposition for and power of knowledge. . . .

I asked my host, as politely as I could, so as not to give offence, for the amount I was indebted to him for his hospitality, the food of my horses, &c.

"Senior" said he, "I am a plain man; I know nothing of the customs of the world, and how a stranger should be treated as he deserves; but I do what I know and feel. I have no account against you. There, you see, is the broad public road; it comes very near my house, from which you can always see it. Whenever you come this way, and you want food and shelter either for yourself or your horses, believe me this house is yours just as much as it is mine, and you are welcome."

So with a hearty shake of the hand, and laughing goodbyes from eyes and lips of the bevy of women at the door, I rode off in charge of the brother of my host, with many "God speeds" and "Pleasant journeys."

And this has invariably been my experience of the country people of St. Domingo. Quiet and inoffensive, devoid generally of education, unaccustomed to the ways of the world; yet they have always shown themselves hospitable to a fault, as far as their means would permit; and their natural intelligence and instincts are so good, that any one would be quickly undeceived who took them for fools, while readily receiving a lesson from them in quiet good-breeding.

Martí's Travel Notes

José Martí

José Martí (1853–1895), the hero of Cuban independence and a prolific writer, visited the Dominican Republic three times in the 1890s. As the Puerto Rican writer José Ferrer Canales said, the "dominicanity of José Martí was fully evident." He saw that Cuba, Haiti, Puerto Rico, and the Dominican Republic shared a common dilemma as small nations in the shadow of the US colossus. He felt that collaboration between them was the only way to confront it. During his last trip, he signed the "Manifesto of Monte Cristi" in that northern town with General Máximo Gómez (1836–1905), a Dominican who became one of the most important leaders of the Cuban war for independence, in which they outlined the goals of Cuban liberation. Martí underscored the fact that true sovereignty required economic independence from external domination and the full inclusion of African-descended peoples as citizens. He was killed in battle in Cuba shortly after he wrote the diary excerpted here, which is composed of a series of character sketches of people he met en route as he traveled from the capital to Monte Cristi by horse and across the border into Haiti. These vignettes demonstrate his commitment to and great affection for rural folk, whom he describes with great admiration and respect. His portrayals of prominent citizens of the countryside around Monte Cristi also include detailed cameos of two important Dominican social types of the nineteenth century. First is the caudillo: men who operated on free-range cattle farms and often took their herds across the Haitian border (or took refuge there when they needed to escape the law). Second is the female head of household: matriarchs who often became highly capitalized figures of authority, given the frequent absences of their menfolk, who were drawn away to migratory labor for the seasonal harvests of cacao, rice, and coffee. By the 1890s the harvests were increasingly of sugar, as US firms developed large plantations that came to dominate the economy by the turn of the twentieth century.

As our horses ate grass to refresh from the ride, and we had a drink from the Yaque River in Eusebio's house, the General made this comment, which embodies a theory of human life force, of health and its necessity: "the horse bathes in its own sweat." Eusebio is a real man. Around his head he wears an old scarf with blue checks, but not to protect himself from the sun, but rather because on the back of his head he has a hole so big it could fit half an egg, which he got from a blow from the butt of a rifle, and above his ear on his forehead he has the scar from a machete, which upon slicing him split into two. He was left for dead.

"And Don Jacinto, is he in?"[1] Our three horses rest with their jaws over one another in the corral. The door creaks open painfully and there is Don Jacinto, reclining in a straw chair, with one thin arm on a large pillow attached to an armrest, and the other above, suspended from two lassos of a new rope, which hangs from the ceiling; against the little window lies a bed frame with two pegs for wine; the ground was dried mud, which opened into cracks; from the table to the door in a row, lying edgeways on the ground, were two glazed bottles of gin and an empty jar with a corn husk cap; the dining room table was shaky and dusty and full of inhaler jars for asthma powder. As for Don Jacinto with his raptor's profile, his green velvet cap pushing his ears forward, he has poultices on his temples; his curved, thick moustache ends in sharp points; his watery eyes pop out of his face, sad and fierce, his socks are stained the color of meat, and his faded slippers are red wool. He was a great man, and a general of the army, who had to leave in a hurry. On fleeing, he left his wife in the care of his compadre, who proceeded to take his woman. On his return and his discovery of the situation, he shot his rifle at the door of his own house, closing his eyes to his unfaithful friend, he said "and to you goodbye! You, [he said to his wife] I won't kill since you are the woman." He then went to Haiti, illegally crossing the border, and he then hooked up with the sprightly daughter of a compadre of the area. Just then a pretty and shy eight-year-old daughter arrives to greet us without socks and in sandals. From the store, which connects to the room, she brings us a bottle of rum and cups. Don Jacinto is in a fight: he has land, which his compadre—the one with whom he took refuge when he fled from the gunfight—needs his herd to cross. "And the world must know that, if they kill me, the one that killed me was. . . . And you can't say to me that God does not pay killers; because once a good day laborer came to me who was being sought after for some money for which he had shot a guy; and another time he had to shoot another one, and he told me that he had been paid for it."

"And those that come here, Don Jacinto? Do they still eat scorpion?"

"This is the thing: if you find yourself face to face with a brave guy, you will get shot." And Don Jacinto's eyes bulge, and his cheeks turn pink. "Yes" he says softly, smiling. And buries his head in his chest.

Everyone talks about Ceferina Chaves in the village. Her home is gracious with a wide front yard, and a large rambling house in the back, where in elegant chairs she greets the lineup of visitors, and gives them sweet wine to drink with her daughter's assistance. She buys local products at a good price, and then sells at a profit, and has her daughters in good schools, and later they come to live as she does in the salubrious bounty of the country-side, in the house from which they control the untamed region with their luxuries and hospitality; for Ceferina it is fame and power from all around. We stop at a corral, as she arrives from far away in her conuco [garden plot], among men who are picking tobacco. The corral is covered with woven dry leaves in an elegant fashion, and she speaks with assurance about her many ideas, saying that if the countryside was a salon she would be its natural owner. Her husband plays a backseat role, doing his own things. Ceferina, who wears gloves and jewelry when she rides to town, is the one who of her own accord and due to her own willpower has been able to improve the land, and cultivate the sweet potato, ripen the tobacco, and fatten the pig. Her daughter will marry a learned man, but will not abandon agricultural labor, nor her pride in it: The armchair and the mortal and pestle. With her porcelain on display in the living room, she spends the morning in the co-nuco. "To the poor, one must leave something, and the divi divi (a fruit) of my land, they can have it." In conversation she has a natural authority, flow and sparkle. Her delicate daughter, her finger shod with a thimble, comes to bring us fresh wine; she has an innocent smile and speaks proudly of in-justices and her dreams. I wanted to steal a portrait of her mother when she said from her armchair "we must see if we can grow good men."

Translated by Lauren Derby.

Note

1. Here Martí provides this note: This Don Jacinto was so strong and of such a beautiful color that he is copied immortally in my pen.

Ulises "Lilís" Heureaux

Américo Lugo

The dictator Ulises "Lilís" Heureaux, born in the picturesque north coast city of Puerto Plata in 1845, dominated Dominican life throughout the 1880s and 1890s. Américo Lugo (1870–1952), a noted historian, jurist, and anti-imperialist essayist, composed this prologue to a biography about this complicated figure in 1919. It is partly a paean to the Dominican Republic and partly a meditation on Heureaux that simultaneously excoriates and admires him.

There is an island, delicious like a fruit, fresh like the morning dew, noble like a princess, lovely like a flower; there is an island created on the seventh day, after the world was finished, solely to embellish and adorn it, if indeed it isn't a precious stone fallen from the crown of God, this divine pearl that the sea displays proudly on her stirred-up chest; there is an island safe and comfortable like a nest, high like a star, splendid like a treasure from the adorable Arabian stories; there is an enchanting island, full of light and of harmonies, beauty of nature, bride of the sky, whose sweet name I am not telling: it stays quiet, I carry it protected, it is hidden, written in golden letters, here in my heart.

In the loveliest, mildest, and most agreeable part of that island whose history is as marvelous as she is, there was once a tyrant, more tyrannical than that of the 1830s, to whom the sword, courage, and audacity granted power rapidly. Black in feelings and in color, white in manners and in mind, a hero in battle, stalwart in adversity, active without equal, affable and discreet to the highest order, ambitious without limits, generous without measure, fastidious about his person, sensual to excess, profoundly familiar with the human heart, superstitious but atheist, of Spartan sobriety and frugality, a Sulla for dissimulation and revenge, such was Ulises Heureaux, body of iron, character of steel, soul of bronze, infernal conscience, intuitive spirit, parabolic verb, sovereign will, dominator of men, peoples, and events, of those who push the wagon of the world and are stamped indelibly in the book of history.[1]

And this extraordinary man deceived everyone, defeated everyone, governed everyone with unlimited authority. He destroyed parties, terrorizing to pacify, [and] he suffocated thought, which is the infancy of action, which is the victory of the mind, and everywhere imposed his jurisdiction, his criterion, his caprice, his instincts, [and] his passions, finally establishing a monstrous centralism in which the Senate, the courts, the public square, the school, even the home, [were] all under his Argive and Briarean presidential control;[2] although he was no president, because the name had ceased to be anything but a mask of the reality that he was a veritable satrap, Cyrus, Cambyses, or Artaxerxes, perhaps the most complete and curious in America, and without doubt one of the most notable for his political capacity, for his leadership, for his natural heroism, for his personal authority, for his almost superhuman strength, [and] for the same seal of greatness that he put on his crimes.[3]

Twenty years, no less, he kept the entire country under his heel, thrashing and struggling there, like Hercules under Antaeus, until one day, assassinated by a group of plotters who perhaps believed they would save the homeland that way, he fell from the throne and from life, like a century-old tree felled by the blows of the axe, causing profound commotion on the ground, horrible stirring in the air, terror in hearts.[4]

Translated by Eric Paul Roorda.

Notes

1. The Roman dictator Sulla (138–78 BC) was said to have combined the qualities of fox-like cunning and lion-like courage.
2. Allusions to Argos, the Greek city-state known for tyrants and the military phalanx, and the giant Briareus, who was one of the Hecatoncheires, the "one-hundred-handed ones," of Greek myth.
3. King Cyrus the Great of Persia founded the Achaemenid empire (600–530 BC); his son and grandson took the name Cambyses. The dynasty later had kings named Artaxerxes.
4. Hercules, at first unable to defeat the gatekeeper Antaeus, who gained strength from being struck or thrown down, finally overpowered him with a bear hug.

Your Friend, Ulises

Ulises Heureaux

The father of the Dominican dictator Ulises Heureaux was Haitian, and his mother was from St. Thomas in the Danish Virgin Islands. A prolific writer, Heureaux left an extensive archive of letters, essays, and poetry in Spanish, English, and French. He rose to military prominence as the lieutenant of Gregorio Luperón, hero of the war against Spain, who often took refuge in Haiti during his military career. After coming to power with Luperón's support in 1886, Heureaux began forcing into foreign exile people he suspected of political opposition to his rule, including Luperón himself. Many of those he expelled went to neighboring Haiti, although Heureaux preferred them to go farther away, because of the long history of Dominican exiles organizing and launching invasions from Haiti. Heureaux kept close tabs on his enemies abroad through a network of spies and his own personal vigilance, as is evidenced in the first letter here, and he monitored, harassed, and sometimes murdered his opponents in exile.

His deep involvement in the details of complicated financial arrangements comes through in the second letter here. During the 1890s, he ran his nation deeply into debt with foreign loans, originating first in Europe and later the United States, in order to pay for his vision of progress, which included railroads, bridges, and urban enhancement, and for his political security, which required an expensive army. This document also suggests the growing influence of the US-owned San Domingo Improvement Company, which came to control the Dominican external debt and take over the administration of its customs service. "El Impruvemen" became an object of the Dominican public's resentment and scorn, as the country's financial disarray took its toll on average citizens.

Despite his counter-intelligence operations and foreign funding, Heureaux's political enemies eventually caught up with him on one of his trips around the country and assassinated him in the town of Moca in 1899.

The second letter is in Heureaux's own distinctive version of English and has not been edited.

San Juan
November 6, 1893

Mr. D. Elias Pereira, Dominican Consul, Port-au-Prince

My esteemed friend,

Your interesting letter of the 2nd was delivered to me yesterday by
Colonel Simeon Montero, the particulars of which I answer here.

I am very happy that President Hyppolite[1] would give you easy access
to the Palace in order that you would be able to conduct your interview
dutifully; and I am very happy that you would be able to send the Dominican conspirators that were found there either to Colon [Colombia]
or Venezuela; I prefer that it would be the former point.

I lament that the conspirators J. Eugenio Villanueva alias Genito,
Gerónimo Nuñez alias Lamanta and Alejandro Deño, have left that
town before your diligence was put into practice. In that regard I ask
you to do everything in your power to achieve, now that your diligence
is directly in practice, immediately sending . . . into effect at St. Marcos,
Gonaive, and Port de Paix, the capture or departure from the country
of the individuals I have indicated, not sparing any expense to achieve
this objective. At the same time you must maintain a weekly communication with Mr. Marsan our Consul in Cap Haitien, giving both him
and me reports of the movements that those individuals might make
anywhere on the coast [so as] to arrive in a definite manner to the end
that I am proposing.

I am aware of the tactic of those gentlemen who have been observed
constantly moving their household, whereby they evade prosecution
and assure their conspiratorial plans. Silence has been maintained with
respect to Mr. Vicente Flores, because it is believed he is exclusively
occupied with teaching in Haiti; but since I have obtained proof that
he writes and dispatches correspondence that comes directed here, I
request you to take all necessary measures to assure that this gentleman
does not leave from that place, except to be sent abroad as soon as an
occasion presents itself.

In the case of Mr. Albert Vargas alias Pereyra, I received information
from Los Matas that he was forming a group of conspirators; but Mr.
José Batista asserted to me a certain kind of good conduct that youth is
observing—I don't want to be hostile to him while he remains in the
same state. I will wait to determine prison or expulsion for him. . . .

It is necessary that you ask all the Consuls for a detailed report of all the expelled ones who reside in different parts of Haiti, so that the measures that you have to take will not be unfruitful.

Get yourself close to President Hyppolite to tell him that the correspondence that I offered to send him as proof of the machinations of the expelled ones against both Governments, was burned, but I kept some from Neyba to give him good details in that respect.

Closely pursue a youth named Wenceslao Sánchez alias Vencito, who was the courier of a message to Neyba to the house of General Pablo Mamá, where that young man remained hidden. That was the cause of that General's death. The correspondence he carried, was burned, and I regret not having the information it could have supplied us; nevertheless my going to Neyba will iron things out and I will then be able to inform you better. . . .

Hoping you are well in the company of your fine family, I repeat to you my firm friendship.

Ulises Heureaux

Translated by Eric Paul Roorda.

S. D. 7 October 1896
To Mr. Charles I. Wells
Paris

My dear Mr. Williams:

Since my last letter of the 14th July, I had the pleasure of receiving your favor of the 18th August. I use this opportunity in order to give you some informations about our general situation here. As far as politics are concerned everything is in a very good condition which I had the opportunity to investigate personally during my last trip to the North, which was a very satisfactory one. Not the same can be said about the financial situation, chiefly as far as are concerned our mutual interest. Both Bank and Regie are in a very difficult and serious position and though I am always most perfectly willing to help even with prejudice to my own interest, I have come to the end of my resources and it is impossible for me to do more.

The Bank has been constantly going back, and notwithstanding the different combinations we have in order to keep her running in a regular way it came so far, that last Monday, the 4th instant, only $600 were left to her in cash.

When M. Duvergé came to tell me so, I ordered him to close the Bank for that afternoon, promising him that I would try to find some silver-money for him for the next day. So I did, and yesterday she opened again with some $10,000 oro mex. in cash. I do not expect that this amount will last a long time, as in this city nearly no drafts can be found, and the merchants who have to remit to the interior are obliged to ship silver coin even, paying the 6% export-duty on this coin. The result is that there is a constant strain on the Bank and as soon as she has some silver in deposit, this is taken away by the commerce. As all this gives me great trouble, moreso as that position is very well known by the merchants, I have come to the conclusion that the only thing which we can do to prevent these constant difficulties is to take up all the outstanding bills and retire the paper money from the circulation. To this end I am studying a combination with Mr. Vicini that he will pay to the Bank a sum of $20,000 mex. monthly to begin in December 96, which amount should be used by her to take up her outstanding bills. In the mean time Mr. Vicini will always be ready to assist the Bank when she needs it.[2] . . . This is the only solution that I see possible and through it we will greatly alleviate our daily troubles.

I repeat once more to you that in the present circumstances in fact there is no use of having a Bank, and by the dispositions that I am taking I am only keeping up the institution in the hope that in a short time the Bank will get its capital back in cash so that at that time by a good management she will be a source of great benefits to all of us and on order to prevent that by a general distrust of the public in the Bank, the possibility of emitting paper money should be lost for ever I have preferred to take these dispositions.

Still one question more.

I am studying the way to make a combination before the end of this year which will permit me to satisfy a great part of my outstanding obligations, and I suppose that I can succeed giving as a guarantee the 1 ½% of War and Public Works, the 6% Recargo Adicional [additional surcharge] and the 3% Recargo Adicional. All these apartados [revenue flows] are belonging to the Government and in the next session of the Congress on December another ½% more will be established which will make a total 11%. Still in order to carry through this scheme I would be obliged to you if you would be good enough to send me a formal declaration from the San Domingo Improvement Co. that these apartados are not affected to any one of the loans under your control and that the

San Domingo Improvement Company approves the destination I wish to give to them and agrees to this transaction.

Do not forget to do all you can to come to see me as soon as possible. We have a great deal to talk together and as my sympathy for you is so heartily meant I should like to see you out of your troubles, and I suppose that some serious talk between us could be of some moral help to you.

With best wishes, I am as ever
Your sincere friend,
General Ulises Heureaux
Presidencia de la República

Notes

1. Florvil Hyppolite (b. 1828) was president of Haiti from 1889 until his death in 1896.
2. The Vicinis emigrated from Italy to the Dominican Republic in the 1870s and invested in sugar cultivation, becoming the wealthiest family in the country by the 1890s.

V

The Idea of the Nation: Order and Progress

The Dominican Republic was a poor country, lagging behind its Caribbean and Latin American neighbors in measures of development such as transportation, agriculture, education, and urban infrastructure. These shortcomings, however, stimulated the growth of a notable intellectual movement in the Dominican Republic, one based on positivism, an ideology of "order and progress" that sought to achieve economic growth along a European model. Even as Dominican politics were mired in contention between rival parties calling themselves Blues and Reds, a core of educators, essayists, and poets formed in Santo Domingo, including the Puerto Rican transplant Eugenio María de Hostos (1839–1903) and the "national poet" Salomé Ureña (1850–1897), whose work called for self-confidence and cooperation to improve the country. These positivist thinkers continue to inspire Dominicans, while the dictator Ulises Heureaux has fallen into disrepute.

The selections here illuminate the changing definition of social and economic progress over the course of the nineteenth century as liberals debated the priorities of nation-building. There was an impressive range of political views, from the utopian protosocialist ideas of Pedro Francisco Bonó (1828–1906) to the vision of a more authoritarian state that Américo Lugo (1870–1952) advocated. We see here the deep skepticism of Bonó regarding elite interests and especially development led by foreign investment in sugar plantation agriculture for export. Bonó put his faith in the smallholding tobacco cultivators of the central plains of the Cibao as the true sentinels of a democratic future (thus anticipating the tobacco-versus-sugar antimony later popularized in the classic work *Cuban Counterpoint* by the Cuban anthropologist Fernando Ortiz). This view contrasts with that of Lugo and Eugenio María de Hostos, who argued that the Dominican citizenry was not yet ready for democracy and still needed to be shaped by strong state institutions such as public schools, which could help forge a culture of democracy. These intellectuals, influenced by racial deterministic tracts emanating from Europe, thought the state needed to lead because the citizenry was degenerate as a result of racial mixture and the tropical environment. Always the optimist, José Ramón López (1866–1922) countered this view, arguing that the real explanation for the backwardness of the campesino was his diet, in particular the overreliance on the plantain as a staple, and that the peasant could indeed be redeemed through dietary reform. These selections show how the reigning optimism about national progress and development in the late nineteenth century collapsed with the coming of the US military occupation and the depression, as liberalism and open markets became associated with the loss of national sovereignty, and a strong state came to be seen as the only path of redemption.

Street People and Godparents

Luis Emilio Gómez Alfau

Father Francisco Xavier Billini (1837–1896), the "Friend of the Poor," spent most of his career as a priest in Santo Domingo (when not in political exile), running a school and establishing charitable institutions: a hospital, an orphanage, a poorhouse, and a mental asylum. The asylum addressed the problem of the mentally ill homeless people in the capital, described in this selection. To fund these humanitarian projects, Billini received permission to set up what became the Dominican National Lottery, which soon became phenomenally popular and remains so today.

Aside from Billini's efforts in the city, there was little in the way of a social safety net beyond the family in Dominican life. One practice that provided some measure of security for children and families was compadrazgo, *or godparenthood, the subject of the second selection here. Both readings come from a compendium of nineteenth-century lore about Santo Domingo.*

Street People

Until the insane asylum was created by the unforgettable philanthropist Father Billini, the numerous demented people called "stupid crazies" were not picked up from the streets of the city.

For the entertainment of rascals, [and to the] scandal of the public and national shame, various maniacs and lunatics swarmed through the city, insolently vociferating, irritated by the many idler delinquents.

José María, mildly insane, with a passion for music, carrying an old euphonium, never missing a military parade, leading the march, paying no attention to the whistles and catcalls of the rascals.

Juana the Nutcase, wandering the streets day and night, becoming enraged when they yelled "Damn the Spanish!" at her. Juanico, who had the nickname "The Little Chamber Pot." [There were] Silly Little Ant, Niní the Gossip, The Rooster, Goya the Gossip, Green Belly, and many other wretched ragamuffins, who begged for public charity.

Soldiers often paraded in Santo Domingo, as in this scene from 1904, with children marching along. "Soldiers on Parade, Santo Domingo City," photographer unknown, black-and-white photograph, c. 1904. Library of Congress, Prints and Photographs Division, LC-USZ62-66342.

Godparents

When an individual selected a godfather to baptize one of his children, he gave proof of his great affection and esteem. If the godfather was rich or suitable, there was no calculating the advantages of the gift or the spiritual connections created by godparenthood to elicit political, social, or economic benefits.

The godfathers were second fathers for the godchild and had duties and rights that allowed them to correct them or punish them. In the case of the death of the father, the godfather took care of the bodily and spiritual health of the godchild, and if the godchild's mother died, too, the godfather adopted the godchild as his own child.

Between a godfather and a godmother there could be no carnal feelings of any sort allowed and in [the] case [of] both of them being single, kindling some interest, no amorous relations could be consummated, because the Church would not pronounce the necessary dispensations through the mouth of any of her ministers.

The negotiations rest[ed] almost always on the word of the persons who verbally agreed to the matter, and it was very unusual to involve notaries, because the given word was the word that sealed the deal.

Translated by Eric Paul Roorda.

From Paris to Santo Domingo

Francisco Moscoso Puello

Most Dominicans see themselves as mestizos, as an amalgam of white and black. This mixed-race mulatto mixture was officialized as indio *during the Trujillo regime, as most Dominicans had* indio *(from* claro *or light to* oscuro *or dark) stamped on their passports, a term that invokes the indigenous people. But most people understand* indio *as a color category akin to* café con leche *(coffee with milk), rather than a historical reference to an indigenous past. As in other mestizo cultures, race and class are inextricably intertwined—thus poor dark Dominicans speak of "improving the race" by moving up in status. Published in the 1930s, this selection by Francisco Moscoso Puello (1885–1959), a doctor and prolific writer from Santo Domingo, explores Dominican identity from the perspective of a member of the old elite who was perceived as a national representative in Paris, where some may have taken him for Haitian because "Santo Domingo" is "Saint Domingue" in French. In this selection we see the complexity of Dominican racial identity, here articulated as a biracial composite from one's parents. While Moscoso Puello accepts the heritage of his mother's blackness, he also demonstrates the mixed-race "racial pessimism" that was characteristic of Latin American positivism. This was due to nineteenth-century theories of racial degeneracy, which presumed that those with black blood were condemned to backwardness. Moscoso must have been familiar with these theories since he was a doctor.[1] Racial determinism led many Latin American elites to solicit white immigration as a means of bringing growth and development.*

Señora: I have to make some transcendental statements today. I have been to Paris, and I have returned silenced, without having been interviewed, without having revealed the motive of my travels, or mentioning what I was doing there. Contrary to the majority of my fellow compatriots [Dominicans] who have had the good fortune of visiting the capital of France, I have always been proud to consider myself a genuinely autochthonous product, without foreign influences, a representative of my race, of my era, and of my country.

Boca Chica, the reef-sheltered beach closest to the capital, was the first tourist destination in the Dominican Republic; a group of Dominican hosts and visiting American guests are shown there in 1899. This beach is still a major attraction for international visitors. Photographer unknown. Frank T. Arms Collection, Photography Collection, Mystic Seaport Museum, #1947/1835/57, © Mystic Seaport Museum.

In Paris, at the Hospital Saint Louis, they used to call me *Monsieur Santo Domingo*. And every morning, in the Laboratory, I received the same greeting: How are you *Monsieur Santo Domingo*? It seems that *Monsieur la France* found me to be very representative, very typical, of my race and my distant Antillean country. It did not annoy me.

However, on occasion, I felt that my friend the Monsieur was completely mistaken, because I, in no way, am a true representative of my country. I am not one hundred percent Dominican, as they say today. Maybe I am representative, if it is race that is being discussed. I say maybe, because, for many of my countrymen, we are a white people, even though the majority are mulattos. The reason for this can be found in the fact that we are descendants of the Spanish, and by gaining independence from Haiti, we reclaimed this noble origin, one that many foreigners unfortunately ignore.

I am 80 percent white, I am three-fourths mestizo; which is to say, more white than black, because of which I can take apart a clock, slog away with screws and complicated machines, read a construction plan, work with electricity, white industry par excellence. And that is why in New York I feel right at home.

But what you do not know is that I do not feel scorn for the black race, and I feel proud to have that be part of my blood. The black has excellent qualities, which the white insists on obstinately negating. I owe my best qualities to that vigorous race. The black veins that I possess I have received from my mother. And this is the moment to talk to you about my genealogy. My father was pure white, a good young fellow, and an excellent man, endowed with many notable qualities: honorable, of generous heart, and very hardworking. He was a man of great intelligence, with honorable physical and moral traits. My father, because of his race, did not have reason to be envious of *Monsieur la France*, who ignored, without a doubt, that for this reason there was a short distance that separated us. Throughout my father's lineage, everything is respectable. I had an uncle, Dr. Elías Rodríguez, who was the Bishop of Flaviópolis, a man of science, about whose life and works I will inquire from the historian Alemar, also a relative, to give them to you on another occasion.

My last name probably arrived in America with Vicente Alvarado de Moscoso, a lieutenant of Pizarro. Notable Spanish singer Carmen Moscoso also had that last name. These facts are neither complete nor definitive. Here, in Santo Domingo, there was an erudite and honorable man Dr. Juan Vicente Moscoso, who did not have children. He was President of the Tribunal of Santo Domingo. And during his tenure he became acquainted with the celebrated procession of the Virgins of Galindo. My paternal grandmother was Doña Mercedes Rodríguez, the sister of the Bishop, already mentioned, without documentation because I do not have it. My father was the son of Juan Moscoso, a painter, and son of Mercedes Rodríguez, and had two sisters and a brother, who passed away years ago, Francisco Moscoso. My great-great-grandfather was a painter and sculptor; as were my father and two of my grandparents. The majority were ordinary people, with the exception of those mentioned, but good people and completely white, absolutely white. It seems that the family vocation was painting. My grandfather carved an image for the church in Jarabacoa, which I believe still exists in that Sanctuary. From there without a doubt I derive my dormant affection for the arts; I am not sure if this is fortuitous or disgraceful.

My father, when he was young, took part in the war for Independence. He participated in the action in Santomé registered and mentioned in the official announcements, according to testimony by Juan de Cruz Rondón, Jacinto Gatón, and Joaquín Montolio. He had the rank of Major. It makes me proud to think that my father enlisted when Dominicans took to arms for noble and righteous causes.

You already know the honor of my father's side, and with respect to that

The Ozama River Tannery, shown in this 1883 engraving, was one of the few industrial concerns in the Dominican Republic in the late nineteenth century. "Tannery on the Ozama in Santo Domingo," engraving by unknown artist, *Frank Leslie's Popular Monthly Magazine* 16, July–December, 1883. Courtesy of the Roorda/Doyle Collection.

which I have received from my mother's side, I do not value it any less so. Almost all of my maternal relatives are of the black race. For that reason, my ascendancy rises from San Cristóbal. They are not very well known. They have left nothing written. My mother's father was a French engineer. My mother, then, was a half blood, but my uncles were pure blooded. I only know that one of them was named Genaro Puello, a tall black, well put together, elegant, and from those who knew him, a good person. There are no details, because blacks do not have history, nor biographers, unless they are Toussaint-Louverture. White pride has no limits.

There is a biological reason to explain these facts. The mixture of races can sometimes enhance the traits of the races that are combined, but, usually, the end result is inferior. This fact has been proven in Santo Domingo. Of the people of pure blood here there have been very few superior men. The reason is, or seems to be, this: the more recent generations of the whites of Santo Domingo, were ungrateful and inferior. Due to the contingencies that they suffered in our country, most whites who stood out in the colony because of their education, lineage, or economic standing had previously emigrated. Those who stayed, therefore, were those who did not have any particular value, and these had to cope and coexist with the blacks, who

A group of gentlemen of Santiago posed in front of their club, the Centro de
Recreo, around 1911. "Santiago, Centro de Recreo," photographer unknown,
black-and-white postcard, c. 1911. Courtesy of the Roorda/Doyle Collection.

surely had nothing to give. The mix of these races gave rise to the Dominican *mestizo*, an inferior person, by and large, in which you find the virtues
of the white race and black race frequently neutralized. Santo Domingo is
the place in this World where you can best study the importance of *mestizaje*
[racial mixture].

But the fact that the *mestizo* may be superior cannot be negated and can
be observed in this country. The majority of men who have distinguished
themselves in the Republic are *mestizos*. However, from this it should not
be said that the *mestizo* is always a cut above. On the contrary, he is inferior
to the two races that have created him, and when, for example, the skin is
lightened, the mind is darkened, and the spirit is impoverished. Whichever
way, this *mestizaje* has damaged my country considerably. The social characteristics, politics, and economics of the Republic are instantly explained
by the fact that it has been populated by this type of men. Only when this
race consolidates will there be hope for the establishment of specific attributes that would permit a social and political evolution that is more uniform and harmonious.

Señora: I think I have overextended myself today. I had wished to discuss
the identity of the one hundred percent Dominican, and I am not sure if I
achieved that. *Monsieur Santo Domingo* has wished to show you that he is
not a true representative of his people. In summary, he is a representative
in parts.

My representative countryman, the culmination of all of this country's social evolution, the man who makes and breaks governments, is, at night-fall, at the door of his hut, sitting on a box, with a handkerchief tied in a knot and a pipe in his mouth, threshing the corn off of the cob, from the harvest of his *conuco* [garden plot], to feed some of the quality chicks that still have not returned to the hut because it is not yet dusk.

He is waiting for his *compadre*, who will bring him the revolver he needs, and they have assured him, that if his Horacio [Vásquez (1924–1930), who represents the perennial caudillo leader] makes a decree at any moment in Moca, to knock down the idiots who have ruined animal husbandry, who have permitted corruption, who charge for state permits and ordinances governing roads, and who have made their relatives wealthy through state appointments, who do not even know what lands to take and fence off—the idiots who are supported by this very government. That is the true *Monsieur Santo Domingo*, who can find himself likewise, at the foot of the mountain, contemplating the untouched virgin forest, where the birds have made their nests for centuries without being disturbed, where you sometimes hear the bark of a dog that hunts wild boars that drink from a spring and that produces the only sound in those awe-inspiring moments of solitude, and where you might cross paths with an Indian one time. That is *Monsieur Santo Domingo* who has not been to Paris, whom I only represent in color.

I am one of the few who think about his sad condition, who lament his state of being, which we have been unable to transform, despite the fact that we have wished for this change with all of our heart, a state of being that will not change for many years to come. That is the one hundred percent Dominican, the one *Monsieur la France*, without a doubt, would take me for, without knowing me, for ethnological reasons already mentioned, and for others I will keep quiet about. I have beneath my skin, the same idea of civilization that the Monsieur cherishes and preserves, over there in the capital of the civilized world.

These are, Señora, the great sorrows of life that sometimes cannot be silenced.

Translated by Lauren Derby and Alex Huezo.

Note

1. José Ramón López, *El gran pesimismo dominicano* (Santo Domingo: UCMM, 1975).

Public Enemies: The Revolutionary and the Pig

Emiliano Tejera

The prominent intellectual, politician, and social critic Emiliano Tejera (1841–1923) linked the problems of political instability and agricultural underdevelopment in the following essay from 1906, in which he blames ranchers and monteros and their free-range livestock for the inability of the country to make progress, which to him would mean settled agricultural development, and which he equates with political pacification of the regional caudillos and thus state formation. What he could not foresee, however, was that legislation curtailing ranching would enable US sugar corporations to move in and dominate the agricultural sector by the early twentieth century.

The revolutionary and the pig are the principal enemies of the country. Both live and want to continue living on other people's property; both prevent the work that would save this lovely though unlucky land. And as total injustice is the certain source of protests, the Ministry in my charge has received the complaints of the foreigners who, the same as locals, were obligated to defend their labors in the military way: with fence posts and strands of thick wire, and more often than not, and shamefully, without any sort of success.

And in truth it is custom alone that is able to make us watch what is happening in the countryside with indifference. The spirit of the herdsmen of the Mesta, passed on to our ranchers, made it so that at the origins of the Republic, when the country was governed by ignorant ranchers, a rural law contrary to our Constitution was passed; and that law continues to the present day.[1] . . . Here there is privileged rural property and rural property that is taxed or enslaved, and the latter can be converted to the former, but not the other way around, when one pleases, even though it would be to the detriment of the nation. The privileged rural property is that which is dedicated to free-range livestock: this gives its owners the right to allow

Very few photographs exist of the elusive *gavilleros*, the Dominican revolutionaries who combined hunting with fighting in revolutions or against foreign occupiers. Photographer unknown, black-and-white photograph, c. 1910. General Subjects Series (F JGG 442), Photography Collection, Archivo Nacional de la Nación, Santo Domingo.

their animals to consume the vegetation and fruits of their land and have the right to consume that which belongs to others, if it is not within a secure fence, and not just the trees in the forest, but all that the farmer plants, if one day his fence suffers any sort of imperfection. The enemy that is the free-range animal, is vigilant, and as soon as a tree, upon falling, destroys a piece of the palisade, or the wind destroys it, or a flood or whatever other cause, the fruit of the farmer's labor, in any state where it is found, is lost to him and the misery will ascend to his family in his house and sometimes leads to cruel hunger. The enslaved or taxed property is that of the individual who dedicates himself to agriculture. Nothing is his except what he has enclosed, and that only while he defends it with an impregnable wall. The rest is for the animals of the rancher. And he that is favored by the law is the rancher, though he spends most of the time in his hammock, plucking his guitar, or visiting his neighbor, and he that is prejudiced by the law is the farmer who nourishes the countryside with the sweat of his face, feeds the towns, and fills giant ships with the product of his industry.

If the law does not establish equality between the two classes of rural property; if it does not say to the rancher: keep within fences your animals

To combat the scourge of free-range livestock destroying crops, some Dominican localities mandated that farmers receive authorization to transport their pigs. The farmer in this photograph is shown being placed under arrest in Cotui because he has "no passport for his pigs." "An Arrest at Cotui, 'No Passport for His Pigs,'" photographer unknown, c. 1904. Hanna-McCormick Family Collection, Library of Congress, Prints and Photographs Division, LC-USZ62-72434.

who are those that wander around and cause damage to the farmer, and in that way you will improve them day by day and will reap the benefit that they provide; and to the farmer: you can work without fencing your crops, so long as it does not come to infringe on another farmer or any rancher, and in that way you will save yourself that enormous work and waste to which until now you have been obligated by an unjust law; if it does not do that, the lawsuits will be interminable, farming and ranching will continue to be at loggerheads and the claims will keep reaching this Ministry from the foreigners who believed that property was equal in the Dominican Republic, according to what the Constitution says, and who find instead the practice of having a privileged property that is less useful and productive, and another enslaved property that is useful and gives abundant returns to the national treasury. And because the evil is ancient and deeply rooted, it is necessary to replace it with a method that is useful and would be such that would cause the least possible damage at the moment. This will involve the skill and wisdom of the legislator.

And it must not be forgotten that our country at present is and for a long time to come will be agricultural, not industrial. We must favor everything having to do with agriculture. A large part of the youth of the cities should be dedicated to agriculture; but why dedicate oneself to that pursuit if the only result in the end is to find ruin, which for a long time all classes have experienced with the ranchers? And above all in many parts of the Republic there is neither real husbandry nor agriculture, only scarcity and often hunger for all—men and animals—when drought strikes the country. What a difference is noted when for whatever reason free-range grazing disappears! Here to eloquently testify are the 300,000 quintals of cocoa beans, produced mainly in the Cibao, in the places where free-range ranching is no longer practiced, or only to a small degree. And [the] coffee plantations of Barahona and sugar mills of San Pedro de Macorís also attest to it. We must favor agriculture and also favor animal husbandry, obliging those who dedicate themselves to it to confine their animals within fences for the purpose, so that they cause no damage, and so that they would be at all times under the close watch of those who attend to them. Reducing the free-range pigs will reduce the revolutionaries, because rarely is the revolutionary a working man who has interests to lose, and there will be more working men when there is no free-range grazing.

Translated by Eric Paul Roorda.

Note

1. The Mesta was a medieval shepherds' union that was granted extensive privileges by the kings of Castile at the expense of settled farmers. The rural law referred to here is the Livestock Law of 1846.

The "Master of Décimas"

Juan Antonio Alix

One of the most popular forms of verse in the Dominican Republic in the nineteenth and twentieth centuries was the décima, a ten-line poem with stanzas and with a complicated yet predictable rhyme scheme. These poems often observed and commented on the contemporary social and political scenes, usually with satire. The most famous décimas in the country are those of Juan Antonio Alix (1833–1918), a prolific poet from the Cibao region, who wrote his verse sometimes in the dialect of that region and sometimes in more traditional Spanish. Papa Toño, as he was known, lived a picaresque existence that is reflected in his work. He participated in the rebellion against Spain in the 1860s, carrying messages to Dominicans in exile in Haiti, and for a decade traveled with a circus. These are his best known poems: "Black behind the Ears," on the subject of race relations, dates to 1883; "The Low-Hanging Mangoes" or "Easy Pickings" is from the first decade of the twentieth century, when Dominican politics was in a particularly chaotic state.

"Black behind the Ears"

> Everyone who's White as snow
> Never sweats about being White
> But not-quite-White has got to fight
> For respect like crazy; if Mulatto Joe
> Goes to a CASINO, he's an Oreo!
> Someone always grinds his gears
> With advice that every White chick hears:
> Avoid a dance with that fellow
> of color, though he may be high yellow,
> 'Cuz he's "Black behind the ears."

> The one who's prejudiced now
> Can go away to La Habana
> 'Cuz on Dominican turf he won't wanna

Stay, where it won't work for him, anyhow,
And a chunk of cheesecake—wow!
The color of honey (when you get near)
Won't be disrespected, not around here,
Because all that stuff's crazy;
Now what's fresh as a daisy?
To be "Black behind the ear."

"The Low-Hanging Mangoes" or "Easy Pickings"

To the likeable and extremely popular *Listín Diario,*
the most interesting and widely circulated newspaper
that the country has.

WE WILL SEE WHAT MISTER MARTIN BIGBRAWL HAS TO SAY

So says Mister Martin Bigbrawl,
who's a really big V.I.P.,
it's the mango he likes 'specially
as a fruit that's most agreeable.
But to clamber up a tree tall
and among those little hearts go,
and a world of trouble there know . . .
because that is so dangerous,
he finds it more delicious
picking mangoes where they hang low.

Mister Martin goes on to tell
that he also likes the chestnut
when it's plucked hot from the pan, but
only when out of the nutshell,
cleanly done by other hands well
with the knowledge only they know;
burning up one's fingertips though
sticking them into the hot flame,
that is something one could not claim
is to pick the lowest mango.

For this reason the bad fortune
of the Homeland won't improve much
since so many people have such
attitudes as Mister Martin.
Silver's what they want to roll in
making such a pretty penny
with monopolies so bonny,
trading goats or contraband, or
as here, in the tale at hand, for
picking mangoes; making money.

When there is a revolution
ne'er-do-wells are first to push to
go to take then to the bush to
take by force a healthy portion.
Some boss sends an expedition,
now they march in order finest,
and the gents are then the quietest;
each stays home, those crafty fellows,
since the aftermath that follows,
is the time for mango harvest.

When the bull's loose in the bullring
toreadors there by the thousand
go to *burladores*[1] closed in
safe from games that danger will bring.
When the bull is killed, expiring
by some other hand, then they all
come out shouting and seem loyal
yelling "viva!," good employees
who alone desire to pick these
mangoes gotten minus toil.

Quit old evil antecedents
sending people to the highland,
to depose a president and
give no cause for the disturbance;
that is not advised by prudence,
if we'd live the life that peace brings
like obedient little siblings

whom it's cost exsanguination
and the ruin of the Nation
caused by taking easy pickings.

See the high price that has followed
the entombment of two powers,
which of thousands were the killers,
victims whom the Earth has swallowed.
Countless are the women widowed,
and the orphans only God knows!
Countless the laments and sorrows!
And the blood has flowed in torrents! . . .
at the root of all this violence
is the harvest of low mangoes.

Now what has to be accomplished
is to let all be forgotten,
and the President who's chosen,
back him so his rule's established.
Evil deeds will be abolished.
No more orphans, no more widows,
no more crime and peccadillos!
And to shirk from work's exertion,
those who would SKIP PERSPIRATION,
still would pick the lowest mangoes.

Long live peace! Long live union!
And down with those who pick the low-hanging mangoes!
Shoo, shoo, go find something to do,
and leave the country in peace.

Translated by Eric Paul Roorda.

Note

1. Enclosures adjoining a bullring to provide protection for bullfighters.

Barriers to Progress: Revolutions, Diseases, Holidays, and Cockfights

Pedro Francisco Bonó

Pedro Francisco Bonó was a prominent figure during the Restoration era, holding political positions that included senator, deputy, minister of foreign relations, secretary of state for justice and public education, and justice of the Supreme Court. His book El Montero *(1856), the first Dominican novel, is a highly romanticized evocation of the backwoods hunter. Moreover, Bonó was also the first Dominican sociologist, a reputation based on his* Notes Concerning the Dominican Working Classes *(1881), a collection of essays, including this selection. First published in 1876 in the Santiago newspaper* El Amante de la Luz *(The Lover of Light) with the title "The Hacienda Question," this piece analyzes some of the ongoing dysfunctions that prevented peace and prosperity in the republic.*

Muscular Work of the Nation

Economists divide vigorous work into various categories; the most productive is that done by *men* in the most hygienic and moral conditions.

Only one-fifth of the available productive force of our male population engages in agricultural labor, distracted as they are because they are perpetually serving in useless wars and civil service. The farmers spend half the year in campaigns or in encampments; they devote the other half to standard gratuitous civil service: on political vigilance rounds; persecuting misdemeanors; in useless weekly inspections; cutting deals, in the mail; negotiating personal loans on the street; doing public work, etc., resulting in the extreme outcome that women and children end up having to do all the rural chores, and, robbed of the male contribution, they are done in an extremely feeble and imperfect way. This is the result of organizing the whole countryside as a permanent standing army.

Hygienic Conditions

The perpetual life in encampments, the repeated slash and burnings, and the constant warfare have kept the better part of the population in the worst of health. The abandonment or neglect of the preventative methods recognized by science and propagated by government has permitted the development of infinite ailments, mortal to some, and making others invalids for the rest of their lives. The country was decimated in 1865 by smallpox, and if through misfortune it were to return today, the death toll would be double. Santiago and its environs are under the scourge of tuberculosis. Macorís, Cotuí, Cevico, Yamasá, are afflicted with tumors, ulcers, or skin infections. Illnesses such as these are more or less easy to prevent or remedy through the medium of good regulations, and [because these are] abandoned . . . today, the population and production are weakened and diminished, [and] thus basic moral obligations cannot be fulfilled.

Religious Law—Time Spent on Work

The Protestant nations observe the fifty-two Sundays of the year, in addition to certain religious or commemorative holidays, whose number does not exceed twenty. The Catholics of Europe are the same case. The Dominicans take up three-quarters of the year with religious observances: Sundays, High Holy Days, days of obligation of the Mass, those of the general and particular patron saints, three of the four solemn days of Easter, the days of the protector, saints of the professions and of the illnesses of the eyes, throat, molars, childbirth, earthquakes, lost objects, etc. Worse still, their absence is not infused with the sacred and pure idea of prayer, virtuous activities, and collective gathering, but rather that of attributing punishment to productive and honest work if done on holy days which they insist must be observed. So this belief strips labor of its sanctity and stamps it with a sinful character, due to workers' and farmhands' opinion that whoever labors on one of these idolatrous holidays would later sustain traumatic injuries or other negative results. This ignorant inheritance is a vice, but the Church could correct it. . . . Because of its deep wisdom and immense influence with both sexes . . . we must call first upon the Church as a powerful and efficient means for our social regeneration.

Police Laws

Among the many bad laws that rule Dominican society none surprises more than those that govern gambling. First a law totally prohibits it, and later, the same law orders and regulates it, and a special administration is created in order to collect a kickback. The town councilmen, the noble town councilmen, are those designated to collect the official payoff and are those who, so that the kickback is maintained, study and take great pains to expand gambling to the fullest extent possible, even multiplying the games of chance by establishing them in every section. Certainly it is admirable to see how such estimable citizens, obliged by the law, strive to raise the bids in this immoral practice . . . so that any price is considered trivial in order to put up a cockfight ring in the countryside.

First of all: in the cockpit stadium, on Saturday, Sunday, and Monday of every week, ten or twelve thousand farmers, sometimes with their wives and children, [are] shouting, gesticulating, wagering, screaming; and surrounding the building [there are] three or four tables for games of chance: here dice, there three-card Monte, yonder blackjack. There is a bar for alcoholic beverages because a little is always needed to quench the thirst of the shouters; there is a permanent dance hall that is quiet during the day and comes to life at night, and close to all of this are trays and troughs of sweets, liquor, cold cuts, cigars, sold by women most of whom are prostitutes. The government representative sanctioned by the law to preside over these honest pastimes walks around observing all of this; and soon you find him dancing and betting and drinking and sometimes collapsing on the floor alongside others under the influence of countless libations or from the impact of a cudgel, which is a common conclusion to the party.

Translated by Eric Paul Roorda.

Food, Race, and Nation

Lauren Derby

José Ramón López (1866–1922) was a very important Dominican journalist and short story writer who brought a pared-down modern style to his literary works. Born in the northern coastal town Monte Cristi and educated in Puerto Plata, he was forced to flee the country by political enemies. In Puerto Rico and Venezuela he continued to write, and he returned to become a senator and state official. This selection discussing López's ideas considers the contrasting meanings of sugar and plantains in Dominican nationalist discourse after the turn of the twentieth century.

While commodities such as sugar had become symbols of US imperialism by the 1920s, traditional food crops have not always been innocent harbingers of *dominicanidad* and signs of a glorious and pristine nation. Indeed, what might arguably be termed the national foodstuff, the plantain, was in the 1890s subject to intense scrutiny and a barrage of criticism. José Ramón López, essayist and social reformer, wrote "La alimentación y las razas" [Food and the races] in 1896, an essay that defined an epoch of Dominican social thought, even though López's disparaging view of the Dominican nation has caused him to be remembered with some ambivalence in the history of Dominican letters. The text is a riposte to social Darwinism and the determinist theories of de Gobineau and Oswald Spengler that conceived of race as the embodiment of national culture, and thus the prime index of a country's potential for development. This conflation of race and nation was particularly pernicious for countries with a predominance of racial mixture, which in this view had no future but one of degeneration. To his credit, López sought to decouple the nineteenth-century link between race and nation, reframing the issue from one of nature to one of culture. The explanation for the Dominican Republic's lack of progress was to be found not in the genetic composition of *la raza* but in diet. Unfortunately, however, in his drive to deessentialize nation, López reessentialized class.

López's argument provides a new twist to the old adage that you are what you eat—that identity is constituted through food. After a survey

By placing Dominican flags on plates in this rustic abode, this installation represents the nickname for the national meal of rice, beans, and meat—*la bandera* (the flag)—which is the ideal daily fare for Dominicans at the main lunchtime meal. It is often accompanied by plantains. "Arro, Habichuela y Cay'ne," installation by Tony Capellán, from *Tony Capellán: Exportadores de Almas. Instalaciones 1994* (Santo Domingo: Museo de Arte Moderno, 1994).

of the globe's dietary routines, he concluded that eating poorly and not enough had produced the malfeasance emanating from Italy and the Middle East; and that nations like Turkey, India, and China would remain stuck in the past until the masses were fed a more regular and balanced diet. Here he took issue with the racialist theories of Cesare Lombroso, the Italian criminologist who contended that certain races (Italians and Jews) were inherently prone to recidivism and criminality. The Spanish colonizers had waged a war of attrition against the swarthy Indian and African, successfully reducing their rations, degenerating the races, and compromising them physically and mentally. The Dominican Republic needed a "food apostle" to teach the people how to eat; the middle class preferred their ran-cid but imported margarine, the poor their anemic plantain, and everyone's nutritional deficit was demonstrated by Dominicans' propensity for coffee and alcohol. For lack of consumption, Dominicans were consumed by vices.

As liberal reformers such as López invested their faith in state formation and urban development, the countryside became the criterion of alterity against which progress was gauged. And the peasant and his plantain became the distillation of rural barbarism. Avid for progress and civilization, Dominican liberals blamed the lack of national development on the peasantry, who, as a result of their hunger and nutritional deficiency, were plagued by a "lack of foresight, violence, and duplicity," as well as hopeless indolence. Poor diet had produced the amorality of the countryside, an ethic of lies, dissimulation, intrigue, and excessive sensuality. The gravest problem, according to López, was the irregularity of the meal, a factor that had reduced the nation to a state of animality. The peasants, most notably the monteros, or mountain dwellers, who engaged in shifting cultivation and who ate great quantities of wild pork, were among some of the most afflicted. For them, the problem "hasn't been limited to the physical and mental degeneration of the race, or the abundance of cretins and peabrains; it has also rendered epidemic the most repugnant of diseases," such that there are entire towns in the interior rotten with contagion. Under a tutelary regime, the state would instruct the peasantry in matters of culture, teaching them to keep their metaphorical house in order, especially at table. Small property holding would be enforced, both to tie the peasantry into the monetary economy and to promote their civilization.

This discussion of the work of José Ramón López was intended to help clarify why the plantain continues to provide such a powerful symbol of Dominican national identity. The fact that the plantain symbolizes the peasantry explains why plantain is said to *embrutecer*, to make stupid, and why *platanizar* (literally, "to platanize") is such a derogatory term. The multivalence of the *plátano* is its national-cum-class resonance; since the eighteenth century the plantain, roasted, boiled, or mashed, has been the quintessential rural Dominican food. Depending on the context, the plantain can either index national nostalgia or it can be a term of denigration for either the urban or rural poor. In a brawl, it might be used to gloss the Dominican nation positively in terms of its masculine virtues, such as virility, courage, honor, and readiness to fight. The plantain today, however, is often paired with the cornflake—held to be the American national starch—as positively and negatively valued national parameters: if the United States has brains, the Dominican Republic has other virtues, such as capacity for love, valiance, and most of all, respect.

Tobacco to the Rescue

Pedro Francisco Bonó

Tobacco cultivation had many advantages for the peasant cultivator. The progressive author and liberal politician Pedro Francisco Bonó summarized the easy entry of a young farmer into the booming tobacco economy in this essay, which he published in the newspaper La Voz de Santiago *(the Santiago Voice) in 1881. His description drew from the observations he made five years earlier as a special agricultural commissioner for the La Vega district, which would become the heart of Dominican tobacco country. He makes the case for tobacco as a crop superior to sugar, coffee, and cacao, due to its local ownership by small proprietors.*

The young peasant clears a plot of land [*conuco*] and fashions a hut with his axe and machete. Now he has shelter and food for a while, so then he marries. The woman shares his worries, his fatigues, but beyond his personal needs she also bears those of pregnancies, illnesses, and children. The family is tired, exposed, naked, sick, without doctors or medicine, and its gaze is fixed on the chief who created it, they all look hopefully to him. From then on comes this other motivation: cut down, knock down, stake out another plot of land, plant it with tobacco and offer it to a storekeeper if he will give him and his family what they need. The storekeeper doesn't have what he asks for because the revolutions devoured his savings, but he sees an opportunity for profit and writes to a foreign merchant to advance him the requested sum. The merchant, who knows that the young peasant has already planted the tobacco and that, it already being in the ground, would require a wait of only four months before it was in the barn and dry, gives the advance to the storekeeper with a surcharge. The storekeeper adds another surcharge and passes it on to the young peasant, which dresses him and his family. After six months everything is covered. The young peasant has paid the storekeeper, who paid the foreign merchant, who paid the State a tax; to the maker his materials, to the banker his money, and all have prospered, including the government.

Comparing now the product [of] tobacco and the products of coffee, cacao, and sugarcane, who can escape the fact that the former is the industry par excellence for the small, poor, inicipient, and thwarted agriculture of the Cibao? Who that plants cacao or coffee sees fruition in six months, and who that is naked can wait years? Can estates thick with sugarcane be created without capital, without the permanent availability of labor, without roads, without personnel skilled in the intricacies of machinery? . . . The farm laborer of the Cibao, under the pressure of moral responsibilities and economic imperatives, has understood most clearly; he insisted on planting tobacco and with that has saved the Republic in all of its misfortunes, is saving it today, and will save it tomorrow, despite droughts, floods, hurricanes, despite daily revolutions of blood and fire like those of this country; despite wars of words, and of internal taxes and external ones like those of the state monopolies, of the foreign customs unions; because to smoke, to inhale, and to chew the tobacco of the Antilles, is a very imperative necessity among Europeans and Americans, like drinking coffee or chocolate sweetened with cane sugar. And the Cibaoeño will insist on that for a long time, because the indispensable basics for another crop to which he could dedicate himself with better results, are not to be discerned on the horizon.

Translated by Eric Paul Roorda.

PER eos dies mirabilis & prodigioſus quidam caſus in illa regione interuenit. Ab ortu enim tanta ventorum rabies coorta eſt, qualem nunquam antea Inſulares ſe vidiſſe, aut audiuiſſe meminerant: inprimis vehementiſſimus Typhon (Hiſpani Huracan appellant) tanto impetu irruit, vt cœlũ ſimul ac terras rapere ſecum & miſcere velle videretur. Omnes improuiſo malo attoniti, præſentem mortem imminere ſibi ante oculos, confundi elementa, & finem rerũ adeſſe, vulgo pauidi credebant. Tum vero ingenti ſono cœlum ſtrepere, & inter horrendos tonitruum fragores crebri micare ignes, aër incendi fulguribus, nox interdiu omnibus noctibus nigrior denſiorq̃, adeo vt per obſcurum alius alij occurſantes, mutuo intueri non poſſent. Errabundi homines defixis præ formidine animis & lymphatis ſimiles per vias perq̃ auia diſcurrebant paſſim ac peruagabantur. Tanta vi interea furentium & horrendo cum ſtridore colluctantium ventorum, vt à radicibus erutæ arbores, & auulſa ſaxa magno cum fragore in planum prociderent, atq̃ ea ruina ingenti villarum mapaliumq̃, ſtrage facta, multos mortales opprimeret. Solidas vero etiam cum incolis domus furioſi illi turbines in ſublime correptas diſſipauere. Paucis horis ingentia detrimenta accepta, vt ne tres quidem naues quæ ad portum ſecuræ in ancoris ſtare credebantur, eius calamitatis immunes eſſent. Ancoris enim ipſis, quanquam robuſtis, fractis, & ancoralibus firmis nouiſq̃ truncatis, cum omnibus nauticis profundo merſæ ſunt. Indi complures ſpeluncis abditi, diſcrimen effugerunt.

Indi

Hurricanes have punctuated Dominican history. One of the most powerful gods in the Taíno pantheon brought the hurricane (a Taíno word). Twin hurricanes in 1494 and 1495 devastated the first Spanish capital at La Isabela. Hurricanes have swept Santo Domingo repeatedly, most notably "Hurricane San Zenón" in 1930 and most recently Hurricane Dean in 2007. Perhaps the most destructive in Dominican history was 1998's Hurricane Georges, which caused massive flooding. "Horrenda & inaudita tempestas," engraving by Theodore De Bry, from *Americae pars quarta* (Frankfurt a.M.: J. Feyerbend, 1594), plate XI. Courtesy of the John Carter Brown Library at Brown University.

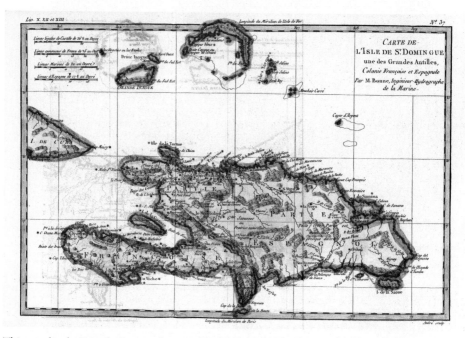

This map by the French cartographer, mathematician, and marine engineer Rigobert Bonne (1727–1795) shows the untamed frontier between the French and Spanish sides of the island of Hispaniola in the eighteenth century. From *Atlas de toutes partes connues du globe terrestre, etc.*, by Rigobert Bonne (Geneva: Pellet, 1780). Courtesy of the Roorda/Doyle Collection.

Ntra. Sra. De la Altagracia

The religious patron of the Dominican Republic is La Virgen de la Altagracia (The Virgin of High Grace), whose image on a painting (c. 1500) is revered at a cathedral in Higüey, where throngs of pilgrims appear on January 21, her feast day, every year. Altagracia, postcard, n.d. Courtesy of the Roorda/Doyle Collection.

A client waiting for a renowned healer and diviner, nicknamed "El Barraco," in a rural township outside of Elias Piña. Note the painted image of the national patron saint, the Virgin of Altagracia (2002). Photograph by Giovanni Savino, "El Barraco lo ve todo con un ojo," © Giovanni Savino Photography.

George Overbury "Pop" Hart (1868–1935) painted a traditional carnival celebration, including parade participants costumed as a devil, a bull, and a king, in a mountain town in 1919, during the first of his two trips to the Dominican Republic. Library of Congress, Prints and Photographs Division, LC-DIG-ppmsca-24787.

"Díos Olivorio lives." Irio Ramírez López and Edwin Pérez, devotees of the healer and nationalist martyr Díos Olivorio Mateo, at his pilgrimage site, La Maguana Arriba, San Juan de la Maguana. Photograph by Lauren Derby, 2010.

A man named Confessor with his prized fighting cock en route to the stadium in Los Toros de Azua (2009). Cockfighting is a major pastime in the Dominican countryside. His cap bears the emblem of the Cibao Eagles baseball team. Photograph by Giovanni Savino, "Los Toros," © Giovanni Savino Photography.

Two boys share a meal of *sancocho* (stew) in the shaded patio of a rural home in Los Toros de Azua (2009). Photograph by Giovanni Savino, "Eating with the Cat," © Giovanni Savino Photography.

Children play baseball and dream of the big leagues in San Pedro de Macorís. Photograph by Eric Paul Roorda, June 2012.

A *colmadón* (corner grocery), which sells beer, rum, and soda, accompanied by loud music, on a side street between Santo Domingo and Baní (2003). Photograph by Giovanni Savino, "Country Club," © Giovanni Savino Photography.

Patrons, Peasants, and Tobacco

Michiel Baud

The rise of the tobacco industry in the Cibao Valley in the late nineteenth and early twentieth centuries transformed the economy, society, and culture of that vital region and impacted other areas of the nation as well. The Dutch historian Michiel Baud closely examines these interrelated changes in his classic monograph Peasants and Tobacco in the Dominican Republic, 1870–1930 (1995). *In this excerpt from one of its case studies, he explores the rural family and the practice of concubinage, which forged bonds across social classes while diffusing matrifocal families.*

The Creation of an Agricultural Region: Villa González
in the Twentieth Century

In 1873, the traveler Hazard could still describe the Villa González region as "uninteresting and unsettled," meaning that it did not have large-scale agriculture. In this period, the major part of the region was covered with forests. The population of the region was sparse and, apart from smallholder agriculture, cattle raising was the principal activity. The legal status of the land was unclear. Most of the land was in the public domain, and, although some land was privately owned, its value was insignificant.

All this changed in the final decade of the nineteenth century, when the Ferrocarril Central was constructed between Santiago and Puerto Plata. The decision to build the railroad was taken in 1890, and the next year construction of the tracks began. The directors of the company decided to follow the trajectory of the existing "main road" (*camino real*). . . . As a consequence of this decision, the line crossed some ten miles over the valley northwest of Santiago before turning northward into the mountains. Although it would take seven years to finish the railroad, the consequences of the project were felt immediately. Land alongside the (projected) railroad became more attractive for agriculture. Las Lagunas was to be the first stopping place for the trains leaving Santiago for Puerto Plata. The railway station became

Against a backdrop of traditional dwellings, this photograph of Puerto Plata in the early twentieth century shows signs of urban progress: a streetlamp and new pavement. Photographer unknown, black-and-white postcard, n.d. Courtesy of the Roorda/Doyle Collection.

the center of an urban settlement situated on flat valley land between the southern slopes of the Cordillera Septentrional and the wide riverbed of the Yaque del Norte. When the place became a proper village with a station building and a church, it was renamed Villa González: after one of its most distinguished inhabitants, Manuel de Jesús González.

Because of the new prospects occasioned by the railroad and the growing population in the agricultural heartland of the Cibao, east of Santiago agricultural entrepreneurs started buying land in the region around the railroad. They took advantage of the low land prices and acquired large amounts of land. These were mainly entrepreneurs from other parts of the Cibao and some recently arrived foreigners. . . .

It was a unique feature of capitalist development in this region that most landowners did not try to expel the smallholding peasantry from the agricultural land. In fact . . . the landowners actively stimulated peasant agriculture on their lands. The fact was that the local landowners lacked sufficient capital and labor to bring their land under cultivation. Especially the absence of a reliable labor force prevented rapid expansion of large-scale commercial agriculture. Local entrepreneurs could not recruit peasant labor by [means of] extra economic coercion and lacked the funds to attract laborers with high wages. They found a temporary solution by integrating peasant production into the exploitation of their property. Unable to clear

A pineapple vendor in Puerto Plata, a city better known for exporting the tobacco of the Cibao Valley. Photographer unknown, black-and-white postcard, n.d. Courtesy of the Roorda/Doyle Collection.

and cultivate their lands themselves, they allowed peasant families to squat there. . . . Nascent capitalist agriculture took advantage of the presence of peasant producers in various ways. First of all, through their slash-and-burn agriculture, the peasant producers helped to clear the land. Second, peasant family members provided a stable, if restricted, source of wage labor. Finally, the peasants produced the tobacco which became the mainstay of commercial activity in the region. . . .

Upward mobility within peasant society usually occurred as a result of nonagricultural activities. Few, if any, persons succeeded in accumulating money solely on the basis of agriculture. Peasant producers who managed to accumulate some capital often were active in mercantile pursuits. Trading was the principal means by which a process of continued accumulation began. Many rich cultivators established small rural shops, *colmados* or *pulperias*, in which basic consumer goods of rural society were sold. This often led to giving small credits to poor relatives and neighbors. In exchange, these cultivators received the debtors' tobacco, which they sold at a profit to larger merchants. In a way the cultivator became a petty intermediary and sometimes a local strongman. . . .

The history of the tobacco-growing peasantry in the Villa González region was closely linked to the emergence of a local elite. Cibao society was relatively homogeneous ethnically, but socially it was stratified. The small elite were called *gente de primera*. Its members considered themselves direct descendants of the Spaniards. Some families could trace their roots directly back to the "old" colonial aristocracy. However, most elite families acquired their status only in the nineteenth century. Possessing land was the principal symbol of social status, but mercantile wealth became increasingly important toward the end of the century. Many members of native elite families married well-to-do immigrants who settled in the country around the turn of the century. In this way a new and rejuvenated elite came into existence in the final decades of the nineteenth century. This occurred on a national scale, but the process was especially significant in the Cibao, where the regional merchants benefited from growth of the export sector. These regional elites consisted of large landholders, well-to-do merchants, and intellectuals. It [the elite] was regularly replenished by successful entrepreneurs but in general was a fairly closed social group. Wealth was important in the acceptance of newcomers, but education, cultural characteristics, and racial features were no less important. In this way a closed, self-conscious, and close-knit regional elite came into existence.

Relations between elite and peasantry were quite ambiguous. The elite in the Villa González region lived close to the peasant producers and in order to procure their labor, established various sorts of personal relations with individual peasants. On the other hand, the elite were clearly distinguished from the peasantry by . . . social position, material welfare, and superior education. The majority of the regional elite lived in the cities, preferring Santiago, but many of the elite lived in the countryside. Continuing dependence on agricultural production gave the Cibao elite a definitely rural character. People used to draw an imaginary circle around Santiago with a radius of some ten miles, where urban and rural societies coexisted. This area was called La Campina: "Among the masses of peasants and workers, small and large proprietors . . . were also very urban people who lived, however, on farms, haciendas, and rural shops; but because of their similar customs, ways of living, social and family status, education, and economic position, they were closely linked to the city, resembling the principal families in Santiago."[1] The clearest material expression of the social and economic superiority of the elite was its housing. In a period when the majority of the peasant population lived in *bohíos* [thatched huts] and slept on beds made of wood covered only by hides, the elite possessed large wooden houses with several rooms, comfortable beds, and furniture. They may have been somewhat shabby and primitive by the standards of the European elite of the day, but their luxury was sufficient to express great social inequalities. The technological advances which shook the world at the end of the nineteenth century and the increasing supply of luxury goods in the country allowed the elite to express its social superiority through other material possessions as well. We may obtain an impression of the lifestyle of this rural elite in the early decades of the twentieth century by citing an observer who wrote in 1917: "The people of the Santiago countryside are normally civilized and wealthy persons, who regularly travel abroad and like to surround themselves in their well-constructed home with all the comfort customary in the cities. They are lovers of music: the luxurious piano, the melodious pianola, or the enchanting gramophone provided with the best pieces of the musical repertory. The culture of the Santiago countryman allows him to frequent the most aristocratic social centers of the city." The piano and the record player, then, served to affirm the social status of the rural elite. In the 1920s, the car became its most outstanding status symbol. Everyone in Villa González, rich and poor, remembers the day that Don Manuel González first drove around in his new car. Traveling abroad was another privilege of the elite in the days before "Nueva York" became a mythical paradise for many poor Dominicans. [The historian Harry] Hoetink stresses the fact that a journey through Europe was "the crowning moment of education" for the Dominican elite in the nineteenth century. It confirmed the high social status of the person involved. When, in the twentieth century and especially during the US occupation, North American culture became dominant in the country, the United States became just as attractive. Until the 1960s, freedom of travel remained a distinct privilege of the wealthy.

Patrons and Patriarchs

One of the most remarkable aspects of rural society in the Villa González region was the close co-existence of the different classes. Rich landowners lived side by side with poor peasant families and were in daily, and sometimes intimate, contact with members of the peasant society. Elite children often maintained friendships with peasant age peers, which could establish a basis for lifelong mutual esteem between members of the two classes. This ambiguity shaped relations between elite and peasantry. It showed itself most clearly in the long-lasting paternalistic interdependence between the two groups.

Peasants and landowners were linked by a complex set of rights and obligations, and patron-client relations proliferated in Cibao rural society. The mutual dependency and vertical bonds between rural elite and peasantry originated in the insecure Dominican political situation in the nineteenth century. The authority of political leaders depended on the loyalty and support of the peasant population. On the other hand, peasant cultivators needed protection against the abuses and constant incursions into their property to which they were exposed. One of the principal threats to peasant society was the forced recruitment of its men. It was very difficult to avoid enlistment, especially when the national army was "detailing groups of soldiers with orders to seize any youths they found in passing."[2] Many peasants cleared their *conucos* [garden plots] as far from the roads as possible, in the hope that roving bands of soldiers would not notice them. The peasants tried to secure protection by entering into vertical relationships with the elite. An influential patron could help one evade expropriation or involuntary recruitment. The paradox, of course, was that one would be expected to fight *for* the patron when he himself got into political trouble . . .

Peasant society itself was imbued with a strong sense of hierarchy, based upon differences in economic power, social status, and manliness. Distinctions in social status pervaded all relations among adult men. This characteristic of peasant culture was related to the masculinist sensibilities often viewed as characteristic of Mediterranean culture. Men had to prove their manhood, to show that they had "balls" (*cojones*), or their social status diminished. Masculine prestige was based not only upon physical courage, however; it depended also upon social responsibility and ability to take care of one's family. The "serious husband" and the man who "honored" his promises was esteemed. Peasant society thus reproduced patriarchal ideology in both its essential sides: an assumed male superiority and social responsibility.

The consequence of this hierarchical ideology was a strict set of rules for "decent" behavior. Respect should be shown by younger to elder, by female to male, by poor to rich. It is significant that the unwritten codes of daily behavior for the three subordinate groups were very similar. Peasants with their landlords, women with their men, children with their parents—none might initiate a conversation, none might show curiosity, and all must "civilize" their language. Children had to kneel down along the road and wait for the benediction of an adult. Women had to submit to whims of their men. Peasants had to approach large landowners as father figures towering high above the humble peasants, all-knowing in their advice, always to be respected. In exchange, they received protection; help in difficult times, and, in some cases, a fraternity transcending class differences and approaching friendship. Thus, the existence of patriarchal relations *within* peasant society functioned to sustain the landowning elite's patriarchal authority . . .

The ambiguity of relations between the rural elite and the peasantry showed itself clearly in one other feature of rural life . . . Sexual relations in Cibao rural society were not confined to members of the same class, despite the great ideological emphasis placed on distance between the classes. It was generally accepted that elite men might have sexual relations with women of lower social status. It may be argued that this acceptance was a direct consequence of the social difference and the patriarchal ideology in which they were embedded. Whereas elite females were kept under close watch and the virginity of daughters jealously guarded, male adolescents were allowed to acquire sexual experience with girls of poorer families.

Both in adolescence and later, sexual relationships outside marriage were easily accepted within rural elite. Three "model cultivators" were interviewed by *La Informacion* in 1925, and all stated proudly that their one "vice" was their attraction to the female sex. [One] was described thus: "As a good countryman, who is reared and educated in the fullness of nature, he is dominated by the eternal female." [Another] boasted that "the spell cast on him by the skirts has led him to make four conquests in one year." The two men speculated that they had some thirty and sixteen children, respectively, "behind the palm tree" (*por detras de la palma*).[3] This behavior—not only the sexual relations, but also the boasting—fit perfectly with the masculinist ideology that pervaded Dominican society. The idea that men could have many sexual relations was also accepted in peasant society. Within elite ideology, such an assumption was complemented by a class-based sense of superiority toward the poor. Elite males often used their social superiority to seduce peasant girls. Even today, mothers warn their daughters against the sweet talk and persuasiveness of rich men. Many do not want their daughters to live as maids in the houses of the rich because of danger of pregnancy. An admonition often heard is this: "They promise paradise, but leave you with a baby."

Despite such interclass sexual relations, members of the elite married only social equals . . . It is astonishing to observe the frequencies of marriages between members of the few influential families of the region . . . At the same time, however, many illegitimate children were born as a result of short affairs between members of the rural elite and young peasant girls. Even when these interclass relations lasted longer, they were hardly ever formalized . . .

Extramarital relations could be serious love affairs and sometimes resulted in the transfer of property to peasants, but they did not threaten the position of the elite. Men were expected to take care of their illegitimate offspring. Because many men did not live up to this expectation, those who fulfilled this responsibility were admired and praised in popular discourse for doing so. The girl or her parents might receive some sort of allowance when the child was born, which might be continued until the child was grown. Some fathers paid for the education of their children, secured a job, or made available a piece of land on which they could live with a family. Illegitimate children could not, however, assert any claim to the possessions of their father, let alone enter the paternal family. Although men often publicly supported their illegitimate children, access to the father's social class was out of the question for mother and children. The father's support depended exclusively on his generosity and had no legal basis. The preservation of elite family capital and class cohesion were first priorities and precluded admission of illegitimate children to the family. The extramarital children of the elite swelled the ranks of the peasantry. They usually ended up in the social class of their mother and shared her poverty . . .

It may be obvious that illegitimate children conceived in these sexual relations did not threaten the coherence and material superiority of the rural elite. On the contrary, they contributed to the growth of the peasantry and swelled the ranks of the poor rural population. At the same time, however, this social mechanism reinforced and perpetuated intimate relations between the classes. Extramarital affairs could not break through the social barriers of Cibao society, but often they generated affective ties across lines. Even though the material benefits were few, blood relationships with members of the elite could be advantageous for individual peasants. The status of a rich father might shadow his illegitimate offspring, subtly helping him to find work or loans. It may be significant that so many rural inhabitants today still trace their descent to important (European) families. The sexual relations, which transcended class boundaries, suggest one dimension of the contradictory nature of elite attitudes toward the peasantry. The rural elite did all it could to maintain and even increase the social distance separating it from the peasantry, but it was unable, and partially unwilling, to give up many of the customs that linked it to the peasant population.

Notes

1. Pedro R. Batista, *Santiago a principios de siglo* (Santo Domingo: Editorial Panamericana, 1976), 151.
2. Ricardo Limardo, "Memoria del Gobernador de la Provincia de Santiago," Feb. 6, 1906, *Gaceta Oficial* 22, no. 1687, May 19, 1906.
3. "Nuestros agricultores de éxito," *La información* (Santiago), March 30, 1925.

Salomé

Salomé Ureña de Henríquez

Salomé Ureña de Henríquez (1850–1897) is not only among the most highly regarded poets in Dominican literature, she may be the most famous woman in Dominican history. In addition to being acclaimed for her verse, she gained renown as a leading educator, feminist, and patriot. The Dominican American author Julia Alvarez brought her to a wider audience with the best-selling novel In the Name of Salomé (2000), a lyrical and historically accurate evocation.

The ideal of progress, which consumed the Dominican intelligentsia during the late nineteenth century, was central to Salomé's work. This circle of progressive thinkers included her husband, Dr. Francisco Henríquez y Carvajal (1859–1935), who is also well known for his long career as a journalist, essayist, diplomat, and statesman. He had to go into exile periodically when political power shifted, as it often did. He served as president during the turbulent year 1916, when the United States invaded the country and began a military occupation. The best known figure among these intellectuals, not himself Dominican, was Eugenio María de Hostos, the influential Puerto Rican writer and educational reformer. He held enormous sway among liberal Dominicans in their efforts to bring about progressive changes in education, politics, urban life, and social relations.

Salomé's status in Dominican nationalist culture is more exalted now than ever before. A new statue of her, slightly larger than life, stands near the ancient Alcazár in the heart of Santo Domingo's Colonial Zone. More ubiquitously, and more telling of Dominican priorities, she is pictured on the very common 500 peso bill, with her son Pedro Henríquez Ureña (1884–1946), who was a famous scholar, author, and critic.

The consuming pursuit of improvement runs through many of Salomé's poems, as is reflected in such titles as "The Glory of Progress" and "Faith in the Future." Possibly as a result of this yearning for advancement, an ambiguous nationalism marks her patriotic pieces, including these two, which celebrate the most important Dominican national holidays: Independence Day, commemorating the separation from Haiti, and Restoration Day, celebrating the regaining of independence after the Spanish recolonization of the 1860s failed.

27th of February

Oh date so generous
which the patriot salutes with reverence;
when floats the free and victorious
banner of the homeland's independence!

Then the voice of fame,
of God and Liberty, summoned to war
the sturdy steel, the spirit aflame,
to triumph or perish, vowed the warrior.

And with her livery of the servant
cast off boldly, with a holy sense,
amid ovations of surprise, giant,
splendid, Quisqueya ascends.

Victory, oh Lord, what glory!
Victory, Homeland, and your illustrious name
with flashes of light inscribes history,
and humanity tributes you with acclaim.

More oh! do you think it sufficient
that triumph of exploits and grandeur?
To a higher level raise your pennant!
By your deeds, another struggle you will endure.

Where the soldier roving,
his nerve ingenious, his power august,
brings order, respect, loving,
he does the work of the graceful and just.

His fields he does not cultivate,
they stretch out under a fiery sun's glow,
in their primitive vigor they await
the fertile peace, the gentle water's flow.

They await the zealous
and active farmer, vast fields of plants
that raising your status prodigious,
would give you strength and hope and perseverance.

A statue of the national poet Salomé Ureña de Henríquez was unveiled at the opening of the "Plaza of Poetry" adjacent to the Alcazár de Colon in the heart of Santo Domingo in October 2011. Photograph by Eric Paul Roorda, June 2012.

Certainly to the cutting edge
will bow down the forest glade,
to give the people refuge,
life to commerce, to the ports trade.

Ay, open new avenues;
let the sun rise, and shine the rainbow's band
and beneficent progress its retail venues
will establish on your deserted strand!

Give welcome to the royal visitor
who approaches you crossing climates,
and lodging worthy of his eminent splendor
quickly raise up on your summits.

Attend, that destiny
unfolds happily for your regions;
and grand, and strong, and powerful, and free,
industry bearing the heraldic escutcheons

that today on your ramparts
on the national ensign, wave in the breeze,
fluttering in the temple of the arts,
of the new glory a monument sees.

16th of August

Reclined luxuriantly
on her bed of floating seaspray
heedless of the thick fog
in which the sky enveloped her glories,
Quisqueya, abandoned, [was] indifferent
to the sound of the waves that lulled her to sleep.

And in her fleeting lethargy,
she did not see the ambition for shiny metal
of the giant hydra,
sacrificing honor and patriotism,
a future of high hopes,
to sink—oh Lord!—into the deep abyss.

Such a fatigued athlete,
she lost her liberty, the true currency;
the sad tropical breeze
folded its spotless wings,
so as not to ruffle, not to stir,
the foreign flag of Castile.

The tall palm tree laid low
turns its brow upward to grow free;
the chest of the gallant
trembles with secret pain;
Quisqueya, the same, apparently calm,
was lulled asleep by the sound of the waves.

More, out of sheer arrogance,
the Iberian dictated servitude and death
by law to the sturdy people,

and Quisqueya shook off her swoon
to squeeze her delicate bosom
into the armor of Pelagius.[1]

Rising up indignantly,
seeking the motto written with her blood;
and upon her rousing call,
sensing the insult to her fortune,
she made the legions tremble that in Granada
saw the crescent at their feet.

The magnificent multicolored flag
showed itself in this contest of the Cross;
in pursuit of eternal fame
a thousand of the faithful gathered in its shadow,
whose triumph immortalized the moment,
as the echoes of the old country died away.

And the cry of victory
rang from valley to mountain,
and in vain, in vain Spain
tried to stifle it with her ferocity:
but Quisqueya dug a grave for her pride
on the fields of glory.

And such a fierce example
and warning perhaps to other nations,
how the land of banners,
uncertain, laid low, and vanquished,
turned the tables on the terrified Iberian,
sent packing by his hosts aroused to war.

Honor, eternal glory
of August to those giant champions,
who in unequal contests,
struggling with the faith of patriotism,
returned greatness to their history,
teaching a hard lesson to despotism!

For them today the Homeland lifts to her brow
a wreath of a thousand laurels,
with ardent affection,
bathed by the sun of hope,
in pursuit of new light, of new life,
to reach an intrepid future.

Translated by Eric Paul Roorda.

Note

1. Pelagius (AD 354–420) was an ascetic, heretical theologian who espoused the free will of man and the primacy of temporal law, rather than religious authority, in bringing about civil order and the performance of good works.

The Case for Commerce, 1907

Dominican Department of Promotion

and Public Works

With the commencement of regular steamship service by the Clyde Steamship Line in the first decade of the twentieth century, and with the imminent opening of the Panama Canal, completed in 1914, the merchant class of the Dominican Republic and their foreign allies—shippers, bankers, buyers, and sellers—looked forward to a more prosperous future. Expositions showcasing material and social progress, often held on significant historical anniversaries, were all the rage during the decades bracketing the turn of the century, including the Jamestown Tercentennial Exposition, held in Virginia in 1907 at the place where the English planted their first settlement in the New World in 1607. The Dominican government sought representation at this fair and produced for distribution there a primer on the country's progress and potential, excerpted here. In keeping with that era of rampant boosterism, the Dominican Republic projected a future role for itself that it was not able to will into existence.

ADVANTAGEOUS SITUATION. The geographical position of the Republic is so privileged that it lies between the Atlantic Ocean and the Caribbean Sea, in other words, on the path of all the ships to or from Europe passing through the Panama Canal. If the prosperity of the Republic is now most promising, no one can foretell what it will be when the Canal is open. The importance of Santo Domingo will increase tenfold, commercially, industrially, and strategically. No ship will cross the Canal on her way to Europe, the western coast of North, Central, or South America and Mexico, or on her way to the Far East, without passing through the Mona Pass, opposite the splendid bay of Samaná. The country lies right in the way, as all other routes to and from the Canal are either less safe or longer than the route through the Mona Pass, between Santo Domingo and Porto Rico. There are other passes, such as that between Cuba and Haiti, the San Antonio pass between Cuba and Mexico, and the various channels between the sev-

A succession of Dominican governments and economic promoters had high hopes for the commercial development of Santo Domingo, pictured here at the turn of the century. However, the city's poor harbor, far removed from major shipping lanes, prevented it from gaining international prominence. "Santo Domingo, 1899," photograph by Frank T. Arms. Frank T. Arms Collection, Photography Collection, Mystic Seaport Museum, #1947/1835/49, © Mystic Seaport Museum.

eral islands of the Windward group. None of these, however, offer the same advantages the Mona Pass affords, not only as the shortest route, but also because the ships taking this route may call at ports in the Dominican Republic for provisions, repairs, etc.

On the other hand, the proximity of the Republic to the greatest marts of the world, makes the country peculiarly suitable for all kinds of investments. There are but two Latin American republics, Mexico and Cuba, nearer the United States than the Dominican Republic; none, however, is nearer to European ports, so that there will always be a market for Dominican products abroad.

VI

Dollars, Gunboats, and Bullets

During the last years of the Heureaux regime, most of the Dominican foreign debt came under the control of a group of investors and lobbyists in New York that called itself the San Domingo Improvement Company. Known popularly as "El Impruvemen," it gained control over the country's customs collection and the revenues it generated as part of a repayment plan. The company enjoyed the backing of some powerful politicians, particularly Theodore Roosevelt (1858–1919), who amended the Monroe Doctrine with the situation in the Dominican Republic uppermost in mind. The Roosevelt Corollary to the Monroe Doctrine states that in cases where "impotence or chronic wrongdoing" on the part of a Latin American state make it impossible for its creditors to collect debts owed to them, then the United States would be compelled to step in as "an international police power." Roosevelt acted on that policy by seizing control of Dominican customs in 1905, taking the San Domingo Improvement Company off the hook for its investment and making the country's debt a responsibility of the US government. The finances of the republic passed into the hands of an American economic advisor and his staff of customs officials, dispatched to iron out the destabilizing debt crisis. The US-run "Dominican Customs Receivership," acting the part of a self-imposed international bankruptcy court, stayed in place for the next forty years.

The 1911 assassination of President Ramón Cáceres (1866–1911), who had been one of the leaders of the conspiracy that had successfully plotted the death of Lilís Heureaux twelve years earlier, ended the hiatus of relative civil order in the country that had occurred during his time in office. Another civil war broke out, making it impossible for the weak government to attend to the mounting debt owed to foreign investors. The instability in the republic attracted the attention of President Woodrow Wilson (1856–1924), who intervened militarily in 1916, beginning an eight-year occupation, as these selections detail.

Uneasiness about the US Government

Emiliano Tejera

As his 1906 essay "The Revolutionary and the Pig" showed, Emiliano Tejera was
skeptical of Dominican progress. But at the same time, he was optimistic about the
intentions of the United States, approving the actions of the Theodore Roosevelt ad-
ministration to take control of Dominican foreign debts. In the essay excerpted here,
also from 1906, a year after the establishment of the US Receivership of Dominican
Customs, Tejera addressed those among his compatriots who feared such interven-
tion. The following year, he helped to negotiate the American-Dominican Conven-
tion of 1907, which formalized the receivership arrangement.

There is a certain uneasiness, a certain misunderstanding in the relations
between part of the Dominican people and the American people, which
luckily has not reached the sphere of official relations. Varied are the causes
that contribute to the fact that there exists in this country a certain distrust
with respect to the methods of the American Government. Some, the skeptical ones, those possessed by the mercantile spirit, do not find it possible
that a people could extend their hand to another people, unless they harbor
the intention to demand the sacrifice of their territory, perhaps the loss of
their sovereignty. . . .

Reason will tell men of good faith who express uneasiness, if they were
to study our affairs dispassionately, that the American Government does
not come to our assistance with complete disinterest; on the contrary it has,
as is natural, a large and powerful interest. The principles of their foreign
policy demand that the European powers do not establish themselves in
America, and to prevent that is the reason they help us. If our craziness
continues, if we do not pay what we owe to European creditors, the day will
come on which, tired of waiting and of demanding payment, the European
Governments will occupy our customs houses, to cover those debts, and
perhaps part of our territory. If it comes to that, the American Government
must act, or renounce its foreign policy, confessing that the Monroe Doctrine is a laughable phantasm, or enter into a war with powerful nations,

or pay the debts or guarantee their payment, taking responsibility itself to cover them. . . . The United States are now, and have been for a long time, the protectors of the Hispanic-American Republics, and in the heart of the patriots of each one of those peoples there is a wound that bleeds, when they remember the humiliations and exactions received each time that that protection has been weakened or when it has not been requested nor granted.

Translated by Eric Paul Roorda.

In the Midst of Revolution

US Receivership of Dominican Customs

Under the American-Dominican Convention of 1907, US government personnel collected, or rather attempted to collect, the customs duties of the Dominican Republic. In fact, the Office of the General Receiver of Dominican Customs lacked the resources to impose order on the nation's finances, because the nation itself was constantly in a state of general disorder. Not only did the Receivership take over the customshouses but also it directed the seaborne Revenue Cutter Service and ran the Frontier Guard, an armed border patrol. The operations of this miniature army and navy led to the death of Receivership employees in the line of duty. With the advent of the Wilson Plan, which demanded peace and stability in the midst of bloody chaos, it was a short step from firefights pitting Frontier Guard members against antigovernment Dominican highwaymen to clashes between US Marines and anti-intervention guerrilla fighters called gavilleros. *The following highlights from the Seventh Annual Report of the Receivership, covering the period August 1913–July 1914, demonstrate the extent to which the beleaguered organization had become involved in the unruly state of political affairs, presaging the invasion Woodrow Wilson ordered two years later.*

The American-Dominican Convention, 1907.
Seventh Annual Report, Dominican Customs Receivership
Clarence H. Baxter, General Receiver.

Office of The General Receiver
Santo Domingo, D.R., October 1, 1914

The Year's Work

The seventh year of the Convention opened in the midst of a revolution, and as it was closing another was in progress. The first was inaugurated during the provisional presidency of José Bordas Valdés, and ended during the latter part of September, 1913, the revolutionists having been persuaded to lay down their arms on the promise of the United States Government that free and equal elections for the presidential electors and members of the constitutional convention would be guaranteed. During that revolution the ports of Puerto Plata, Sánchez and Samaná were blockaded by the federal forces.

The largest of the three ports and the second in importance throughout the Republic, Puerto Plata, was also blockaded during the second revolution of the year, which had its inception on April 13, the end of the provisional term of President Bordas; and the custom house was absolutely closed from April 23 until the cessation of hostilities on August 9. This second blockade was accompanied by a siege of the city under the leadership of President Bordas himself.

No other one effect of the revolutions accomplished so much towards the great decrease in the Receivership collections as the blockades of Puerto Plata. During both revolutions the Government-owned railroad extending from Puerto Plata to Santiago was out of commission, and this was true of the only other railroad of the Republic, known as the Samaná and Santiago Railway, which is owned by British capital, and operated from Sánchez to La Vega, another important town in the Cibao. These two roads are the only carriers for the richest section of the Republic.

The second revolution was due to the dissatisfaction of the people with the Bordas Government, which had been elected to carry out constitutional reforms and call elections for a definite successor. The fighting rapidly spread to all parts of the Republic, and even the capital did not escape. Siege was laid to the city by the revolutionists during the latter part of the Fiscal year, which was lifted however on the 28th of August, 1914, after the appointment of the new Provisional President. On the 18th of August an American Commission . . . came to present a plan of conduct locally known as the "Wilson Plan," having been suggested by the President. The plan proposed the resignation of Bordas, a general disarmament, the selection of a provisional president by the chieftains of the several political parties, a reformation of the election law by the President pro tem., and the calling of elections for presidential electors and members of the constitutional convention. José Bordas, president *de facto*, resigned, and Doctor Ramón Báez was appointed to the office of Provisional President on the 27th of August, 1914. Efforts are now being made towards the convocation of elections during the month of October.

It is estimated that the Bordas administration contracted debts amount[ing] to $7,000,000 which includes the unpaid salaries of that period. From July 1913, until Doctor Baez assumed office, a very small part of the budget, save the military, was attended to. . . .

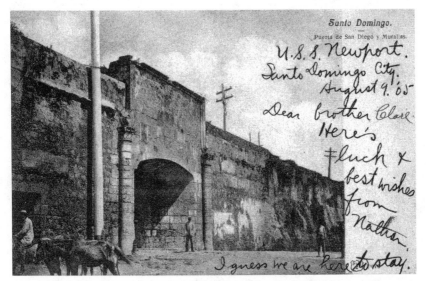

Santo Domingo.
Puerta de San Diego y Murallas.

U.S.S. Newport.
Santo Domingo City.
August 9. '05
Dear brother Clase.
Here's
fluck &
best wishes
from
Nathan.
I guess we are here to stay.

A sailor aboard the USS *Newport* made this prediction to his brother in August 1905, just as the US Receivership of Dominican Customs went into operation: "I guess we are here to stay." He chose a postcard showing the San Diego Gate in the ancient city walls, the main entrance to Santo Domingo from the Ozama River port. Photographer unknown, black-and-white postcard, c. 1905. Courtesy of the Roorda/Doyle Collection.

It gives me pleasure to report that the Receivership Annex has at last been completed, and the General Receiver, his Deputy, and the American personnel are comfortably housed therein. A great drawback that has heretofore prevented the Receivership from retaining for any length of time the service of capable young Americans has finally been overcome. Now they have comfortable and homelike living quarters, and, through the careful saving of the General Receiver of Dominican Customs, the Dominican Government has a building that will some day be to it a substantial piece of property that can be used for many purposes.

The old house was, as [are] most houses in the Capital, very insanitary and uncomfortable as a home. There sickness was the rule rather than the exception, three cases of typhoid fever and several cases of malaria being recorded during the year, and it was necessary to keep a trained nurse in almost constant attendance during the Seventh Convention Year, as well as an American Doctor for the Receivership during a portion of this time. All of these expenses have been lopped off, and the American Government's representatives under the Convention are not suffering any longer the usual hazards of disease in the Tropics, in addition to the dangers of the revolutions. During the siege of Santo Domingo, when most Americans retired within the walls of the city or left for Porto Rico, the new annex, although outside of the city walls, was constantly occupied by the General Receiver and his assistants, and the work of the central office within the city went on without interruption. Almost every night Government outposts near the annex indulged in hap-hazard firing, and on one occasion several cannons blazed away in the darkness without the city in the direction of the annex. However, there were no casualties amongst the personnel, and the building was only struck by one bullet, so far as is known.

Revenue Cutter Service

It will be seen from the table herewith that two of the revenue cutters traveled more than ten thousand miles each during the Seventh Convention Year. This establishes a record for the little vessels, and the total mileage of the five cutters is also a record as well. We must remember that Nos. 1, 2, 3, and 4 are seventy-five feet by ten feet, with a draft of three feet, and were only guaranteed by the builder for five years, whereas, they have been in a continuous service for eight years, and two of the vessels are still worth retaining in the service. No. 1 and No. 2 will have to be soon discarded; but during the latter part of the year a larger boat was purchased at a cost of $25,000, with the funds saved by the Receivership from the five per cent allowance. She has been named the *Patria,* at the request of the Government, and has been in service since June 17, 1914.

During the year the cutters assisted twelve merchant vessels in distress, transported upwards of two thousand rifles and one hundred and eighty-one thousand rounds of ammunition, besides medical supplies and money for the payment of the Government troops. So far as transportation goes, this was the best year in the history of the Dominican Revenue Cutter Service as well as the most strenuous, on account of the political disturbances; and I am pleased to report that there has not been an accident of any importance nor a single life lost in the service. During the past revolution the cutters were of inestimable value to the Government as transport boats, but of less value to the Receivership and the public in general on that account, although by means of the cutters we were enabled to keep in communication with the outside world when all cable service was cut off, by carrying cables to Macorís from the Capital, from whence they were transmitted by wireless to Porto Rico, and in carrying mail from steamers and other ports to the Capital. On several occasions steamers from New York were met by cutters at Puerto Plata, and the mail for the Capital and southern ports was transported from said port, thus saving many valuable days for the trade of Santo Domingo. They were also used in distributing the Porto Rican "observers" to various points on the Island during the election of December, 1913.

It is hoped that the use of the boats as transport vessels of war by the Government will be discontinued. Besides being a great hindrance to the ordinary work of guarding the coasts, it has also been very dangerous; and it is a wonder that no lives have been lost on the cutters. On numerous occasions the boats have gone to sea with as many as seventy-five passengers aboard, while there have never been more than two small rowboats attached to the life saving apparatus.

Frontier Customs Service

In the fall of 1912 the Frontier Guard was reorganized, at the request of the Dominican Government and under the direction of the Receivership, and since that time it has been operated along the Haitian border in connection with the customs service. This small body of men patrols one hundred and fifty miles of as wild and uncivilized a district as exists anywhere at the present day. It has proved very efficient, although it embraces no more than one-third in number than formerly and costs the Government but one-half. The guards under Receivership control can not take part in political activities, while under the Government they were compelled to.

This year has been more turbulent than ever for the Frontier Customs Service. With the overthrow of the Haitian Government by the Zamors early in the year 1914, one revolution came to an end, only for another to begin, led by Davilmar Theodore and ably assisted by Dosilien. The latter had fought in both the Haitian and Dominican revolutions of the past, and was feared by both peoples. With his headquarters at the village of Ouanaminthe, Haiti, which is directly across the river from Dajabón, he terrorized the whole district.

Before the last revolution in Santo Domingo broke out, there was some little trade in ammunition between the two republics, but when the two revolutions got in full swing it was carried on more or less freely and openly in defiance of the Frontier Customs Service. In the south the Dominican revolutionists did business with the Haitian Government representatives, and in the north the Dominican revolutionist chieftain traded first with one side and then with the other. Affairs finally culminated in an attack on the custom house of Comendador by an armed force of revolutionists. The attack was made in order to divert the attention of the customs authorities from a large amount of rifles and ammunition that the Haitians were attempting to smuggle across the border for the benefit and with the aid of Dominican revolutionists. On account of the vast superiority in numbers of the revolutionists over the customs force, the American Inspector of Customs was forced to abandon the custom house, and under orders from the Deputy Receiver, he proceeded to Dajabón and joined forces with the mounted inspectors there.

Dosilien, the Haitian, repeatedly threatened to attack the custom house at Dajabón with his force of revolutionists, more than three hundred in number, but the Deputy Receiver there, although he had under his command only about twenty-five men, handled the situation fearlessly but with tact, and the threatened attack was never realized. In June, Dosilien and his forces were surprised and he was killed by Haitian Government troops.

The only death in the personnel of the guard occurred in this district during the latter part of July, 1914, when four mounted inspectors sought to confiscate a quantity of rum and flour that had been smuggled over the border and was being used at a vaudoux feast in a small community of Haitians living on the Dominican side. The feast had been in progress three days, and the participants numbering about sixty, refusing to give up the contraband. When the inspectors attempted to seize it, they were attacked by the whole crowd of drunken men and women with knives and machetes. Fortunately, only one of the inspectors, Martin Pérez, was killed. The other three succeeded in escaping after killing half a dozen of the Haitians. When a larger force of inspectors returned to the scene, the feast was ended and the guests had all departed. The body of Pérez was identified by a small piece of his uniform that was found on his arm. His body had been mutilated horribly and then burned.

Since the organization of the Receivership, two Americans have been killed while on duty in the Frontier Customs Service, and three wounded, while among the Dominican personnel there have been fourteen who have lost their lives, and twenty-three who have been wounded.

Note

Thanks are due to Cyrus Veeser for this selection.

Gavilleros

Listín Diario

A wide assortment of men joined the armed resistance to the United States occupation; they came to be known as gavilleros (bandits). The term was not new; it referred to the mountain-dwelling highwaymen who had plagued the countryside in the years preceding the US invasion, but it took on a different connotation under the circumstances of 1916. Gavilleros now meant the rebel forces of General Arias, disbanded Dominican government forces, and local monteros; whatever their origin, the US Marines called all of them bandits. Pursued by the Marines during the early months of the US takeover of the country, the guerrillas supplied themselves at the expense of the civilian population, as is reflected by these two reports from the nation's leading newspaper, Listín Diario *of Santo Domingo. The arrival of airplanes in 1919 doomed the gavilleros, because marines flying overhead could locate the gavillero bands in rough terrain and drop bombs on them, allowing ground forces riding horses and mules and armed with modern Springfield rifles and machine guns to catch up with and kill the survivors.*

The first news report concerns a band of about eighty armed men under the command of General Chucho García. After US forces chased them from the environs of Baní, they resorted to targeting civilians. The account picks up after the Marine attacks had driven García's men out. The second report pertains to a group of former government army soldiers, disbanded by the Marines, who operated as gavilleros near Cotuí.

16 September 1916

. . . All of those who had risen up in revolt in the mountains began to pillage from the outskirts of the town, and the peasants who headed there carrying their product to market, were attacked and robbed of everything, fruits, animals, etc. One contingent of the rebels went toward Baní, and arrived at Yaguate among the hard-hit ones, the vendors, and the ranch-owning Cabreras, who, with the help of some friends, managed to capture two of the three gavilleros [found among them]. . . .

19 October 1916

GAVILLEROS MENACE PEASANTS. We have been informed by persons who merit complete credence, that in the surroundings of Cotuí a chief with a group of armed men is going around extracting money or other goods from the peasants. Those who refuse are threatened with being forced to be a soldier or shot.

Some have been forced to dig a grave. Seeing this, the authorities of La Vega and surroundings have gone about suppressing that brigandage; but the time will come when one cannot travel on those roads for fear of being robbed. We have previously been informed that this chief extorts $5 from each one, saying it is to raise the tax that the Government does not pay.

Translated by Eric Paul Roorda.

A Resignation and a Machine Gun

Frederic Wise and Meigs O. Frost

Fourteen years after a contingent of US Marines seized control of Santo Domingo, the commander of that force penned his memoirs in blunt language. Appropriately entitling his book A Marine Tells It to You, *Colonel Frederic Wise recounted his participation in what the US Marine Corps still today refers to as its "colonial small wars" in China, the Philippines, Mexico, Haiti, and the Dominican Republic. The chapter "San Domingo" offers his perspective on the chain of events in May and early June 1916, when the Marines took over the capital city and extended their control to Monte Cristi and Puerto Plata, en route to taking Santiago de Los Caballeros in July. Wise, who held the rank of captain at the time, earned a reputation as "a strict disciplinarian with a volcanic temper" among his men, who nicknamed him "Dopey." Such a man was ill suited for diplomacy but adept at violence. His narrative in the following selection, with its casual racism and brutality, demonstrates the mentality of the Marine occupation from its outset, and suggests why the Dominicans resented so deeply the bullying of men like Frederic Wise.*

Admiral [William B.] Caperton put me in command of the expedition. One hundred and fifty men strong, the two companies of Marines went aboard the *Prairie*. . . .

The *Prairie* came to anchor in the open roadstead off San Domingo City [on May 5, 1916], a mile or two beyond the mouth of the Osama River. . . . We landed at the Custom House, walked out through a gate in the wall, and called at the American Legation, which was in a suburb outside the wall. Peter Russell, the American Minister, was an old-timer in Latin American affairs. Then we learned the situation ashore. It was a complicated one.

President Hernandez [*sic*; he was actually Juan Isidro Jiménes] of San Domingo had left his capital for a vacation at his country home some miles from the city. Minister of War [General Desiderio] Arrias [*sic*] saw his chance. He proclaimed himself president. The Army stood about fifty-fifty. But Arrias' forces held the city and the fort, which contained the Arsenal. The troops loyal to President Hernandez were short of ammunition. Arrias was supposed to have about a thousand men in the town. At the corner of San Domingo City where the Osama River flowed into the open roadstead, was Fort Osama, with thick old Spanish walls on which modern guns were mounted. President Hernandez with his thousand men was in camp just outside the city walls. They had no artillery. They were supposed to be our allies.

Minister Russell's dope was that Arrias would never leave the city unless he was run out of there. It was my job to accomplish that. . . .

Here was the situation we faced:

A walled city had to be captured. In it were a thousand well-armed men with plenty of ammunition, some artillery, and gunners who knew how to use it. They were fired with the fresh enthusiasm of a revolution that looked successful. Arrias' men, knowing what had taken place in Haiti [occupied by the Marines the previous year], had the added spur of hatred for foreigners who were the allies of President Hernandez. The Dominicans had been a free people for some sixty-five years since they had won their independence from Haiti. And their pride was even more sensitive than the Haitians'. Also they had much more white blood in them. Their whole history ever since they achieved independence, had been just one revolution after another, too.

It didn't look so good. Particularly because I didn't know how far I could trust the President's men. I went down to Fort Geronimo with Mr. Russell and we went in to talk it over with President Hernandez.

The President of San Domingo, a tall, dignified old man, received us in a bare little apartment. He spoke Spanish. Mr. Russell interpreted.

From what I had learned and what he said, I could see he was in a bad fix. He wanted his presidency back. He wanted his capital back. But he didn't care much about getting it with the aid of Americans. That meant that later he was going to be in a jam with his own people.

He put it up to me to go into San Domingo City with Mr. Russell, see Arrias, and demand he surrender without bloodshed. I told him Arrias would laugh at me. He asked if I'd try it anyhow. I told him I would, on the proviso that if Arrias didn't agree to it, we would attack the town in the morning and he would pledge that his troops would fight alongside mine. It was agreed. . . . We drove into town.

Leaving the carriage outside the great gate of iron-studded planks [of Fortaleza Ozama], we were conducted by a guard into Arrias' quarters. He was a taller man than the President and much darker. He received us very graciously.

I told him that this damned business of having revolutions in San Domingo had to cease; that he must get out and let the President come back into the capital without a row; that the United States meant business and if he didn't do it we were going to put him out.

"I do not intend to leave," he said.

"Oh, yes, you will," I told him.

He shrugged his shoulders and smiled politely.

"The days of revolutions in San Domingo are over," I told him. "The State Department has made up its mind that the President is coming back, and under no conditions will they ever recognize you. These revolutions have got to cease and you Dominicans have got to run a good government."

He looked at me and smiled again.

"Has the United States sent people down here to teach us how to behave?" he asked.

I knew what he meant. The Dominican Customs, under American control for several years, had recently been reorganized and the posts all filled with [Secretary of State William Jennings] Bryan Democrats. As I had met with some of these, I didn't have any comeback.

We left, then. Back to Fort Geronimo we went to see the President. He was very much distressed at the outcome of the negotiations. He flung out his arms in a dramatic gesture.

"I cannot keep my word to you," he told me. "I can never consent to attacking my own people!"

"You've put me in a jack pot," I told him. "At your solicitation we have gone in and made another cheap bluff."

He agreed with me.

There I was under orders to help a President who at first accepted our help and then insisted he didn't want to be helped, and who, anyway, was utterly powerless to dislodge Arrias.

"The only thing for you to do is resign, if you don't want the help of the United States," I said.

The President paced up and down for a moment. At last he turned to us.

"Very well," he said. "I will sign my resignation in the morning."

"You'll do no such damned thing," I told him. "You'll sign it right now."

He sat down, had his secretary write out his resignation, and signed it. Right from Fort Geronimo, Mr. Russell sent that resignation into San Domingo by messenger to a printing shop. Thousands of copies were printed. Within an hour the city was plastered with them. . . .

Before daybreak we marched from our camp around in back of the city, formed in line of skirmishers, and at dawn advanced through those broken places in the wall.

Returning from the campaign to capture Santiago, US Marines posed on the train they requisitioned for the purpose. Photographer unknown, black-and-white photograph, 1916. Courtesy of the Roorda/Doyle Collection.

It was Vera Cruz all over again, minus the Navy's first day of fighting.[1] House by house, block by block, we combed San Domingo City from that wall clear to the beach. Not a shot was fired at us. Not one of our men fired a shot. We never found a weapon in all those houses.

Arrias and his army had departed the night before.

By nine o'clock that morning the town was ours, Marines were patrolling the streets, [and we] had established headquarters in Arrias' quarters in Fort Osama. . . .

Two weeks after the capture of the city we started after Arrias. The first step was to be the capture of Monte Christi. . . . It was to be my job to take the town and establish the base. . . .

I went ashore [on June 1] and looked up the American consular agent, a Mr. Petite, a native of St. Thomas. His summary was brief.

"The rebels are in control of the town under a native named Miguelito, one of Arrias' lieutenants. They have run the governor out. But there haven't been any outrages. The town is running along in a normal manner."

On August 29, 1916, a calm day two months after the US invasion, a series of rogue waves, generated by two distant storms, unexpectedly began to roll into Santo Domingo. The ninety-foot crests drove the armored cruiser USS *Memphis* onto the jagged shoreline, killing forty-three sailors and wrecking the ship. A large crowd of citizens came to the scene, some of them risking their own lives to rescue the survivors. The US consul, Carl M. J. von Zeilinski, took this photograph of the scene the day after the disaster. "USS Memphis Wrecked at Santo Domingo, August 1916," black-and-white photograph, August 30, 1916. Courtesy of U.S. Naval Historical Center, photograph #NH 46219.

I found Miguelito in the Town Hall. He was rather a well-dressed native of heavy stature. A pistol was belted to his civilian clothes.

"We intend to run you out of town," I told him.

"You won't have the easy time you had over in Haiti," he told me.

"We won't have any trouble when we make up our minds to take the town," I informed him.

I left him and made arrangements with Mr. Petite to give me some horses so I could ride around the next morning and see the place thoroughly. . . .

Next morning we landed and occupied the town without any opposition. Miguelito and his army of about a hundred and fifty men cleared out and camped by the ferry. I took up quarters in the room in the Town Hall where I had met Miguelito, and the men occupied the forts. . . .

The second night we were ashore, the Dominicans from the hillside back of the town saluted us with several volleys. It was the first time American Marines had ever landed at Monte Christi, and they were resenting it. None of us were hit. I paid no attention to it. . . .

Then the Dominicans started their old trick of stopping all food coming into the town. That didn't bother the Marines. We had our supplies from the ships. But it was rough on the population. They complained that I had caused all this trouble and that I must devise a way for them to get food.

I knew the only way to do it was to disperse that camp out at the ferry. This we proceeded to do next day.

I took one of the ship's detachments, a machine gun—it was a French weapon—and went over toward the ferry to see what was going on. . . . I left the main detachment, took a squad and a mule which carried the machine gun. After we had traveled a short distance, I saw a group of Dominicans armed with rifles, under a tree. I had an idea that was an outpost from the main body.

We were on a hillside about three hundred yards away from them. I didn't want them to know I had a machine gun. We opened up on them with rifles. Several got away. I had an idea they would soon return with their friends. We got the machine gun off the mule and set it up. The scrub brush, about waist-high, concealed it. There we waited on that hillside. We had seen them last disappearing over a ridge of that other hill three hundred yards away. Between us ran the road that led to the ferry.

In about twenty minutes, some hundred and fifty of them came over that ridge. In a ragged, irregular group, holding their rifles high and free arm, and shooting as they came, they ran down the hill toward the road. In the midst of them I recognized Miguelito, mounted on a roan mule. I suppose the eight or nine of us looked uneasy to them.

We let them come till they got to the road. Their front extended over a hundred yards. Little groups of three or four of them, with intervals of a few yards between. No order. No discipline.

When they reached the road we opened up with the machine gun and sprayed it up and down their line.

To one side of the machine gun, I was sitting on the hillside, my elbows on my knees, my field glasses to my eyes. The whole picture was brought to my vision at very close range. Evidently it was the first time they had ever encountered a machine gun.

I could see sheer amazement on their faces. The gun was functioning properly. All up and down the line I could see them dropping. Then they turned and ran. We kept shooting at them until the last of them vanished over the ridge. I went over to the road to see what damage we had done. I found thirty-nine casualties.

It was impossible to pursue them through that kind of country, and I was pretty well satisfied, anyway, that we'd never have any more trouble with what was left of the gang. We returned to town and I had the natives go out there and get the wounded.

The food blockade ceased. Life in Monte Christi went back to normal.

Note

1. The Mexican port city Vera Cruz was occupied by the US Marines for six months in 1914.

The "Water Torture" and Other Abuses

US Senate, Hearings before a Select Committee

on Haiti and Santo Domingo

The Marine occupation of the Dominican Republic was sullied in the US public eye by revelations of brutal methods employed by the occupying forces in their attempts to pacify the countryside, where the insurgents called gavilleros *found havens in the rough terrain and among the peasants. Atrocities committed by Americans emerged during 1920–1921 from the fog of war into the glaring light of Senate investigative hearings, some conducted in the Dominican Republic. Eyewitnesses gave testimony that marines, in particular the infamous Forty-fourth Company, had tortured prisoners, murdered civilians, and carried out scorched-earth tactics against the peasantry. The most damning evidence about this brutal conduct did not emerge until the publication in 1922 of the hearings, from which this selection is taken. The interlocutors in the transcripts are mainly the three senators Atlee Pomerene (D-Ohio), Joseph Medill McCormick (R-Illinois), and Wesley Jones (R-Washington) and the attorney Horace Knowles, who made a career out of being a gadfly of Dominican causes. As demonstrated in the exchanges between the testy senators and various witnesses, many of them victims of the abuses to which they testified, the senators were slow to acknowledge the depth of the depravity that many marines had exhibited during the occupation.*

Statement of Dr. Alejandro Coradin, of Hato Major

DR. CORADIN: On the 22nd of June, 1917, I saw an old man dragged, tied to the tail of a horse—an old man by the name of José María Rincon. . . . a man 80 years old, generally esteemed, due to his conduct as a good man. . . . he was taken prisoner in the drug store by Mr. Peralez, who was operating with the forces of the occupation.

MR. KNOWLES: Do you mean operating or in charge of?

CORADIN: He was a lieutenant. There were other officers of high rank I did not know. Under the imputation or accusation that the medicine which had been prescribed for healing some skin disease was for dressing the wounds of the men in rebellion in the hills, of course—I add to-day to what I stated yesterday that this man was tied.

KNOWLES: I want to get this clear as to this point. You mean to say that the medicine that was found in his possession was intended to dress the wounds of his compatriots who were outside the city, and who may have been wounded in contact with the marines?

CORADIN: That was an accusation made by the forces of occupation, because the medicine was not intended for dressing the wounds of those men.

KNOWLES: What was that?

CORADIN: I state today and stated yesterday that the medicine was for healing a skin disease, and that the marines stated that it was for dressing wounds. That is what I said.

SEN. POMERENE: Can you give the names of those marines who stated that?

CORADIN: I have said more than once that I don't know the marines. I know Mr. Peralez. . . .

POMERENE: Are you sure he was a marine, or did he belong to La Guardia?

CORADIN: He was a marine. He was with the marines and dressed like a marine.

KNOWLES: Was he the man, Peralez, who was in charge of that detachment or body of men that operated in the city at that time?

CORADIN: No; as I stated yesterday, there were officers of higher rank.

KNOWLES: Were they present during all the happenings that you have described?

CORADIN: Yes; there was a doctor, a captain, and another captain.

SEN. JONES: Two captains?

CORADIN: Two captains and Lieutenant Peralez.

JONES: Oh, Peralez was a lieutenant?

CORADIN: Yes.

KNOWLES: Was Rincon a strong man?

CORADIN: A man of 80 years can not be a strong man. . . .

KNOWLES: State to the Senators exactly what happened when they stopped there with the man, and the condition in which he was.

CORADIN: It is easy to suppose the condition in which that old man must have been after having been dragged by the tail of a horse at full speed through the town. When Peralez stopped with him I can state that he was dying.

KNOWLES: And then what happened?

CORADIN: And then Peralez shot him. And then with the same rope he tied him and hung him from the branch of a tree.

KNOWLES: Was that in the presence of all the other marines?

CORADIN: A short distance from the camp.

KNOWLES: In sight of the incident?

CORADIN: Yes. . . .

KNOWLES: Before closing, I wish to present the commission with one of the victims of the water torture. . . .

Statement of Mr. Pedro Hernández Rivera, of Hato Major

. . . MR. RIVERA: I was confounded or mistaken for a man by the name of Pedro Rivera . . . I was asked how much ammunition I had sent to the men in the hills. That was all the questions asked. They did not allow me to speak . . .

KNOWLES: In whose hand was the rope that was tied around your neck?

RIVERA: A marine on horseback, but Capt. Merckle was there . . .

KNOWLES: You were arrested and tied in the city, Mr. Rivera?

RIVERA: Yes, on the street.

KNOWLES: How many marines and officers were in the group that took you to this place?

RIVERA: About 10 or 12.

JONES: Did they take any other prisoners at the same time?

RIVERA: Yes . . . two more . . .

JONES: All of the marines were Americans?

RIVERA: Americans . . .

KNOWLES: Will you please describe again exactly what happened when you arrived at the destination of the officers and marines who were taking you?

RIVERA: About an hour after I arrived I was placed on my back, with my face to the sun, and was kept there for about two hours while water was poured through a funnel at intervals, and when I refused to open my mouth they forced it open with a stick.

KNOWLES: Were you fastened to a stake or tied to anything?

RIVERA: Yes. [Indicating with his arms out at right angles and his feet separated.]

KNOWLES: And each hand and foot bound to a stake?

RIVERA: Yes.

SEN. MCCORMICK: Lying on his back?

RIVERA: Lying on my back.

KNOWLES: How many men were present when the funnel was put in your mouth?

RIVERA: Americans?

KNOWLES: Yes.

RIVERA: About eight Americans. My feet and arms were held by an American. My head was held by an American. I still have the scar (pointing to his right temple). I did not feel it at the time.

KNOWLES: Who was it, if you could see, that poured the water in the funnel that entered your body?

RIVERA: A marine. I did not know him. He kept it over my mouth.

KNOWLES: How long did they continue to pour this water?

RIVERA: Two minutes. They poured water in the funnel until I became unconscious. Then some minutes they poured again after I revived.

KNOWLES: How many times was that repeated?

RIVERA: I believe it was about three times.

KNOWLES: Why did they stop?

RIVERA: I don't know, because I suppose they did not wish to give me any more.

MCCORMICK: Now let me ask a question. He said, if I remember, that there were two other companions taken at the time. Were they similarly treated?

RIVERA: Yes.

KNOWLES: What happened to these men?

RIVERA: They threw water in the same way as I have stated.

MCCORMICK: Well, they are here, so they will testify.

KNOWLES: How long did they keep you at the stake there after they finished?

RIVERA: I was tied by a rope around my neck to the trunk of a tree. That night I slept in the same state, with my right hand loose and the other hand tied.

MCCORMICK: It is needless to say that the other members of this committee share in the expressions of regret which was given by the chairman of the committee.

Statement of Mr. Emilio Suárez, Hato Major

KNOWLES: Had you any connection or position with the army or guard under the military government?

MR. SUÁREZ: No. I acted only as a guide.

KNOWLES: For what time period?

SUÁREZ: A year and two months . . . Capt. Merckle obliged me to accompany him . . . from April, 1917, up to July, 1918 . . . In June we left Hato Major with a detachment of marines . . . under the command of Capt. Merckle and Lieut. Simmons of the Forty-fourth Company. . . . On arriving opposite a place called Santana, Capt. Merckle . . . obliged the people in that place to declare where the bandits were to be found, tying women, men, and children, and threatening them with death if they did not state where they were to be found. With that end they were all taken to San Lorenzo . . . Capt. Merckle ordered that the prisoners be blindfolded.

KNOWLES: How many were at that time prisoners?

SUÁREZ: About 25—women, children, and men. . . . After that he went out in the country, setting fire in El Candelaria, in Pedro Sánchez, in Margarita, and in San Francisco, burning many houses, perhaps about 200 houses. . . . Col. Thorpe ordered the reconcentration of the whole eastern Province. After that there were about 1,500 marines in Hato Major. . . . After that Capt. Merckle called me and told Amador Cisnero, the second chief of police of San Pedro de Macorís, and me that we had to kill many prisoners in the country, so as to put a stop to banditry. On the 27th of September we left with a detachment of marines for Dos Ríos, passing by Matapolacio. When we got to Matapolacio he ordered that the whole town of Matapolacio be burned. Only one house was standing at that place. . . . On reaching El Salto, which belongs to the Macorís Sugar Co., a town with a good many houses, Capt. Merckle ordered all of the houses to be burned. After that I and the marines in examining, found on the river bank a man wounded in the thigh, and we took him to Capt. Merckle, who told him that he ought to state where his companions were. He told him that he had been wounded and had been interned in the colony [sugar plantation], for 10 days, maintaining himself by eating sugar cane. He told him that was not sufficient, that he should tell the truth as to where his companions were, and he stated that he didn't know. Then he took that man and took a big trunk of a tree and placed him face downward on the trunk and cut another stick about that thickness [indicating] and beat him on the buttocks and all over the body. Cut off his ear, wounded him on the chest in two places.

KNOWLES: How did he wound him?

SUÁREZ: Making crosses on his chest.

KNOWLES: What with?

SUÁREZ: With a knife. He poured salt into the wound and orange juice. . . . Then he took that man and mounted him on a horse and tied his legs tightly under the belly of the horse, and we left for Dos Ríos. We

This rare action shot of field operations depicts US Marines detaining and interrogating two Dominican civilians in August 1916. It bears the ominous caption "Two Rebel's Captured." Photographer unknown, black-and-white postcard, August 1916. Courtesy of the Roorda/Doyle Collection.

arrived there in the afternoon, and then the chief at Dos Ríos told Capt. Merckle he knew where there were two fugitives, and that he wished to capture them. . . . The following day, pretty early, he appeared with the two men as prisoners, one of them had yaws.

KNOWLES: Do you know what that is?

INTERPRETER: It is a tropical skin disease.

KNOWLES: Proceed.

SUÁREZ: These men stated that they had not come to town, because they were suffering with that bad disease, and they might infect the people of the city. His companion stated that he had not come because he was keeping company with his sick friend, as on a former occasion his sick friend had done the same for him. That night Capt. Merckle and Amador ordered us to kill the man suffering with yaws with our knives. We told him we would not do so, because the man had not offended us, and he had many rifles and machine guns and could use them on him. Then he sent a sergeant of marines and an enlisted man, and the sergeant fired one shot. He fell on the ground alive, then the enlisted man drove a pick-ax through his head from one side to the other. . . . We left for Hato Major with the three prisoners [Dominicans who had been accused of stealing], with the man who had been tortured, and the companion of the man who was suffering from yaws and had been shot the previous

This unfortunate Dominican, staring balefully at a marine's camera, had been identified as a "Bandit Cheif [*sic*]." Photographer unknown, black-and-white photograph, c. 1920. Courtesy of the Roorda/Doyle Collection.

night, mounted on a horse the same way he came from Dos Ríos. On reaching Mata Lambre, Capt. Merckle ordered that the three young men and the companion of the man who had been suffering from yaws, be shot, and he ordered them to be released one by one, and he stood off with a machine gun and killed each one, only leaving the man whose ears had been cut off and whose chest had been marked with crosses. Then he shot each of those men through the ear and left them dead on the plain near the road, and the bodies were eaten by the pigs or the hogs and dogs. Then he ordered Armado Mejía, whose ears had been cut off, to tell him where his companions were, saying that if he did not tell him, he was going to shoot him. He said that he could not state where they were. Then he set fire to the leg in which he was wounded and burned the trouser on that leg. After that we left for Hato Major. . . . He ordered 10 marines to throw oranges at Mejía and to strike him all over the body. Sometimes he fell on the ground, and he remained breathless for a time, and he asked them to kill him and not torture him so much, but they stated that he was a bandit and should die little by little, and that [Merkle] would not give him anything to eat until he died of hunger and thirst. . . .

The Land of Bullet-Holes

Harry Franck

The travel writer Harry Franck (1881–1962) and his wife, Rachel (1893–1986), made their way from New York through the islands of the Caribbean in 1919–1920, going by train, boat, and automobile along a route passing through Haiti and the Dominican Republic, both under US Marine Corps occupation at the time. The Francks traveled in the company of an armed American marine and an unarmed Haitian gendarme while crossing the border between the two countries in a durable Ford "flivver." In Franck's account of their trip, first published as a serial in Century *and then as the book* Roaming through the West Indies, *which is excerpted here, the casual racism and sexism of the imperial perspective is present in a particularly concentrated form. However offensive his characterizations of race and gender may be, they were assumptions that underpinned the military occupation of the Dominican Republic by the US Marines (1916–1924) and their war against the gavillero guerrilla forces, which Franck described. His description of the Dominican National Guard as a gang of criminals presaged the rise to power of the dictator Rafael Trujillo (1891–1961), whose disreputable past did not prevent him from receiving a commission in the military trained by the US Marines.*

Unlike the Haitian shacks behind us, the dwellings of Dajabón [in the Dominican Republic] were almost habitable, even to the exacting Northern point of view. Instead of tattered and ludicrously patched Negroes of bovine temperament lolling in the shade of ragged hovels of palm-leaves and jungle rubbish, comparatively well-dressed men and women, ranging in complexion from light brown to pale yellow, sat in chairs on projecting verandas or leaned on their elbows in open windows, staring with that fixed attention which makes the most hardened stranger self-conscious in Spanish-America, yet which, contrasted with the vacant black faces of Haiti, was an evidence at least of human intelligence and curiosity. The village girls, decked out in their Sunday-afternoon best, were often attractive in appearance, some undeniably pretty, qualities which only an observer of African ancestry could by any stretch of generosity grant to the belles of Haitian *bourgs* behind us.

Even the change in landscape was striking. Whether the Spaniard colonized by choice those regions which remind him of the dry and rarely shaded plains of his own Castile and Aragón, or because he makes way with a forest wherever he sees one, he is more apt than not to be surrounded by bare, brown, semi-arid vistas. . . . The great plain that stretched out before us in Dajabón was almost treeless. . . . In contrast to *caco*-impoverished Haiti, large herds of cattle wandered about the brown immensity, or huddled in the rare pretenses of shade. . . . Clusters of thrown-together huts, little less miserable in these rural districts, it must be admitted, than those of Haiti, jolted past us now and then, their swarms of stark-naked children of eight, ten, and even twelve years of age scampering across the broken, sun-hardened ground to see us pass. Yet in one respect at least even these denizens of the wilderness were superior to their Haitian prototypes—they really spoke their native language. Familiar as we had both been for years with French, it was rare indeed that we got more than the general drift of a conversation in Haitian "creole." The most uneducated *dominicano*, on the other hand, spoke a Spanish almost as clear and precise as that heard in the streets of Madrid. . . .

It was not until morning that we caught full sight of the chief feature of the plaza and the pride of Monte Cristi. By daylight a monument we had only vaguely sensed in the night stood forth in all its dubious beauty. In the center of the now deserted plaza rose a near replica of the Eiffel Tower, its open-work steel frame crowned by a large four-faced clock some fifty feet above our dizzy heads. Well might the Monte Cristians pride themselves on a feature quite unique among the plazas of the world.

Those who glance at the top-heavy structure from the south are struck by a jagged hole just above the face of the dial, midway between the XII and the I. It is so obviously a bullet-hole that the observer could not fail to show surprise were it not that bullet-holes are as universal in Santo Domingo as fighting cocks. Thereby hangs another tale.

In the early days of the American occupation the choice of commanders of the *Guardia Nacional* detachment in Monte Cristi was not always happy. It was natural, too, that a group of marine officers, bubbling over with youth, sentenced to pass month after month in a somnolent Dominican village, should have found it difficult to devise fitting amusement for their long leisure hours. Pastimes naturally reduced themselves to the exchange of poker chips and the consumption of certain beverages supposedly taboo

Monte Cristy - (Rep. Dominicana) - Vista parcial de la Ciudad

The clock tower of Monte Cristi, a focus of civic pride built at great expense, sustained damage when a drunken marine fired his gun at the clock face. Photographer unknown, tinted black-and-white postcard, c. 1920. Courtesy of the Roorda/Doyle Collection.

Harry Franck excoriated the Dominican national guard in his description of the US Marine occupation. A company of the Guardia, with its American commanding officer, is seen here at rest in an unidentified town. Photographer unknown, black-and-white photograph, c. 1919. Courtesy of the Roorda/Doyle Collection.

in all American circles and doubly so in the Marine Corps. The power of Dominican joy-water to produce hilarity is far-famed. It came to be the custom of the winning card player to express his exuberance by drawing his automatic and firing several shots over his head. This means of expression would have been startling enough to the disarmed Dominicans had the games been played in the open air with the sun above the horizon. But the rendezvous was naturally within doors, usually in the dwelling of the commander, and the climax was commonly reached at an hour when all reputable natives were wrapped in slumber. The sheet-iron roof that sheltered us during our night in Monte Cristi corroborated the testimony of the inhabitants that they had frequently sprung from their beds convinced that yet another revolution was upon them.

One night a difference of opinion arose among the players as to the hour that should be set for cashing in of chips. The commander offered to settle the problem in an equitable manner. Stepping to the door, he raised his automatic toward the famous $16,000 clock and fired. The decision was made; the game ended at twelve thirty. It is not particularly strange under the circumstances that the inhabitants of Monte Cristi are not extraordinarily fond of Americans or of marine occupation . . .

Santo Domingo under American Rule

As in other lands under temporary or permanent American rule, from Haiti to the Philippines, a native constabulary was organized. The *Guardia Nacional* of Santo Domingo, consisting at present of a company of eighty men in each of the fourteen provinces, has the same organization as the Marine Corps. . . . Their uniform lacks only the hat ornament and somewhat more durable dye-stuffs to [be] an exact copy of that of our "leather-necks." . . . The officers are marines, usually sergeants, except in the higher commands and a very few natives who have climbed to "shave-tail" rank. . . . The native rank and file of the Guardia have a cocky, half-insolent air quite foreign to their simpler fellows in Haiti; they look as if they would be better fighters, more clever crooks, and not so easily disciplined.

The *cacos* of Santo Domingo are called *gavilleros*, *caco* in that country meaning merely thief or burglar. They are usually armed with *pata-mulas* [mule hooves], which are rifles that have been cut down into revolvers. . . . Not until the Americans came were these anti-governmental groups called bandits; they were dignified with the title of revolutionaries. . . . The *gavillero* situation had been bad before the Americans landed. It became worse under the occupation, for reasons that we shall see. . . . The forces of occupation might in some ways have handled this bandit situation better than they did; largely because of ignorance of local customs, partly because of inefficiency and a certain amount of brutality, they made something of a mess of it, or at least let it become more serious than it need to have done. . . .

The rascally, brutal, worthless, "Diamond Dick" class of American sometimes gets into the Marine Corps as into everything else and tends to destroy the good name of the majority. Boys brought up on dime novels and the movies saw at last a chance to imitate their favorite heroes and kill people with impunity: some of them, too, were Southerners, to whom the Dominicans after all were only "niggers." The great majority of the forces of occupation were well meaning young fellows who often lacked experience in distinguishing outlaws from common citizens, with the result that painful injustices were sometimes committed.

These ignorant, or movie-trained, young fellows were sent out into the hills to hunt bandits. They came upon a hut, found it unoccupied, and touched a match to the *nipe* thatch. They probably thought the hovel was of no importance anyway, whereas it contained all the earthly possession of a harmless family. In their ignorance of local customs they could not know that the entire household was out working in their jungle yucca garden. Or they found only the women and children at home, and burned the house because these could not explain where their man was. Or again, they met a man on the trail and asked him his business, and because he could not understand their atrocious imitation of Spanish, or they his reply, they shot him to be on the safe side. In still other places they burned the houses of innocent accomplices, because bandits had commandeered food and lodging there. If one can believe half the stories that are current in all circles throughout Santo Domingo, the Germans in Belgium had nothing on some of our own "leather-necks."

A parish priest of Seibo, who seemed, if anything, friendly to the occupation, told me of several cases of incredible brutality of which he had personal knowledge. . . . The Guardia, he asserted, included some of the worst rascals, thieves, and assassins in the country, men far worse than the *gavilleros,* and these often egged the naïve Americans on to vent their own private hates. Scarcely a month before a sad personal experience had befallen him. On Christmas Day he had gone with acolytes to another town to attend a fiesta, when a drunken marine fired his rifle twice into the wattled hut where it was being held and killed a boy of ten who was at that moment swinging the censer.

American Sugar Kingdom

César J. Ayala

United States sugar corporations came to dominate the Dominican sugar industry in the early twentieth century, with far-reaching effects. The Dominican Republic became part of what the historian César J. Ayala calls an "American sugar kingdom" that stretched from Cuba to Puerto Rico. Under the control of a handful of US-owned sugar companies and banks, with their interlocking directorates, the output of Dominican sugar soared during the years of the US Marine occupation. This selection, from Ayala's book American Sugar Kingdom: The Plantation Economy of the Spanish Caribbean, 1898–1934, *documents how the burgeoning sugar industry permanently changed the country's landscape, social structure, and economy.*

Vertical Integration: The Dominican Republic

The development of the sugar industry of the Dominican Republic, unlike that of Cuba, does not date back to the early nineteenth century. Sugar was of relatively minor importance in the Dominican Republic, beginning its ascent in the second half of the century as a result of two external factors. First, the Spanish reoccupation of the Dominican Republic in 1861–65 brought Spanish and Italian immigrants interested in the development of the industry. Second, the immigration of Cuban planters during the Ten Years' War of 1868–78 in Cuba introduced to the Dominican Republic the technology of the Cuban mills and steam power for refining and transport. Sugar production began to expand in the 1870s, but production figures were even smaller than those of Puerto Rico. The primacy of sugar in the export basket of the Dominican Republic was consolidated by the North American occupation of 1916–24. . . .

Under the combined influence of a favorable military government and high international sugar prices during World War I, the North American interests in the Dominican Republic propelled the expansion of Dominican sugar production from its prewar level of 86,734 tons in 1913 to 371,419 in 1926. In 1920 sugar exports amounted to $45 million, or 413 percent greater than that of the other three largest crops combined. In 1926 sugar represented 88 percent of the export tonnage and about 60 percent of export value. The sugar companies claimed that the Dominican government received 65 percent of its income of $7.4 million from sugar-related taxes.

The sugar estates and the power of the corporations were consolidated during the military occupation, but the expansion of North American sugar interests predates the military intervention of 1916. Central Romana, for example, began to grow cane in 1911 with the purpose of shipping it over the Mona Passage to grind in the Guánica mill of the South Porto Rico Sugar Company in Puerto Rico. Nevertheless, the real growth of the sugar-producing latifundia occurred mostly in the period 1917–20 under the American occupation. . . .

In 1907, of the fourteen ingenios [sugar plantations with mills] in operation, four belonged to the General Industrial Company (Vicini Group), three to Bartram Brothers and associates, and two to Hugh Kelly. Together, these nine ingenios accounted for 67 percent of the land planted in cane in the republic, taking into account the lands of colonos [sugar-producing farms without mills] associated with the mills. Foreign capital was represented by seven ingenios belonging to North Americans and one to Cubans established in the republic, which together accounted for 62 percent of cane lands. The General Industrial Company of the Vicinis was incorporated in New Jersey. . . . Geographically, sugar production was concentrated in San Pedro de Macorís, with its seven ingenios accounting for 67 percent of cane lands; in Santo Domingo, with three ingenios representing 16 percent of the cane lands, and in Puerto Plata with one ingenio representing 2 percent of the cane lands. It must be underscored, however, that all these enterprises were individually owned and the corporate phenomenon was still unknown.

Sugar still did not have the overwhelming predominance in the Dominican export basket that it acquired after 1916. In fact, in 1907 and 1908, the value of cocoa exports, a peasant-produced crop, surpassed that of sugar. Regionally, El Cibao continued to be a land of tobacco, cocoa, and petty commodity producers. Coffee, the fourth export by value, was spread throughout the republic, while sugar was concentrated in the east, particularly in San Pedro de Macorís.

The uncertain state of land titles in the Dominican Republic opened opportunities for US capital to acquire vast estates. The process of conversion of *haciendas comuneras* [commonly held agricultural lands] into private property under the laws of the Dominican Republic allowed foreign corporations to acquire vast expanses of relatively unpopulated land for the development

San Pedro de Macorís grew more than any other city as the result of the boom in sugar production in the early twentieth century, as attested by these scenes of two principal thoroughfares of the thriving port. The main feature on Calle Duarte is the tower of the elaborate Victorian firehouse, dating to the 1890s. The Royal Bank of Canada, constructed in 1914, stands at the left on Calle Sánchez. "Calle Duarte" and "Calle Sánchez," photographer(s) unknown, black-and-white photographs, c. 1920. Courtesy of the Roorda/Doyle Collection.

of sugar production. Through the acquisition of haciendas comuneras the Barahona Company, organized in New York in 1916, soon became the owner of the second largest sugar estate in the Dominican Republic, with an extension of 49,400 acres of land. The expansion of this estate occurred through the extensive "purchase" of *pesos comuneros* [shares of commonly held land] and through the acquisition of extensive water rights. By 1917 the Barahona Company owned 10 percent of the land in Barahona Province. Although the titles to many of the lands were false, Barahona could afford to hire the best lawyers in the country. The land speculators in effect deprived many peasant households of land, as Bruce Calder argues, by "taking advantage of the ignorance and poverty of the inhabitants of the Neyba Valley who, for lack of unity and financial resources, cannot hire a good lawyer to defend their legal rights." The Barahona Company also acquired rights under the Ley Sobre Franquicías Agrarias to the waters of the Yaque del Sur River, against the protestations of the peasant communities along the riverbanks. The protesters claimed that ten thousand people would be left destitute and would be forced to become tenants of the Barahona Company if the government granted its demands for water rights. As in Cuba, however, the beneficiaries of North American rule were North Americans. The actions of the company were legal and favored by the local elite, who believed that the Barahona Company's multimillion-dollar investment would improve the economy of the region.

In some instances foreign sugar companies obtained titles to whole villages. In 1921, the Central Romana estate, a subsidiary of the South Porto Rico Sugar Company, burned to the ground two hamlets, El Caimonal and Higueral, which stood in the path of its expanding fields. One hundred fifty families were left homeless, the company having made no provision for them. The degree of land concentration which the United States military occupation of 1916–24 brought about can be appreciated in the fact that out of the 438,182 acres of land owned by the sugar estates in 1924, 326,416 were owned by the five largest mills. The Central Romana alone owned 144,418 acres of land. . . . This concentration of land is misleading. Actual concentration in the sugar industry was much higher. In the Dominican Republic, three groups of investors were in almost complete control of the industry; out of nineteen large centrales the Cuban Dominican Sugar Company owned ten, the Central Romana (South Porto Rico Sugar Company) owned two, including a truly gigantic one, and an Italian-Dominican group (Vicini) owned three estates . . . the links with the oligopolistic sugar refining network were organized through institutional connections which implied close ties with banking capital (City Bank, House of Morgan) as in Cuba.

The Universal Negro Improvement Association in San Pedro de Macorís

Officers and Members of the Association

One of the main areas of operation for the US Marines was the vicinity of San Pedro de Macorís, the heart of the increasingly US-dominated sugar industry. The US corporations that owned and operated the plantations and refineries in the area facilitated the immigration of West Indian workers as contract laborers—men to work in cane processing, women to serve as domestics—to provide a secure labor force, since Dominicans resisted this poorly paid work. Degraded as cocolos (coconut-eaters), they faced discrimination from native Dominicans and harassment from US Marines. One group of Barbadian immigrants in San Pedro attempted to establish a chapter of the Universal Negro Improvement Association, an organization founded by the Jamaican Marcus Garvey (1887–1940) for the empowerment of people of African ancestry all over the world. The US military authorities, dominated by US southern whites, would have none of the Black empowerment message of the Association and proceeded to deal with its members as they might have in the Jim Crow South. The injured parties protested their unfair treatment in this letter to Rear Admiral Samuel S. Robison (1867–1952), commander of the US occupation forces. The original spelling has been left unedited.

September 5th, 1921

Sir:

We the undersigned do hereby thru these presents solicit your attention to hear us in the following occurrence which took place on the evening of September 3rd at 9 o'clock P.M.

Owing to our grievance we desire to bring to your notice that on the 23rd of December we obtained the necessary permission of the Military Governor and of the Civil Governor of this locality for the organization of our Society known under the name of united improvement association of negroes.

We therefore organized ourselves as a civil and law abiding people according to the Mandate of the Constitution of said Society of which we have the honor of presenting your inspection.

After been on a working basis from the aforementioned date, we have been unfortunately forcibly led to face a disappointment from the fact that on Septber 3rd our President, General Secretary and Members including females and minors were arrested, Chart Documents and Building seized, whilst Officers and Members of the afore mentioned Society were singing sacred pieces.

The President asked the Military and Civil Officers on what grounds they were arrested, but the only reply that he received was, "close your mouth." They were all marched to prison where they are detained and kept up to this moment without knowledge of having committed any crime or violated any of the Laws issued by the Military or Civil Governor.

We therefore pray that your Excellency will give this matter your kind attention and Judgement for we believe that there is no just cause for it. We remain, Sir,

Yours respectfully,
Thomas Duruo, James Cooks, Charles P. Lundy,
Jonathan Isaac Bowman, Henry Cardoso, Abraham
Labega, Louis I. Machavous, Alan Jordan, Martha
Labega, Eudarie James, Martha Harnsford, Agnes
Branch, Victor Burnet, John Felix Lavrist

The Crime of Wilson

Fabio Fiallo

President Francisco Henríquez y Carvajal (1859–1935) was a Renaissance man. As a student of Eugenio María de Hostos, he studied Constitutional law and philosophy at the seminary of San Tomás in Santo Domingo and medicine at the University of Paris, where he earned his doctorate. He became a surgeon, educator, newspaper editor, and advocate for women's rights. He also became involved in politics, holding a number of different government posts at home and abroad, in between stints in exile when his political opponents were in power. Dr. Henríquez is probably best known for having married Salomé Ureña, the celebrated national poet.

Henríquez became president under unprecedented circumstances, and was literally never permitted to take office. He had been on a diplomatic mission to Washington, D.C., dispatched by beleaguered President Juan Isidro Jiménes (1846–1919), as the threat of an invasion by the United States arose. He continued on to Buenos Aires for the Pan-American Conference on Finance, where he learned in May 1916 that the first US Marines had been sent ashore in the Dominican Republic. He immediately returned to Washington, to lodge ineffectual protests, and then went to Cuba, where he learned in July that he had been appointed president of the republic in absentia. He dutifully made his way back to Santo Domingo, but the Marines barred him from assuming power in any capacity. In November, Wilson declared the occupation official, so Henríquez left again for Cuba, while the Marines went about setting up a military government excluding Dominican citizens.

The US occupation generated a wave of protests of all kinds among the Dominican population, in particular verbal condemnations, despite the USMC's efforts to suppress dissent. The list of authors who wrote books or articles decrying the Yankee presence reads like a who's who of the Dominican intelligentsia of the time: Federico García Godoy, Francisco Peynado, Julio Cestero Burgos, Rafael Damirón, Max Henríquez Ureña (Francisco Henríquez and Salomé Ureña's son, who became the best known of the talented family internationally), even the bandleader and musicologist Julio Arzeno, among many others.

Another opponent of the occupation was "Ñico" Lora, born Francisco Antonio Cabrera (1880–1971), a composer, singer, and accordionist who helped to popular-

ize merengue, now considered the Dominican national dance rhythm. Lora wrote the merengue, "The Protest," soon after the Marine invasion. The song is still performed today, with the title "The Invasion of '16":

In the year 1916, the Americans came,
Trampling with their boots the Dominican soil.
Francisco Henríquez Carvajal, defending the flag,
Said, "The Yankees cannot rule our land!"

We'll make them go, giving them machetes.
The Americans, the abuser.

One of the most eloquent voices to speak against the occupation was Fabio Fiallo (1866–1942), who denounced in his book The Crime of Wilson in Santo Domingo the loss of sovereignty and lack of respect the United States showed President Henríquez. Fiallo was a poet, novelist, journalist, and politician. In 1899, when the dictator "Lilís" Heureaux was still in power, Fiallo began publishing the incendiary newspaper the Free Flag, which eschewed foreign firms' advertising as a revenue source. Despite being jailed by Juan Isidro Jiménes in 1900, he kept publishing it until 1916, when the US Marines jailed him again, this time at hard labor in the infamous Torre del Homenaje, with its dungeons dating to the early 1500s. Later, in the early 1930s, he fell afoul of the dictator Trujillo, who jailed him a third time. He went into exile afterward in Havana, where The Crime of Wilson in Santo Domingo came out in English translation in 1940. By then the Marine occupation had been over for sixteen years, and the Trujillo dictatorship, which came to power using the military force the occupation left behind, had been in place for a decade, with another twenty years still to go. Fiallo died in exile in Havana in 1942, arguing to the end of his life against the US Marine occupation and the dictatorship it spawned. Fiallo eventually returned to the Dominican Republic, but not until long after his death, in 1977, when his remains were transferred from Havana to Santo Domingo to be reinterred with other heroes of the nation in the "Altar of the Homeland." President Joaquín Balaguer (1906–2002) arranged for the repatriation of Fiallo's remains. This was an ironic and cynical gesture coming from Balaguer, a man who was a notorious enemy of freedom of the press himself. This selection from The Crime of Wilson in Santo Domingo begins in November 1918, when Henríquez traveled to the peace conference at Versailles.

When in 1918 the Teutonic colossus fell, vanquished at last under the blows of the most formidable coalition of all times, the Dominican people, sequestered as they were from universal intercourse by their omnipotent rulers,

breathed a deep sigh of relief and hope. It was not that any sensible Dominican could build any illusions on the righteousness of the beautiful principles
which the victorious governments had written on their banners to satisfy
the aspirations and maintain the fervor of the peoples who had been thrown
into the terrible fire of the conflict. Too well could the sincerity of the principle of "free determination," which President Wilson had proclaimed with
evangelistic unction, be measured by those who had seen soldiers of that
lofty pretender cowardly assassinate a nation and seal that crime with torrents of innocent blood. But all had deduced that upon the termination of
that tremendous conflagration the world would at last emerge from the
regime of lies, of forced silence and slaughter which had imprisoned for
more than five years, as an immense cloudy funnel, all the light and all the
dignity of civilized life; and that the bloody account of the victor and the
vanquished had been settled, the glances of the world would be turned in
astonishment to the forgotten corner of the Caribbean Sea where the forces
of a great power had perpetrated behind the back of the world and of its
own people the most iniquitous act of international piracy of modern times.
It was vaguely felt in the midst of the bitterness and anguish of that hateful
slavery that when the silence reigned over the battle fields of ruined Europe,
the silence which weighed on the unhappy captive whom the Yankee sergeants held under their knees to prevent cries reaching the conscience of the
world, would be broken.

However, although it was easy—perhaps too easy—to organize at that
time a grandiose manifestation of indiscreet rejoicing for the victory of the
allies, which was also the victory of our executioners, it was yet impossible
for any one who did not wish to uselessly risk his life to initiate within the
national territory any public activity for the purpose of conveying our protest and the livid light of our tragedy to free peoples from whom we were
isolated by the most vile and brutal censorship ever used by a conceited and
bloody despot. All the glances and all the pallid hopes of the country were
turned in consequence toward the patriots who, residing on free soil, could
with more or less success, champion our cause, and especially towards that
noble and austere citizen who still carried on his shoulders the sacred inves-
titure of the Republic. . . . It was thus that Dr. Henríquez and the friends of
the Dominican cause in Cuba took up the task of raising funds to pay [for]
the trip of our President to Versailles. . . .

The League of Nations accepted in its constitution a humiliating reserva-
tion whereby all matters relating to the American continent were placed
without the scope of its jurisdiction, thus abandoning these republics to
the arbitrary sovereignty of the United States. History will never be able

Dominican resistance to the US occupation grew steadily until the withdrawal of the Marines in 1924. This protest tableau of 1921 employed a cigar store Indian, representing the freedom-loving Taíno chiefs, to decry US abuse. Unknown photographer, black-and-white photograph, 1921. General Subjects Series (F JGG 301), Archivo General de la Nación, Santo Domingo.

to explain how the hands of the diplomats who signed this monstrous renunciation of national dignity did not wither and fall of shame. Only two countries—Mexico and the Argentine—were resolute enough to maintain their status as real nations, refusing to associate themselves in that false international agreement in which our peoples could not enter except cowering under the gallows of submission and slavery, and from which we could expect no protection, morality, justice nor right.

In such an atmosphere of force, deceit and rapine, with the spirit of the world still torn and troubled by shock of the immense drama whose epilogue was being brought to a close at Versailles; with all attention focused on the struggle which had arisen between the victorious nations in settling the vast problems of misery and confusion that had accumulated during four years of destruction, how could the voice of Dr. Henríquez be heard? His voice—the weak voice of that far-off victim in the Caribbean Sea was lost in the vortex of colossal interests, like the biblical voice of the prophets who clamored for justice in the desert. He requested an audience within the conceited Yankee Imperator—his equal in the hierarchy of souls—and it was refused. After much effort, he obtained an interview with the Chief of the Latin-American Division of the Department of State whom Wilson had the foresight to take with him to Europe to direct the gestures of his tropical puppets, but he merely voiced the unappealable decision that American affairs must be taken up in America.

What must be done in the face of such gross injustice? . . .

The second half of the year 1920 and the first quarter of 1921 were the most arduous and emotional periods of our struggle against Yankee occupation. A resolute phalanx of orators and journalists, filled with war-like ardor, had launched through the narrow road, sown with mortal threats, which the modifications of the censorship had opened up for us, unexpectedly violent attacks against the intrigue of the Military Government toward a protectorate or annexation and encouraged the people against any compromising manoeuver which might affect the independence and sovereignty of the Dominican Nation. . . .

The imprisonment and, above all, the trial of the journalists was the most resounding victory of Dominican patriotism against the iniquitous tyranny of the Military Government. The right to impose the death sentence . . . caused much astonishment and general indignation.

As was natural and unavoidable, that stupid ostentation of iniquity provoked the strongest reaction which had been heard against the Government of the United States up to that time. Starting from Havana . . . in less than a week it extended like a giant wave of fire over the entire continent, causing admonitions and protest in the press which daily became more and more violent, warning Wilson that the "Case of Santo Domingo" was already the "Case of America," and that it was drawing criticism from the entire continent against him and his sergeants who had been converted into the executioners of an unarmed people. . . .

Wilson had no alternative but to issue an order releasing all the newsmen. . . . The dike broken, the national conscience spread in a series of manifestations which carried the echoes of our decided opposition and irreconcilable claims throughout the world, which claims were not to be satisfied or terminated except by the recognition of our rights and the termination of the Occupation. . . .

Now in order to better enlighten my fellow citizens in regard to that stubborn and painful struggle, which day by day and hour by hour the Nationalist Commission [formed to negotiate an end to the occupation] had waged against its omnipotent enemy, the imperialism of Washington, I wish to transcribe here some notes from my diary during the short time I had the honor of forming part of that Commission. May I state in passing that my days in the jail at Homenaje under the cruel Yankee bayonets—notwithstanding the fetid water I had to drink, the wormy meat I had to eat, my continual association with dirty, evil smelling and depraved men among whom I was placed—were days of fiesta and contentment in comparison to those days through which I lived in Washington under the mortal anguish of a cruel disillusion at every instant and brutal deception each minute. . . .
May 23rd 1921:

Interview with Dr Henríquez and Mr. [Secretary of State Charles Evans] Hughes. Hughes expressed the willingness of the American Government to withdraw from Santo Domingo on the following bases:

1. Election of a regular Government by the people.
2. Approval of all acts of the Military Government.
3. Loan of $2,500,000.
4. Acceptance of a treaty which regulates the *right of intervention* . . .

Dr. Henríquez indignantly pointed out that these demands . . . had been rejected by two consecutive governments and by the Dominican people who would never accept them now nor at any time.
June 2nd:

Held my last conference with Mr. [Assistant Secretary of State Sumner] Welles under the pretext of bidding him good-bye to return to Santo Domingo. From this conference, as in the two previous ones . . . I got the first impression, which was now a conviction, that the Department of State in

truth sought a man, a man with whom they could make an agreement for the prompt withdrawal of troops from Santo Domingo, but this man could not be Dr. Henríquez, nor I, but some one whom they thought would be willing to grant the right of intervention which they eagerly sought. It is a bridge over which they wish to remove their troops from Santo Domingo; but a bridge whose supporting end on our coast belongs to them by right of intervention. Who will be this man? Really, I do not see him, in spite of the dangerous impatience of some of our politicians to secure power.
June 3rd:

My conversation with Dr. Henríquez on my departure was sad. The situation is summed up by the expression: "We seek a man. Who will be this man?"

No, no. Born on Dominican soil! I swear such a man does not exist.

VII

The Era of Trujillo

Although Fabio Fiallo wrote that there was not a Dominican who would accept the terms the United States dictated to end the Marine occupation, Horacio Vásquez (1860–1936) did just that. Don Horacio, a veteran caudillo of Dominican politics, had the support of followers known as *horacistas*. The winner of an election organized and administered by the Marines in 1924, he presided over the transition from foreign military rule to national civilian governance that year.

Rumors of coups distracted the new Dominican government. When President Vásquez had to seek expert medical treatment in the United States, his opponents moved to undermine his authority, with the assistance of ambitious army leaders. The most ruthlessly ambitious of them all was General Rafael Trujillo, who had risen from a childhood of impoverished obscurity to command of the armed forces through a mixture of cunning and violence. He had a seamy background as a cattle rustler and an overseer of underpaid and abused Haitian workers on a sugar plantation, but Marine Corps recruiters accepted him into the inaugural class of the makeshift military academy they established at Haína near Santo Domingo. After graduating from the Haína Military Academy, Trujillo was credibly accused of raping a teenage girl but was acquitted of the outrage in a court-martial by a tribunal of US Marine officers. This was the man who forced his way to the top in the Dominican Republic in 1930.

Trujillo rode the crest of what seemed to be yet another popular challenge to metropolitan rule mounted from the restive Cibao, a region long associated with revolutionary foment. But this "revolution" Trujillo orchestrated and manipulated from behind the scenes. He surreptitiously armed an insurgent caravan from Santiago that burst into the capital on Dominican Independence Day, February 27, 1930. While publicly averring his loyalty to Vásquez, Trujillo clandestinely acquiesced in the rebels' success, ordering his forces in the field to allow the Cibao rebels into Santo Domingo without opposition. The upheaval of February 1930 began an artfully concealed coup d'état that installed Trujillo as the unquestioned master of the Dominican Republic. He stood as a candidate in the elections that were called for May 1930 and then unleashed on his political opponents a paramilitary squad of urban roughnecks personally loyal to him, a gang who called themselves "La 44" after the most notorious of the Marine units that had served during the occupation. "La 44" attempted to assassinate the leading rival candidates before the election and on Election Day itself attacked the electoral commission before the judges could condemn the tainted election results, which showed Trujillo with a virtually unanimous mandate from the cowed populace. So began the "Era of Trujillo," which lasted thirty-one years, indelibly marking the Dominican Republic with its unique brand of authoritarian rule.

The Haitian Massacre

Eyewitnesses

In October 1937, Trujillo unleashed a genocidal assault known as the Haitian Massacre, which killed approximately 15,000 ethnic Haitians, mainly in the northwest border region. Most of them were murdered by Dominican army troops, using machetes to make it look as though civilian peasants had perpetrated the slaughter. But in this selection we see that many Dominicans actually helped save Haitian lives during the unspeakable atrocities of 1937. Fifty years after the bloodshed, the historians Lauren Derby and Richard Turits interviewed survivors living in Haiti, some still residing in towns that had begun as refugee communities set up by the Haitian government, and recorded forty hours of these survivors' grim recollections in Kreyòl mixed with Spanish. One town where Derby and Turits located eyewitnesses to the genocide was Ouanaminthe, located on the Massacre River across from Dajabón, Dominican Republic, the epicenter of the disaster. There they found the poignant public school record that begins this selection, which is followed by two of the narratives they collected.

From the Log of the Ouanaminthe School

The number of students with parents disappeared is now 176 [of 267 students]. The poor creatures are all in tears. In the evening one hears nothing but cries and wails from the houses of the whole town. The Dominicans, without doubt awaiting an immediate riposte, have evacuated the civilian population in Dajabón for eight days. . . . Father Gallego of Dajabón has lost two-thirds of his population. . . . In certain parishes, in Loma and Gourabe, 90 percent of the population has disappeared; instead of 150 to 160 baptisms a month, there is not even one. Some schools which had fifty students before now have no more than two or three. It's grievous and heartbreaking what has happened.

Anonymous Man in Ouanaminthe

When the massacre happened, I missed becoming a victim as a child. When the massacre started, I was at school; I went to a religious school. The brothers had a choir for all the children who sang; and they had a group of kids who knew how to sing, and I was always singing with the brothers. When the massacre started, the children were in school, and I was at choir. And October 7th, the day of the patron saint festival at Dajabón, the brothers took us over there, since the border was free to cross, and no one was afraid to cross the border at that time. So the brothers took us to go to mass there, so that we could sing in the choir at mass there. And while we were in the church, I saw a band of Dominican military who were milling about outside while we were in church. Since we were children, we didn't understand anything. What was happening was that the military wanted to kill people at that very time, right in daylight—to take people from the church and kill them. But what happened was the brothers were foreign, they were French, and I think because of them, they didn't do this. But when night came, around six, around that time, they started killing people. They started killing people at six o'clock, while people started crying out for help, people started running, they came wounded, they crossed the Massacre River, they all came wounded, they killed a lot of people. A lot of people who were saved came here. And so, this is how I came to Dosmond colony. When people started arriving, the Vincent government rounded up people in the Dominican Republic. The war began with a lot of people dead, a lot of Haitians were taken when war came to the frontier. They finished killing people after one week, a week later. The Vincent government sent for the rest of the Haitians. Then Trujillo sent his men to gather and haul out the rest of the Haitians left behind. They brought the war to the border. In Ouanaminthe, when you looked at the river, it was completely a sea of people and donkeys—it was completely full!—because many of the people—in fact most of the Haitians on the Dominican side—were afraid to live in the Dominican Republic any more. They were forced to leave although they didn't have a place to go to in Haiti since they had never lived there. When they arrived in Haiti, they were homeless refugees. So the government had to make colonies for them because Dosmond was a big savanna, a place where I knew everyone by name. My father had a beautiful garden in the savanna. It really was a savanna—there weren't any houses at all, nothing like it. The place was a desert. Before the massacre, in the frontier, although there were two sides, the people were one, united. All the tradesmen in Dajabón—all the cobblers and tailors—they were all Haitian. And even today there are

A group of "Santo Domingans," possibly of Haitian origin, regarded the camera in this photograph taken near San Pedro de Macorís in 1940. "Sto. Domingans. San Pedro de Macorís, St. Domingo," photographer unknown, c. 1940. Library of Congress, Prints and Photographs Division, LC-USZ62-65418.

Haitians all over Ouanaminthe, even though they still die today, there are still Haitian children there today, crossing the border daily. Haitian children, even if they were born in Dajabón, they still went to school in Haiti, every morning they would cross the border to go to school, every afternoon they would return. Their parents lived in Dajabón, but they came to school here. Haitians have always liked the French system of education, and the Catholic schools. Even the Dominicans love the French language, and the French language helps them a lot to speak Kreyòl.

Irélia Pierre, Dosmond/Ouanaminthe

I was born in the Dominican Republic. When the massacre broke out, I was very small. I remember that I had been in school a while. The day of my brother's marriage, after the ceremony was over, a Dominican arrived at the reception. The reception was the morning that the massacre broke out, and people started fleeing. That night we hid. The next morning when we woke up, some of the older people said "Be careful if you go out." So we stayed at home. Everyone came to my grandparents' house. They said they were going to Haiti because a revolution had broken out, and that they were killing Haitians. They all slept at my grandparents'. During the night, a woman said to me, "You come with me to my house." I said, "No, I'm going to stay with my mother—I can't leave her here." So we went to the garden where my mother was working, and she cut some bananas and put them in her bag. I carried a tree branch.

Suddenly, I looked over and saw a lot of guardias [Dominican soldiers] getting off their horses, and I heard them say, "There's one over there in the garden." Then they entered the garden and killed the girl. When I saw that, I ran. It was night. While I was running, I saw an uncle of mine, who took me into his house to protect me. When I arrived at his house I was terrified. They didn't let me sleep; they took me to another place. That morning at four o'clock they all took their bags, and we started to march toward Haiti.

While we were walking, some Dominicans told us to be careful and not go through Dajabón, but to pass around it, since they were killing people there. When we arrived at the Dabajón savanna, we saw a guardia. When we saw him I said, "Mama, we're going to die, we're going to die!" She told me to be quiet. Then a guardia screamed *"Está preso, está preso!"* [You're under arrest, you're under arrest!]. After that they had us all stand in the sun in the savanna. When we said we were thirsty, they said they would give us water soon. While we watched, we saw one guardia on a horse who had a rope to tie people up. When he saw that if he tied up too many people they started to run, he began to kill them and throw them into a hole.

He killed everyone; I was the only one who was saved. They thought I was dead because they had given me a lot of machete blows. I was awash in blood—all the blood in my heart. After all these tribulations, it's thanks to God that I didn't die. They killed them all in front of me. They tied them up, and after they killed them, they threw them down. I was small when I lived through all this, but I remember it all too clearly. I remember calling out after the guardia had left, "Mama!" but she was dead; "Papa!" but he was dead. They died one after another. I was left alone in the savanna without anything to eat or drink. There were a lot of small children who were thrown up in the air and stabbed with a bayonet, and then placed on top of their mothers. They killed my entire family, my mother, my father. We were 28—all were killed. I was the only one to survive that I knew of. After they finished cutting me up, it was a group of older men who had come from Haiti who found me on the ground in the sand along the banks of the Massacre River. They picked me up and returned with me to Haiti. They brought me to Ouanaminthe, but they didn't take me in—they said they couldn't take care of me, so they said they would send me to Cap-Haïtien; when I arrived there, there would be people there to take care of me. I spent a month in bed in the hospital, after which time they sent me to live in

Ouanaminthe. When I arrived here, I didn't have any family to receive me, so I went back to Cap again. I stayed under the auspices of the state. After about a year, they sent me back to Ouanaminthe again, at which time I lived there with some other foreigners. God gave me the strength to survive. Now I am married and have four children, but my entire family died during the massacre. Both my mother and father were born in the Dominican Republic. We lived in Loma de Cabrera. My father worked in agriculture, growing manioc, peanuts, rice on his own land—land that he had bought. He had ten karo of land (32.5 acres). He also kept some cattle, pigs, chickens, and goats. We grew enough food to feed the family (we never bought food at market) but also to sell. I used to go to market with my mother where we sold everything—peas, rice, bananas, corn. I only spoke in Kreyòl since we lived among Haitians. I hardly spoke in Spanish at all. There were some Dominicans in the area where we lived, but not many; there were mostly Haitians. There were both marriages between Haitians and Dominicans, as well as concubinage. There were no problems that I remember between Haitians and Dominicans—for example, no jealousy for Haitian land.

Message to Dominican Women

Darío Contreras

The Trujillo regime adopted maternalism and eugenics as official policy; they thus followed the 1940s trend in Europe and the United States to seek to increase and improve the population through state intervention with measures ranging from prizes to mothers with many children to penalizing infanticide. Simmering beneath these policies, however, were historical concerns that Haiti had a larger population in a smaller territory and was poised to engulf Dominican territory; a position that was officialized in the writings of Joaquín Balaguer and Manuel Arturo Peña Batlle (1902–1954) after the 1937 Haitian massacre. Darío Contreras Cruzado (1879–1963) was a key figure in the articulation of a public health agenda under the Trujillo regime. He completed his medical training in France, where he was trained in eugenics, the pseudo-science of racial improvement and the idea that the state must adopt an activist role in ensuring the health of its future citizens. These public health initiatives held a mixed legacy for women, since they did mobilize women to participate for the first time in state initiatives as social workers and empowered them as state agents, thus bringing middle-class women into the regime; but simultaneously expanded measures that penalized poor women accused of infanticide or diseases associated with prostitution. This address by Contreras, who was at one point denounced by the Trujillo regime and would later become Trujillo's personal surgeon and operate on his life-threatening case of anthrax, was read at an event convened by the Feminine Section of the Trujillista Party (Partido Trujillista), held in Ciudad Trujillo in September 1942.

Inspired by the Ideals of the Benefactor of the Motherland:
Message to Dominican Women

A healthy birthrate and good health: those are two of the conditions that make nations powerful and respected.

With good birthrates we will obtain the number of citizens sufficient to defend the rights and liberty of *la Patria*. With this we will have more children who are well prepared for the honorable struggle and constant progress that is obtained with honest work.

With good health we will obtain familial joy, the happiness of the people, and the well-being of the Republic.

The great preoccupation of all good governments is to increase the population using all resources; hence all the facilities offered to arriving immigrants—grouping them in colonies, with hygiene, schools, churches, exemptions from customs taxes, medical dispensaries, hospitals, and everything that serves to conserve health and give joy to individuals who have been transplanted from one country to another.

The protection of maternity and infancy, this series of works for the public good promoted with such auspicious magnificence by our Honorable President the Generalísimo Dr. Rafael Leonidas Trujillo, of his Era, can be evaluated by considering the maternity wards in this capital, Santiago, Samaná, and other locations; the orphanages, such as the "Angelita" [Trujillo's daughter] and the "Presidente Trujillo"; the reformatories in distinct regions; juvenile delinquency courts; the milk stations for the good and scientific nutrition of infants; hospitals for children, such as the "Ramfis" [Trujillo's son], which has just been expanded with the addition of a beautiful building that was previously occupied by the Dominican Red Cross, with its depository always full of medicine to combat the most frequent infantile diseases, such as the terrible diphtheria and other dangerously contagious diseases.

But all this magnificent work of a great Leader will never bear the maximum fruit that his effort has the right to expect if all mothers do not contribute, each one injecting her individual determination, so that the protection of infancy will bring about the perfection, always greater, of the next generation of Dominicans.

Civilization has complicated and intensified life. The simple life, without vanity or pretensions, of other times has disappeared. In earlier times wives were devoted to the home, and the wife's greatest satisfaction was seeing herself surrounded by numerous progeny, healthy and happy.

Today, social evolution obligates women to have an active life, to work, and to play sports that were formally unknown to them, and since women's rights have become equal to those of men, she occupies a seat in the legislative body, the municipal council, and other elected posts. Her social obligations are now greater than before and this has had repercussions on offspring.

Wives today prefer to limit the number of their children to one or two as

A large family posed outside their combination rural store and home sometime in the 1950s. Photographer unknown, black-and-white photograph, c. 1950s. Courtesy of the Roorda/Doyle Collection.

in France. Maybe this limitation is one of the causes of the setbacks that are now being suffered by the nation of France. That is why it is necessary for our density of population to be numerically well balanced.

But we will never reach that numerical balance if we do not ultimately counteract an evil that concerns the statisticians who guard the national destiny. It is the case that many of our women expel from their wombs the fruit of their love affairs as soon as they become aware that they are carrying future citizens, who should have come to form the rank and file with us in the struggle for greatness, happiness, and defense of the Motherland.

This, which we reveal with sorrow, is a social problem whose solution requires the cooperation of all women. Because if it is true that unscrupulous doctors lend themselves to criminal operations, destroying these lives in embryo, it is also true that these doctors would not have the opportunity to commit their crimes if women did not seek to abort their blossoming fruit.

It is you, the women, whose responsibility it is to restrict and eliminate such an odious and dangerous practice; odious because it constitutes a crime, and dangerous because impeding the increase of the population condemns women's own children, already raised, to a disaster that could occur in the future.

Only ignorance of the damage that is done to the organism, or a lack of reflection and examination of one's conscience, could excuse the cold blood with which future mothers frequently direct themselves to the doctor's office, which in this case is equal to the gallows, where they go to surrender . . . their own children, to the medical executioner who aborts them, and then they return home satisfied and happy after the abortion, far from thinking that they have committed a crime and as if they had done a good deed.

Dominican Mothers: Think of the future and the dangers to which our nation's own children are exposed; think about our population's own health, which will be shattered, making us eternally sickly beings, mutilated, to lose the delight of life and even life itself, as has occurred on not a few occasions, caused by the criminal practice that our own conscience condemns.

Señoras: If you have listened to me with the interest and faith with which I have written this message for all of you, I shall be happy and secure in the knowledge that you will view with horror and disgust those professionals who dedicate themselves to destroying our Dominican children, in our own wombs, stealing our precious health, destroying our happiness and home, and committing a crime against the Motherland within our society.

Dominican women, let this be your slogan: For my health and for my homeland I will not let a conceived child be snatched from my womb.

Translated by Melissa Madera.

The Sugar Strike of 1946

Roberto Cassá

Facing international criticism for the Haitian Massacre of 1937, Rafael Trujillo re-linquished the titular presidency of the Dominican Republic to puppet replacements while retaining all of the authority and public recognition of being The Chief. As head of the armed forces, he committed the Dominican Republic to the Allied cause immediately after Pearl Harbor, declaring war on Japan and Germany. U-boats sank both ships of the fledgling Dominican Merchant Marine soon after, though a stream of equipment and financing from the US Lend-Lease program and the Export-Import Bank offset these losses. Generalísimo Trujillo became president again in 1944, the centennial year of Dominican independence, at a reinauguration that the US am-bassador termed a "coronation."

When World War II ended, the flow of arms to the Dominican Republic did, too, with high-ranking US State Department officials stating that the reason was the un-democratic nature of the country's government. In response, the autocratic Trujillo allowed the formation of opposition political parties and labor unions, which he had hounded out of existence in the early 1930s. The period that followed became known as the "interlude of tolerance" during the repressive Era of Trujillo. The highlight of the period was the sugar strike of 1946. The workers in the canefields around the southeastern cities of San Pedro de Macorís and La Romana sparked the strike, and it spread to other sectors of the economy. In this selection, the eminent Dominican scholar Roberto Cassá, director of the Dominican National Archive, analyzes that exceptional moment. The interlude ended shortly after the famous strike, when the dictator reasserted his usual intolerance, again clamping down on labor leaders and political opponents.

More than a sugar strike, the one that began on January 7, 1946, was, in a certain measure, a regional strike, at whose core were found the sugar workers. This characteristic was not foreseen by the organizers of the strike. And the fact is that the social conflict in the east brought the entire population together in opposition to the sugar companies. These were the owners of the great majority of the wealth, and they generated a multitude of social conflicts with the proletariat, the peasantry, the petit-bourgeoisie, and the bourgeoisie. Such a state of affairs united these classes in support of the strike led by the industrial and agricultural workers of the sugar mills.

The strike came to be the moment of explosion of the tensions the population of the region had held in for a long time. The expansionist tendencies of the foreign corporations had created a suffocating atmosphere, made worse by the international crisis of 1929–1934. That event prompted an exodus of portions of the population, both urban and rural, now that the level of subsistence demanded to reproduce the different social classes was no longer attainable. It is revealing that the population of San Pedro de Macorís grew by little more than 1,000 persons in fifteen years (between 1935 and 1950). An anxious feeling seized the people, and the primary responsibility for it was unanimously attributed to the foreign companies.

To make up for the drop in prices, the factories acted to take over everything, displacing local interests: during the 1930s they significantly expanded their territorial base on the coast with new expropriations in the countryside, . . . appropriated many of the small sugar holdings of small-scale growers who had survived the collapse in sugar prices in 1920, implemented the system of paying workers in scrip and vouchers, directly imported most of the food and manufactured goods their employees consumed, and produced the most basic necessities, such as meat, milk, bread, cheese, butter, ice, lumber, and so on.

A number of large businesses gave donations of food. In La Romana, the House of Hilari Mallol, the principal commercial enterprise, distinguished itself, actively offering sustenance to the strikers in the amount of 25,000 pesos, according to the rumor that circulated at the time, which appears to have been well founded. People in the middle class organized to take up collections. In other cases, the small store-owners agreed to grant credit to the strikers. Even so, resources were limited, and one of the [movement's] weak flanks was the difficulty of survival for the strikers, who were dependent on weekly paydays; this was particularly evident in La Romana, where the strike was prolonged [to] almost three weeks, while in Macorís it lasted eight days. . . .

In all of that what stood out was the exasperation of spirits, so that the people resolved to run the risks that mobilization entailed. It is certain there were gradations among the sugar mills, from the most cautious attitude at Santa Fe to the most violent at Consuelo. In the latter, workers armed themselves with clubs and machetes and convened assemblies almost every day. In the words of Barbarín Mojica, "no one had ever seen that." Without doubt the planners of the movement themselves were not only surprised, but overcome by the fullness of the social response. In mills, *bateys* [sugar workers' communities], and cities, groups of mobilized strikers maintained themselves and frequently staged demonstrations at which they reiterated their slogans.

The verve of the masses, nevertheless, did not have a political leadership of great range. It fundamentally expressed the state of moral indignation that resulted from the exploitation in the form of an explosion of contained rage, but restricted to levels that would not provoke the authorities too much. But this was not destructive violence, like burning the cane fields, as the administrators of the sugar concerns had expected. What solidified this unusual mobilization was the decision not to tolerate the appalling conditions of misery any longer. When the local federation in Macorís announced that they should return to work, the Haitians did not believe it and were not in the mood to do it; the personal order of "Papá Mauricio"[1] had to arrive for them to come to agreement. In La Romana the suspicion was yet more dramatic: [the strike leader] "Nandite" had to visit one *batey* after another in order to convince the cane cutters that they had obtained their demands.

The masses did not mobilize directly against the state, but against the enemy that they saw closest to them: the North American administrators. The resolution that the strike had to be prolonged until all demands were met was unequivocal. These demands fell into two categories: the eight-hour work day and the daily minimum wage of one peso, with bonuses proportional to the categories on the wage pay scale.

When the strike exploded, the companies did not resist the implementation of the eight hours, but they did resist a general raise in wages. In the first discussions, Central Romana in particular contended that the reduction of the work day by four hours amounted to a wage hike, so no additional pay was justified. The regime had to exert direct pressure at that point through negotiations undertaken by the Commission on Wages.

In those discussions the delegates of the unions and the labor lawyers of the two provinces demonstrated leadership. They exposed in a shattering manner the situation of exploitation, the illegal mechanisms that the companies utilized, and they rebutted the allegations of the company representatives point by point. It is notable that the position of the principal government functionaries participating in the Commission was inclined to give credence to the allegations of the labor representatives, albeit with the necessary formalities. . . .

The pressure of the regime on the companies brought about a preliminary result, an agreement whereby wage increases would come to be recognized that in general ranged around 60 percent and in some extreme cases approached 100 percent. The first and sharpest debates took place with respect to the neuralgically sensitive areas of Central Romana, while the strike unfolded on that estate. Another point that generated tensions was setting the level of payment per ton of cane. At last, when the factory called West Indies resisted following the example of Central Romana in the decisions it had taken, [the head of the Wage Commission] had to affirm its position in a special document intended to pressure that company to comply. . . .

What stands out is that the percentage increase in the wages of the cane cutters was less than that obtained in the nonagricultural areas. At least, the cutting and transport of cane were the activities that earned the smallest relative increases. From the 36 centavos that had been fixed for a ton of cut cane during the harvest of 1945 and from a fixed rate of 45 centavos at the moment of the negotiations, it rose to 50 centavos under the terms of the resolution the Commission adopted at its meeting on January 22. While the raises for nonagricultural activities normally were between 55 percent and 65 percent, for cane cutting the increase was 11 percent over the prevailing rate and almost 40 percent with respect to the previous harvest.

It is certain that in previous years the cutting and transportation of cane had received raises relatively higher than those in the industrial area, possibly because of the scarcity of workers. In all ways, the cane cutters were the least favored by the general strike. When the union asked that the price per ton of cut cane be set at 60 centavos, the companies showed themselves to be inflexible on that point. They argued that substantial increases had been conceded recently. With respect to this issue there was a difference in how productivity was calculated, because the companies considered six hours to be sufficient time to cut 2.5 tons of cane, whereas Raúl Chardón, the union representative from La Romana, maintained that eight hours were necessary to cut two tons of the best sugarcane.

The meager increase in the rates for cane cutting and transportation was seen to be partially compensated for by the increases accorded to the other diverse tasks, which were the least remunerated because of the machinations carried out by the administrators. For example, in December 1945 a wage of 35 centavos per day was normal for clearing underbrush, which more than doubled when the minimum wage went to 1 peso per day. But even taking into account these major raises outside the cutting and transport of cane, the overall agricultural wage level experienced a substantially smaller increase than nonagricultural work. . . .

In spite of the forcefulness of those resolutions in support of the interests of the workers, the fact that many pending points remained to be clarified, even in various areas and offices that were covered by the resolutions, revealed the differences between the respective positions taken by the labor federations of Macorís and La Romana. The former came to the conclusion that with the preliminary agreements and verbal guarantees offered by the representatives of the state, the majority of the petitions were satisfied, and for that reason they proceeded to lift the strike, so that it ended on the eighth day after it began. In La Romana, by contrast, the unions, following a general sentiment of the masses, understood that the resolutions taken in the capital did not satisfy their expectations, and that the strike had to be prolonged in spite of the exit of the *macorisanos*.

In the position of the *romanenses* two very marked aspects appeared. The first was the belligerent attitude that was employed to keep up the pressure for ample and diverse concessions; it was seen as necessary to obtain everything all at once. Among the *macorisanos*, on the other hand, the leadership succeeded in imposing a certain sense of moderation that held that they had to seek basic victories. This mediation channeled the state of exultation, in the beginning similar to that of La Romana, although less visible . . . in any case, differences in expression and rhythm between Macorís and La Romana were evident. In the former, the separation of the majority of workers from urban life was initiated, and their dispersal among seven different sugar estates. A second aspect resided in the hidden political plans of the principal leaders from La Romana. They sought to create conditions, more or less in the short term, for a popular uprising, supported by the state of intransigence that had overcome the [owner] class because of the protests. There are indications that in particular they manipulated the possibility of the rapid arrival of an expedition. . . .

The government officials did everything possible to eliminate all points that remained unresolved or confused, so that the Federation of La Romana would accede to lifting the strike. They asked Mauricio Báez to come to that city to act as mediator, because he had won the respect of his class comrades in the neighboring city. But even so, the strike was not lifted, because at times unexpected things were requested, which suggest that the leadership was artificially prolonging the conflict. At least, they considered the petition to prolong the strike prepared by "Fello" Dalmau, an *antitrujillista* known to the chiefs of the Federation, who one Friday, when the strike was at the point of being lifted, announced that he was certain that an expeditionary force would arrive the following Monday. In a measure that was certainly linked to that [announcement], at a moment when a complete agreement was at hand, at a multitudinous assembly of all the unions of the entire sugar industry, an initiative reached the floor calling for the strike to be prolonged for two more days, because the arrival of an expeditionary contingent was imminent.

Mauricio Báez, to whom, through his role as mediator, devolved responsibility for the conduct of the assembly, decided to run the risk implied by extending the strike without having a cause to justify it. Immediately before that, a popular demonstration had been convened, accompanied by new closures of businesses, which earned them [these businesses] the title "defender[s] of the people." Colonel Flores, the government representative at that phase of the negotiations, understood that the *macorisano* leader had gone back on his word, dealing him a slap in the face. This prompted a subsequent hardening of policy on the part of the government.

To make evident the political context underlying the strike, the regime turned away from cautious treatment [and] toward the eventual employment of drastic measures. For such a purpose, the generals Felipe Ciprián ("Larguito") and Frank Félix Miranda were sent to consider the situation and use corresponding methods. "Larguito" tried to intimidate the leaders, ordering that they be given beatings. Afterward, Miranda went to the point: he made it known that he had orders from "El Jefe" to eliminate the leaders who resisted the immediate return to work. This directive was intended by means [of this designation] to confirm the order for the assassination of Mauricio Báez, which accidentally became known in Macorís thanks to a telephone operator connected to the Dominican Revolutionary Party. [The strike leader] Del Orbe had to hurry to La Romana to look for Báez to save his life, taking him [to Cuba] to seek diplomatic asylum. . . .

The rumor of an expected armed expedition ran through the population, such that the government mobilized a strong military contingent, equipped with armored vehicles, with visible preparations for going into action. The leaders had to lift the strike in a precipitous manner, under the threat of being assassinated. Even when a portion of them hastily came to an agreement to give the order to end the stoppage due to the dangerous circumstances, among the masses that decision was renounced, and suspicions were expressed about the moral quality of those who had thusly acted.

Translated by Eric Paul Roorda.

Note

1. Mauricio Báez (1910–1950) was the charismatic leader of the strike. He fled to Cuba, where Trujillo's agents hunted him down and killed him.

Informal Resistance on a Dominican Sugar Plantation

Catherine C. LeGrand

In her densely textured study of a single large sugar estate, Catherine C. LeGrand challenges the stereotype of sugar workers in the Dominican Republic as being mainly powerless Haitians. This selection from her work provides a detailed portrait of the complex society and complicated operations of a large sugar plantation during the Trujillo regime, as well as the anonymous forms of popular resistance to the injustices and indignities of everyday life there.

A few years back I was fortunate to stumble on the records of Ozama, a Dominican sugar plantation owned by the British Columbia Sugar Refining Company from 1944 through 1955. . . . They reveal that a significant proportion of the cane cutters on the Ozama estate were not seasonal migrants from Haiti, but rather Dominicans and Haitians resident in the Dominican Republic, many of whom were also peasants. Furthermore, the Ozama records indicate that the foreign managers were not all-powerful. Administrators often complained of worker insubordination, and they had trouble dictating when, where, and how cane cutters would work. . . .

Like other Dominican sugar plantations, Ozama was a small country unto itself. The "nerve center" of the Ozama plantation was the *batey central*, located one kilometer north of the Carretera de Mella, a paved road that ran from Santo Domingo east to San Pedro de Macorís. Here stood the sugar mill, which, during the harvest, ground up to 1,800 tons of sugar a day. Here also were the railroad and machinery repair shops, the carpentry shop, the sawmill, the company store, and the office of the medical assistant (*practicante*) hired by B.C. Sugar to treat ailing workers. West of the sugar mill, the lodgings of the factory and railroad workers, mechanics, and carpenters spread out along a series of narrow, dusty streets. On the eastern side of the mill, the Canadians built spacious homes for themselves, with carefully watered flower gardens, a country club, a swimming pool, a golf course, and a schoolhouse where the younger children of Canadian administrators could study in English. Sixty kilometers of railroad tied the central mill to the canefields, and from the mill, oxcarts piled high with sugar bags moved slowly to the plantation's private wharf on the Ozama River. From the wharf a fleet of small boats plied the river, transporting the sugar to ocean steamers waiting at the port of Santo Domingo.

Although it was not part of the plantation proper, no description of Ozama would be complete without mention of the independent village of Sabaneta located just off plantation land, ten minutes by foot west of the central *batey*. Sabaneta mushroomed in the 1940s with a cluster of rickety bars and brothels, Sunday cockfights, and independent shopkeepers who tried to compete with the plantation stores, keeping their doors open when the company's stores closed for the night. Sabaneta may have been rowdy, but it was also autonomous.

The plantation itself stretched for more than 60 kilometers north and east of the central *batey*. The outlining areas, where the land was too rolling for sugarcane or too distant from the rail lines, were devoted to pasture. The livestock operation was essential to provide horses for the administrators, overseers, and plantation police and oxen for the cane haul. In the 1940s and early 1950s, hundreds of wooden carts, each pulled by six oxen, transported the cane from the fields to the rail depots.

The fields of sugarcane, located closer to the mill, were divided into six sections, each with its own village for laborers (*batey*), company store (*bodega*), and Dominican overseer (*mayordomo*). The sugarcane harvest (*zafra*) lasted five months, from late December or early January until the beginning of June; and the plantation produced between 25,000 and 30,000 tons of sugar each year. Although some independent cane farmers (*colonos*) sold cane to Ozama for processing, the Ozama Sugar Company itself grew more than 85 percent of the cane it ground. During the *zafra*, the plantation's work force swelled from about one thousand to nearly two thousand as cane cutters flooded into the *bateyes*. We do not know what percentage of cane cutters were Haitian and what percentage Dominican, but an informal company survey in 1947 during the off-season indicated that approximately 50 percent of the field workers were Haitian citizens. . . .

To understand the success of field workers' initiatives, we must keep in mind one basic factor: labor scarcity. Throughout the 1940s and 1950s, labor shortages plagued the Ozama Sugar Company and, judging from the fragmentary information that exists, the Dominican sugar sector in general. This situation has several explanations. First, British laws impeded the free importation of workers from the British Antilles. Second, the migration of

Haitians slowed after the Dominican army killed between 10,000 and 20,000 Haitians, mainly along the border, in October 1937. Meanwhile, the Trujillo government took stern measures to enforce Trujillo's "Dominicanization of labor" laws, which required industrial and agricultural establishments to hire a majority of Dominicans. But cane cutting was seasonal, and harvest wages were not high enough to attract a plentiful, stable work force of Dominican residents. Finally, Ozama had to compete for workers with the other foreign-owned sugar plantations and with Trujillo's public works projects. What is more, the Canadians made every effort to increase sugar production on the estate, resulting in a growing demand for cane cutters during the 1940s.

To make the plantation as productive as possible, B.C. Sugar's strategy was to use the maximum grinding capacity of the mill by increasing the supply of cane. This involved both growing more cane and eliminating all obstacles to efficient delivery from the fields to the mill. The aim was to keep the mill grinding at full capacity 24 hours a day during the *zafra*, so as to shorten the harvest period yet still produce the maximum amount of sugar. For an efficient, profit-seeking sugar company, this strategy made good business sense. . . .

While the administrators wanted cane cut and delivered to the mill every day during the *zafra*, they could not persuade the field workers to do so. Most workers refused to cut cane the day after payday, which fell on a Saturday every two weeks, and the work force usually did not return to full strength until the following Tuesday. Also, almost no one would work on religious or certain national holidays: Día de los Reyes (January 6), Día de la Virgen de Altagracia (January 21), Día de Duarte (January 26), Día de Candelaria (February 2), San Blas (February 3), Viernes de Dolores (one week before Good Friday), Día de la Cruz (May 3), and so on.

Furthermore, B.C. Sugar had difficulty keeping a full contingent of sugar cutters over the entire five-month harvest. The company could not start the harvest before Christmas because it could find no one to cut cane; around Easter the shortage of workers became acute. Some workers went on pilgrimage to Higüey or returned to their home villages to celebrate Holy Week with their families. The rainy season began around Easter, and when the rains fell, Ozama's administrators noted, Dominican peasants planted their rice crops. It seems that at Eastertime many cane cutters abandoned the sugar plantations to work their own *conucos* [garden plots].

Other laborers worked only for the first part of the sugar harvest to make enough money to purchase the identity cards (*cédulas*) that the Trujillo dictatorship required each citizen to carry. The identity cards had to be renewed every year with a cash payment in March or April, under threat of imprisonment or forced labor for noncompliance. Still other workers left sugar plantations toward the end of the harvest when the poor quality of the remaining cane lowered the income the cutters could expect as piece-workers. Off they would go to seek employment on another sugar planta-tion where the harvest might last a few weeks longer. . . .

. . . The Ozama Sugar Company could not raise wages in order to at-tract labor because wages were set, at first by the Dominican Association of Sugar Producers and from 1945 on by the Trujillo government (through the Comité Nacional para Regular los Salarios of the Secretaría de Estado del Trabajo). The company therefore resorted to non-monetary incentives to attract and retain its labor force. It made efforts to improve housing on the estate by building small cement houses for workers, with communal kitchens, bathrooms, showers, and, in the central *batey*, electric light. It also allocated credit in the company stores and Christmas bonuses to workers as an incentive to return for the harvest. And—a morbid benefit—the com-pany awarded free coffins to the families of workers who died in its employ.

When labor was particularly scarce during the *zafra*, management occa-sionally shut down all other activities on the plantation, directing construc-tion and railway repair workers to join the cane-cutting effort. But many of these people categorically refused to do so. Though the company offered pay equal to their other jobs, they regarded cane cutting as socially unac-ceptable, indeed degrading, work. Finally, despite the desire to keep the mill running around the clock during the *zafra*, the administrators admitted de-feat. Every two weeks on the Sunday following payday, management closed down the sugar mill, recognizing that no cane would arrive from the fields that day. Those Sundays were devoted to cleaning the machinery.

A second form of resistance involved robbery and destructive careless-ness bordering on sabotage. Some reports of theft on the plantation seem to support the idea that the cane cutters, like the surrounding peasant popu-lation, were primarily concerned with subsistence. The Ozama report of July 16, 1948, for example, complains that workers were forever trampling the new cane shoots agronomists planted in experimental plots; and when the cane grew a bit larger, the workers ate it. The company lost thousands of fence posts, which workers and local people took for their cooking fires; as well as cattle, which the workers slaughtered at night to eat. Company reports also mention problems with the theft of horses, tools, and light bulbs.

Cases of vandalism are harder to identify because they often appeared to be accidents. For example, frequent derailments on the plantation rail

Típicos Dominicanos. Carretón de Cañas.

While the sugar industry burgeoned and modernized during the Trujillo years, many aspects of it remained unchanged, such as the use of manual labor to cut the sugarcane and oxen to transport it to the mills. "Sugar Wagon," Trujillo Years (F IE 0009), Archivo General de la Nación, Santo Domingo.

lines damaged the cane cars and delayed the delivery of cane to the mill at harvest time. Many derailments resulted from wet or defective tracks or malfunctioning switches, but switch problems often stemmed from worker error. Plantation administrators generally attributed such derailments to worker negligence, but sometimes they suggested that an accident must have been intentional. . . .

Another example of possible sabotage relates to the frequency of knife chokes in the mill. If cane stalks were cut too long, they obstructed the mill's mechanical knives, sometimes shutting down the grinding process for hours until the blockage could be removed. Administrators note that more problems with knife chokes appeared after the company began to mechanize the cane haul, using tractors instead of ox-drawn carts. It seems that the attempt to mechanize the cane haul provoked some worker opposition. . . .

The Canadians at Ozama tended to attribute the frequent accidents not to the native workers' hostility but to their lack of intelligence, and specifically to their inability to handle modern technology. Managers described the Dominicans and Haitians with whom they worked as childlike, superstitious, and incapable of mastering or even really understanding North American technology. Implicit in their reports is the idea that the company was helping to modernize the Dominican Republic by introducing new machinery and agricultural methods but that locals were fundamentally incapable of making productive use of such technology. Modernization would occur despite the Dominican people.

Occasionally the Ozama reports provided a glimpse of how local people attributed their own cultural meanings to the new technology. One night the Canadians were roused from a deep sleep by a cacophony of locomotive horns. They rushed outside, fearing that the racket signaled fire or some other catastrophe, only to find that the locomotives were "wailing" to mourn the death of a switchman in a dance hall in Sabaneta and that this wailing of locomotives was a customary sign of mourning on the estate. . . .

At Ozama, many canefields suddenly went up in flames, particularly during the harvest period before the rains began. Some of these cane fires were accidental, started by a casually discarded lighted cigarette butt, sparks from the railroad, or the negligence of nearby peasants who, burning off weeds before planting, let their *conuco* fires get out of hand. But some were obvious cases of arson: administrators found packets of candles in the fields. Such fires may have been set by individuals with particular resentments against the company. The majority, however, can only be understood in terms of the informal negotiation of pay rates.

. . . Burned cane gives good sugar only if it is ground within 24 hours. To avoid losing the burned cane, Canadian administrators paid higher wages to cutters who were willing to harvest it immediately. These bonus wages, of course, were transitory (they lasted only as long as it took to get the burned cane loaded). But by 1948, cane fires had become so frequent that the company decided not to harvest some of the burned fields as a strategy to discourage arson.

Cane cutters also balked at company efforts to reorganize the labor process to complement the mechanization of the cane haul. Mechanizing the haul meant replacing oxcarts with tractors and trucks to transport cane from the fields to the rail depots. . . . After a few weeks, the company declared the new cutting system a great success—it was fast and cost-efficient. But the workers disliked it and refused to cooperate; they complained repeatedly, and their numbers diminished as cutters gradually drifted away from the tractor-haul district. . . . By 1950 the company had abandoned its efforts to mechanize the cane haul.

The Ozama reports occasionally mention other incidents, with less direct economic consequences, that nonetheless suggest another facet of worker resistance: satire, humor, and insult. For instance, oxcart drivers always called their oxen by name, and some named their animals after Canadian administrators ("Mr. Tony," "Mr. Smith," "Mr. Angus," and so on). Drivers frequently whipped and swore at their animals, but if the Canadian named took offense, the carter would say, "I'm not talking to you, I'm talking to my bull." In another example, workers asked a new Canadian administrator for the packing crates in which his personal belongs had been shipped, so as to use the wood for building material. The administrators, whose name was stamped all over the crates, consented. Some weeks later, a new brothel appeared in Sabaneta with a board on which the administrator's name was stamped prominently displayed on the portal. The Canadians could not help but see it every time they drove along the main road from the plantation into Santo Domingo. These stories convey an image of the workers independently commenting on (and indeed talking back to) their foreign bosses and getting away it. . . .

Biography of a Great Leader

Abelardo Nanita

As part of his cult of personality, Rafael Trujillo generated a national industry of praise for his person, his family, and his purported accomplishments. The daily press was filled with panegyrics to the dictator, and books approaching the level of hagiography, paid for by the regime, rolled off the presses not only in "Ciudad Trujillo," or Trujillo City, as Santo Domingo was renamed in 1937, but also in New York, in English translation. The most prolific author in this genre was Abelardo Nanita, who wrote "Silhouette of President Trujillo," his first admiring essay about Trujillo, in December 1932, soon after he had seized power. Nanita went on to make a career as a supersycophant, serving in various government positions—senator, cabinet member, and secretary to the president—and writing books about his boss. His literary oeuvre, amassed over a quarter century, consists almost entirely of volumes extolling Trujillo. His titles included A Full-Size Portrait of Trujillo, Trujillo and the Post-war World, A Hero of San Cristóbal *(Trujillo's birthplace), and the magnum opus* Trujillo, *which went into five editions in Spanish and three in English. The publishing campaign apparently reached its intended target; a copy of Nanita's* Trujillo *was among the books President Harry S. Truman kept in his private study. These selections come from the 1957 English edition of the work, published by the government of the Dominican Republic. The first comes from a chapter entitled "1937," which says nothing about the most salient event of that year, the Haitian Massacre, but claims that Trujillo was too great to be held to "universal standards." Later in the book, the author more directly exculpates Trujillo from the slaughter, justifying it by blaming the victims.*

1937

Throughout the years, whether as Generalissimo in 1937, General in 1927 or Lieutenant ten years earlier, Trujillo has remained one and the same. Essentially, time has wrought no change in the man himself. . . .

His friendship, though generous, is never depreciated by exaggeration; though severe in meting out punishment, he is devoid of cruelty. Never wittingly unjust, he is at times unyielding, and certainly always sincere. His pragmatism and apparent skepticism notwithstanding, his idealism is sensitive and impassioned, more so than one might expect in a person so unfathomable and cautious as well as withdrawn and aloof. He is relentless with traitors, and yet tender in his affections. He is a friend to reckon with, and an enemy to reckon with. Profoundly human, every inch a man. And he is more—a leader. . . .

Geniuses act independently of norms. Only average men leading average lives conform to the rules of general mediocrity. Mediocre men adapt themselves to universal standards; the great men of history are those who tower over the masses.

Trujillo's greatness consists, however, not only in towering over his fellows, but also in the encompassing nature of his achievements. His is not the loftiness of a granite column but rather that of a majestic mountain range.

Portrait Study

. . . He is very neat about his person. His wardrobe reveals care and good taste, combining simplicity with elegance, and might well be envied by a prince. His collection of neckties is famous. The best tailors in New York, London, and Paris fashion his clothes.

His manner is urbane, and is readily adapted to any situation. On occasions he is gallant and attentive; when among simple countryfolk he is plain and jovial. Either in uniform or in mufti, he would be an immediate success at any gathering of society in Europe or in the United States.

Women delight him. He is unfailingly gallant, attentive, and considerate toward them. He enjoys being in their company. He is genuinely impressed by feminine beauty. Handsome and of striking bearing, it hardly need be added that his enormous popularity with the fair sex stems from something other than politics. When he makes his way through enthusiastic crowds, many a look of admiration from feminine eyes is sent his way for the man he is, independently of his being a national hero.

Well built, soldierly without being pompous, of average height, the President cuts a good figure. His winning ways not only assure receptiveness on the part of his hearers, but are such as to influence even his enemies.

On two occasions, leaving behind his astonished aides and at grave risk of his life, he penetrated alone into an enemy guerrilla encampment. His personal magnetism and his power of persuasion won the day without need of using any weapons. The guerrillas laid down their arms.

Another of Generalissimo Trujillo's remarkable assets is his ability as a conversationalist. Spiced with a mordant sense of humor, his words come in a free and easy manner. Neither pompous nor stuffy—in the company of intimates he does not stand on protocol—his joviality rises to the surface effortlessly in a natural and spontaneous manner, and the arguments he puts forth in cordial tones of camaraderie usually carry the day. When he speaks in public his remarks are punctuated by appropriate gestures and delivered in a tone that, though gentle, has a ring of command, and the conviction underlying his every word moves his audience to genuine enthusiasm.

He is free of fetishes and quirks. He likes animals but not exaggeratedly.

A Political Figure but Not a Politician

Taking the word in the meaning which we generally give it, Trujillo never was what is known as a politician. . . .

Life has made him a devotee of discipline. Obedience, punctuality, self-control, and a subconscious habit of being always attentive and awake to the voice of conscience are second nature in him. He has a firm conviction that without discipline order is impossible, and that without order peace is impossible. For this reason he is harsh in punishing any breach of discipline, which he feels borders on disloyalty.

It did not take him long to realize that one of the most serious defects among the Dominican people was a lack of discipline, and that only through strict discipline could their unruly and rebellious nature and their individualistic tendencies—so independent of guidance—be corrected or modified. He viewed the rigorous imposition of discipline as a *sine qua non* in order to obtain positive and effective results for his country.

A Permanent Boundary

. . . Protected by our cordiality and circumventing our immigration restrictions, more than 100,000 Haitians from the lowest strata of society—for cultured Haitians emigrate only to France—invaded our farm lands, our valleys, and our hills. They infiltrated into the huts of our peasants, our sugar plantations, the villages and towns, the workshops; into our very homes, replacing our peons, workmen, and domestic servants, performing all sorts of work for unfairly competing wages and lowering our standard of living, degenerating our language and our customs, filling our highways and our byways with beggars, introducing savage rites and exotic heresies, with succeeding administrations in our country patiently looking on and no one nor anything apparently capable of halting the shadow cast by their invasion. . . .

The events of 1937, which were so misinterpreted in certain sectors for lack of adequate information on what had transpired before, constitute one of those typical cases shared by the peoples of both countries that unfortunately have taken place for centuries. . . .

The Trujillo-Hull Treaty, whereby he gave back to our country the financial sovereignty it had lost, and the Treaty with Haiti, which made possible the Dominicanization of our frontier, rescuing a vast extent of territory that the neglect of earlier administrations had given up to the insatiable ambitions of our neighbors, are two everlasting monuments to Trujillo's glory. With the former he put an end to the American meddling that dated from the imperialistic era; with the other he ended once for all the pacific but illegal invasion by Haiti, drawing a permanent boundary that delimits in a fixed manner the respective jurisdiction of both countries and leaving to each that portion of the earth where it is to fulfill, without molestation or fear, its God-given historical destiny.

A Diplomat's Diagnosis of the Dictator

Richard A. Johnson

*The US Foreign Service officer who filed the following report profiling Rafael Tru-
jillo drew from several years of personal experience with the man when he recorded
his views of him in 1953 and 1954. Richard A. Johnson, a career State Department
diplomat, served as first secretary of the US Embassy in Ciudad Trujillo, the second-
ranking position on a staff of more than 100. For part of his time in the Dominican
Republic, he took the role of chargé d'affaires, acting as ambassador when that official was away. Although the ambassador was the official chief of the diplomatic mission, the first secretary had more intimate knowledge of the country. This was due
to the fact that the ambassador was usually a political appointee with no diplomatic
training; often was absent from his post for one reason or another; and rarely spoke
serviceable Spanish, if any. First Secretary Johnson sized up both the Dominican
dictator and US foreign policy toward his regime in his unusually lengthy, detailed,
and candid summation. The report, which Johnson compiled with the help of the
Embassy's naval attaché and two diplomats with the rank of second secretary, had a
prophetic quality, foretelling the personal animosities Trujillo incited among many
of his erstwhile allies. These grudges provoked a conspiracy among some of those
who felt wronged by Trujillo, leading to his assassination eight years after Johnson
sent this dispatch to Washington.*

Generalísimo Rafael L. TRUJILLO, dictator of the Dominican Republic,
suffers from a progressive megalomania which may ultimately prove fatal
to his regime. His basic policies derive from compulsions to improve his
international reputation, win applause and enforce obedience at home, establish a dynasty, legitimize his arbitrary actions, and satisfy his incredible
greed. . . .

Generalísimo Trujillo could say with substantially more accuracy than
did Louis XIV, *"L'etat? L'etat c'est moi!"* Current Dominican affairs and trends
can best be understood, therefore, by studying them through the facets of
his personality. . . .

Implications of Trujillo's Increasing Megalomania

Important American businessmen with long experience here affirm that the dictator's megalomania is progressive. A retired Foreign Service Officer, Dr. William DUNN (who served as one of his financial experts in the early Thirties) received some of the most striking confirmation of this. When he congratulated Trujillo recently on evidence of progress since his last visit to the Dominican Republic, the Generalísimo replied with sublime solemnity, *"Yo lo hice todo solo, todo solo!"* ["I did all of it alone!"]. . . .

The progressive nature of the *Jefe*'s illness may also cost him the loyalty of competent subordinates. His custom of exalting and debasing his followers periodically did not alienate too many able assistants in the past because he always held out to those in disgrace the possibility of regaining his favor. However, recent decrees forbid reappointments to the armed forces, police, and foreign service. This indicates that the *Jefe* now demands such blind loyalty that any able person who slips even once will be lost to the regime forever. Furthermore, as he becomes more easily offended and greedier for adulation, only his more sycophantic and less competent followers will be able to please, and this may produce a substantial, unorganized opposition in the Dominican Republic, to which previously apolitical elements will gravitate as his psychopathic tendencies become more obvious.

A further observation to be drawn from the progress of Trujillo's psychosis is that it may cost him the respect of his followers and the public. His enormous hunger for ornate uniforms, decorations, monuments, palatial housing, and ceremonies of all kinds have long made him appear ridiculous to foreigners. . . .

Since the Dominicans are not without humor, their *Jefe*'s increasing need for fore-and-aft ostrich-plumed hats, gold braid, exaggerated publicity, and fantastic eulogies may eventually undermine their respect and even fear of him.

A strong element of cruelty, which makes Trujillo relatively insensitive to the feelings and needs of others, will be dangerously exaggerated by his increasing egoism. Thus far, his Neronic excesses have been mostly sexual, but he has, at times, shown sadistic tendencies. On one occasion he compelled a crippled gentleman of good family to execute grotesque dances in public, and, quite recently, his insensitivity to the grave problems of the poor led him to require the wearing of shoes in Ciudad Trujillo and other municipalities. During the last quarter of 1952 he countenanced thousands of arrests of working-class Dominicans on the most trivial charges, and he ordered the eviction of scores of others from their homes for his personal gain. Although the masses still separate Trujillo from the brutalities of his government and do not trace such acts to him, additional mistakes of this nature may ultimately cost him the sympathy of the people now persuaded by propaganda and occasional . . . gestures that he is vitally interested in helping them. . . .

The Generalisimo's greed is only exceeded by his love of power, and both are closely inter-related. The methods he employs to milk the public and the public treasury are as thorough as they are numerous and as lucrative as they are immoral. Even foreign policy is perverted to serve his private ends. He also engages in a wide and growing range of businesses, his interests in which he usually tries to conceal. This makes it difficult, and in some cases completely impossible, to verify either the existence or the extent of his local investments. His holdings abroad are reportedly enormous but completely unverifiable here. Unfortunately, his greed, far from approaching satiation, grows with the years. . . .

Trujillo's insatiable hunger for adulation has induced the development, over the years, of a national eulogistic cult penetrating all aspects of Dominican life and embracing all manner of panegyrics. The President of the Republic and the poorest *campesino* operate under a common compulsion to pay him obeisance, a compulsion that highlights any failure to laud or even to display originality in superlatives. . . .

So voracious is the Jefe's demand for praise that the task of supplying it has had to be institutionalized. The Partido Dominicano for years has been charged with organizing meetings, lectures, and competitions for his greater glory. It is still highly active in these spheres, but it is now assisted by the Instituto Trujilloniano. . . . The Instituto's principal tasks in its first full year included the organizing of a competition for a hymn to Trujillo, the publication of four issues of *Renovación* (a periodical devoted to the publication of speeches and articles on Trujillo), the formation of a committee to plan the celebration of the first quarter century of the era of Trujillo, and the sponsorship of three major lecture series in Ciudad Trujillo and one in Santiago, covering various phases of the political, economic, and educational policies of Trujillo.

Trujillo's appetite for public acts of allegiance, laudation, and obeisance far surpasses that of the average Latin American dictator. May 16 (the anniversary of his first election to the presidency), August 16 (the anniversary of his first inauguration), October 24 (his birthday), and December 18 (the date of his entry into the army), have long been featured by nation-wide *actas* and demonstrations. The national holiday, February 27, has lost its real

Busts of the dictator proliferated across the republic during the self-proclaimed "Era of Trujillo," serving as sites for innumerable ceremonies honoring him, like this 1958 event involving young women. Photographer unknown, black-and-white photograph, 1958. Courtesy of the Roorda/Doyle Collection.

The most ambitious of Trujillo's projects of self-glorification was this enormous monument erected in Santiago in 1944, the centennial year of Dominican independence. Photograph by the Dominican Travel Bureau, 1954. Courtesy of the Roorda/Doyle Collection.

significance under the compulsion to accord Trujillo no less praise than the liberators. . . .

We estimate conservatively that no less than a hundred and fifty public demonstrations or large meetings were staged in 1953, in addition to those six national days. This implies an average of a meeting per month per province.

The demonstrations follow a standardized pattern, whether held out of doors or in public halls. They usually begin with a mass dedicated to the Generalísimo. Music is provided by military, police, or fire department bands. The speakers (sometimes as many as fifteen) throw all restraint to the winds in eulogistic competition. Party workers and government employees must attend these orgies of adulation and are severely reprimanded by their superiors and by the omniscient *Foro Público* of *El Caribe* [a vicious gossip column in the government mouthpiece newspaper] if they let their attention wander, or even if their dress does not conform to required standards. . . .

Trujillo's thirst for publicity equals or surpasses his hunger for public manifestations. . . . He insists on an unbelievable volume of press and photographic coverage of all his current activities . . . we can report with absolute assurance that not an issue of either paper appeared [in 1953] without at least one verbal or pictorial tribute, and that the space devoted to him or to demonstrations honoring him probably averaged, at the very least, a page per day in each newspaper. . . .

Trujillo's publicity is obviously intended and undoubtedly helps to sustain his regime; but only an advanced egomaniac could stomach the surfeit of adoration and falsification and still demand more. . . .

Trujillo's vanity requires durable manifestations of his greatness in astounding numbers. All public offices have long been adorned with his pictures and busts, some with two or more of each. Every community has its bust, statue, or monument and some have several. The five stars which symbolize the Benefactor are omnipresent in stone, metal, paint, and print. During 1953 they even appeared in neon lights on the Hull-Trujillo Monument, together with a flattering neon slogan. . . .

No estimates are available of the number of busts, portraits, or five star clusters installed in 1953. The most interesting signboard discovered by Embassy officers last year bears the legend "We owe everything to Trujillo." It adorns the grounds of the National Insane Asylum. . . .

The most convincing evidence of the Generalísimo's progressive mental illness is afforded by recent indications that he aspires to deification. The proliferation of busts, monuments, and emblems already noted would, in itself, imply his intention to fix himself in the public mind as an eternal and omnipresent force. Moreover, some of these monuments . . . convey a definite impression that Trujillo is super-human.

Embassy officials who have visited the Monument to the Peace of Trujillo in Santiago report that one of its Vela Zanetti murals is a modernized version of the scene in the manger, the principal differences being that the "Holy Family" is placed in the doorway of an unpretentious thatched cottage, and that five stars, instead of one, cast their rays on the family group.

Another mural terminating a series illustrating pre-Trujillonian Dominican history shows representative Dominicans receiving from an angel, with awe and reverence, a Dominican flag with the Generalísimo's five stars conspicuously superimposed.

The slogan of God and Trujillo has been in currency for some time. During the past year employees of the Embassy noted on a few occasions that enthusiastic Trujillistas had reversed the word order, apparently without incurring any penalties from the civil or religious authorities.

Since deification also implies a ritual of worship it is not surprising that the Institute Trujillonian established a special committee on April 10 to study a project for a competition "for a hymn to Generalísimo Trujillo, inspired by his life and work." The hymn, according to the local press, will be played on dates connected with Trujillo's life, when his personal flag is raised, when he makes official visits, and on appropriate dates in schools.

The apotheosis of Trujillo has already given him the semi-divine heroic status already achieved by the fathers of Dominican independence. . . .

A British View of the Dictatorship

W. W. McVittie

As the chief representative in the Dominican Republic of Great Britain, the major consumer of the all-important sugar crop, the British ambassador W. W. McVittie had a close view of the Trujillo regime at its height in the late 1950s. The sardonic and succinct report he sent at the end of May 1958 provides a miniature portrait of the excesses of the ruling family.

McVittie refers to two widespread cultural practices: giving gifts and compadrazgo, godparenthood, which have interrelated religious significance in the Dominican Republic. The giving and receiving of gifts has multivalent meanings there, which encode power relationships in complex ways, depending on circumstances. The tradition of a godparent giving valuable gifts to the godchild, items that the biological parents would be unable to provide, is a central element of the system of compadrazgo. The word itself, which has a meaning in Spanish something like coparenthood, is the term given collectively to the intricate networks of patronage and deference wherein well-to-do godparents, their godchildren, and the children's parents enter into a complicated relationship that has deep social and religious importance.

Near the end of his dictatorship, Trujillo allowed his younger brother Héctor, nicknamed "Negro" because he had the darkest complexion of the Trujillo clan, to take over as president. Like previous individuals to hold that office at the pleasure of his domineering brother, Héctor was a puppet president, virtually ignored in that office. The ambassador's report, which refers to him as "the President," illustrates just how irrelevant the Dominican presidency was during the Trujillo regime unless the Generalísimo himself held it.

May 30, 1958

Dear Department,

1. The Activities of the Trujillo family have the same importance here as those of the Royal Family of an absolute monarchy in medieval times.

The Trujillo dictatorship was so intrusive that families were expected to display a sign proclaiming "In this house, Trujillo is the Chief." This special edition brass plaque dates to 1955, a year of excessive commemorations of the dictator's twenty-five years in power, including a yearlong extravaganza, the World's Fair of Peace and Brotherhood, held in Ciudad Trujillo. The plaque reads "In this house, Trujillo is the National Symbol." Artist unknown, c. 1955. Courtesy of the Roorda/Doyle Collection.

2. This month, the Generalísimo has devoted much of his time to acting as godfather at mass baptisms. He has "done" as many as 250 babies in one day, standing in his chapel for two or three hours in full uniform in spite of very hot and damp weather. The expenditure for presents to his thousands of godchildren must have reached a tidy sum. My French colleague says that this strange activity is not a gesture toward the Vatican, but is due to the superstitious nature of mulattos of peasant stock.

3. The Generalísimo's favourite daughter, Angelita, is expecting a child and the Generalísimo is simply trying to ensure that the birth will be auspicious. I shall express very courtly congratulations when the great event takes place.

4. The Generalísimo's mother, aged eighty, Excelsa Matrona, has also been photographed many times this month with groups from schools, societies, social clubs, etc. who have presented a bunch of flowers to her.

5. The President has, as usual, been effacing himself. He did not appear when the Generalísimo opened a new highway named after the President. His only public function was one related to foreigners; he had to shake hands with 250 hearty members of the American Society of Travel Agents.

Yours ever,
W. W. McVittie

Exile Invasions

Anonymous, Armed Forces Magazine

Two failed attempts were made to organize an invasion of Trujillo's Dominican Republic in the late 1940s. The first fizzled in 1947: a group of exiles were training on the Cuban island Cayo Confites, until the Cuban government decided it would be prudent to pressure the would-be rebels to disband before they could launch their attempt. The second got off the ground in 1949 from a base in Guatemala but met disaster at the hands of superior firepower at the little port of Luperón, on the north coast of the island west of Puerto Plata.

With the success of Fidel Castro's insurgency in Cuba in January 1959, which began with a small-scale invasion launched in a pleasure yacht in 1956, the idea of doing the same thing in the Dominican Republic came to seem workable. Picking up where the Cayo Confites conspiracy had left off, Dominican exiles began organizing another invasion attempt from Cuban soil with the support of the new Castro government. On June 14, 1959, fifty-six commandos trained in Cuba, most of them Dominicans, boarded a C-46 transport airplane flown by a Venezuelan pilot and took off from their base in Pinar del Río province in far western Cuba. Their intention was to land near San Juan de la Maguana, but poor visibility there diverted the landing to the mountain-girded Constanza Valley, where they landed at the military airport and, as the airplane took off again, exchanged gunfire with soldiers and then escaped into the surrounding hills.

At the same time as the aerial foray into the mountains at Constanza, a two-pronged amphibious expedition set out aboard two recreational yachts, the Carmen Elsa *and the* Tinina, *that were not unlike the* Granma, *the boat that had carried Castro and his followers from Mexico to Cuba. The Dominican boats headed for inlets on the north coast of the country, near where the Luperón invasion had been destroyed a decade earlier. Their landing was delayed until June 20, when the* Carmen Elsa *approached Maimón and the* Tinina *neared Estero Hondo; both small craft were crowded with men. Spotted by elements of Trujillo's powerful air force, the invaders stood little chance. Strafing by airplanes and bombing from shore sank both vessels, and the survivors who made it ashore perished in a conflagration ignited along the beach by the Army's shelling, apparently with civilian loss of life as well.*

Meanwhile, Trujillo's air force tried to bomb the insurgents near Constanza, which resulted in more civilian casualties without hitting the rebels, who split up and sought refuge among the peasants in the mountains, as Castro's men had done in Cuba after landing from the Granma. But instead of harboring the invaders, the local people turned them in or killed them, in order to collect large cash bounties offered by the government. Many of the men and women who did so appeared in the pages of the July and August 1959 issues of the Revista de las Fuerzas Armadas *(Armed Forces Magazine), posing with their machetes, which some of them had used to dispatch rebels. The cover of the July issue featured one such campesino shaking hands with a soldier. The August issue included the editorial translated here, supposedly reprinted from a Mexican periodical, which credited the poor hill people for their service to the nation, praised Trujillo for knowing the people would rise to his support, and ridiculed Castro for backing the invasion. The piece failed to mention the bombing that was part of the government response to the invasion attempts and that caused civilian deaths both in the mountains and along the coast.*

Although the triple invasion attempts of June 1959 failed, with all the men involved either killed or captured to face heinous imprisonment and show trials, their example inspired further internal opposition to the Trujillo regime. A clandestine organization calling itself the 14th of June Movement came together after the debacle. The movement gradually drew in the charismatic Mirabal Sisters, setting off the chain of events leading to their kidnapping and murder at the hands of the dictator, an event that provoked international outrage. That crime combined with others, especially Trujillo's attempted assassination of President Rómulo Betancourt of Venezuela and his use of violence against the Catholic clergy in the Dominican Republic, caused Trujillo to be ostracized from the international community.

The People, Not the Soldiers, Crushed the Invasion of the Bearded Ones of Fidel Castro Ruz

Demonstrating once again that the Dominican Republic has been converted into an anti-Communist bulwark of America, the people materially crushed the Cuban invaders who thought they could plunge the Dominican Republic into the kind of chaos taking place in Cuba.

Castro Ruz has convinced himself already that he is the military supergenius of the 20th century trying to enthrone himself like a creole Napoleon. And now Mr. Castro Ruz is booted out on the street. His soldiers, who are more like little pirates out of an adventure story than soldiers, believed that to land on the coast of another country and take to the woods, would be child's play. They thought about the North American movies, where the invaders from distant lands go wherever they want, and they were completely

The construction in the 1940s of the Jaragua Hotel, designed by the Yale-trained modernist architect Guillermo González Sánchez, marked the beginning of modern tourism development in the Dominican Republic. The internationally acclaimed hotel was one of the first and finest resort hotels in Latin America. Artist unknown, color postcard, c. 1946. Courtesy of the Roorda/Doyle Collection.

mistaken. Generalísimo Trujillo, knowing how his people think, did not mobilize a single soldier. The Dominican Army with its Maximum Leader at its head, stood by as spectators. The inhabitants of the areas around Constanza, Maimón, and Estero Hondo, in the extensive region of the Cibao, knew the grandiose intention of the bearded ones and agreed with the prophetic words of Generalísimo Rafael L. Trujillo when he advised the Cubans what would happen if they tried to invade his country by flying in eggheads [*sesos,* literally "brains"] and bearded villains [*barbas*]. And they fulfilled the words of their commander. They crushed the invasion without the intervention of the army. That indicates a pronounced popular decision for anti-Communism. In the Dominican Republic Communism is rejected in the courts, in the written word, and in the act of war.

What damage they inflicted, ultimately, those reckless soldiers of the lunatic Castro Ruz. Puppets moved by two strings. One pulled by Dr. Castro from Cuba. The other manipulated from the Kremlin in Moscow. And that they went to die on foreign beaches, departing for the invasion in barges like cages for beasts, directly to the slaughterhouse, is a crime for which Castro Ruz must answer before History.

This gentleman did not make real the notion that the organized people stand ready to throw away by the shortest route their life, their work, their effort, and their tranquility to abet a movement alien in all of it ideals and customs. The Cuban people already have noticed that Castro Ruz, storm bird of the Sierra Maestra, does not have sufficient capacity to put on trial an era of peace and abundance. On the contrary: he has plunged his people into chaos; he has drowned them in blood and has placed himself like the god of death atop a pyramid of cadavers. And that is not governing.

Translated by Eric Paul Roorda.

I Am Minerva!

Mu-Kien Adriana Sang

The arrest and brutal murder of three of the four Mirabal sisters was a watershed moment in the history of the Trujillo regime. Born into an educated, elite family, the Mirabal sisters joined their husbands to form a clandestine political organization called the 14th of June with the intent of bringing down the Trujillo regime. Their code name within the movement was the "butterflies." They were tortured and raped in jail, and their death at the hands of the regime mobilized many against the brutality of the regime at a time when its violence was entering a new phase of ferocity, as it lashed out at the Catholic clergy and women, targets that had been off limits previously. The historian Mu-Kien Sang channeled her own deep identification with the Mirabal sisters into the book excerpted here, which became a runaway theatrical success when it was adapted as a play. Written in the form of a letter from Minerva Mirabal (1926–1960), returned as a ghost, to her surviving sister Bélgica "Dedé" Mirabal-Reyes (1925–present), the book tells the story of her political coming of age, her run-in with Trujillo, her persecution, and the pain she felt as she left behind her small children when she was arrested.

I don't know how I have returned to this world that forced me to leave. I see so many young people in a hurry. How different it is! You can breathe freely now. There is no fear of speaking. How frightened we felt when we were at university! How I had to struggle in order to study law! I had to win thousands of battles. Papa didn't let me come to Santo Domingo. Finally I was able to. I entered in 1952. Study! Study! But the dictator, villain, and tyrant Trujillo could not forgive me my contempt, nor my ideal of freedom. When I wanted to enroll the second year, I received a strong blow. Superior grades didn't matter. The problem was not academic, but political. He sought me out to humiliate me. If I wanted to continue studying, I had to make a compensatory speech to Trujillo. Me, Minerva, who had protested and screamed that I never liked him, who preferred to remain behind shattered, rather than submitting to him. Biting my tongue and with profound grief in my guts, I had to recite a laudatory speech for el Jefe! I will never forget that cursed day the 24th of October 1953, the birthday of the demon called el Jefe. When I uttered those words, I wept mercilessly and in silence from the depths of my painful soul. I remember each moment and every word I pronounced. How could I forget?

In this house I remember several sad episodes, my dearest Dedé. I still hold onto the image of the time in October 1949, when on el Jefe's order, they came to get my father and me to send us to prison. This was my first time in jail. Trujillo did not allow my indifference toward him. What did he want? That I faint before his gallantry? Who did he think he was? God? They say that he became fixated on me at that party in Santiago that July. They say that he could not forget me, that I was stuck in his mind like an obsession. . . . I did not even feel his gaze or notice it. A month later he invited us to the inauguration of the Hotel Montana. My mother didn't want to go. But as things unfolded, I went to accompany Papa. I danced with Ramfis and with Trujillo. I never hid my views, and I believe that I did not give any kind of hope to this wretch, who I found contemptible due to his love for power and domination. But really it was that very October in 1949 when my differences with Trujillo arrived at their most critical point. We went to another party at one of the country mansions of the dictator in Villa Borinquen, a few kilometers from San Cristóbal. Mama insisted that I should not go. Her intuition was truly powerful. Her prayers were ignored. We took the car, with Jaimito driving and accompanied by Dedé. The rest of the group was Papa, Pedrito, Patria, and I.

We thought it was a day party, which is why we left Salcedo at 4 A.M. Remember? When we arrived they told us it was that night. We spent the day eating and chatting. We arrived at the house where the party would be. It was located on the top of a hill, and we saw from the first instant the spectacular view. They assigned us to a table near the door, and now I know why. They wanted a place where Trujillo would see us immediately. The dictator made his spectacular entry. His sycophants stopped and yelled "El Jefe!" His face had a thick covering of pink powder and rouge. This was his way of whitening himself and hiding the blackness that he had behind the ear and up front and center and that he refused to accept. That night he passed the limits of toleration and he was laughable—he looked like an enormous scarecrow that spoke.

After much insistence, I danced, reluctantly, with Manuel De Moya. It was part of a sinister plan. Suddenly Trujillo took over the dance. They played the piece "Ay Tana, la maricutana!," when De Moya passed me into the arms of that man. The music stopped and they played two Merengues more. For two pieces I was forced to dance with this monster who I so detested. We started to dance and he took every opportunity to court me. I pretended to be indifferent and responded evasively. I told him that I dreamed of marrying my knight in shining armor. In response he told me with his effeminate, high-pitched, and whistling little voice: "I will send you young men for your conquest." I responded simply "And if I conquer them?" He wanted to keep going but I cut him off. Until I told him to leave my friend Pericles Franco alone. I cannot forget the tension in his face. The response was simple, but direct. "Are you a Communist?" he asked me. I responded simply. "As Communist as you are." This response made me an enemy of the regime. The dance ended, and I went directly to the table. I recounted what had happened. Everyone turned pale. Prisoners of their panic, they decided to abandon the party. We left in a rush. They say that Trujillo passed the whole night in a rage. What happened at the party had the family worried. How sorry I am Dedé! On the recommendation of Juan Rojas, a notorious Trujillista, Papa accepted writing a telegram asking forgiveness for what had happened.

Apparently the telegram did not arrive in time. It was not enough for the tyrant to imprison my father and me. He also arrested and interrogated my friends. It wasn't long before Trujillo's intentions became clear. He returned to court me again. He sent Manuel De Moya as an emissary, this nobody, this lowly henchman, to ask me if I would go to the Hotel Jaragua to a rendezvous—alone!—with el Jefe. My response, of course, was negative. "I am not going! I would prefer to kill myself! I will shoot myself right here and now. I am not going! I am not going!" I screamed desperately.

In revenge, Trujillo detained us for many days. My mother and I were all right, buried in the Hotel, but fine. My father, however, was utterly changed by the new prison. It was the vengeance of the tyrant, subjecting us to the worst, using his power. The family was worried and with the pressure of many insistences from the Trujillistas the dictator agreed to meet with us. He spoke with my mother and ignored me. Afterward in a mocking tone he asked me what I wanted. I responded calmly, "To be tried. Everyone who has been taken prisoner has the right to be tried, so I ask for the right to be tried for the crime that you accuse me of having committed." Trujillo did not respond. He stared at me with disdain. He did not free us.

Those days were very sad. The experience of jail had completely transformed my father. Some time later Trujillo let us go. We arrived here at our house at Ojo de Agua, totally transformed. I had decided to struggle to topple this regime, which stomped so cruelly on human dignity. When we arrived nothing was the same. Did you see how our fine business started to peter out? Our previous well-being was failing. Life here was not, nor could it be, the same. Our father was sick, depressed, taciturn, and wandered around the rooms aimlessly. He was slowly dying. Relatively young, he was becoming old. A man full of life, converted into a melancholic. This house, Dedé, is a coffin of memories, some of which are heartbreaking. This is where the life was sucked out of Papa. He died in 1954.

They arrived full of patriotism
In love with a pure ideal.
And with their noble blood on fire
The magnificent call of liberty
Your sacrifice that God blessed
The entire patria will glorify
As an homage to the brave
Who died there for freedom

In 1960 the struggle commenced in earnest against the tyrant, which nothing would stop. The year started with the most important meeting of my political life. The 10th of January, we met in the house of Patria and Pedrito, in San José de Conuco. We had to define a plan of action. We could not stop. Then we decided to continue another day, but in Mao, in the house of Charles Bogaert. There the name of our group was born: 1J4, in memory of the fallen. We started to plot. We decided to open up the movement in order to confront forcefully the tyrant-assassin. Someone from the SIM (secret National Intelligence Service) detained us. Some people say it was Andrés Norman Montero, a medical student who had a lot of influence among the workers and peasants of Porvenir sugar mill. One by one we started falling by the wayside.

January 13th we were at our house in Monte Cristi, when they took Manolo [Minerva's husband, Manuel Távarez] prisoner. I remember that in order to comfort Manolette [their younger son], I threw our bed pillow on the ground. How could I sleep comfortably while he was on the floor? They arrested me eleven days later. It was peaceful; they let me be taken away by the gendarmes. Manolo's mother and his sister Angela brought me mints and chocolates in their pockets, as well as some underwear. I only asked that they take care of my kids. When I left, Minou [Minerva's daughter] grabbed my legs, crying, saying "Mommy don't go! Mommy don't go!" I held back my tears, gently peeled off her arms and got into the car. I yelled "Take care of Minou! Take care of Minou!" The scene did not move the gorillas at all. Immune to our tears, they continued with their work. They first took me to Santiago, then to Fortaleza San Luis, and then I was transferred to the hellhole of La Cuarenta [a notorious penitentiary].

A few months later, in May of 1960, they came to take María Teresa and me prisoner from Conuco. They took us straight to La Victoria [prison]. We spent three months subjected to their torture and humiliation. Our *compañeros* [comrades] in the movement, among them our spouses, remained in jail. The women were let out first after being in prison a long time. Thanks to the OAS [Organization of American States, which pressured Trujillo to stop human rights abuses], we were let out. They let us go without trial. The men did not have this luck. They were taken to court, "tried," and "condemned" to thirty years of prison. There were many prisoners. Besides Manolo and Leandro were Cayeyo Grisanti, Freddy Bonelly, Marcos Troncoso, "La Cuca," who was Manolo's driver, Pipe Faxas, Julio Escoto, Luis Gómez, Weceslao Vega and Guido Cabral, and others I cannot recall. This seemed to be the culminating moment of the tragic comedy of the regime. I tried to mask the devastation of the experience of my time behind bars; I wore an elegant blue jacket and I went there to accompany them. They were taken to the Palace of Justice, they entered from behind so that they did not face the crowd that awaited them. It was frightening how skinny they were, with the visible signs of their torture. When they were taken into the room, they could see their family and friends, who smiled at them, greeted them and waved to them. It was a way of saying, "We're with you." We needed to raise their spirits, shake them up, so that they felt the solidarity and joy that we felt for their courage, and starting softly, but firmly, we sang the national anthem. At first my voice sounded buried, then other voices chimed in, until all those present could sing with spirit and emotion. Who would have thought that the anthem could be a song of protest? Afterward, under the pressure of the OAS, they were taken to trial, and due to an "absence" of proof a few were absolved, but the leaders, Manolo and Leandro, did not have this privilege.

I remember one night when we could not sleep and were sitting on the floor in jail, we were asked if we had thought of death. María Teresa responded that we had not, maybe because we were young. The question surprised me. It left me thinking. Maybe due to our youth, we had a deep conviction that our people needed freedom. I threw myself into the struggle against Trujillo without fear, and why not? Sometimes perhaps I acted imprudently, without seeing or considering the real and grave consequences of my political actions. I remember that I heard from María Teresa, that some people called us "heroines" and "butterflies." Truly I believed that more than heroines, we were martyrs, since the only thing we did was suffer, suffer a lot.

Translated by Lauren Derby.

VIII

The Long Transition to Democracy

A group of men who had different reasons to hate Trujillo conspired to kill him on May 30, 1961. That night, eight gunmen in two cars laid in wait for him on a lonely stretch of coastal highway not far from the scene of the triumphant "International Fair for Peace and Brotherhood" that he had staged in 1955 to mark his quarter century in power. When he drove past, alone except for his chauffeur, they ambushed his car, blocked the highway, and opened fire. He went down in a hail of bullets. Some of the assassins used rifles that CIA agents attached to the US Embassy in Ciudad Trujillo had supplied to them.

The opportunity to celebrate the end of "The Era of Trujillo" publicly was slow to come, as the dictator's sons, brothers, and military comrades and the figurehead president, Joaquín Balaguer, all jockeyed for control. When the celebratory moment finally arrived, amid high hopes for a rapid transition to democratic rule, it proved to be fleeting. Instead, the Dominican Republic entered into another turbulent political period. For the next five years a series of governments came and went, each with a different form: an interim Council of State arranged through international mediation; a freely elected presidency; a triumvirate installed by a coup d'état; a military administration imposed by a US occupation; and finally an authoritarian regime led by Balaguer, whose extended rule was the main legacy of that US intervention. The selections here begin with the time of the chaotic aftermath of Trujillo's assassination and continue through the recent administration of Leonel Fernández. The popular Leonel's twelve years in office combined high levels of stability with political participation, whereas Dominicans in the past had usually had to sacrifice one to achieve the other.

"Basta Ya!": A Peasant Woman Speaks Out

Aurora Rosado

Here a peasant woman from the central Cibao region offers some reflections on politics and economics, voicing a critique of the era of Trujillo, and her concerns about the problem of economic inequality today.

Aurora Rosado, Club Las Mercedes, Paso Bajito-Jarabacoa

Trujillo was a man who enslaved the whole country because he believed he was a god, while exploited and marginal women had no liberty; but they had their land, and no one could avoid work.

Today it's the opposite. We have freedom but are crushed because in terms of work for the peasantry, there is no land in the Dominican Republic; the land is all in the hands of some sick landholders that never think of death, only their happiness, and they don't care if the peasantry lives or dies. Here he who has property counts, and the others, they believe they are gods on earth and that all these poor people should be done away with.

Sirs, I repeat that we are almost the same way off as with that cruel tyranny that seems to be repeating itself. It seems that the roots of that tree have not yet dried up and they have bloomed again, now with even more force and much cruelty. They don't kill us with a shotgun or take people to jail, but what with the rising prices there is starvation. . . .

As for the history of Trujillo compared with today, it's not strange that they are very similar, the only thing is that women have improved their lives and they are not as marginalized as we were in the past, when they could not vote or buy in the *colmado* [corner grocery]. Sirs, that was huge what our grandmothers lived through. . . .

And that is nothing,—I will tell you even more. That disarmed man who believed that he was a king and the worth of his wife didn't mean anything, he treated his women like pigs that were only there to birth his babies, and the government even gave prizes to those who had more children.

If Trujillo liked a girl she had to be his; to him the value of the girl did not matter at all—ay so many women were raped! Everywhere there were spies to hear what people said, and if the authorities did not like someone they would invent a reason to throw them in jail, as their sad families cried and said goodbye to their loved one because they knew the tyrant would do away with his life. . . .

If today a similar tyrant returned to the country, he would have to constrain himself; he could not kill any defenseless person without reason, because the women of the countryside are the revolution, and we are learning to defend our rights, and we will never allow any Don Juan to take our women if he wants them. We are on our feet in the struggle, and we will never allow tyrants to destroy us. We ask God who watches us from heaven that a country so beautiful and peaceful never again be governed by a king like Rafael Leonidas Trujillo.

Translated by Lauren Derby.

Without Begging God

Joaquín Balaguer

Joaquín Balaguer was arguably the most important figure in twentieth-century Dominican history. Although Rafael Trujillo is widely regarded as the dominant figure
in the country during that time, the influence of the longer-lived Balaguer may be
seen as more pervasive.

Balaguer, the son of a Puerto Rican immigrant, attended the University of Santo
Domingo and briefly the Sorbonne, earning a law degree, and then began his political career in 1930, at the outset of the Trujillo regime. He held a variety of government positions, mainly diplomatic posts, including periods as ambassador to Colombia, Ecuador, and Mexico and as secretary of foreign relations, but his longest
stint was for six years as secretary of education—not the typical career track for a
future authoritarian. In 1957, he became vice president for Trujillo's brother Héctor (1908–2002), whom Trujillo had placed in the president's chair five years earlier.
When the elder Trujillo forced his younger brother to resign in 1960, in response to
growing international criticism of the regime, Balaguer succeeded him as puppet
chief executive for "El Jefe," who was clearly still the man in charge right up until
his death.

Balaguer was a member of an intellectual cadre who supported the Trujillo regime with ideological, historical, and statistical arguments. As he rose from one
post to another in the Trujillo government, one constant in Balaguer's career was his
role as an eloquent apologist for the regime. As acting secretary of foreign relations
when news of the Haitian Massacre of 1937 broke in the international press, it fell
to Balaguer to explain the event in a full-page paid advertisement in the New York
Times, in which he justified the bloodshed on the grounds of self-defense, asserting
that the Haitians were cattle rustlers. Balaguer's piece cited census figures to claim
a Haitian casualty count in the dozens, not the thousands.

Balaguer remained a constant in Dominican political life from the 1930s until
his death in 2002, by which time he was a completely blind but still lucid and influential ninety-two-year-old. The personal transition he experienced paralleled the
journey of the Dominican state from dictatorship to democracy. During his career,
Balaguer went from being a puppet president in a totalitarian system to being an

authoritarian strongman, then a paternalistic chief executive, and finally a facilitator of peaceful transfers of government power. He was president of the country for a total of twenty-six years: for two years around the time of Trujillo's assassination; for twelve years following the US military occupation of 1965–1966; and for another twelve years culminating in 1996. Along the way he became an extremely divisive figure. His numerous supporters in the right-wing political parties he headed revered him as a strong leader who maintained order and enhanced infrastructure. But those on the Left reviled him as the willing servant of a tyrant and an election-stealing murderer.

A diminutive, bookish man, he was in many ways an unusual figure among Latin American strongmen. He was a prolific writer of poetry, biography, essays, and fiction. While Simon Bolívar set the precedent for caudillos composing poetry, Balaguer's literary work was particularly voluminous, with nearly sixty books to his name. Whereas "The Liberator" and others in his mold mixed intellect and the fine arts with raw machismo, the bachelor Balaguer lacked a hypermasculine persona. Without a military background, his scholarly demeanor contrasted with the martial comportment of Trujillo and his ilk, and his dark suits and horn-rimmed glasses stood out among the elaborate uniforms that usually surrounded the seat of power. Far from a physically imposing figure, Balaguer eventually lost his sight and became physically dependent on others, but he remained firmly in political control, his mental acuity seemingly undiminished.

While in certain respects Balaguer was unlike figures such as Bolívar and Trujillo, he resembled them in having an immense ego. That trait is reflected on a grand scale in the following poem, which he wrote in 1919, when he was only thirteen.

I

I am made of iron. All the force is gathered in me just as all evil is
  gathered within Satan, because of this it does not matter to me if my
  garden has no perfume or if I do not hear Pan's moans,

My songs are the roars of furious lions, and I want to be a furious poet
  with a male soul, and not a silly rhyming forger of false hope that fears
  the taunts of the hostile crowd,

I hold all the pride of my indomitable race, which is why my miserable
  body has not been withered away by those that would wish that I kept
  silent,

I am made of iron. And because of this with pride I sustain all the force and audacity and valor that I have without begging God for anything. . . .

Translated by Lauren Derby.

The Masters

Juan Bosch

Juan Bosch (pronounced "Bo") (1909–2001) became the countervailing force to Joaquín Balaguer in Dominican political history. He was a dissident writer jailed at the infamous Nigua Prison by Trujillo. He fled the island after his release and was one of the exiles who formed the Dominican Revolutionary Party in 1939. After twenty-four years abroad, Bosch returned to his home country soon after Trujillo was assassinated. His long record of anti-Trujillo activism while living in Cuba, Venezuela, and Costa Rica made him a hero on the Dominican Left, helping him to be elected president in a landslide victory in 1962. He was a prolific writer whose work spanned the genres of history, criticism, political theory, and fiction and who taught the Colombian novelist Gabriel García Marquez in a seminar while in exile in Cuba. This short story, titled "The Masters," reflects his social realism and his attention to the problems of the rural poor.

When Cristino couldn't even milk a cow any longer, Don Pio called him over and told him he was going to give him a gift. "I'm going to give you half a peso for your walk. You look very ill and can't continue working. Return if you feel better."

Cristino extended his trembling, yellow hand. "Thank you very much, Don. I would like to start walking already, but I have a fever."

"You can stay here tonight, if you'd like, and you can even make medicinal *cabrita* tea for yourself. It's good."

Cristino had taken off his hat and his hair, so abundant, long and black, fell against his neck. His scant whiskers looked as if they were dirtying his face, which had such prominent cheekbones.

"Alright, Don Pio," he said. "God will repay you."

He slowly walked down the steps, covering his head again with the old black felt hat. When he got to the bottom of the staircase, he stopped for a while and looked at the cows and calves.

"That small calf is so lively," he said to himself in a low voice.

He was talking about the one that he had cured days before. He had had worms in his navel and was now running around and jumping happily.

Don Pio walked out onto the balcony and also stopped to look at the cattle. Don Pio was short and chubby with small, rapidly moving eyes. Cristino had been working for him for three years. He paid him one peso a week to milk the cows, which was done at dawn, attend to the duties of the house, and take care of the male calves. He had been a good worker and a calm man, but he had become sick, and Don Pio did not want to keep sick people employed in his household.

Don Pio lifted his eyes. At a distance were the bushes that covered the path of the brook and above those bushes were clouds of mosquitoes. Don Pio had ordered that wire screens be placed on all the doors and windows of the house, but the settlement of huts where the farmhands lived had no doors or windows; there were not even any hedges. Cristino was moving around down there, on the first step of the staircase, and Don Pio wanted to make one more suggestion.

"When you get to your house put a treatment on, Cristino."

"Oh, yes, of course Don Pio. Thank you," he heard him respond.

The sun was boiling on every tiny leaf of the savanna. From the hills of Terrero to the ones of San Francisco, lost in the north, everything shone under the sun. At the border of the cattle ranch, very far away, there were two cows. They could barely be distinguished, but Cristino knew each and every one of the cattle.

"Look, Don," he said, "that cow over there must have delivered last night or this morning because I can't see her belly."

Don Pio was walking around up there.

"Do you think so, Cristino? I can't see her very well."

"Get closer to that side and you'll see her."

Cristino felt cold and his head began to hurt, but he continued looking at the animal.

"Take a little walk over there and make it fast, Cristino," he heard Don Pio say.

"I'd go get her but I don't feel well."

"The fever?"

"*Unju*, it's getting worse."

"That doesn't matter. You're already used to it, Cristino. Go and bring her back to me."

Cristino held his chest with both his bony arms. He felt the cold begin to dominate him. He lifted up his forehead. All that sun, that small calf. . . .

"You're going to bring her to me?" the voice insisted.

With all that sun and his trembling legs and those bare feet covered with dust.

"You're going to go get her for me, Cristino?"

He had to respond, but his tongue felt heavy. He tightened his arms over his chest a little more. He was dressed in a dirty striped shirt of fabric so thin that it couldn't keep him warm.

Footsteps resounded from upstairs and Cristino thought that Don Pio was going to come downstairs. That scared Cristino.

"Yes, Don," he said. "I'll go. Let the cold pass from me."

"It will go away with the sun. Do that favor for me, Cristino. Look, that cow will leave and then I could lose the calf."

Cristino continued to tremble, but began to walk.

"Yes, I'm going, Don," he said.

"It took a turn around the brook," explained Don Pio from the balcony.

Step by step with his arms over his chest, bent over in order to keep warm, the farmhand began to cross the savanna. Don Pio looked at his back. A woman slipped onto the balcony and stood next to Don Pio.

"What a beautiful day, Pio!" she commented in a singing voice.

The man didn't respond. He signaled toward Cristino, who was walking further away with clumsy footsteps as if he were going to stumble.

"He didn't want to get me the small cow that delivered last night. And just a moment ago I gave him half a peso for the walk."

He was quiet for half a minute and looked at the woman, who appeared to demand an explanation.

"They're so ungrateful, Hermania," he said. "It's not worth treating them well."

She gave him a look of agreement.

"I've told you that a thousand times, Pio," she commented.

And they both continued to watch Cristino, who was now sadly barely a stain over the green of the savanna.

Translated by Melissa Madera.

The Rise and Demise of Democracy

CIA Reports, 1961–1963

After the assassination of Trujillo in May 1961, Balaguer managed to remain president for the rest of the year, trying to balance the demands for democratic reform made by President John F. Kennedy (1917–1963) and the Organization of American States against the need to placate Trujillo's family, who intended to maintain their complete control of the country. When the dead dictator's oldest son and two of his brothers threatened to oust Balaguer, Kennedy sent warships to Santo Domingo to stop them, and they soon left the country. But Balaguer reneged on his promises to reform, so the Kennedy administration pressured him to resign from office in January 1962, and he went into exile in the United States. The provisional government that followed Balaguer, called the Council of State, inherited the complex set of problems left behind by Trujillo. The Council organized elections for December 1962.

The candidate of the Dominican Revolutionary Party, Juan Bosch, won the election, regarded as the first free election in Dominican history, beating out the candidate of the conservative Union Cívica party in a landslide. Bosch was inaugurated on Dominican Independence Day, February 27, 1963, taking over a government that had been bankrupted by years of Trujillo's kleptocracy and the economic sanctions imposed by the United States and the Organization of American States. He guided a new constitution to passage in April 1963 that guaranteed many of the freedoms that had been denied during three decades of dictatorship and outlawed Balaguer's practice of sending opponents of his government into forced exile. But seven months after Bosch took office, a wing of the Dominican military still dominated by Trujillista officers seized power from him, under the pretext that he was a Communist, although this internal report demonstrates that inside observers knew these accusations were false.

Observers in the CIA filed weekly summaries of the situation in the Dominican Republic throughout this turbulent period that provide a concise and prescient account of what happened. This selection depicts the rapidly moving events beginning with the attempts by the Council of State to gain control of a chaotic situation in the late autumn of 1961 and continuing to September 1963, when the military ousted President Juan Bosch.

Dominican Republic

20 October 1961

In recent weeks the three major Dominican opposition political groups have shown increasing intransigence toward the Balaguer government. All three have rejected Balaguer's most recent offer to accept them in a coalition government, a step which the President considers essential to his liberalization program. The opposition's stiffer attitude seems to stem not from any increase in provocations by the government—which have in fact declined—but from mounting self-confidence. The police showed unusual restraint in dealing with the student rioting that began in the capital on 16 October and spread to other cities. Nevertheless, the rioting, initially to protest the naming of a pro-Trujillo university rector, had a clear antigovernment character and further exacerbated the political situation. It led the government to close the university until next January.

Opposition elements, including the majority of the upper middle class as well as students and other groups, remain suspicious of United States intentions in the Dominican Republic and fear that the United States will end in backing another dictatorial regime.

12 January 1962

The seven-man Council of State, installed on 1 January with President Balaguer as temporary head, began almost immediately to tackle the difficult economic problems inherited from the Trujillo dictatorship and the seven months of political instability that followed. All assets of the Trujillo family—including two thirds of the country's sugar-producing capacity and numerous other important businesses—were confiscated. Steps were taken to halt the outflow of foreign exchange; much of the country's reserves had been removed by the departing Trujillos last November.

Friction has developed within the council, however. The most pressing complaint is the continued interference by the armed forces.

8 June 1962

The seven-man Council of State, the Dominican Republic's caretaker executive, can be credited with important accomplishments since it came to power five months ago. After more than 31 years of Trujillo tyranny and the seven months of confusion that followed the dictator's assassination a year ago, the bases for democratic government and moderate socio-economic reforms are being laid and the principle of civilian supremacy over the military has been at least tentatively established. Next August a constituent assembly is to be elected to revise the constitution.

There is a threat of subversion from extremes of right and left: the Trujillo remnants, most of whom are in exile; and the Communist-influenced 14th of June party and smaller groups.

9 November 1962

The 30-year Trujillo dictatorship left the country without political leaders tested in democratic rule. The two major presidential candidates have serious political shortcomings. The 67-year-old Viriato Fiallo, a respected physician, nominated by the National Civic Union, on occasions has displayed a lack of political acumen. Juan Bosch, a temperamental and opportunistic writer who became a professional revolutionary exile after opposing Trujillo in the early 1930s, is the nominee of the Dominican Revolutionary Party, which represents the moderate left.

7 December 1962
Pre-election Outlook in the Dominican Republic

The Dominican Republic is to choose a president and a bicameral legislature on 20 December in its first democratic election in more than 30 years. The relative calm prevailing in the final three weeks of the campaign suggests that the voting will take place on schedule. Earlier, however, a tense atmosphere over a period of two months had resulted from the activities of extreme leftist parties boycotting the election and of Trujillo remnants, and from the wrangling of inexperienced party members. . . .

Former President Joaquin Balaguer recently failed in a well-publicized attempt to return as a presidential candidate [redacted]. Now in the United States, Balaguer has been unable to book passage because commercial airlines face heavy fines if they land him at Santo Domingo.

28 December 1962
Post-election Situation in the Dominican Republic

The chances for peaceful and orderly transition to constitutional government in the Dominican Republic have been substantially improved by the heavy victory of the Dominican Revolutionary Party in the national election on 20 December. President-elect Juan Bosch will take office on 27 February. He has indicated that he plans a reformist domestic policy, and a "dynamic, different, and democratic" foreign policy not unfriendly to the US. Various groups that had been plotting to seize the government will probably lie low, at least for the time being, and President Duvalier of Haiti apparently has thought better of getting involved with exiled remnants of the Trujillo family in order to try to make trouble.

The US ambassador to the Dominican Republic regards the success of the country's first free election in 38 years as "fantastic." An estimated one million people, or about a third of the population, voted on 20 December in an atmosphere of relative calm. Just before the election, fears had been aroused by the rough campaign tactics of the two main parties and by reports of plotting by exiled Trujillo elements with the connivance of Haitian dictator Duvalier. Still other opportunists were known to be trying to thwart the electoral process in order to gain power for themselves later.

The threat that these forces would produce chaos appears, at least for the moment, to have receded. The two-to-one margin of victory of Juan Bosch, the President-elect, and his Dominican Revolutionary Party (PRD) over the National Civic Union (UCN) should give pause to several groups that were considering plans to prevent the elected government from assuming office on 27 February.

The five other parties that participated received less than 10 percent of the vote. Armed forces leaders have expressed pride in the elections and awareness that an economic and social revolution is inevitable and that it will be better for it to occur under an elected government.

Bosch told reporters during the elections that his party's objective "is the welfare of the little man," and that his foreign policy would not bring a renewal of the relations with Cuba or the USSR. He reportedly said some Latin American governments had erred in handling the Cuban situation in a fashion that showed that they are under US influence. He indicated that he favored the Alliance for Progress, but placed greater emphasis on self-help measures.

Bosch has mapped out a reform program intended to cope with the country's disorganization inherited from the passing of the Trujillos. Not the least of Bosch's problems is arranging a means of equitable distribution of former Trujillo properties, which are estimated to comprise over 50 percent of the country's most productive lands and industry. These properties are now in the hands of the state. His program—which seems virtually assured of legislative enactment because of his overwhelming congressional majority—is ambitious. It provides for a large-scale redistribution of farming land to peasants; the organization of cooperatives to assist sugar growers, cattle raisers, and fishermen; and the encouragement of industrial development by native and foreign capital. The most controversial plans are for the introduction of "people's stores" in rural areas and the extension or cancellation of certain mortgages.

These latter devices are aimed at destroying inequitable forms of landholding dating from early colonial times, and are regarded as especially drastic by the business and professional classes which form the backbone of the opposition UCN.

21 February 1963
Pre-inaugural Situation in the Dominican Republic

The President-elect Bosch of the Dominican Republic, just returned from a two-month trip abroad, has attacked what he calls "vested interests" and may be preparing action that would lead to a major political crisis. . . .

Bosch's remarks on the proposed constitution, which he said should be "revolutionary," gave an impression that he backs those features that appear hostile to private property, business, and foreign investment. He is apparently already at sword's point with members of the outgoing regime.

The Embassy comments that Bosch's comments on the constitution "can only have succeeded in frightening the business and propertied classes." In general, his remarks appeared to clash with, and may damage the fruits of, his own efforts in the US and Europe to get development aid for the Dominican Republic.

The majority of Dominicans favor, or have become reconciled to, the need for social and economic reform. Members of the propertied classes and conservative-minded leaders of the outgoing administration, however, were deeply alarmed over the new constitution draft's lack of specific guarantees for property rights and over its broad framework—which if fully used would amount to a radical reform.

Officers of the armed forces almost unanimously expressed their apprehensions that the proposed constitution would discourage foreign investments necessary to the country's economic progress, and many of the military termed it a "Communist document." The armed forces although they still appeared disposed to support the incoming government at the time of Bosch's return, have been put on their guard and will be alert to any trend they consider likely to lead to the left. Widespread reports that Bosch may give important positions in his government to some of the several extreme leftists and persons with unsavory reputations who have been seen in his entourage will increase apprehension among the military. . . .

14 June 1963
Potential Problem from Dominican Extreme Left

Recent press accounts of startling Communist gains in the Dominican Republic are exaggerated, although President Bosch's continued tolerance of Castro-Communist activity is a serious potential problem.

Ambassador [John Bartlow] Martin does not believe that Bosch or other leaders of the ruling Dominican Revolutionary Party (PRD) will go the way of Castro. Nevertheless, Bosch refuses to restrict Communist activities on the ground that this would lead them to undertake the kind of terrorist campaign going on in Venezuela. This tends to underestimate the non-violent troublemaking potential of the nearly 100 well-disciplined Castro-Communists who recently returned from exile. . . .

19 July 1963

Dissatisfaction among certain military leaders with Dominican President Juan Bosch seems to be increasing, and he also may be heading for a collision with his most dangerous potential political opponents.

27 September 1963
Overthrow of Dominican President Bosch

The chief instigator of the 25 September coup d'etat that overthrew Dominican President Juan Bosch was army Colonel Elías Wessin y Wessin. . . . Wessin previously has been described by US military officials as a tough and virulent anti-Communist, backed by a group of the more reactionary young officers. Bosch's demand early on the morning of the 25th that Wessin be removed for antigovernment plotting reportedly led to the coup. . . .

The end of Bosch's seven-month-old government—the first freely elected democratic regime in the country in over 30 years—does not augur well for Dominican political stability.

The police have cracked down on Castro-Communist parties—which were outlawed by the military immediately upon ousting Bosch. The arrest of numerous extreme leftist leaders may deter significant anti-military action by their followers for the time being. However, the new regime's repression of the left has also removed the only moderate leftist parties from the political scene. . . .

"Ni Mató, Ni Robó"

Juan Bosch

Kennedy did not intervene after the coup removed Bosch, as he had when the "Wicked Uncles" of the Trujillo family had threatened to claim power. Bosch, initially favored by the administration and supported with funds from the Alliance for Progress, had lost Kennedy's support. One high-ranking policy maker, George Ball, called Bosch "unrealistic, arrogant, and erratic . . . incapable of running even a small social club, much less a country in turmoil." Bosch went back into exile but would return to become the leading left-wing political figure in the Dominican Republic for the next three decades. In contrast to his nemesis Joaquín Balaguer, who defeated him in tainted elections in 1966 and 1990, Bosch is praised by his supporters for having never killed or robbed anyone: "Ni mató, ni robó."

Juan Bosch expressed his views on Dominican politics in an interview recorded in June 1964, nine months after the coup that removed him from elected office. The former presidential counsel Lloyd N. Cutler conducted the interview for the John F. Kennedy Presidential Library.

CUTLER: Tell me, why do you think it is that the Latin American democratic intellectual groups, of which you are a leading member, have always been reluctant for their governments to adopt a strong position towards Cuba . . . ?

BOSCH: . . . In the particular case of the Dominican Republic, the situation is more complicated because Dominican young people, I would say—I speak of the responsible youth from the middle class, which is the responsible class, and for that very reason the dangerous one—I would say that out of every one hundred young people who were fifteen years old in 1956, ninety-nine have dreamed of being Fidel Castro. Not Fidel Castro the Communist leader, but Fidel Castro the revolutionary leader who overthrew a dictator named Fulgencio Batista; the image of a guerrilla who went up into the mountains and came down victorious. He still lives in the hearts of nearly all Dominican young people and all the parties. It is very hard to touch that image without producing a reaction prejudicial to democracy. But those Dominican young people don't know what democracy was. They thought democracy was Trujillo, Batista, and Pérez Jiménez,[1] and the entire corrupt spectacle of Latin America dictatorship. The word democracy is associated in Latin America with the worst political periods of our countries because those dictators always spoke in the name of democracy, and because in the United States itself, the democratic country, they were referred to as the rulers of the free world, and in the Dominican Republic, these young people had to learn what democracy was before democracy was pitted against the hero that they admired then and continue to admire now. . . .

CUTLER: Now, I will ask you a harder question. Looking back, do you think there is anything which you could have done or should have done that would have helped your government to stay in power?

BOSCH: Perhaps. Perhaps I made many mistakes, but it is very difficult for a head of state not to make mistakes. Now, there is one thing about which I am very much pleased, and that is that the fundamental error of my government was to establish a democracy that was too broad. Yet that experience is what has saved Dominican democracy for the future. I must say that when I received the news of President Kennedy's death, I reflected that it had been good fortune for me personally to have been overthrown before President Kennedy's death. Because, with such an example, no one knows what might have happened in the Dominican Republic. . . .

CUTLER: . . . it seems to me from my experience in the Dominican Republic that after the election there was no feeling of drawing together on either side. Did you consider, for example, a cabinet of national union, or making some effort to bring all of the parties into the Cabinet, or coming to terms with the business people or the military people in an effort to consolidate in a new administration?

BOSCH: Yes. I offered posts in the Cabinet to all parties, including a party such as the Union Cívica. I offered two posts to parties that had polled only twelve thousand votes, as in the case of Dr. Jiménes Grullon. I offered him a post in the Cabinet. I wanted to form a national coalition cabinet, but they all refused. Only the National Party accepted, taking the post of labor. But what happened was that unconsciously they still looked with favor on Trujillo, which is one of the reasons why I had to maintain a very broad democracy in the Dominican Republic, and why I could not, under any circumstances, accuse anybody of being a Communist. Because Trujillo had accused everybody of being Communist and harassed everybody, I had to create an entirely different image in Santo Domingo, so that the people could gradually realize that democracy was not Trujillo. Those politicians continued to look with favor on Trujillo, but today the majority of the people knows that democracy was something quite different from what it was under Trujillo.

CUTLER: But were the people ready to accept democracy? And by the people, I do not mean simply the majority of voters, or the poor *paisano*, but the people who have power and education and play a prominent role in the life of the country. Were they really ready to accept democracy?

BOSCH: At this moment, I would say that a part, which might be estimated at more than 50 percent, of the physicians, engineers, lawyers, and businessmen would be willing to support a democracy. But there is the other 50 percent that would not be willing, now or ever, because they were trained under the dictatorship and because their interests are stronger than the Dominican people in general. Now, democracy does not teach the way a school teacher does. Democracy teaches through practice. Of this 50 percent that today would support democracy, there is a high percentage that would support it because by experience they know that when democracy in Santo Domingo disappeared, they were hurt. Not because they are intellectually or emotionally convinced that democracy is better, but rather because the absence of democracy has hurt their interests. But that is how one learns democracy.

CUTLER: What groups were represented in the "golpe" that overthrew you? Was it only the military?

BOSCH: No, no.

CUTLER: Was it also the Union Cívica leaders?

BOSCH: Yes. Union Cívica. The former Council of State. . . .

CUTLER: The business community?

BOSCH: Yes. The businessmen and some of the industrialists and a very small number of the military leaders. Nevertheless, all together they held the power. They had more power than the government. Never in the history of the Dominican Republic had the people held the power, and the people would still need many years before they could hold the power.

Note

1. President Fulgencio Batista (1901–1973), former dictator of Cuba, and General Marcos Pérez Jiménez (1914–2001), former dictator of Venezuela.

Fashion Police

Elías Wessin y Wessin

The US Senate Internal Security Subcommittee (SISS) had a long history of Red-baiting on foreign policy topics going back to the days of Joseph McCarthy (1908–1956), when it ruined the careers of "China hand" diplomats whom it accused of allying with Mao Zedong (1893–1976). In the early 1960s, the SISS harassed several State Department officials with experience in Cuba, charging them with aiding the rise to power of Fidel Castro (1926–present). The subcommittee turned its attention to the administration of Juan Bosch in 1965 as part of their ongoing investigation into the situation in the Caribbean, which they addressed in their report "Communist Threat to the United States through the Caribbean."

The lead counsel for the SISS was J. G. Sourwine, a dedicated Red-hunter with many years of experience in conducting Senate investigations and orchestrating hearings. He directed his questions at Brigadier General Elías Wessin y Wessin (1923–2009), who had played the lead role in the coup against Juan Bosch. The general's answers reflect the hysteria harbored by the most powerful opponents of the Bosch administration.

MR. SOURWINE: Did the situation get particularly bad in the capital city, formerly Ciudad Trujillo, I think at the time called Santo Domingo?

GENERAL WESSIN: Yes, sir.

SOURWINE: How bad did that situation get?

WESSIN: It deteriorated on account of the political demonstrations that took place against the Government.

SOURWINE: But just how bad did it get? I have in mind something that you told us during the staff conferences, and I was hoping you would repeat it, because it was very descriptive.

WESSIN: When they discovered the question of the formation of the peasant militia, and the peasant fraternity ordered by Angel Miolán, when I saw with my own eyes forty schools of Communist and Marxist-Leninist indoctrination, the trip, with all expenses paid by the Government, of the students who went to Havana to celebrate the 26th of July—when a citizen could not put a coat and a tie on to go to a section of the city—when all the Government buildings were taken over to give quarters to militants of the party, when all the unions were dominated by Communists, this brought on as a consequence a general strike of the merchants, and a protest of all the Dominican people against communism.

SOURWINE: Sir, do you mean the situation actually got so bad that a man who put on a necktie and a coat was unsafe in an automobile in the streets of the poorer class sections of town?

WESSIN: He was in danger. They threw stones at him. They would say, "Enjoy your car, because soon it will be mine." When the strike began, the person who Juan Bosch sent to act as a spokesman for the Government at the radio station controlled by the Government was the president of the 14th of July Movement—Dr. Manuel Távares Justo.

SOURWINE: All right. I will have a question or two about him in a minute. But I want to pursue this matter of the actual danger of a person who wore what you might call the middle-class badge of the coat and the necktie. Do you recall that President Bosch coined a new word in his conferences and speeches which was picked up by the mobs and used as a rallying cry when they attacked these citizens whose only fault was a civilized appearance?

WESSIN: He invented the word "tutumpote." [1]

SOURWINE: What does that word mean?

WESSIN: A bourgeois.

SOURWINE: Was that, do you know, a corruption of the Latin words totum potet, meaning omnipotent, all powerful?

WESSIN: It is a corruption of the Latin words totum potet.

SOURWINE: But it was used in a derogatory sense by Mr. Bosch and by the mobs to mean a grasping for and an exercise of excessive power by those who were better off?

WESSIN: He used it to awaken hatred of the mob against the well-to-do people. . . .

Note

1. *Tutumpote*, meaning "big-shot" or someone from an elite family, while popularized by Juan Bosch in a speech of 1963, is actually an old slang term in the Dominican Republic. It may be a reference to "totem pole."

The Revolution of the Magi

José Francisco Peña Gómez

The charismatic José Francisco Peña Gómez (1937–1998) was a tragic figure in Do-
minican politics. He was left a virtual orphan when his parents fled the Dominican
Republic at the time of the Haitian Massacre of 1937. Adopted by a family whose
name he took as his own, he went on to enroll at "La UASD," the Autonomous
University of Santo Domingo, founded in 1538, which was the first university in the
hemisphere. La UASD would play an important part in the Dominican politics of
the 1960s and 1970s. Peña Gómez took a job as a radio announcer and became a sup-
porter of Juan Bosch. He gained influence in 1965 as the voice of national discontent
in the wake of Bosch's removal. Peña Gómez used his Santo Domingo radio show to
announce the outbreak of the Constitutionalist Revolution on April 24 of that year,
which would become his most famous and controversial broadcast.

After the failure of the revolution, Peña Gómez spent twelve years in exile; he
then returned to the Dominican Republic and became the leader of the Dominican
Revolutionary Party. He lost tainted elections to Joaquín Balaguer repeatedly, while
riding out the splintering of his party, becoming a kind of martyr to popular politi-
cal aspirations along the way. Hugely popular with the rural and urban poor, he
was denied power through a variety of means, until he died of pancreatic cancer at
sixty-one.

Presented here is a transcription of Peña Gómez's broadcast of his radio program
Democratic Tribune on January 6, 1965, the holiday of Epiphany, or Three Kings'
Day. This holiday is the most important of the various celebrations surrounding
Christmas in the Dominican Republic and is more important than Christmas Day
itself. This episode was among the most incendiary that he broadcast during the
prelude to the actual outbreak of violence.

Sixth of January, Day of the Magi, day of happiness for all children except
Pedrito, who at 6 in the morning stood melancholy without a revolver,
without a whistle, because the Magi had left him nothing.

It was 6 in the morning, and I had just awakened, not because I wanted to
get up but because of the children to whom the Magi had left something had

started a procession, and they were awakening their friends in their homes, knocking on doors, saying, "Get up, the Magi left me two revolvers, and to me a shotgun, and to me a car."

Pedrito was looking for all this under the bed, in the corners of the house, but without finding anything. Finally the boy went out in despair to answer the call of his friends with empty hands.

"What happened, the Magi have not left you anything?" A bitter "No" was the answer. "They have left you nothing because you misbehaved," they answered. "This is not true, because I am an obedient boy, and I was never absent a day in school, I respect my father and mother, I love you and all my friends, and if you wish you can ask my father and mother about it."

The children did not waste any time in doing so and asked if it was true what Pedrito was saying. The father could not answer them, because there were tears in his eyes; because he knew that his son had spoke the truth, and because he had promised that if he behaved, the Magi would bring him a car, a bicycle, a revolver, and a baseball mitt. But he had not fulfilled his promise, not because he did not want to do so, but because of the cruel Government's fault. He was an employee of the Public Administration, and he had been separated [fired] just a month before the feast of the Magi because of the quirk of a man who decided to separate him.

The father told Pedrito: "Do not be in a hurry, Pedrito, because at 9 the Magi will bring you something." The boy innocently asked: "Why at 9, father?" "Do not ask me, son of my soul." And he gave him a kiss.

He left the house with a radio in his hand and went to pawn it for 10 pesos, and bought Pedrito his gift.

The boy, full of satisfaction, said innocently, "I knew that the Magi would come to me, because when they promise something they fulfill their promises." Despite this, the father was thinking of what the family would eat today and tomorrow, since that radio was the last thing of value that remained, and he already had pawned it to buy Pedrito's gift. He was without work, and everything else he owned was pawned. The father was thinking and talking aloud:

"This world is not well divided, since we have nothing, while there are many who have more than they need.

"What hopes can my son have for tomorrow? He is 8 years old, and I am unemployed, without means to educate him, to feed him, and give him the rearing that he merits."

He suddenly got up and said: "We have to make a revolution, so that the workers can work, have bread and freedom, so that there will be no more exploitation and poverty; so that the country can develop; so that our sons can grow up in a democratic system, get an education, and become good citizens; so that there is no more unemployment, and the riches of this country can go to those who work for them and not to those who sell the country, as it is happening now. This system of exploitation set the country back, this country that has been trampled upon a thousand times.

"Arise, people, and unite into one bloc; let's start a democratic revolution for the good of our country."

United States Intervention
in the Revolution of 1965

William Bennett

After the coup against Juan Bosch, the Dominican military established a "Trium-virate" of civilian politicians to head the government. Cliques in the armed forces continued fighting for control behind the scenes in the uncertain political climate, with only one branch of the services clearly backing the Triumvirate. That branch was the powerful Armed Forces Training Center, commanded by General Elias Wes-sin y Wessin, leader of the coup against Bosch. The headquarters of his elite infantry unit, which possessed all the tanks in the army, was located near Santo Domingo at San Isidro, where the most advanced airplanes also were based, along with some 4,000 men, all subordinate to Wessin.

When a conspiracy of Dominican junior officers led a revolt against the Trium-virate on Saturday, April 24, 1965, the poor neighborhoods of the capital, which had given Juan Bosch their overwhelming support, rose up to support them. Several military units stationed near Santo Domingo followed suit, entering the city the next day. The "Constitutionalists," as they became known, seized the Presidential Palace and forced the Triumvirate president to resign. The Constitutionalists' pri-mary demand was Juan Bosch's return from exile in Puerto Rico, his resumption of the presidency of the republic, and the revival of the 1963 constitution, which the military had suspended. On Tuesday morning the "Loyalist" forces of the govern-ment responded with air attacks on the National Palace and other strategic points in Santo Domingo, as well as the rebel military bases, sparking a civil war. They did so with the support of resident US diplomats, who opposed Bosch's return and claimed that Communists controlled the rebellion. The main battle occurred on the Duarte Bridge across the Ozama River, where Constitutionalists used guns supplied by their military allies in a bloody but vain attempt to prevent the Loyalist tanks, commanded by General Wessin, from crossing over into the city. Meanwhile, Ameri-can citizens awaiting evacuation to the US navy ships that had arrived offshore were assembled at the exclusive Embajador Hotel on the outskirts of the city when a group of armed Constitutionalists entered the hotel searching for a prominent Loyalist, fired guns into the ceiling, and menaced the expatriates.

The afternoon after the Duarte Bridge battle and the incident at the Embajador Hotel, Ambassador William Tapley Bennett (1917–1994) met at the US Embassy in Santo Domingo with the leaders of the rebel forces: José Rafael Molina Ureña (1921–2000), installed as president by the Constitutionalists two days before, and Colonel Francisco Caamaño Deño (1932–1973). This telegram is Bennett's report to Washington on the exchange. Caamaño subsequently became the main rebel commander; Molina sought political asylum immediately after this disheartening exchange with the US ambassador.

12:26 AM, April 28, 1965
Confidential
Joint State/Defense Message

Molina Ureña appeared at the Embassy shortly before 4 PM, accompanied by gaggle of some 15 or 20 whom he introduced as his principal political and military . . . Col[onel]s Hernándo Ramirez and Caamaño were with him. Following security practice I have instituted, I required all weapons to be checked at entrance.

Molina Ureña, nervous and dejected, was trying hard to carry himself as constitutional president and failing miserably. While all emoted democratic principles and some sought breathe fire, it was clear they realized forces arrayed against them were superior and they said prepared negotiate settlement.

In meeting lasting almost one hour, various members of group asserted their people still prepared to resist, but they felt their action necessary in interest preventing further bloodshed. I made clear our emphatic view senseless shedding of blood must end, at same time reminding them that it was their action on Saturday [distributing weapons to pro-Bosch citizenry] which initiated this fratricide and called forth counter-reaction. I recalled to them US had loyally supported Bosch to end of his government and beyond and had made clear its emphatic disapproval of his overthrow. That had happened, however, more than eighteen months ago. Latest effort to restore Bosch was obviously unsuccessful and at some point one had to start anew. I made clear to them we were talking in similar terms to both sides and, while meeting was going on, word was brought in that Navy–Air Force bombardment had ceased. I suggested it was high time they approach other side for talks.

Both in full group and in private conversation with Molina and one or

PÁLACIO DEL EJECUTIVO
Ciudad Trujillo, Rep. Dom.

The grandiose National Palace, constructed by Trujillo in the early 1940s, became an arena of extended political conflict in the early 1960s, which reached a bloody climax in April 1965. "Palacio del Ejecutivo, Ciudad Trujillo, Rep. Dom.," photographer unknown, black-and-white postcard, c. 1950. Courtesy of the Roorda/Doyle Collection.

two civilian cohorts, I underlined and reiterated there was no question communists had taken advantage of their legitimate movement, having been tolerated and even encouraged by PRD [Dominican Revolutionary Party]. I noted that in spite of fact PRD Democratic Party they had in effect given communists free rein, especially through military distribution of arms to civilians in large numbers, their tolerance of widespread looting and physical mistreatment of innocent persons. I said there was much talk of democracy on their part, but this did not impress me as road to get there. . . .

As regards their request that we dissuade Wessin from crossing bridge and get air force to call off bombing, I reminded them embassy staff had been successful four times yesterday in getting air force to hold back and had thought early this morning truce had been worked out. They had in fact tried to take advantage of each situation. Then I came down strongly on disgraceful incident at Hotel Embajador where American lives were wantonly placed in peril this morning. Was this an example of democracy in action? . . .

Meeting finally dragged to close with Molina leaving accompanied by small group and several others, principally military, lingering as though they trying to avoid going out again into cruel world. . . .

The President of the United States Chooses the Next President of the Dominican Republic

Lyndon Johnson

This transcript of an Oval Office recording reveals the casual way that President Lyndon B. Johnson (1908–1973) changed the trajectory of Dominican history. In a conversation with the State Department undersecretary and noted Latin American specialist Thomas C. Mann (1912–1999) on the morning of April 26, 1965, Johnson hinted at the decision he was about to make to intervene militarily in the Dominican Republic. The exchange demonstrates that he made the move expressly in order to prevent Juan Bosch from returning to the presidency he had won at the polls and to install the most prominent Trujillo protégé of all, Joaquín Balaguer.

PRESIDENT JOHNSON (LBJ): What is the word on Dominican Republic this morning?

SECRETARY MANN: Well, it isn't good this morning. We were hoping last night that the Army would be able to get together. But they are split. The Wessin group and the Air Force are in one camp; the Army, that's a large part of the Army that is in Santo Domingo the capital itself is supporting the rebel government; and the loyalties of the troops outside the capital are still uncertain. They haven't gone over to the rebels yet, and presumably they will split, too. The Wessin forces are separated from the center of town by a river, which is commanded by the rebels; the bridge over the river, there is only one, is commanded by the rebels. The guns controlling the bridge are being strafed by the air force. And Wessin has not yet tried to move across that bridge with his main troops. In the meantime, looting is going on in the city, a lot of chaos. They've got about fourteen hundred marines on board these ships standing offshore. I just asked that we alert Defense that we might have to airlift, in case things got very bad, some people out in the southern portion of the U.S. Presumably marines could get control of . . .

LBJ: Southern part of the U.S.?

MANN: Well, by air.

LBJ: What'd you mean—repeat that statement.

MANN: I say we've—

LBJ:—alerted Defense.

MANN:—alerted Defense to, against the possibility of having to airlift some additional people down, in case the fourteen hundred are needed and are not enough.

LBJ: OK.

MANN: I don't think there's anything we can do right now, except wait it out. I don't know how it will go. They're not likely to do too much shooting, at least they never have in the past. Either the troops on one side or the other are likely to cave. We heard last night late that they were moving to Wessin's side and they apparently stiffened during the night and early this morning.

LBJ: Abe Fortas,[1] I went out to see him last night just to visit with him on the general picture. He had had a call from a fellow that Bosch lives with, or visits with, down in Puerto Rico, it was their lawyer, said Bosch wanted to know whether he should go back or not, and he'd about concluded that he couldn't go back 'cause the field's closed and it might be dangerous, and so he was gonna' stay in Puerto Rico for a while.

MANN: Yeah, I don't think he could get in right now. I don't think anybody could get in right now.

LBJ: What's our ambassador, he's cut off, huh?

MANN: Well, he was asked to come up on consultation by the Bureau [of Inter-American Affairs of the Department of State], who were worried about this deteriorating situation. They didn't expect it to come so soon. . . .

LBJ: Uh, we are really gonna' have to set up that government and run it and stabilize it some way or other. This Bosch is no good. I was down there.[2]

MANN: He was, he is no good at all. And the tragedy behind all of this is the price of sugar, which you can't do much about. You can't try to raise the price of sugar without putting Castro firmly in the saddle. They're both sugar economies. I think what we're going to have to do is to pour even more money into Santo Domingo to offset this low sugar price right now. This is what's hurtin' 'em. And if we don't get a decent government in there, Mr. President, if we get another Bosch, it's just going to be another sinkhole.

LBJ: That's what you're gonna' do, so that's your problem. You'd better figure it out.

MANN: Therefore, I think we'll know in the next six or eight hours how this fighting is going. If Wessin comes out on top, the man to get back, I think, is Balaguer. He's the one who ran way ahead in the polls.

LBJ: Well try to do it, try to do it some way or other. I see where they claimed last night that we were in on the shooting of the Palace and that we were supporting this government, the ones that are resisting Bosch. Is that right?

MANN: Well, no, it isn't right, I saw that in the paper this morning.

LBJ: ABC was puttin' it out. We ought to correct that.

MANN: Everybody you, yeah, everybody you have an aid program with, you're quote supporting them, and that's nonsense.

LBJ: We supported Bosch.

MANN: We supported Bosch, we support every Latin American . . .

LBJ: Why don't you call in the AP, or whoever it was, ABC, and point out this is not in the interest of our government to be saying these things. 'Cause we supported Bosch, we support this government, and we're not supportin' one against the other in one of these violent things we don't take any part in.

MANN: It's the nation, the economy.

LBJ: That's right. Will you do that?

MANN: I will do that.

Transcribed by Eric Paul Roorda.

Notes

1. Fortas (1910–1982) was a longtime political ally of Lyndon Johnson, who appointed him to the Supreme Court in October 1965. He served until 1969, when he resigned amid a corruption inquiry.

2. Johnson visited Puerto Rico in July 1962, but not the Dominican Republic.

Operation Power Pack

Lawrence A. Yates

Pouring into Santo Domingo in the last days of April 1965, US Marines and Army airborne troops drove through the center of the ancient city from two sides, clearing an armed cordon called the Line of Communication, which linked their two landing areas at the Embajador Hotel and the San Isidro air force base. They also sealed off an "International Security Zone" in the area of the US Embassy. This cordon and zone separated the combatants in such a way as to stifle the insurrection in the poor neighborhoods and support the Dominican military forces surrounding them. By the end of May, Loyalist troops had regained control of rebel-held neighborhoods outside the armed corridor, while the Constitutionalists trapped inside of it could respond with nothing more than sniper fire. The Organization of American States voted to support the US action, with troops from Brazil and a handful of other Latin American nations arriving to join what became known as the Inter-American Peace Force. "Operation Power Pack," as the occupation was code-named, lasted until September 1966, smothering the Constitutionalist Revolution. More than 3,000 Dominicans died in the war, most of them prior to the US intervention, which involved 24,000 US troops and claimed the lives of twenty-seven marines and paratroopers killed in action. While the initial goals of the operation were unclear, eventually the US forces adopted a peacekeeping role, geared to the counterinsurgency tenet of "winning the hearts and minds" of the people and employing "psychological warfare," food aid, and still-secret covert operations to do so. The results were mixed at best, as indicated in this excerpt from an official US Army study published twenty-two years later.

U.S. occupation of the power plant made it possible for those running the installation to provide some critical services and, on occasion, to indulge in some mischievous fun: aside from being able to bring electricity to Santo Domingo on a sporadic basis, the troops could shut down [Constitutionalist commander] Caamaño's air conditioners at will.

Whether manning an observation post, going on patrol, or simply cross-

As the Landing Zone of the Marines, the polo field outside the Hotel Embajador, a luxury hotel built in 1954 for Trujillo's vaunted World's Fair of Peace and Brotherhood, held in Ciudad Trujillo, was the focal point of the US invasion and the staging area for the evacuation of US citizens. Photographer unknown, color postcard, 1954.

ing an exposed area to get to the power plant or some other facility, Americans located within sight of Constitutionalist territory quickly learned that the greatest threat to their personal safety was not an all-out Constitutionalist attack on U.S. positions (an unlikely prospect) or a projectile launched by an angry Dominican demonstrator; rather, it was the ubiquitous rebel sniper whose harassment of the foreign invaders became a routine but dangerous fact of daily life.

Sniper fire accounted for the majority of American casualties during the intervention. . . . The troops at first returned the sniper fire, but the rules of engagement restricted their choice of weapons. The 106-mm recoilless rifle was the largest weapon that could be employed. The advantage of the 106-mm was that it not only killed the sniper but usually destroyed his cover as well. The disadvantage was that sometimes an entire building would be leveled to kill one man. Furthermore, a 106-mm round would sometimes pass through three or four shanties grouped together, thereby increasing the risk of killing or wounding innocent civilians. The back blast of a recoilless rifle fired in one of Santo Domingo's narrow streets or alleys could also destroy poorly built houses in a friendly area. All told, the 106s were best reserved for knocking holes in substantial structures or in the walls of

In the aftermath of street fighting in the Colonial Zone, a disabled tank remains stranded on a narrow street, bearing graffiti of the pro-Bosch forces: "Constitution" and "People." This may be an example of "the rebels' antiquated armor." Photographer unknown, May 1965. Courtesy of the Roorda/Doyle Collection.

buildings soldiers wished to pass through during the course of a patrol or attack. The recoilless rifle was also ideal for use against the rebels' antiquated armor and against large groups of isolated rebels. . . .

The M79 grenade launcher and the .50-caliber machine gun and spotting rifle served much better as antisniper weapons. The grenade could easily destroy a room in which a sniper was operating and do it without the collateral damage of the recoilless rifle. The .50-caliber machine gun had much the same effect, as its bullets could penetrate the most common construction materials in the Dominican Republic. When U.S. troops could actually see a sniper, the .50-caliber spotting rifle on a 106 presented a "surgical" way to eliminate the problem, either by targeting the sniper himself or by placing a round where he was likely to be standing, usually to the immediate right of a window. . . .

Dominicans wishing to pass from northern Santo Domingo into Ciudad Nueva, or vice versa, invariably had to traverse the LOC [Limit of Control], where makeshift barricades of concertina wire, sandbags, and oil drums shut off side streets and alleys, channeling pedestrian and vehicular traffic into a series of checkpoints and roadblocks erected at five or so strategic locations. Nearly 50,000 people a day traversed the corridor making congestion a chronic problem that was compounded by the "undisciplined driving habits" of Dominican cabbies and by an insufficient number of Spanish-speaking troops at the critical bottlenecks. Military police, supported by Army troops and Dominican policemen, manned the checkpoints, where they looked for "subversive" agents and, more important, weapons. The intention was to prevent the flow of arms in either direction across the line. No Dominicans (with the exception of national policemen) could enter the corridor with a weapon, a rule that disrupted the Constitutionalists' efforts during the first half of May to send arms north for the purpose of using them against pockets of Loyalist troops or simply of caching them for retrieval at a later date should the Americans take over Ciudad Nueva.

The rebels refused to be deterred by U.S. surveillance measures and adopted several ruses to achieve their objective. Guns were placed in automobile gas tanks. Hearses and ambulances loaded with concealed weapons instead of bodies cleared checkpoints without being searched, often as American soldiers removed their helmets out of respect. After the subterfuge was discovered, the treatment accorded such vehicles at roadblocks became anything but respectful: MPs undertook vigorous searches, even opening coffins that did not appear completely sealed. Another rebel tactic was to create a diversion or mount a full-scale sniper attack during which a vehicle containing weapons would attempt to run a roadblock during the confusion. Again, frustrated American traffic controllers devised countermeasures. The rapid emplacement of emergency barricades during such disruptions discouraged speeding cars and trucks, as did the occasional lobbing of a grenade from an M79 launcher into their paths.

One rebel deception for smuggling arms across the LOC lent itself to no immediate counteraction. While all Dominican males entering and exiting the corridor were frisked, females were spared the procedure lest the indignity of it incite a riot. Thus, women and young girls wearing loose-fitting dresses or maternity clothes could easily slip grenades, pistols, and ammunition through the checkpoints. Efforts by U.S. authorities to obtain female inspectors failed, while less delicate suggestions for eliminating the practice were dismissed out of hand. Reports written during the last part of May claimed that the problem still lacked a solution, although photographs of checkpoint activity indicate otherwise. One photo in particular shows an American soldier with a mine detector and a determined look dutifully passing the device in the vicinity of a young woman's skirt.

Having difficulties crossing over the LOC, the rebels decided to go under it via the city's sewer system. A highly successful ploy at first, the Americans eventually realized what was happening and once again devised counter-measures. A Special Forces team acquired a plan of the sewer system and passed it to corps and division. The Green Berets also assisted the 82d in reconnaissance missions in the sewers, while Army engineers emplaced a series of booby traps that included mines, grenades, barbed wire, trip flares, and, according to some sources, chemical agents. During these preparations, the two sides would often meet, and an underground firefight would ensue. After the engineers installed the obstacles to underground traffic, soldiers above ground removed the manhole covers, lowered lights on wires, and began maintaining a 24-hour watch (in twenty-minute shifts) over the open holes. Underground infiltration fell off markedly after that. . . .

In mid-May, U.S. Special Forces personnel in Santo Domingo received new orders. Described in an after-action report, the mission was " . . . to assist the 82d Airborne Division civic action program. This overt civic action mission was a cover for many covert Special Forces activities, and was designed to create an impression that Special Forces was primarily engaged in a civic action mission in the Dominican Republic."

What constituted the "many covert" activities is not clear from the available evidence. Sources concerning the civic action program, on the other hand, are readily available, thanks to the efforts of civil affairs officers to preserve them. A civic action–civil affairs program began as soon as marines and paratroopers established positions in and around Santo Domingo. Something had to be done to alleviate the deplorable conditions in the city and suburbs. Garbage and bodies littered the streets, electrical power outages were frequent, potable water was in short supply, and a starving and war-weary population required food and medical attention. Hospitals were crowded, with physicians practicing by candlelight. At first, the U.S. military's response to the shortages and human suffering consisted of little more than the voluntary sharing of C rations with hungry Dominicans or the providing of impromptu medical treatment. On 3 May, a bonafide civic action program supplanted voluntarism, as marines and the 82d distributed rice, powdered milk, cornmeal, beans, cooking oil, water, and clothing to the population. At the Embassy's request, Washington authorized the distribution of food to people on "both sides" in the civil war, so long as they were unarmed. In all, over 15,000 tons of food and 15,000 pounds of clothing would exchange hands, not only in Santo Domingo but in the countryside as well.

At first, troops unfamiliar with civic action procedures exercised little effective control. As mobs of hungry Dominicans stormed distribution points, several members from a single family could each make off with a full family allotment. Some Dominicans, after having received their initial handout, simply hid it close by and returned for more. As soldiers distributing food and clothing gained experience, they enacted measures such as ration cards to curb such abuses. Free medical clinics also enjoyed a high volume of business, although the crowds requiring the doctors' attention were much better behaved. . . .

The civic action and civil affairs programs sought to provide humanitarian aid, assist in stabilizing the country, and win the "hearts and minds" of the Dominican people. The last two goals coincided with efforts undertaken by Army psychological warfare specialists. . . .

When the 1st Psychological Warfare Battalion arrived in the Dominican Republic, it brought with it mobile printing presses, mobile broadcasting facilities, a loudspeaker capability to broadcast from trucks and from the two c-47s, and ultimately, heavy, mobile printing equipment. The loudspeaker trucks proved more effective than the aircraft in imparting information. Wherever the trucks would stop, hundreds of Dominicans would gather round to hear the latest news and receive leaflets and pamphlets, which by the end of May were being printed at the rate of 70,000 per day. On 5 May, the battalion's mobile broadcast, "The Voice of the Security Zone," hit the airwaves and was powerful enough to be picked up deep in the interior. In addition to these highly visible activities, battalion propaganda analysts helped interrogate rebel detainees to gain feedback on the PSYWAR [psychological warfare] effort and to uncover areas in which rebels and civilians alike were vulnerable to propaganda. . . . Leaflets bearing pictures of Presidents Kennedy and LBJ and pamphlets extolling the virtues of the OAS and the evils of communism became standard, if innocuous, fare. Some propaganda, however, was blatantly false, as USIS [US Information Service] officials tried to convince the population that the intervention was a benevolent undertaking. One of the battalion's after-action reports listed among the USIS-imposed propaganda themes such fictions as the "landing was made only for peaceful and humanitarian ends," and the "US government supports neither side nor has it given military or material aid to either faction." . . .

Undoubtedly, the food, clothing, and medical programs won friends among locals who had initially opposed the intervention. According to one 82d report, "Civil assistance has been the single most important factor in building a favorable image of the airborne soldier." Personal contact was indispensable to this goal, and fact sheets issued to the soldiers instructed them on proper conduct. But despite this and other efforts to promote good relations, some friction between Dominicans and U.S. troops was inevitable. To begin with, the marines and the 82d were resented as an occupation army. The use of U.S. troops to break up demonstrations, despite the restraint exercised in doing so, also created hostility, as did "the immorality of some American soldiers who did not distinguish between professional prostitutes and ordinary Dominican girls." (The incidence of venereal disease in the Dominican Republic was high enough to make a lasting impression on several officers who tried various measures to curtail their troops' sexual liaisons with women other than the ubiquitous and "clean" camp followers.) In day-to-day dealings with Dominican citizens, a racial slur or an ugly incident could also undo a great deal of good will in seconds. In one particularly tragic occurrence, a soldier requesting an Alka Seltzer of a teenager who worked in a drug store thought that the boy had poisoned him. He shot and killed the teenager on the spot. A visit by General [Robert] York to the neighborhood to offer his personal condolences could not assuage the bitterness caused by the tragedy.

In a more positive vein, many Dominicans simply appreciated the fact that, with few exceptions, the intervention reduced the previously uncontrollable bloodletting of the civil war. While in a crowd, locals would often hurl abuse or more tangible objects at soldiers manning the front lines. Alone, a Dominican would often offer the Americans beer and whisper words of appreciation for the job they were doing. Perhaps indifference—or more aptly ambivalence—best describes the feelings of most Dominicans once Americans became a familiar presence among them. Few U.S. troops who served in the country fail to recall the words of a piece of graffiti that became more and more common as the intervention continued: *Fuera Yanqui—y lléveme contigo* (Yankee go home—and take me with you).

The Twelve Years

CIA Special Report

Moving between New York and Washington, the exiled Joaquín Balaguer cultivated his ties with US policy-makers, putting himself in a position to benefit from the 1965 invasion. He suggested a plan to his contacts at the State Department that called for a cooling-off period under a provisional government, to be followed by presidential elections. The Johnson administration adopted this course of action without attributing it to Balaguer, setting June 1966 elections as part of its exit strategy from "Operation Power Pack." Returning to the Dominican Republic, Balaguer campaigned publicly to be president and maneuvered privately to assure his election over Juan Bosch, also back from exile. With cooperation from US officials, who increasingly identified Bosch with Castro, Balaguer won the election. He was sworn in as president of the Dominican Republic for the second time on August 16, 1966; the last of the US troops left the following month.

With the Trujillista military establishment now firmly under his command rather than undermining him, Balaguer set about purging his political enemies in a reign of political violence akin to those Trujillo had periodically unleashed. Government agents kidnapped and murdered as many as 5,000 of his critics during the period known as "the Twelve Years," a Dominican dirty war that has yet to be fully exposed, which spanned Balaguer's tenure in office from 1966 to 1978. The victims of "Operation Cleanup," as this campaign of violence was called within the death squads, included Francisco Caamaño Deño, the leader of the Constitutionalist revolt. He attempted to trigger a revolution against the Balaguer regime with a Castro-style commando landing from Cuba, where he had gone into exile after the US intervention, followed by a guerrilla campaign in the mountains. His group came ashore and made it into the Central Mountains, but government forces located them in February 1973 and wounded, captured, and executed him.

This CIA special report provides a succinct portrait of Balaguer's regime at the beginning of his second term in office.

The New Balaguer Government

Outwardly there is little in either personnel or policies to distinguish the ten-month-old second administration from the first. As he had done in 1966, Balaguer again offered posts in the government to members of opposition parties. No real "government of national unity" was achieved, or intended, however. Authority is centralized in the president's hands, and no member of the government exerts any real influence on presidential decisions. Bringing members of the opposition in to the administration did not give the opposition a voice in government; rather it has contributed to the weakening of the appointees' political parties. The post election appointments and reassignments that Balaguer made in the military appear to have achieved the dual end of dispersing authority to prevent only one officer from becoming powerful enough to challenge the government while retaining the military's support. . . .

The concept of a loyal opposition is foreign to the Dominican experience, and nonpartisan cooperation for the good of the nation has never been attractive to practitioners of what has been called "the politics of annihilation." Balaguer's discouragement of opposition activity to protect his administration is understandable in the Dominican context. Such a policy, however, if continued indefinitely, endangers future political development and the administration itself to some extent. Government is increasingly centralized in the President's hands. The interests of much of the population are unrepresented. Most political parties are spurned by the majority of the youth—about half the population of the Dominican Republic is under the age of 20—and those who want to act look to the revolutionary left for inspiration. . . .

In February there was a general strike in San Francisco de Macorís to force the transfer of the local police chief. There is some evidence that the PRD [Dominican Revolutionary Party] and members of extreme left political groups were involved. On 24 February, Balaguer delivered a major television address in which he accused Bosch and the PRD, as well as others, of trying to destroy constitutional government through "psychological terror" and of trying to impose Communism on the Dominican Republic. He warned that the government would use undemocratic measures if necessary to preserve order.

The speech was believed by some to be a carefully calculated maneuver to polarize the country politically and to confront the people with a contrived political choice between constitutional government and Communism. It was an unmistakable warning that the government would not tolerate political agitation that disturbed domestic tranquility.

Three months later *La Banda,* a police-sponsored, anti-Communist terrorist group, provoked outraged public reaction and widespread criticism in the press as a result of its activities. These included the invasion of private homes, schools, and at least one church in search of "subversives" as well as open participation with the police in a raid on the headquarters of an important labor union. *La Banda* and the government publicly disclaimed any relationship, and the chief of the National Police, who had countenanced the formation of *La Banda,* pledged that the government would not tolerate terrorism from any quarter. The assumption that *La Banda* had only suspended operations very temporarily was confirmed in June by reports of new forays by the group.

In the past, President Balaguer has escaped being held personally responsible for particularly outrageous incidents of antiterrorist police action. After his speech in February and the emergence of *La Banda,* however, the fiction of presidential ignorance or innocence has become difficult for the government to maintain.

Why Not, Dr. Balaguer?

Orlando Martínez

Perhaps the most publicized crime of Balaguer's Twelve Years was the murder of the journalist Orlando Martínez (1944–1975) in March 1975. Martínez was editor-in-chief of the magazine Ahora! *and the author of "Microscope," a widely read, harshly critical column in the newspaper* El Nacional. *He wrote many exposés of the Balaguer government's corruption and human rights violations. In the biting editorial presented here, he invited the president, for the good of the country, to board a plane and leave. Soon after the publication of this bold piece, four members of the Dominican military stopped Martínez as he drove down a Santo Domingo street and shot him at close range. The crime went unpunished, as did all the crimes of the Twelve Years, until Balaguer left office. Then a new inquiry began, which led to the trial and conviction in 2000 of four gunmen, including one of Balaguer's generals. It was the first conviction for any of the crimes committed during the Twelve Years and the first time in Dominican history that a high-ranking military officer was brought to justice for murder. The ringleader received the maximum thirty-year prison sentence, but Balaguer himself was not subpoenaed, nor were any of the top four generals, known as "the Uncontrollables," who served him. This despite the fact that Balaguer had already admitted he knew who the killers were in his 1988 book* Memories of a Courtesan in the "Era of Trujillo," *which included a blank page to be filled in after his death with details of the Martínez murder. (Like much else about Balaguer's Twelve Years, that page remains unwritten.)*

Why Not, Dr. Balaguer?

Mr. President of the Republic, since you now prevent an artist of the prestige and moral quality of Silvano Lora from living in his homeland, since you now send Dominicans into foreign exile to please yourself or for political gains, I am going to permit myself to make certain recommendations to you.[1] I hope that, above all, you will meditate on the last of them.

Because you have said, and you seem to be certain, that in this government corruption stops at the door of your office, why not kick all the corrupt ones out of the Dominican Republic?

Because there is here a galloping inflation of delinquents without uniforms and, because of you, also in uniform, why not order the thugs [*calies*] of the regime to be arrested and put them on an airplane?

Why not tell the half-breeds who run the airport not to arrest those who carry one or two marijuana cigarettes, but instead arrest the fat wise guys in the drug traffic?

Why not send into exile those who receive commissions to negotiate contracts that give away our riches to multinational corporations?

Why not put on a boat the big landholders, those who prevent their country from leaving behind underdevelopment and the situation of collective misery that goes with it?

Why not put on the same boat those in the city who are the ideological support of those land barons?

And also those who are their armed backing: those who beat, imprison, and torture peasants who fight for their rights.

Because you are so close to the *norteamericanos*, why not ask them to send an aircraft carrier here to take away the numerous thugs who live on the people's labor? In case your friendship with the United States is even closer than we suspected, why not ask the Pentagon for a rocket of the latest model with the scientific objective of creating a colony of thugs on the Moon?

Why not remove from the sight of honorable Dominicans, who are the majority, all the deadbeats in this government who get paid without working?

Why not, to sum it all up, deposit in a toilet bowl first the irresponsible functionaries who act like contemporary Fouchés and in the hour of need don't show their faces?[2]

And my final recommendation:

If it is inevitable that this situation will continue, if it is impossible to avoid undignified and miserable deeds such as took place last Sunday at the airport, why, Dr. Balaguer, don't you decide to board the airplane or boat and disappear once and for all from this country along with the others I have previously mentioned?

Translated by Eric Paul Roorda.

Notes

1. Silvano Lora (1931–2003) was a Dominican painter who gained international fame as part of the *arte povera* (poor art) movement of the late 1960s, which used common materials and found objects to make political statements. Known as the "Quixote of Dominican Culture," his focus on human suffering and the struggle against oppression got him into trouble with the Balaguer regime, which forced him into exile by refusing him reentry at the Santo Domingo airport just before Martínez composed this piece.

2. Joseph Fouché (1759–1820) led a long career of notorious cruelty and cunning, surviving throughout the period of the French Revolution and Empire. As a Jacobin revolutionary, he led the de-Christianization campaign that ransacked churches; he then earned the sobriquet "The Executioner of Lyons" for the slaughters he ordered there. As Napoleon's minister of police, his agents were ubiquitous. His actions reflected his motto: "Terror, salutary terror."

Dominican, Cut the Cane!

State Sugar Council

The economy of the Dominican Republic surged in the early 1970s, with the annual rate of growth above 9 percent during that half decade. Joaquín Balaguer's policies of opening the country to foreign investment in the sectors of tourism and manufacturing accounted in part for what some referred to as the "Dominican Miracle." But a high price for sugar on the international market greatly benefited the economy during the heart of Balaguer's "Twelve Years" period (1966–1978). During the 1973 harvest season, the Balaguer government's State Sugar Council pushed for a record harvest of Dominican sugarcane. This was in order to take full advantage of surging sugar futures prices, which would soon reach their historic high of 65.2 cents per pound in November 1974. This selection is representative of a series of full-page advertisements the government published in the most widely circulated Dominican publications, exhorting citizens to overcome their traditional disdain for cutting cane and to take to the field in a vigorous demonstration of patriotism. (Fidel Castro mounted a similar sugar harvest campaign around the same time.) In 1985, the world price for sugar futures fell to 2.35 cents per pound, its all-time low. The economic hard times brought on by low sugar prices spelled doom for the Revolutionary Party, which took power in 1986 when Balaguer's "Twelve Years" ended. At the same time, longing on the part of the Dominican electorate for the good old days of sugar prosperity in the 1970s helped to propel Balaguer back into office in 1986.

State Sugar Council

The Dominican feels himself attracted to the cane harvest, inspired by President Balaguer's sugar policy.

Each day that passes more Dominican arms are dedicated to the cutting of the cane, because the State Sugar Council gives its workers better social conditions.

Dominican, cut the cane of your country!

Translated by Eric Paul Roorda.

The Blind Caudillo

Anonymous

Facing pressure from President Jimmy Carter (1924–), Balaguer permitted the 1978 electoral count to proceed, having suspended it when the poll numbers began to run against him on the night of the May election. As a result, the Dominican Revolutionary Party (PRD) won its first election since Juan Bosch's victory in 1962. But the PRD succumbed to corruption and inefficiency during its two terms in power, from 1978 to 1986. Both of the PRD presidents during that time ended their tenure in shame and failure; one committed suicide, and the other was indicted on corruption charges. Bread riots and strikes disrupted life in the cities at intervals while the PRD was in control, pitting police against dispossessed city dwellers in scenes reminiscent of the worst days of the 1965 revolt. Hoping for a return to relative stability, anxious voters brought Balaguer back to the Presidential Palace in 1986, and he rewarded them with a campaign of civic improvements.

Balaguer traveled around the country to inaugurate public works in person, associating himself with the new infrastructure in the minds of many citizens. His most ambitious construction project, the monumental "Columbus Lighthouse," hearkened back to his political origins in the Trujillo regime, when the idea was hatched of building a giant recumbent cross near Santo Domingo. The Great Depression killed the campaign in the late 1930s, but not before a panel of famous architects chose a design, which appeared in publications and postage stamps around Latin America for several years. The lighthouse was envisioned as a final resting place for the reputed remains of Columbus, which had resided in the Santo Domingo cathedral, and as a symbol of unity among the nations of the Americas. The project drew criticism for many reasons, including that it required the destruction of the entire Las Americas neighborhood and diverted funds that could be better spent in other areas in need of development in the Dominican Republic, such as medical care, education, electricity, and water systems. Despite being a waste of government money, the Faro de Colón opened before the 1992 quincentennial of the Great Navigator's first voyage to the Americas, which Balaguer hoped would stimulate tourism.

Balaguer had won another term in office in 1990, defeating Juan Bosch again, but tainted electoral returns elicited widespread protests. The vaunted five-hundredth anniversary of Columbus, preceded by a cleanliness campaign, the construction of a cruise ship terminal in the port of Santo Domingo, and general refurbishing of the city's Colonial Zone, was a flop. The wave of tourists failed to materialize. The giant Columbus Lighthouse, designed to project an illuminated cross into the night skies, operated sporadically. It drained power from the weak electrical grid and proved to be subject to blackouts, and seemed to mirror the dark prospects for Balaguer's reelection in 1994. Nevertheless, he clung to power tenaciously, manipulating the poll that year in ways even more blatant and widespread than he had done in the discredited 1990 election, according to an international election observation team led by the former president Jimmy Carter, whose intervention in the election of 1978 had persuaded Balaguer to step down then.

Resisting international pressure, this time Balaguer refused to yield to the apparent winner, the very popular PRD candidate Francisco Peña Gómez. The Balaguer camp charged that Peña Gómez, with his dark complexion and Haitian parentage, was in league with Haitians who wanted to reunite the island. In the wake of the stolen election, to stave off international criticism Balaguer offered a compromise called the Pact for Democracy. He agreed to halve his term in office to two years and allow a special election for a new president in 1996. Almost ninety years old and nearly completely blind by then, he was not quite through with politics yet. He abandoned his own party's nominee in 1996, throwing his weight behind Leonel Fernández (1953–), the centrist leader of the Party of Dominican Liberation, which Juan Bosch had formed in the 1970s. With the votes of many of the Balaguer faithful, Leonel Fernández won a narrow runoff election in 1996 amid sporadic violence. The outcome denied Peña Gómez and the PRD the presidency once more and assured Balaguer's own continued influence on national politics for another four years. The Fernández administration subsequently left the former president off the list of those subpoenaed in the case of Orlando Martínez when it reopened his case in 1997.

After running for president one more time in 2000, Balaguer died in 2002 at ninety-five. He remains a highly controversial and divisive figure in the Dominican Republic today. Many Dominicans excoriate his subversion of democracy and the violence and repression of "the Twelve Years." Many others revere him for different, contrasting reasons: for overseeing the transition from Trujillo's totalitarian state to the democratic republic of the present; for perpetuating important aspects of Trujillismo; and for his extensive public works projects, as reflected on an internet website devoted to his memory, which contains this page.

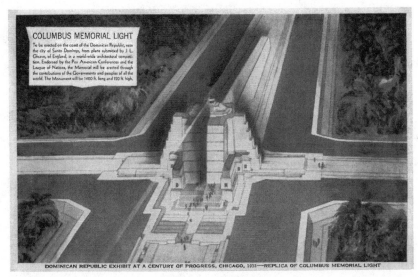

COLUMBUS MEMORIAL LIGHT

To be erected on the coast of the Dominican Republic, near the city of Santo Domingo, from plans submitted by J. L. Gleave, of England, in a world-wide architectural competition. Endorsed by the Pan American Conferences and the League of Nations, the Memorial will be erected through the contributions of the Governments and peoples of all the world. The Monument will be 1400 ft. long and 120 ft. high.

DOMINICAN REPUBLIC EXHIBIT AT A CENTURY OF PROGRESS, CHICAGO, 1933—REPLICA OF COLUMBUS MEMORIAL LIGHT

The Columbus Lighthouse, pushed by the Dominican government for decades, finally took shape in time for the five-hundredth anniversary of the Admiral's landfall in 1992, using the same design as this model, which was first exhibited in 1933 at the Chicago "Century of Progress" World's Fair. "Columbus Memorial Light," photographer unknown, color postcard, 1933. Courtesy of the Roorda/Doyle Collection.

His Works of Government

On this page we would like to present a mosaic of the visionary work in material infrastructure with which Dr. Joaquín Balaguer endowed the Dominican Republic.

We exhibit here a minimal or representative number of [his] works, all of which we have not included because of space limitations, which in their totality constitute a legacy to be evaluated and valued by future generations and by posterity. . . .

The Columbus Lighthouse
Hoyo de Chulín [sprawling apartment project]
Juan Pablo Duarte Olympic Center [built to host the 1974 Central
    American and Caribbean Games]
National Aquarium
Jiguey-Aguacate Prison
Central Cibao Aqueduct
Botanical Garden and Zoo
Santiago Palace of Justice

Joaquín Balaguer constructed scores of public works during his terms in office from 1966 to 1978 and again from 1986 to 1996. Photos of the most prominent of them from the former period are seen on the cover of an LP of political merengues extolling Balaguer and his Reform Party. Cover of *Lucía*, named for a song Balaguer wrote c. 1929, campaign album for the Partido Reformista, c. 1978. Courtesy of the Roorda/Doyle Collection.

Irrigation Canals
Plaza of Health [hospital]
Santiago Sports Palace
Cathedral of La Vega
Basilica of Higüey
Avenue of the Port and Bartholomew Columbus Marine Plaza [cruise
    ship terminal on the Ozama River]
Puerto Plata Mountain Cable Car
North Seaview Park [in Santo Domingo]
Regional Theater of the Cibao
International Airport [located east of the capital, now named Francisco
    Peña Gómez International Airport!]
National Library
Neighborhood Streets

Translated by Eric Paul Roorda.

The "Eat Alones" of the Liberation Party

Andrés L. Mateo

Leonel Fernández's victory in the election of 1996 brought the Party of Dominican Liberation (PLD) to power for the first time, yet in the eyes of some there was little change from the partisan politics of Balaguer's Reform Party. The PLD faced charges to that effect, as is reflected in this essay by the Dominican historian and social critic Andrés L. Mateo on the genesis and runaway success of the term of popular opprobrium comesolos *(eat alones) as a moniker for the PLD. This anecdote reveals how important food sharing is for Dominicans; it also provides a taste of the remarkably creative popular oral culture in the country.*

Comesolos: *A Reading*

The impact of the term "comesolos"—the eat alones—in the last electoral campaign is indisputable. The term was converted into a powerful weapon of persuasion, and a very effective sobriquet. It is important to explain the genesis of this expression, and how it operated in the popular imagination.

The birth of the epithet "comesolos" in the political arena was a product of the Reformist Party cadres' reaction to the system of distribution of the food handouts that was adopted by the Party of Dominican Liberation [PLD]. Providing these food handouts, of course, had been a signature activity of the Balaguer regime. This term did not arise through marketing; it was not part of a political campaign strategy, and notwithstanding the fact that in the end it was used in a television commercial, its power lay in its popular conception.

I have studied philologically the gestation of this popular label. The PLD thinks that the expression was unfair, and they thought that the Reformistas invented it to refer to personnel ousters in the administrative bureaucracy. To be fair, the PLD did not fire many Reformistas from state posts. Rather, the term emerged because of a contradiction between a form of populist Reformista political clientelism that the PLD wanted to adopt, and the closed structure of the party in practice.

A veteran Reformist militant Lluberes, who calls himself an "expert in handouts," explains the origin of the term "comesolos": "The PLDistas wanted to reorganize the distribution of the handouts in the barrios, and ordered their committees to update the rosters of poor recipients. Their idea was to appropriate the distribution system. Yet once in the barrios, they quickly realized that their tactics would have to change, because their new system did not work, and the lists would have to remain in the hands of the PLD party militants. Some of those in charge of making the handouts had gotten a job in the new government, and handed out the bags at night, so they were called *cocuyos* [fireflies]. But for Balaguer the only thing that was red—Reformista—was the handout; it was organized in the light of day, regardless of who the militants were."

Lluberes then took me to a Reformista center so that a guy named Papito could tell me a story. Papito told me that the nickname "comesolo" was born because a PLD activist brought a bag of food home to his house that his wife received happily. But after a short time, the PLDista noticed that Papito's house did not appear on the list, and someone came to take the bag that had been allocated by mistake. Lluberes says that he was there, and heard Papito say for the first time: "Those guys—the PLD—what they want is to eat alone." The term took off like wildfire in the barrio, and became at first a timid expression of resentment which those excluded from handout distribution would use more and more frequently as a disparaging term against the new regime of Leonel Fernández.

But according to Lluberes the establishment of "Comesolos" as the definitive party insult was during the first Three Kings' Day [January 6, the day Christmas gifts are presented in Latin America] that the PLD government gave out gifts. The PLD allocations had been organized in such a way that each person had been assigned a ticket allocated by the neighborhood PLD committees to the party members. The ticket also assigned a time when children were supposed to be taken to collect their presents. The traditional Balaguerista event had been a degrading free-for-all. Poor people from the barrios slept outside on the sidewalk the night before at the door of Balaguer's residence. This form of mocking the poor was part of the messianic sensibility of Balaguer's regime, in which only on condition of being ready to be beaten and pummeled with a gun butt could the poor receive their toys, and the PLDistas, wishing to avoid this, tried to avoid this spectacle with improved organization.

Notwithstanding this handout's resemblance to previous ones, the majority of those who struggled to get toys for their kids (or get them to sell them later) did not have vouchers. Lluberes says that he has never seen so many people angry, and that right then and there the expression "come-solos" spread as people adopted it spontaneously. Even Lluberes, a party stalwart, became a target of this term of abuse. When Lluberes arrived at the place where the toys were allocated, Lluberes was asked for a voucher, which in fact no one had received, and when people pushed him out of the line, they yelled "Comesolos, comesolos"!

This etymology of the expression explains its semantic meaning, but it cannot explain its significance for the PLD once it had a semiotic meaning. The two modes together—the semantic and the semiotic—would give shape to the epithet, but only the PLD would be identified by it.

The nickname is a form of denomination that starts by unifying an attribute (positive or negative) with the object of discourse, and that term makes it unnecessary to name the word itself. On hearing the term, the reader or the listener knows what it refers to.

Translated by Lauren Derby.

The Election of 2000

Central Election Commission

Dominican voters in 2000 had to return to their places of birth to take part in the election, in which three candidates ran, including Joaquín Balaguer. For weeks in advance they received elaborate instructions, published in the newspapers and on posters, about how to cast their ballots on election day. Lines at the polling places turned out to be serpentine on May 16, which was fiercely hot. Yet despite the complications, voters turned out in droves—women in the morning, many of them carrying umbrellas against the sun, and men in the afternoon, as prescribed, to wait hours for their chance to go through the sixteen steps of preparing and submitting their ballot. The result was an upset victory for the Dominican Revolutionary Party, and with it the definitive end of the Balaguer era.

Steps to Vote

1. To register: women will have to arrive at their polling places, or "electoral colleges," between 6:30 and 8:30 am and men from 1 to 3 pm.
2. You will form a line in each shift.
3. You will hand your national identification card to the first official.
4. The official will verify that you are on the definitive list of voters and register you in the special roster of participants.
5. After you have been noted in the register, they will return your ID to you.
6. At the end of registrations in each shift, the roster will be closed, with a line drawn across it.
7. Remain in line until the beginning of the voting. The first to be registered will be the first to vote.
8. The women vote from 8:30 am until 1 pm, the men from 3:30 until 6:00 pm, or in each shift until everyone on the registration roster has voted.
9. Enter the voting area with your ID in hand.

10. We will give you a ballot that is stamped and signed. Proceed to the voting booth.
11. Mark inside the box of your favored party, never outside, and you can do so with a cross, a horizontal or vertical line, or an X.
12. After marking it, fold the ballot over twice so it cannot be seen, leaving the stamp and signature on the outside.
13. Deposit the ballot in the box.
14. Sign your name on your stamp and put your fingerprint on the definitive list of voters.
15. Dip your fingertip in the dye and they will return your ID to you.
16. And now depart the polling place.

Voting is easy at an electoral college!
The country is counting on your vote.
Central Election Board

Translated by Eric Paul Roorda.

The Sour Taste of US-Dominican Sugar Policy

Matt Peterson

United States corporations continue to play a major role in the production of Dominican sugar, most of which finds its way to the lucrative American market, whose annual consumption amounts to more than sixty-five pounds per person. Gaining and maintaining a quota of the US sugar market was an obsessive foreign policy goal for both Rafael Trujillo and Joaquín Balaguer. Sugar diplomacy was a priority for Leonel Fernández, as it will be for his successors, beginning with Danilo Medina, who took office in 2012. This analysis cogently explains this complicated relationship.

For people in the Dominican Republic identified as Haitian, many of them sugar workers, the situation has deteriorated further since 2009, when this article appeared. The Dominican Constitution of 2010 invalidated the citizenship of everyone born in the country to parents from Haiti, all of whom are considered to be "in transit" according to immigration law. A Supreme Court ruling in October 2013 ordered a review of all birth certificates going back to 1929, in order to identify this population and strip them of their citizenship rights as native-born Dominicans. They lose government health care and public schooling, and face deportation to Haiti, where most of them have never been.

Sugar: An Unfair Fight for American Market Access

Unlike [the case of] crops such as corn and cotton, American support for sugar does not take the traditional form of direct subsidy payments to farmers. Rather, the government establishes a minimum price for domestic sugar by offering low-cost loans to producers, payable in sugar on default, and by tightly restricting the flow of sugar into the United States through a combination of high tariffs and import quotas. The result is a domestic price for sugar that is typically double the world price. Not only do American consumers pay considerably more for their sugar, transferring their wealth into the hands of highly profitable agribusinesses, but those same businesses are encouraged to overproduce and sell the excess to other countries, thereby putting downward pressure on the world price. . . .

378

The Dominican Republic has long benefited from the highest U.S. import quota for sugar. In fact, almost all Dominican sugar goes to the United States. The Dominican sugar industry is also struggling. . . . Production costs are relatively high, and production volumes have fallen from their peak of 1.2 million tons in 1982 to just over 500,000 tons in 2008.

Dominican sugar survives largely by the grace of the American taxpayer, since its exports to the United States are purchased at the inflated U.S. domestic price rather than the deflated world price. This is perhaps unsurprising given that one of the biggest Dominican sugar companies is owned by the Florida-based Fanjul family who also own Flo-Sun and its Domino subsidiary. The Fanjuls happen to be major political donors—to the tune of $650,000 in 2008.

Unfortunately, the corporate welfare for producers in the Dominican Republic does not trickle down to the laborers who are the backbone of the industry. Sugar cane cutters there earn about $2.50 for each ton of hand-cut sugar cane; the young can cut as much as three tons per day, but the elderly and infirm often struggle to cut even one. Working twelve-hour days or longer, many live in company shantytowns known as *bateyes*, without sewage systems, running water, and electricity.

Almost all are undocumented Haitians despite having lived in the country for decades or having been born there—cane cutters are thus continually under threat of arbitrary arrest and deportation. They seek out this misery to avoid an even worse fate in Haiti, where last year [2008] 46 percent of the population was undernourished and 78 percent survived on less than what $2 could buy daily in the United States in 2005. . . .

The Link between Trade and Labor Standards

Here, then, is the multifaceted problem of American agriculture support. First, it plays favorites among international corporations, arbitrarily handing a lifeline to Dominican sugar. . . . Second, in the Dominican Republic, and other countries enabled by U.S. agricultural policy, the failure to include meaningful labor standards in trade agreements contributes to massive abuse of labor rights. Third, the creation of an inflated and exclusive U.S. internal market, and the subsequent deflation of the world market, condemns hundreds of thousands of [sugar workers worldwide] to needless poverty.

Leonel, Fidel, and Barack

Leonel Fernández, Fidel Castro, and Barack Obama

The crossroads election of 2000 returned the Revolutionary Party to power, but the struggles of the administration of President Hipólito Mejía (1941–) after his underdog victory stoked public indignation against him in the run-up to the 2004 contest. Worst among these were the problems of runaway inflation and chronic electrical shortages, with resulting blackouts. The "White Party" took the blame as well for deteriorating public safety, especially in the poorest neighborhoods of the capital and other large cities, where many of its supporters lived. With the "Whites" (the Revolutionary Party) under a cloud and the ranks of the "Reds" (the Reform Party) having thinned since the death of its leader, Joaquín Balaguer, the "Purples" of the Party of Dominican Liberation (PLD) swept to a landslide victory in May 2004. The popular Leonel Fernández, universally known simply as "Leonel," reprised his successful 1996 campaign strategy of taking centrist positions and courting the support of Dominicans in the United States, who were permitted to vote for president while living abroad. Leonel himself had grown up in the Upper West Side of Manhattan, giving him the ability to connect with the Dominican diaspora or "Dominican-yorks" on a personal level. Winning an unprecedented 57 percent of the vote, he took the oath of office for the second time in August 2004. His return to the presidency marked the third consecutive peaceful, transparent electoral process and transition of federal power in the Dominican Republic. His reelection in 2008 further demonstrated the vitality of Dominican democracy in the post-Balaguer era.

As president, many of Leonel's signature achievements have been in the field of international diplomacy, where he has helped to facilitate the settlements of several regional disputes, including a peaceful resolution to the constitutional crisis in Honduras in 2009. He also confronted the shattered Dominican economy, with less success. But he will probably best be remembered for building the Santo Domingo subway, the first in the Caribbean, an apt symbol of a highly urban vision of progress, yet one that has left the rural classes in the dust.

In the arena of foreign relations, Leonel has been congenial to both sides of the dominant Latin American regional alignment, which pits the United States against an informal coalition of nations opposed to American domination. The first of this group was the Cuba of Fidel Castro, whose half century of defiance of the United States has inspired other national leaders to take their states in the same direction, most notably and volubly President Hugo Chávez (1954–2013) of Venezuela. In accordance with this neutral stance, Leonel took to the road. In March 2009 he traveled to Havana, where he paid a visit to the elderly Castro, and in July 2010 he went to Washington, where he met with President Barack Obama. The first selection here is Castro's own report of his time spent with Leonel, as posted in English on the Cuban Revolutionary Youth website Juventud Rebelde. The second is the transcript of a "photo opportunity" with Leonel and Obama at which each made brief remarks alluding to the conversation they had just finished and indicated their differing priorities for the bilateral relationship between the Dominican Republic and the United States.

My Meeting with Leonel Fernández of the Dominican Republic

I had met him in the Dominican Republic when he was elected for the first time as president [in 1996]. He was especially courteous to me. He spoke of his first efforts to increase the capacity for generating electricity with much less consumption of fuel oil, whose prices were rapidly growing.

Nobody handed him the job on a platter; he got there through a kind of process of natural selection by virtue of which he went up the political ladder while historical events were unfolding.

He is the son of a Dominican woman who had emigrated, like many of her compatriots, to the United States, and he was taken along with his brother to New York City, where he learned how to read and write.

He was lucky in that his mother would closely follow the problems in their homeland and she communicated revolutionary opinions and criteria to him that would condition him for the new times the Dominican people were living through.

He arrived at his own criteria [in a] different [way] from me, but they determined his attitude in regard to situations that were similar [to] and at the same time very different from those I had gone through in Cuba. . . .

Where the conversation with Leonel acquires its greatest dimension is when he deals with the subject of the cost of the current crisis. Starting with that instant, his mind doesn't stop reasoning for a minute, expressing each one of the main chapters in the cost of the current crisis with exact figures. . . .

He doesn't even pause to go on explaining about what Bush spent on the war in Iraq, added to the annual deficit in the budget of that country, which he calculates one after another, until next March 19th; he immediately adds Bush's bailout plan; and he follows this with the Obama bailout plan and so on.

In this case, he limits himself to what the crisis is costing the United States. [Then] he begins calculations of how much this is costing the European countries in turn, first those in the Eurozone supported by the European Central Bank, and then all the countries in eastern Europe, and finally Great Britain and Sweden.

Not missing a beat, Leonel goes on to review the costs to [the] countries in the rest of the world.

He complains of the GDP of the United States and other nations. He adds them all up. He calculates the deficits proposed in each one of them. He goes on to calculate the loans taken on by the banks to sustain the production of each of the producing companies, the times money deposited in the banks is loaned, the grand totals of loans, generators of toxic derivatives, and the escalation to figures that equal hundreds of trillions of dollars.

Leonel states that financial speculation rules everywhere.

"Persons who do not produce are speculating."

"One person sells oil he doesn't produce and another person buys oil he doesn't intend to consume."

"The same is happening with food."

"And so it goes with everything."

The mortgage becomes a stock that is bought and sold on the market, he continues, without the homeowner knowing about it. He could lose his home because of an operation that is carried out in some faraway country.

"Neoliberalism is collapsing on its own."

"Returning to Keynesian principles does not solve the current crisis."

"That implies looking for new ideas."

Leonel knows that the figures are mind-boggling; he is concerned about the necessity for such sums to be understood, even though they appear absurd, and he promises to go on supplying data.

I would define Leonel's thesis just as he sees things: capitalism is a system that oozes poisonous toxins through every single pore.

With the passion heard in his voice, I deduce that the Yankees will curse the arithmetic taught to Leonel in New York when he was learning to read and write. . . .

Fidel Castro Ruz

Obama Holds Joint Media Availability with Leonel Fernández
of the Dominican Republic

July 12, 2010

OBAMA: Hello, everybody. Good afternoon.

President Fernández and I just had an excellent conversation. We first met and I think forged a good working relationship and friendship at the Summit of the Americas last year, and we have built on that relationship, as have our respective administrations on a whole host of issues.

We had a wide-ranging discussion. One of the first messages I wanted to deliver was my appreciation for the role that the Dominican Republic played in helping the international community respond to the crisis in Haiti after the devastating earthquake there. And I think that the Dominican Republic's role, President Fernández's role in particular, in helping to facilitate a rapid response was extraordinarily important. It saved lives. And it continues as we look at how we can reconstruct and rebuild in Haiti in a way that is good, not only for the people of Haiti but also good for the region as a whole.

That was just one example of the leadership that President Fernández has shown. He and his government have been extremely helpful in resolving the political crisis that existed in Honduras, and we discussed ways that we can manage that process so that Honduras can once again be fully integrated into the regional groupings and organizations in a way that is respectful of democracy. We coordinated closely between our two countries on that issue.

We discussed the critical issue of drug trafficking and crime, and how that has the potential to be destabilizing throughout the region. And we have already seen great cooperation between our countries through the Caribbean Basin Security Initiative, but more needs to be done. And so President Fernández and I discussed how we can do a better job coordinating through multinational groupings to address what is a scourge on so many countries. And that involves us dealing both with the supply side of the equation, but also the demand side. . . .

We talked about how, working together, we can expand trade opportunities, commercial opportunities, business opportunities. One area that I expressed to the president that is of particular interest to me is clean energy . . . sugarcane-based ethanol, the possibilities of real energy independence in the region, I think those same opportunities exist for the Dominican Republic. President Fernández and I discussed how we can work more closely together around energy security issues, something that my administration is very interested in partnering with Central American, Latin American countries to work on.

So the main message I have to the people of the Dominican Republic is thank you for your friendship. I think the American people appreciate greatly the bonds between our two countries, bonds that express themselves, obviously, in an extraordinary Dominican population—Dominican American population that we have here in this country. And, obviously, I've got to note that we've got some pretty good baseball players here from the Dominican Republic.

[*laughter*] . . .

FERNÁNDEZ: Thank you so much. Well, first of all, I would like to thank President Obama for his kind invitation to come here to the White House and speak on issues that are of mutual interest for the US government and for the Dominican Republic.

As the president has indicated, we have agreed on several issues, some bilateral issues for the US and the Dominican Republic and also on regional issues.

We do appreciate, Mr. President, that with all you have on your agenda, with all the international issues, with all the crises, with the economic situation that's affecting [so many countries] worldwide, you have put on your agenda the Caribbean, Latin America, and the Dominican Republic. I think this is evidence that you do have an interest for the region and the problems that affect not only the Dominican Republic, but the region as a whole.

As you have indicated, one of our major concerns has to do with drug trafficking, with transnational crime, all the violence related to all these criminal activities. I think that the Caribbean Basin Security Initiative has been the right path forward. I commend you for that, Mr. President. And I think now we should move into a more collaborative environment with the other Caribbean nations, Central America, and Mexico. It is only by coordinating our efforts that we can really defeat this epidemic that has become overwhelming to all of our countries. Whatever we can do, from the supply side, as you said, or the demand side, will be of great significance to the safety and security of our people.

Other issues, like you said, related to clean energy, we're working on that in the Dominican Republic, with wind energy and with the potential production of ethanol in our country.

We'll move on also with trade. We have a free trade agreement between both of our countries, [from] which we have not benefited fully because of the global financial crisis and how it has affected trade. But we can look into the future, hopefully, and we will increase our trade activities and more investments coming from the US into the Dominican Republic.

So once again, Mr. President, I thank you for your friendship. I thank you for your vision, for your leadership, and for your commitment to the region and the Dominican Republic.

Transcribed by Eric Paul Roorda.

IX

Religious Practices

The remaining parts of this anthology treat the subjects of religion, popular culture, and immigration, mainly from contemporary perspectives.

Most Dominicans define themselves as Catholics and contend that Vodú is practiced only by Haitians, a vision belied by the anthropological work on popular religion, which demonstrates a porous dividing line for adepts between Catholicism and Vodú in both religious practice and belief on the ground. Like the population itself, Dominican religious forms are an amalgam of influences drawn from a diverse range of sources. Beliefs and rituals originating in Europe, in Africa, and on the island of Hispaniola itself flow together in the spiritual life of the Dominican Republic. The paucity of Catholic priests in the interior meant that for centuries the lay brotherhoods or *cofradias* provided the sinews of Catholic faith through patron saint festivals and pilgrimages, which highlighted the presence of popular religious features, from miraculous sightings to rites of healing and purification. The Catholicism of early modern Spain, the gods of the Kongo people of Central Africa, and the heroic legends of Taíno tribal leaders who resisted the invasion of their land are some of the elements to be found in the religious practices of the Quisqueyans.

Mercedes

Flérida de Nolasco

Two representations of the Catholic Virgin Mary share the role of religious patroness of the Dominican Republic: Our Lady of Mercy, or Mercedes, and Our Lady of High Grace, or Altagracia. Mercedes is the older of the two, having first appeared in the year 1218 to St. Peter Nolasco, who was inspired to establish the Mercedarian Order of monks as a result of his encounter. But it was her supposed appearance in March 1495 to the troops of Columbus at the height of the Battle of Vega Real that made her a venerated figure among the colonizers. This battle was the culmination of the rebellion led by Taíno cacique Caonabo, which intensified after his capture by the Spanish, under the leadership of cacique Guarionex. Guarionex's army of several thousand warriors met a force of 200 Spanish soldiers, reinforced by their Taíno allies under the cacique Guacanagari, at a small promontory called Santo Cerro. On this hill, which overlooks the "Royal Plain" or Vega Real, Columbus made a stand and was encircled by his enemies. Facing defeat, his men were encouraged when Our Lady of Mercedes appeared above a cross their commander had planted in the ground. The Taínos tried to burn the cross, but it would not ignite. The inspired Spanish broke out from Santo Cerro and routed their opponents, capturing Guarionex and extracting from him a promise of complete capitulation. The unburned cross became an object of veneration, and Our Lady of Mercedes became the first patroness of the Dominican Republic. Her standing was confirmed in 1615 when a violent earthquake and a long series of aftershocks hit Santo Domingo and the city's survival was credited to the public's prayers to her.

The legend and pilgrimage site of Santo Cerro is more fully explored in this account by the pioneer folklorist Flérida de Nolasco (1891–1976).

Traditional Devotions

While in the small towns the traditional customs have been preserved, in the capital and the other cities of relative importance they are being forgotten, to the point that frequently nothing remains of them except the memory. Nevertheless, we still have in our capital a sector that goes on being faithful to the traditional customs. That is the religious sector. The devotions that at present are practiced in this capital are the same that were observed in the earliest times of the Colony. The continuity of the traditional devotions—compact, integral, and unanimous—is, in these days, an unmistakable seal of popular approval; and it is a tie that binds, a knot that unites the Dominican people in a single spirit; a force and stimulus that shakes and awakens the shattered national character with powerful efficiency.

The chronicler Alcocer says: "In the Convent of the Sisters of Mercy there is a *miraculous* sacred image of Our Lady of Mercy, to which the city is very devoted, and which is venerated on the high altar with curtains drawn across it, and it is uncovered on various occasions, at which time the faithful offer their devotions."

At the same time we hear of the great devotion of the Dominican people to the Virgin of Mercy—to the same image that still graces her chapel in the Cathedral—and of the countless and special favors granted through her intercession, from the prolix Tirso de Molina,[1] who assures us that it was the first image of Our Lady that arrived in the Indies. And from that time until the present day, it has been honored with solemn rituals and taken on processions of public and private veneration. The altarpiece where it is located is covered in silver ex voto offerings.

In the Chapel separated from the body of the church was what was called the School of Christ, with the title of Our Lady of Peace, and in it a religious society was established to attend to the Sacred Burial rites held on Good Friday. The Sacred Burial continues to this day. . . .

Nothing, not [even] those happenings most opposed to traditional sentiments, has been able to alter this devotion. . . .

Many miracles are attributed to the historic image of Our Lady of the Rosary, and its devotees take it on processions twice a year. Today the venerated image that Dominicans honored with their devotions is missing from the altar of its chapel, and we see now an image of modern manufacture as a substitute for the historic image of the Virgin, which could not have been much less ancient than that of Our Lady of Mercy. What a shame that such a worthwhile image would be disparaged, which not only represented for us an incomparable history of love and sacrifice but also, like all works of the colonial period that have been preserved, had an intrinsic artistic value. . . .

Overall, worship of the Virgin Mary in the form of Our Lady of High Grace, goes as far back in the Capital as it does in Higüey, where the oldest religious Sanctuary in the Americas is venerated.

The Sanctuary of Santo Cerro

At the foot of the cross that he himself had planted, the Great Admiral is said to have expressed his joy in a speech; and he recommended in his testament that a Chapel be erected on the same spot where he had invoked the Holy Trinity. It is the Sanctuary of Holy Hill [Santo Cerro].

Crowning the hill is the Sanctuary. From a distance, Holy Hill seems suspended between the sky and the woods. From the summit of the Hill the view commands the entire valley, and is still the most beautiful that eyes can see in all of the Indies. The sky, on crystal clear days, is a mirror reflecting the grandeur of God; and on the hillside below, giant trees rise straight up until they graze our feet, seeming like they want to take flight to escape from the ground.

"Blessed be the mountains and the hills of the Lord, blessed all the plants of the earth!"

On contact with the True Cross, as they called it, miracles multiplied; and the story of so many marvels echoed in other places in the Americas and in Spain. Emperor Charles V himself wrote to the Pope giving him an account of the wonders effected through the medium of the Cross of Holy Hill, and he supplicated for papal authorization of the devotions of the faithful to the miraculous Cross.

A piece of it is venerated in the Sanctuary, kept inside a golden crucifix; and another piece of it is in our Cathedral, kept inside the cross of silver filigree, which . . . continues to give solace to the people in times of tribulation. . . .

In addition to the traditional devotion of the Holy Cross in the historic Sanctuary of Holy Hill; who does not go up there to implore for the favors of the Virgin of Mercy? The image that wakens the most spirited devotion is this ancient one, made of wood, which arrived in the earliest days of the Colony, as a memento of the legendary and unforgettable apparition.

Place of miracles and joy. It was there where in past centuries, redolent of incense, celestial canticles were heard, and where mysterious processions of fervent souls were seen to pass in the wee hours of the night, in the grand and impressive silence of the night, with burning candles that, as they were consumed, marked the road they traversed with warm drops of white and fragrant wax, like tears, that fell as they passed.

Later, men learned many things, they knew so many things about the land, that they forgot their dreams, and the beautiful mysteries fled forever. But the miracle of faith lives on.

Translated by Eric Paul Roorda.

Note

1. Tirso de Molina (1571–1648) was a Spanish monk of the Order of the Blessed Virgin Mary of Mercy who wrote dramas and poetry in the baroque style. He visited Santo Domingo between 1615 and 1617.

Altagracia

Anonymous

The cult of Nuestra Señora de Altagracia, Our Lady of High Grace, goes back almost as far as that of Mercedes. The physical artifact at its heart is a painting of the Holy Family produced by an anonymous hand in Spain sometime before 1500. The story of the painting, which depicts a Bethlehem manger scene, has several versions, one of which credits Alonso and Antonio de Trejo, Andalucian brothers reputed to have established the first sugar-producing facility in the New World, with ownership. The painting is said to have disappeared from their house, only to be found hanging in an orange tree, which became a sacred site. Another tale says that a young woman from a good family asked for a painting of the "Virgin of Altagracia," whom no one had ever heard of, but her father, wanting to oblige her, set out for Santo Domingo to look for such a thing. When he paused to pass the night in the little town of Higüey, an old man approached him with a rolled-up canvas, which he gave to the girl's father, saying it was what he was seeking. The picture on the canvas showed the Virgin Mary admiring the infant Jesus in the foreground, with Joseph hovering in the background. The next morning the old man and the painting had vanished, but the father found the artwork in an orange grove nearby, and brought it to his daughter. Whatever the painting's origins, Higüey became a major pilgrimage site, and celebrations for Altagracia on her feast day of January 21 spread across the colony, drawing devotees from as far as Haiti. Pope Pius XI crowned the miraculous image of Altagracia personally in 1920, and Pope John Paul II crowned her again on his visits to the Dominican Republic in 1979 and 1992. Now the nation's official patron saint and "The Queen and Protector of the Hearts of the Dominicans," the Virgin of Altagracia remains the most important official and popular national icon in Roman Catholic observance in the Dominican Republic today. This prayer is taken from a prayer card by an anonymous author.

Prayer to Our Lady of High Grace, Patroness of the Dominican People

Our Virgin and Mother of High Grace, receive our prayers that we offer to you this day. Moreover, to obtain better fruits from our petitions, we must remember these words of the Father: "Give and you shall receive."

What are we able to offer to this sweetest Mother? Sin makes us unworthy of you, my Mother; but your great mercy inspires our confidence, and we offer you all the good that there may be in our thoughts, words, and works, we are yours, and under your maternal protection we will stamp our works with the magnificent apostle of Love.

Yes, my Sweet Mother, we will publicize your goodness to show you the love of the mortals. How sweet it is to love and to feel loved by the beloved being! We believe that you, Virgin of Altagracia, Mother of the Dominican People, interest yourself in favor of your children and that your devotion is necessary to save us, because God does not grant a grace that does not pass through your most beautiful hands.

Grant us, therefore, Mother of love, your powerful intercession and support, and defend our Fatherland, bless our homes; make it so our families imitate the virtues of that Holy Family that your miraculous image represents, love of wife and of mother; love of husband and of father; love of child. You, beloved Virgin, will teach us to feel these loves so that for you Jesus reigns in our Fatherland, in our families, and in our hearts. Amen.

Translated by Eric Paul Roorda.

The Catholic Bishops Say No to the Dictator

The Five Bishops of the Dominican Republic

The Catholic Church supported the Trujillo regime for three decades. However, toward the end of his rule, when violence began to spill into the corridors of the Church to an extent that could not be ignored, the tide turned. This letter by the archbishop and bishops of the Dominican Republic forcefully states, in response to a request from the government, that they cannot give the title "Benefactor of the Church" to Rafael Trujillo. It was a remarkable act of resistance to the regime's violence, and sending it at the height of Trujillo's rule meant risking grave consequences.

To Dr. Joaquín Balaguer, President of the Republic,
and to the Members of His Cabinet . . .

6 February 1961
Your Excellency Mr. President and Honorable Secretaries of State,

We have the honor of referring to the important letter that Your Excellency and the members of the Cabinet directed to us last 16th of January, inviting us to give our support to the initiative in progress to grant the title of Benefactor of the Church of the Republic to the Generalísimo Dr. Rafael L. Trujillo Molina, Benefactor of the Patria and Father of the New Nation.

We have read and considered the proposal which Your Excellency expounds in the letter referred to with great interest. And we are honored by the recognition proffered by the Generalísimo Dr. Rafael L. Trujillo Molina for the "benefits, favors, and thanks that the Catholic Church has received in our country," as stated in your letter, for the care for the spiritual needs of our community of faithful. For this, the gratitude of the Clerics and the Catholic people is well known.

His Excellency the Metropolitan Archbishop of Santo Domingo, Monseñor Ricardo Pittini, has given testimony of this gratitude in many speeches and documents, as have also the members of the secular clergy and the faithful on the occasion of the construction and repair of buildings, or through concessions ordered to facilitate the spiritual mission of the church. You

Religious life was intertwined with political life during the Trujillo regime. In this 1950s photo, a Catholic monsignor blesses the new vapor lights installed in one of the many Trujillo Parks around the country, in this case in Moca, in front of a bust of "The Benefactor," mandatory for all such public spaces. Photographer unknown, black-and-white photograph, c. 1950. Courtesy of the Roorda/Doyle Collection.

Trujillo donated this statue of San Miguel (Saint Michael), a figure powerful in both Christianity and Vodú, to the Church of the Rosary in Moca in the 1950s. Photographer unknown, black-and-white photograph, c. 1950. Courtesy of the Roorda/Doyle Collection.

yourself recognize, in the letter to which we refer, that our gratitude has always been manifest.

You can be completely sure, Your Excellencies, that we privately and publicly give thanks for these "benefits, favors, and thanks" granted to the public good; since gratitude is the virtue of every Christian heart; and we will continue to demonstrate it in every way that is within the ambit of Our possibilities, and within the range of Our rights and duties.

Regarding the issue that You have requested, we must recognize the limit of Our power, however. This request surpasses Our jurisdiction, and thus we cannot grant or even support this initiative; but rather it could only be the Holy See that could evaluate granting titles of this nature.

Octavio A. Beras, Assistant Archbishop, Apostolic
Administrator of Santo Domingo
Hugo E. Polanco Brito, Bishop of Santiago
de los Caballeros
Francisco Panal, Titular Bishop of La Vega
Juan F. Pepen, Bishop of Altagracia
Tomas F. Reilly, Titular Bishop de Temisonio
and Prelate of San Juan de la Maguana

Translated by Lauren Derby.

Liberation Theology

Octavio A. Beras

Inspired by Vatican II, when the Latin American priesthood began to translate the Bible into a blueprint for social change, the Catholic Church made an about-face, shifting allegiance from the state to the poor. Far from the conciliatory role played by the Catholic Church during much of the Trujillo regime, this text offered a rallying cry for the Church to address the grave social ills facing the peasantry in the 1960s, from lack of access to land and credit to exorbitant rates of interest, issues that were pushing peasants into urban areas seeking jobs. The situation of the peasantry had barely changed since the death of Trujillo, as large landed properties had grown over time, fragmenting peasant lands to the extent that family subsistence was no longer possible for the majority. As a result the bishops began to speak out stridently in favor of land reform, which had been promised since the early 1960s. This declaration, which they issued in 1967, is an example of the new role of the church as a social advocate for the poor.

The Problem of the Dominican Peasantry

1. The basic aspiration of the Dominican peasantry is to be able to live free of ignorance and poverty, or cast in a positive light, to find the means to ensure a life worthy of all mankind including: a home, food, their children's education, etc. Hundreds of letters from all regions of the republic have been sent to the Literacy Programs conducted by the bishops, which prove that these are the goals of our peasantry.

2. The poverty in which hundreds of thousands of peasant families live is no longer accepted by them as if it were inevitable, which is their fate and thus faced with "religious" resignation, and certainly God's plan is that man submits the land to his control. The experience of the parish priests with our peasants, especially the youth, confirms that for us the recent words of the Pope[1] are worth repeating: in nations "in which the economy is almost exclusively agrarian, the poor are

overcome by anxiety: the peasants also have become conscious that they do not deserve their poverty."

3. Concretely the sources of the peasants' concerns are:
   a. *The lack of sufficient land* to maintain a *family in a dignified way*
   b. *The high interest rates of the short-term land rental contracts* that loom over many peasant families like a prophesy of gloom
   c. The uncertainty of property titles of small farms and consequently the *fear of eviction, although they have never lived anywhere else*
   d. The impossibility for the rural working class to find a *just living wage, notwithstanding minimum wage legislation*
   e. The *difficulties* faced by small farm owners or renters to *obtain on their own easy access to agricultural assistance, in terms of credit or technical help.*

4. The Dominican peasantry has come to realize that it must *unify* in order to better its economic situation and in order to publicly validate its rights and aspirations. When the peasant organizations are truly democratic, they do not inspire hatred as a motor of social change—which is certainly incompatible with the true spirit of Christ—nor do they deploy violence as an arm of social change. They are determined to have their rights and desires fulfilled within the law, even if they do hope that the law, adapting to the changing situation of Dominican society, is each day more just. Some of these organizations actually have an explicitly Christian inspiration.

5. The peasantry does not only want more land, more education and more work security; it wants above all to *be more*, which is to say, "it wants to participate even more in the responsibilities, outside of all oppression and situations that offend the dignity of man." They don't want to be given special favors or handouts, they want help developing themselves. In other words, they want to have an active role in the decisions that affect them.

The Church Response

6. The Bishops of the Dominican Republic support wholeheartedly the efforts of the peasantry to overcome the condition of poverty and ignorance in which many find themselves. It is a duty of every man to develop the various talents that God has given them: economic, cultural, moral, and religious. To reduce genuine human development to merely the moral and religious is equivalent to a defacement of God's

plan for mankind, as would be limiting his development to solely the economic domain.

7. Authentic human development is also *collective*. It is not enough that each peasant as an individual can improve his economic, cultural, or religious situation. The peasants must support one another as they seek their own advancement; they must unite through their own initiatives and select their own representatives in economic organizations—such as cooperatives and labor unions. To impede or create obstacles to these sound efforts when created by free peasant organizing would negate the social character that God himself has imprinted on humanity.

8. We the Bishops feel as our own the anxiety and insecurity that many peasant families are forced to live in due to a lack of their own land, and stable and just terms that are rarely found in the rental contracts, as well as the actual payment of the legal minimum wage, which could easily be challenged by agricultural organizations.

We are fully conscious that the state of these grave problems implies profound changes in the nation's socioeconomic structures. These structural transformations cannot be introduced in a disorderly fashion, nor imposed through an insurrection, which "would engender new injustices, and inequalities and would provoke new destruction. You cannot combat an evil at the price of a worse one." The people and especially the Dominican peasantry, through what we would call a Christian instinct, rejects change induced through the use of armed warfare and disrespect for the law. These socioeconomic changes must thus be realized in a lawful manner and—although these are changes in the socioeconomic structures of the country—through new legislation. These laws imply on the one hand taking into account technical, economic, legal, and financial considerations, which cannot be improvised lightly without frustrating the end result. But on the other hand, and precisely due to the complexity of the problems that need to be solved, the study and implementation of solutions is necessary "without further delay." One cannot toy with the hunger, suffering, and distress of many thousands of Dominicans.

The technical or legal consideration of these laws is not in the realm of our pastoral competence. Our obligation is to ask in the name of Christian justice that these serious problems are resolved in a legal and orderly way, to the maximum extent of our generosity. We wish to recall the *Church doctrine* of these issues:

a. God has intended the land and its fruits for the use of *all* people and not only a few, so that property in land is allocated to everyone fairly.

b. All the other rights, *whatever these may be*, including those of private property and free trade, are subordinate to the fundamental right that all people can use God's property so as to live with dignity.

c. The right of *private property* legally acquired is not unconditional or absolute. "There is no rationale in reserving land in excess of basic needs for exclusive or unconditional use when others are lacking."

d. When a conflict arises between the rights of private property and communitarian needs, *it is up to the public authorities* to find a solution, with *the active participation of the people and popular organizations.*

e. "The collective good demands sometimes the *expropriation* of large rural landholdings either due to their size, their lack of use, the poverty of the population, or the grave harm to the interests of the country." Always when the common good requires an expropriation, it must be effected in an equitable way, taking everyone's situation into account.

f. "Within the *fundamental rights* of human beings is the right *to freely organize workers' associations which genuinely represent the worker* . . . as well as the right to *freely participate in the activities of these associations, without risk of repression.*" These fundamental rights are supported explicitly by Church doctrine for peasant cooperatives and trade unions.

g. The "authentic representation" of the peasantry by these organizations only arises if these do *not* "become a form of patronage by which they freely assume the right to dispense of the worker's labor and property." The organizations must represent the peasants and not the reverse, placing the peasants at the service of the organizations.

h. The peasant organizations "must work within the judicial-moral orbit." Their objective is not to destroy the legal order by taking justice into their own hands—which would harm the legitimate rights of others—but rather to represent the rights of the peasants before public opinion and the authorities.

In sum: the moral principles that the Church proposes as its own contribution to the solution to the problems of our peasantry—land ownership, land rental contracts, the payment of a just minimum wage, easy access to technical input, and credit—are basically the following: above all else, the primacy of the right to subsist in a dignified way, the competence of the state to resolve conflicts between individual rights and the interests of the majority, and the active participation of the freely constituted peasant organizations in the decisions that affect the peasantry, when they respect the rule of law.

9. For these reasons, the Bishops of the Dominican Republic regard with profound sympathy the efforts on the part of the peasants to join cooperatives, community development, and professional organizations such as trade unions. These organizations should enable peasants to learn how to make technical improvements, which on their own they would not be able to learn or afford. The greatest yield of these new approaches would be an increase in young people's love of agricultural work, and this would contribute to their ability to gain a decent livelihood in rural areas and thus prevent them from emigrating in massive numbers in desperation to the cities to live a life on the margins of the economy and society. Finally, these peasant organizations can contribute effectively to the creation of the social conditions necessary such that many unemployed men of the countryside are willing to take work, such as cutting sugar cane, that often presupposes living in conditions irreconcilable with human dignity.

Octavio A. Beras
Archbishop of Santo Domingo
President of the Dominican Diocese

Translated by Lauren Derby.

Note

1. Pope Paul VI (1897–1978) convened the Second Vatican Council (1962–1965).

To Die in Villa Mella

Carlos Hernández Soto

Just twelve kilometers north of the capital city of Santo Domingo, the town of Villa Mella (originally Sabana Grande del Espíritu Santo) was founded by a group of fugitive slaves fleeing Saint Domingue in 1678. The area became notorious when Wolof slaves from West Africa there, owned by Columbus's son Diego Colón, led the first slave revolt in the Spanish colony in 1521. Villa Mella later received migrants from nearby San Lorenzo de los Minas, a squatter settlement of refugees from enslavement in Saint Domingue that was named for Los Minas, the Gbe-speaking peoples from the Bight of Benin. In the nineteenth century Villa Mella received more Haitian migrants, in particular the Moreno family, which arrived with Haitian troops during the Haitian occupation in the 1830s. Proximity to the Ozama waterway enabled residents to cultivate, fish, and sell their foodstuffs downriver in the capital.

This community has long practiced a series of distinctive mortuary rituals that fuse Catholic elements such as the use of Latin prayer with Central African–derived elements such as invocations to Calunga, the head of the underworld, and a sense of close proximity between the dead and the living. Belief in Calunga as god of the sea and the dead probably originated in the Kongo region of Central Africa, from which the majority of slaves arriving in the eighteenth century hailed. This selection describes the banco, *the rite that finally ushers the soul of the dead into the netherworld a few years after death and one that was explicitly proscribed by colonial law. It is unique to Villa Mella, although many features of the mortuary practices related here are characteristically Dominican and found throughout the country. Between the date of death and the banco the soul is in a kind of purgatory and can attack relatives if the proper rites are not adhered to. The banco is organized by a lay brotherhood or* cofradia, *mutual aid societies that organize pilgrimages, patron saint festivals, and above all, burials, which until recently were costly for the poor. These brotherhoods were formed by free blacks and Africans of particular ethnicities, both of whom were prohibited from joining the cofradias of whites during the colonial period. Lay brotherhoods provided the backbone of Catholicism, especially in the interior, where priests had a fleeting presence until the twentieth century. The cofradia at Villa Mella is called the Cofradia de Espíritu Santo, or the Congos, and has been named a world heritage site by UNESCO. This selection describes the banco as carried out in Villa Mella in the 1980s.*

The cofradia is named for the drums, the congos, which are attributed to the Holy Spirit. They say that the Holy Ghost appeared with these drums on his shoulder in Villa Mella. The instruments called congos used by the cofradia are the main drum, the minor drum or *alcahuete*, the little canoe, and several pairs of maracas. The little canoe or *canoita*,[1] an instrument exclusive to the Congos of Villa Mella, is made of two clacking sticks, like a clave. With these instruments, the Congo Cofradia executes their "twenty-one drum patterns." In reality, there are more than twenty-one.[2] But twenty-one is a sacred number in keeping with the idea of the divine origin of these instruments, which they say are the "property of the Holy Ghost and personification of the Holy Ghost."

Right after death, the cadaver and the house are prepared for the wake. The body is covered with a white shroud and socks, but without shoes. The "tomb" or "altar of the nine" is prepared in the house. On the first level, corresponding to the table, a candle and a flower are placed in each corner. In the middle of the table, propped up on the second level, they place chromolithographs of the saints or "mysteries" (spirits), a glass of holy water, a sprig of basil or rosemary, which they will use to sprinkle holy water, a rosary, a bell, and a donation plate. On the last level they place a doll or what they call the "soul vigil."

After the prayers, they play the first round of ceremonial drummings of the cofradia, which are danced until the ninth day. The first drumming is called "Bembé Yaguá," which is rigorously followed by the others, called "Palo Mayor," "Camino Reale," and "Calunga." Later they can follow up with any of the beats, but they will always finish with "Calunga," which is the most suggestive and sacred one, to the point that when a person dies they will say that they are "singing Calunga for her." Around five PM, the drums resonate with Calunga, the words of which are "the time has arrived" (for the death and farewell) and improvisations are made with which they give thanks to the one who leads the prayers. The essence of these rites is to request the eternal rest of the deceased and cleanse it from evil (with holy water or incense). The ritual cleansing extends to everyone present so that the deceased does not harm them.

As part of the purgatory rites, the lay priest or one of his assistants undoes the ritual tomb, taking apart the levels, and removes the tablecloth and the crepe paper adornments. They then make several left turns toward the bedsheet, which served as a tablecloth for the tomb. The crucifix, the candles, and the donation plate, which were on top of the tomb, are placed outside the front door of the house, as are the crepe paper decorations. After the final prayers to send off the soul, they burn all the paper that was used to adorn the tomb, sweep the house, and take apart the canopy in the yard used to shelter the tomb and have a celebration.

During the transitional period before the soul has been purified and dispatched, the relatives of the dead are obliged to celebrate the nine days of prayers and the first-year anniversary of the death and take care of the other prescriptions (such as on the day of the dead cutting the grass and painting and adorning the grave site with flowers). They may also be prey to attacks from the soul of the dead and are subject to the norms and prescriptions of mourning, particularly women. During mourning, the dead and their anguished living relatives constitute a special group, located between the world of the living and that of the dead. One of the objectives of the banco is precisely to finalize the state of mourning. The sensation of potential contagion and danger is aggravated by the fact that during the first nine days the dead person is said to be in the house. During the day the corpse cannot act due to the light. At night, however, it can do harm. For this reason, a candle is kept lit below the altar in front of which they say the prayers for nine days, "so that the corpse stays there and doesn't bother anyone." The candles, which they arrange on the altar table and on the tomb, function, according to those interviewed, "to light the path toward Christ, so the way can be seen clearly." Beneath the tomb they place a glass of water next to the candle for the dead and a little cup of coffee. All of the informants said this was "the glass of the dead" for the soul to drink and refresh itself, to quench its thirst. Among the objects arranged on the tomb is the "donation plate," where participants leave a small voluntary contribution for the expenses of the nine days, the year anniversary rite, or the banco. At the end of the ceremony, they count the money and publicly announce how much money was collected. They believe this number is good luck, and they will play it in the lottery.

Translated by Lauren Derby.

Notes

1. The canoe symbolizes the boat in which the soul of the deceased crosses the river that divides the world of the living from that of the dead.
2. The number of divisions of *luas* in Dominican Vodú is 21.

A Tire Blowout Gives Entry into the World of Spiritism

Martha Ellen Davis

Martha Ellen Davis is an ethnomusicologist and leading expert on Dominican popular religiosity, healing practices, pilgrimage, and music. In this essay she recalls one of her first forays into the world of Dominican religiosity and discusses its relationship to Haitian vodou, as well as Espiritismo—a school of European-derived belief characterized by mediumship and trance possession that became very popular in Cuba and Puerto Rico in the late nineteenth century.

One day in Santo Domingo, I was on my way downtown to the firehouse stop in a *carro público* (jitney car), when a tire blew out, and the passengers all had to find another means of transportation. One young woman I had been talking to on our way, very nice indeed, was interested in my research in Dominican folklore and music, and we continued talking after we got out. She suggested that I meet her mother, a respected spirit medium. And that was how my entry into the world of Dominican spiritism and *vodú* began.

The conversations with that medium and my observation of sessions at her house have helped me to understand a bit about Dominican *vodú*/spiritism. As the medium explained, "The spiritual world is very broad." I could not pretend to understand it deeply. But it was essential to study aspects of religious devotion in order to understand the purposes and contexts of much of traditional Dominican music.

Dominican *vodú*/spiritism represents a fusion of practices similar to Haitian *vodou*—a manifestation on Hispaniola of African-American popular religion—with European spiritism, so named and set forth by the Frenchman Allan Kardec, *pseud.* (1804–1869) in *The Spirits' Book* (1857) and *The Mediums' Book* (1861). Spiritism is more prominent in upper- and middle-class urban practice, and *vodú* in lower-class and rural practice, but both share elements although in different proportions. Haitian *vodou* itself represents a mixture of elements from various parts of Africa, principally West and

Doña Bircía, who leads the *cofradía* (religious brotherhood) of the Virgin of Carmen in Porto Blanco, Elias Piña, in front of her altar. Photograph by Lauren Derby, July 2011.

Central Africa, integrated with aspects of Catholicism. Here it should be noted that, within the African-descended populations of the Americas, certain areas of Cuba and Brazil have counterparts closer to specific African ethnic groups than the more eclectic *vodou* of Haiti. Haiti broke away early from both Africa and Europe with its independence in 1804; therefore it has developed a folk religion more its own.

In the Dominican Republic, what researchers call *vodú* and practitioners call devotion to the *misterios*, or, in the urban, upper and middle classes, *espiritismo*, has more European elements, in accord with the cultural composition of that country: Christian elements on one hand; and, on the other, aspects of spiritism that perpetuate pre-Christian European beliefs. These are supposedly based on Celtic or rather Druidic heritage, and others originally from the Middle East. Kardec dedicated himself to reinterpreting Christianity through spiritism in his famous book, *The Gospel according to Spiritism* (1864), initiating the fusion between Christianity and spiritism.

The mixture and simplification of Haitian *vodou* in its Dominican manifestation are seen in the spatial organization of the altars and folk temples, the social organization of the practitioners, the beliefs themselves, and the ritual. To characterize the nature of Dominican *vodú* in contrast with Haitian *vodou*, Professor Enrique Patín Veloz writes, "Dominican *vodú* practitioners on the whole do not have their own temples, they do not

Detail of the altar for an annual saint's festival sponsored by a spiritist/Vodú medium. Important icons pictured: Lower level, left to right: the Virgen de la Altagracia, the national "protector"; Jesus; Dr. José Gregorio Hernández, a Venezuelan physician (1864–1919), who continues to heal in death as an elevated spirit. None of these three "incorporate" (manifest through possession) because of their spiritual elevation. Upper level, above Jesus: San Miguel, the most commonly depicted saint on Dominican Vodú altars, who incorporates as "Belié Belcán." The offering in the black bowl consists of roasted peanuts (*maní*), corn, sesame, and chopped coconut, in this case with little vanilla wafers. At the end of the ceremony this offering is strewn in the air and then distributed in handfuls to those in attendance as a good luck memento, to be eaten or saved. Photograph by Martha Ellen Davis, Cabral, Barahona, 2007. Used by permission.

practice [real] *vodú* ritual, they do little animal sacrifice, they do not have an organized priesthood, they do not have secret societies, etc. And what is even more curious, they do not believe themselves to be voodooists rather 'material spiritists' because they call *vodú* 'material spiritism' and the *luas*, the *vodou* deities, 'material spirits.'" By "material," such practitioners refer to earthy expressiveness in contrast with "spiritual," "elevated" expressions. Here Patín was describing upper- and middle-class altars of Santo Domingo, and specifically the altar of my new friend's mother, where he personally assisted in interpreting clairvoyant messages during private consultations.

The mixed nature of Dominican *vodú* is noticeable in the physical appearance of the altar. Describing the altar of my friend's mother, there is a cross, and there are chromolithographs and commercially-produced plaster statuettes of Catholic saints, each one representing a *vodú* entity: Saint Enrique, or *Olisá Bayí*, the head of altars; the Virgin La Dolorosa, or *Metresilí* (a Dominican contraction of the Haitian Maitresse Erzulie); *Ogún Balenyó*, represented by Saint James ("San Santiago"). There is also a statuette of Doctor José Gregorio Hernández, a Venezuelan medical doctor who died in 1919 and has been beatified; he is found on many altars of Caribbean spiritists as a great healer. In front of Doctor Gregorio there is a handbell used in Christian prayers and also in *vodú* to invoke the deities, *misterios*, or *seres* in the terms of spiritists.

In the center of the spiritist altar is a water-filled glass goblet, which functions like a crystal ball to perceive the presence of any *seres* or *misterios*, spirits of the dead (as in spiritism), and the spiritual essence of mortals in attendance at the "session" (or of an individual in a private consultation). On each side of the altar there are kerchiefs of various colors, each one representing a *misterio*; they are used by their respective entities when they "manifest" through spirit possession in the "mediums" (called *servidores* by more "material" practitioners); they self-identify when they come by selecting their color of kerchief and tying it across the shoulder like a sash or on "their" (*i.e.*, the medium's) head. There is a vase of flowers to please the *"metresas"* or female *seres*, and a dry seaweed "flower" called the "Flower of Jericho" that opens when it is watered to symbolize the "opening of the path."

In summary, studying this altar, one can see Catholic symbols, many with dual meaning in *vodú*—such as the representations of saints and the handbell; purely Christian articles, like the cross; purely *vodú* articles, like the kerchiefs; articles from European spiritism, such as the goblet; and articles unique to Caribbean spiritism, such as the representation of Doctor Gregorio and the use of the "Flower of Jericho." The Dominican spiritism/*vodú*, as I observed in this upper- and middle-class altar of Santo Domingo, has much in common with Brazilian Umbanda; both represent a mix of African-American popular religion with Catholicism and spiritism. In both countries, African-derived religion was more developed in places with a larger concentration of slaves. In Hispaniola, it is more ubiquitous in Haiti and the southern region of the Dominican Republic, in contrast with the cities of Santo Domingo or Santiago.

Because these urban centers are culturally more hybridized, they have religions that likewise are more eclectic. And because large cities are the focus of economic and social change, there is more sensitivity there to the spiritual necessities of the residents of such an environment.

Although the mixture represented by Dominican *vodú,* like Brazilian Umbanda, might give discomfort to religious conservatives of mainstream Catholicism, this type of religion deserves respect. On the one hand, it is the result of great spiritual power because it incorporates the wisdom and strength of many religious traditions of the peoples of the New World. On the other hand, more objectively, any religion that successfully responds to the psychological, physical, and social needs of its followers should be considered meritorious.

The sensitivity to believers' needs shown by such religions is possible because of its flexibility, for *vodú,* as a popular religion, is neither controlled nor standardized by any governing body; every spiritual center functions independently. This is the same feature that renders many Protestant sects attractive and accounts in part for the great rise in Protestantism, as well as Spiritism, in Latin America today.

Note: The author has remained friends, in fact adopted family, of the young woman she met in the *carro público* in 1973 and with her mother, the medium, for over forty years.

Translated by Alex Huezo and Martha Ellen Davis.

Díos Olivorio Mateo: The Living God

Irio Leonel Ramírez López

Olivorio Mateo was a fence maker and day laborer in the southwestern region around San Juan de la Maguana in the early twentieth century. As his fame as a faith healer grew and he developed many followers, the US Marines concluded that he was a bandit and assassinated him. Today he is venerated as a popular creole saint in the region. This selection is from an interview with a contemporary faith healer who is a devotee of Olivorio Mateo (Liborio). He is a member of a cofradía or religious sodality, which holds fiestas de palos (saints festival) and makes pilgrimages to the major patron saint festivals.

My name is Irio Leonel Ramírez López. I have carried this religion since birth. My father was what they called a "cavalrio" [religious leader] for Olivorio Mateo. My great-grandparents visited Palma Sola.[1] They had a very big religious community there, but when the military destroyed it [in 1962], they were forced to leave. I have a little baton from Palma Sola, one that was used by the Liborista guards. This was used to drive away the demons making people ill and giving them bad fortune; it would drive them away. One of those old people gave me this as a present, as a memento from Palma Sola, although I did not go there. I was born the day of the Virgin of Mercedes, and I like to carry out this religion. I am a humble person, a good person; I like to help people. There are people who feel pain and they come here for me to give them remedies. I heal people by passing this little baton across their bodies and if there is something evil in them this will drive it away. Olivorio used a stick of pine to heal people; this is a *palo de cruz* [lit. "stick of the cross" or "sacred stick"]. We are here to continue serving the powers of Olivorio Mateo. I mostly work with the herb that Liborio used, *Yerbabuena* [mint]; he also used *Anamú* for baths [used for spiritual cleansing], and he used *ruda, Apasote, albahaca, Altamisa,* and *sábila.*[2] There are many things used for healing the various diseases that people have. We also go to water springs to pray for people's health, like the Olivorio

Photo of Olivorio Mateo with sacrificial offerings on the altar at his pilgrimage site, La Maguana Arriba, San Juan de la Maguana. "Altar for Díos Olivorio Mateo," Photograph by Lauren Derby, 2010.

Mateo spring, which is in Naranjal, La Maguana, and Arroyo de Limón, los Tres Hachos, los Botones, various places. We also go to the sacred cave of San Francisco and the Santo Cerro of La Vega to share the religion of Olivorio Mateo, who, as a good father, is a God to us.

So you define yourself as a Liborista?

Yes, very Liborista. Our group is called the Angels of Olivorio Mateo.

Can you tell me what Liborio means to you?

To me, Liborio is a living presence who did a lot of good and for me this image of Olivorio is alive. I adore him.

Can you tell me how Díos Olivorio Mateo is different from the other gods?

There is no difference because the other saints gave Olivorio his powers to help others. God gave him the power, the fortitude, so that he can do good things on earth.

If Liborio is the intermediary between God, the saints, and us, then can we say that Liborio is kind of like Jesus Christ?

We call him the second God. Everyone called him Papa—Papa Liborio. He is a creole god. I am a devotee of Liborio because when an elderly person died he would say "stand up" and they would stand up. For this reason I am a believer in Papa Liborio.

Does the fact that he fought the US Marines figure in his popularity among the faithful?

Yes, he tried to save the nation. He also gave a lot of advice before leaving this earth. Before dying, he told everyone to save a *hacha de cuava* [hatchet for kindling] and a *palo de cruz* [a medicinal shrub] and salt and sugar and have candles ready because there would be a time when everything would become dark, and there would be cyclones and there would be nowhere to go. And during Cyclone Georges [September 1998] more than five thousand people died here in San Juan de la Maguana and the darkness that he predicted came about here. I saw it. It became dark suddenly one day. He also spoke of an earthquake and that Haiti was going to be buried. And that happened [in January 2010]. So for us he is a God on earth. And for those of us who worship him, we are protected. I hardly even felt that earthquake. We have the powers of God and Liborio. We feel few things.

If you sense that there is an evil spirit present I can help. For this reason God and Olivorio Mateo as our father from San Juan de la Maguana gave us a kind of power so that we can help humanity. We can even combat the bacá.[3] Let's say that I want to become a millionaire through these evil ends, a bacá can be made with an egg laid from a chicken on Good Friday which becomes a bird. You take this egg on Good Friday and (people tell me because I have never done this and will never do it) they bury it in the ground with four chicken feet; then they take a black chicken head or that of a rabbit or a dog or cat and say some prayers and bury it. They grow this evil thing—the bacá—with their mind and that of the owner of the bacá in order to harm someone. So the owner of the bacá sends it to pester your enemy and rob other people's houses and thus to become rich. Those of us who have spiritual knowledge, such as myself, can kill that bacá. I take a black chicken and I prepare it with *rulo* [a species of plantain] and cooked ashes and I prepare the house with several different holy waters from springs and from the botánica and we take the point of a knife and a new needle and nails and we beat that chicken and we kill the chicken, and with it, break the spell—with the knowledge that Olivorio Mateo gave us.

Interview conducted and translated by Lauren Derby.

Notes

1. On the death of Trujillo, a large community of faithful congregated at Palma Sola, a rural parish near San Juan where it was said Olivorio's spirit had descended on a pair of sacred twins, León and Plinio Ventura. The community grew until it was attacked by the military in 1962.

2. *Petiveria alliacea L.*, *Ruta chalepensis*, *Chenopodium ambrosioides L.*, *Ocimum gratissimum L.* (basil), *Artemisia domingensis urb.*, and *Aloe vera*. *Palo de cruz* is *Isidorea Pungens*.

3. A bacá is an infernal spirit demon that can be used to create money for its owner or punish one's enemies.

Jesus Is Calling You

Frances Jane "Fanny" Crosby

In recent decades, evangelical Protestant religion has gained tremendous popularity and untold numbers of adherents in the Dominican Republic, as it has across Latin America. In Santo Domingo, the former theater district has become a zone of fervent spiritual revival, with congregations of worshippers crowding into the old movie houses, now churches, singing gospel songs. The world-famous Juan Luis Guerra, who is among the born-again Dominican population, releases CDs of Christian music and fills the baseball stadium with fans for concerts of his hymn-like merengues and bachatas. Much of the musical canon of the Pentecostal, Seventh-Day Adventist, and other evangelical denominations active in the Dominican Republic consists of traditional music, much of it from the United States, loosely translated into Spanish. The following well-loved revival tune was the work of the widely published American composer, songwriter, and poet Frances Jane "Fanny" Crosby (1820–1915), a blind childhood prodigy who gained celebrity as an adult, becoming the first woman to speak publicly on the floor of the US Senate, where she recited one of her poems. "Jesus Is Tenderly Calling You Home" was translated into Spanish as "With Tender Voice" and appears here translated back into English from the Spanish adaptation of Crosby's very different text. This translator heard this particular song resounding from a rooftop place of worship in the Las Américas neighborhood of Santo Domingo, now the site of the Columbus Lighthouse, in 1986.

Jesus is calling you with tender voice:
your invitation to love's purity.
Why do you turn from the call to rejoice?
Sinner, how deaf will you be?

Chorus:
He calls you today, he calls you today, come to Christ today, and tell him:
"I give you my soul."

Jesus invites you, the weariest one:
sees your desire, He feels your pain.
Bring Him your burden; it will be undone,
you, the Lord God will sustain.

Chorus

Jesus is guarding you every day
so much to hope for, love to attain.
Burdened one, come, at his feet you may lay
all your temptation, your pain!

Chorus

Translated from Spanish by Eric Paul Roorda.

X

Popular Culture

These selections explore a few characteristic elements of Dominican popular culture, including music, festivals, barrio culture, and superstitious beliefs. Isolation and rural autonomy have forged a persistent culture of informality, one in which leisure-time diversions are socially important. As in other former slave societies, male autonomy is highly valued and has given rise to the valorization of popular male figures, such as the *tíguere*, that celebrate the everyday arts of male bravado, repartee, upward mobility, and prowess.

The operations of race in the Dominican Republic have long perplexed outsiders who expect to find a two-tier racial system as in other former sugar plantation societies. But the Dominican pattern was very different. Slaves arrived early, and the plantation model dissolved rapidly, enabling a majority of freedpeople to emerge by the eighteenth century—very early in regional terms—which meant that African-descended people moved throughout society and there was a greater chance of upward mobility. This can be seen in the striking career of Eduardo Brito, who was born illegitimate and worked as a shoeshine boy yet rose to become a world-class operatic baritone who performed at the Waldorf Astoria Hotel in New York singing "Lamento esclavo," a melancholic song about a slave who pines for freedom. The fact that class stratification was not acute made for greater intermarriage across the color line, as did the institution of the "casa chica" or concubinage, which was a natural byproduct of an itinerant male labor force and often created cross-class family ties. Occupations such as cattle ranching, wood felling, and farming of smallholdings of tobacco and cacao, which used few slaves, combined with poverty, also meant that labor relations between masters and slaves were far more intimate, and slaves were not segregated apart as in Cuba or Haiti, where slave majorities developed at the height of the sugar boom. Finally, the arrival of large numbers of Haitian and West Indian laborers to cut sugarcane in the early twentieth century also reinforced the idea of Dominican creole or mixed identity, as opposed to that of the darker skinned migrants, who were associated with an occupation redolent of slavery. These features of socioeconomic development help explain the absence of racial consciousness that outsiders have found so peculiar, although the growth of a large diaspora to the United States has changed the meaning of race in recent decades.

Carnival and Holy Week

Luis Emilio Gómez Alfau

The week before Lent and the week before Easter are now the occasions for large, long parties across the Dominican Republic. These two selections from a short popular history published in 1944 show that Carnival parade celebrations in the nineteenth century were similar to those today in that they involved groups of dancers called comparsas, even if other traditions, such as the pelting of eggs filled with powder for St. Andres, are no longer practiced. Holy Week observations have changed dramatically, however; whereas in the 1800s the focus was on religious processions and abstinence, now all eyes are on the country's beaches, which Dominicans re-take from the tourists during Semana Santa, with throngs of people camping by the water and having fun for the whole week, often taking time off from work.

Carnival

Carnival was celebrated with great enthusiasm for the three days before the beginning of Lent.

The right people, of the best society, formed their comparsas, and they allowed the girls, under the care of a chaperone or some respectable person, to give expression to their lively ingenuity.

The mask has always transformed the woman, the guise of the masquerade displacing that of the hypocrisy imposed by convention and social restrictions.

These comparsas set out in the afternoon and at night to visit their friends and make noise with the cheerful ringing of bells. There was almost always someone in the group who could play the piano and would be the life of the party during those hours of happiness. The owners of these houses, visited by storm, toasted the invaders with vanilla guava or other refreshments, during the concourse from house to house between eleven and midnight.

During the shady afternoon hours of Carnival, the streets were populated with masqueraders. Comparsas dressed like red or blue devils, like sick people from the hospital, pregnant women covered with yellow pow-

The queen of a Carnival celebration showed off her fabulous couture at an elite gathering in the Capital in 1928. Photographer unknown, black-and-white photograph, 1928. Trujillo Series (F MP 86), Archivo General de la Nación, Santo Domingo.

der [the color of adultery], with big gowns, as monks, as [Taíno] Indians, as Apaches, as imitations of [the machete-wielding folk hero] Concho Primo, as nuns, as gardeners, as cooks, and as Dutch girls. Other comparsas danced in a line to the rhythm of an orchestra or mimicked the [chants that] echo from a convent, reciting ingenious verses.

The elegant youth rode through Carnival in elegant coaches. The girls, happily seated on display in the doorways of their houses, showered the young men who came their way with a rain of confetti [made of] rice painted different colors, of sweets, of little cookies and fine candies, delicate essences dispersed by atomizers, a veritable deluge of caramels, and so on. A swarm of boys of the street followed behind, and the retailers and the coachmen had their harvest during the days that Carnival lasted.

In the neighborhoods splendid dances took place, also *en masque*, and in the cabarets the people of the good life consumed the nights in dances, *sancochos*, and cocktails.

Holy Week

The religious practices mandated by the Church were rigorously observed by the faithful, and, consequently, the families did not neglect to attend Mass every Sunday and [the other] days of observance. During the season of Lent, everyone in the community confessed and took Communion; there were days of gathering and prayer, the carnal appetites were conquered with a rigorous diet, there was no dancing, and no festivities of any sort took place. In foods red meat was not mixed with white fish, and there was no swearing. During those days there were few who failed to eat fresh or salted fish, sweetened broad beans, stewed balls of ripe plantain with sesame, and other dishes reserved for the occasion.

During Holy Week, the Church celebrated with ritual functions [and] with total solemnity, with the traditional processions leaving from the churches and following a Way of the Cross through the city with an order and silence of complete fervor.

On Palm Sunday, the procession commemorating the entrance of Jesus into Jerusalem departed from the Cathedral, and the columns of marchers were fed by the whole population, rich and poor, those at leisure and those in need. Later, the procession of the image of Jesus in the Garden set out. On Holy Monday the religious offices and submissions to Jesus at the Whipping Post took place in the Cathedral, under the patronage of the brotherhood [responsible for the image], led by the owners of the image, the prestigious Guerrero family, who at that time owned and lived in the house today occupied by the Columbus Hotel. On Tuesday the image of humility and patience, called Jesus of Pain by the people, paraded through the streets, celebrating the corresponding festivities in the Church of Santa Barbara: masses, motets, dignified cantatas, and so on. On Wednesday, in the church of Our Lady of Carmen, the great day of the Nazarene, for which we still reserve great devotion, attracted numerous [members of the religious] brotherhood. On Thursday, the Solitude procession went from the chapel of Our Lady of Mercy. During the night of that day, lavish monuments or the pious steps of the Way of the Cross were erected in all the churches. A large crucifix was placed where the worshippers could kiss it and deposit alms in a little plate. On Friday the procession of the Fifth Anguish left from San Carlos. This procession and that of the Solitude were held after ten or eleven at night, and the neighbors along the route illuminated their doors and windows. On Resurrection Sunday, two processions took place: that of the Holy Sacrament in the Cathedral, at four in the morning, and that of the Resurrection; the first, after leaving from the Cathedral, flowed together on Silversmith Street with the other procession, which [had] left from Our Lady of Mercy and in which figured the images of Our Lady of Sorrows, St. John, and the Marías.

From ten in the morning on Ash Wednesday until more or less the same hour on Saturday of Glory, the city remained under curfew, no one raised his voice, in no part of the city was anyone heard to undertake to sing or play an instrument. The police made sure to keep horseback riders from coming inside the city walls and prevented vehicles from circulating. If for some reason the transit of quadrupeds was permitted, their hooves were wrapped with rags so that their hoofbeats would not make noise. The doctors who had to visit the sick did so on foot, covering distances, and likewise on foot all of the necessary articles of consumption—the bread, the milk, the charcoal—were brought home. Public establishments did not open their doors. All activity ceased voluntarily. The ritual bell-ringing of the churches was done with a rattle. The military drums were silenced and the soldiers marched to the beat of a deaf echo. When the Cathedral let loose its famous bells, ringing out "Glory to God in the Highest," a great commotion and jubilation was raised in all the neighborhoods. The churches burst with joyous peals of bells, fireworks, missiles, and sparklers split the air, getting confused with the shrill factory whistles and the whistles and cowbells of the rascals. . . . The windows and balconies were filled with showy curtains, the coaches, horses, burros, and carts were put into action, each attending to its business, the commercial establishments reopened their doors, and all of life was reborn.

Translated by Eric Paul Roorda.

Tribulations of Dominican Racial Identity

Silvio Torres-Saillant

Notions of race in the Dominican Republic, which are unique in the community of nations, defy easy explanation. The complex racial categorizations in practice there, marked by the consistent denial of African lineage, are largely the result of the country's history. Silvio Torres-Saillant has considered the relationship between that troubled past and contemporary constructions of race among Dominicans, both on the island and living abroad, in his voluminous work. This selection is from his 1998 essay "Tribulations of Blackness: Stages in Dominican Racial Identity."

Dominican society is the cradle of blackness in the Americas. The island of Hispaniola or Santo Domingo, which the Dominicans share with the Haitians, served as port of entry to the first African slaves to set foot on Spain's newly conquered territories following Christopher Columbus's eventful transatlantic voyage in 1492. Nine years into the conquest of what thenceforward became known as the New World, King Ferdinand and Queen Isabella appointed Fray Nicolas de Ovando governor of Santo Domingo, authorizing him to bring "black slaves" to their colony. Marking the start of the black experience in the western hemisphere, the arrival of Ovando's fleet in July 1502 ushered in a social and demographic history that would lead in the course of five centuries to the overwhelming presence of people of African descent in the Dominican Republic today. Blacks and mulattos make up nearly 90 percent of the contemporary Dominican population. Yet, no other country in the hemisphere exhibits greater indeterminacy regarding the population's sense of racial identity. To the bewilderment of outside observers, Afro-Dominicans have traditionally failed to flaunt their blackness as a collective banner to advance economic, cultural, or political causes. Some commentators would contend, in effect, that Dominicans have, for the most part, denied their blackness. Faced with the population's tolerance of official claims asserting the moral and intellectual superiority of Caucasians by white supremacist ideologues, analysts of racial identity in Dominican society have often imputed to Dominicans heavy doses of "backwardness," "ignorance," or "confusion" regarding their race and ethnicity. I would like to invite reflection on the complexity of racial thinking and racial discourse among Dominicans. . . .

Dominicans of African descent possess what one might call a deracialized social consciousness whose origins date back to the decline of the plantation economy in colonial times. After generating a widespread and massive influx of black slaves in the early sixteenth century, the Hispaniola sugar industry declined dramatically. The evanescence of the industry, concomitant with the constant exodus of white settlers, marked the texture of race relations in the context of the colony's ensuing impoverishment. . . .

Worsened by the effects of Governor Antonio de Osorio's depopulation of the eastern territories in 1605, occasional foreign invasions, pirate raids, and various natural disasters, the Santo Domingo economy deteriorated to the point that slavery became untenable and the rigid racial codes engendered by the plantation virtually broke down. The number of free blacks, a segment that had begun to surface toward the end of the sixteenth century, grew to a majority as the social distance between blacks and whites shrank significantly. The testimony in 1763 by Archbishop Fernández de Navarete about the scarcity of pure whites, affirming that the majority of the free population "including landholders, was of mixed blood," highlights the pervasiveness of racial intermixture in Santo Domingo.

The decay of the plantation and the virtual destitution of whites helped to break down the social barriers between the races, stimulating interracial marital relations and giving rise to an ethnically hybrid population. The racial integration and ethnic hybridity that characterized seventeenth-century Santo Domingo explain the emergence of the mulatto as the predominant type in the ethnic composition of the Dominican population.

Interestingly, despite the large presence of people of African descent at the time, many of the eyewitness accounts of the precarious state of the colony bewailed the scarcity of blacks as a primary cause of the decay. We begin to recognize here a tendency to limit the term *black* to people still living in slavery or engaged in subversive action against the colonial system. . . .

Gradually, the sphere of blackness became associated exclusively with slavery and subversion, fostering a conceptual space that permitted free blacks and mulattos in Santo Domingo to step outside the racial circumscription of their blackness in configuring their identities or aligning themselves politically.

The disruption of the plantation economy and its demographic impact on the population facilitated a split between biological blackness and social blackness. As the racial oligarchy originally generated by the plantocracy

A fishing family with children near San Pedro de Macorís in 1929. Fishing nets spread out to dry, as in this photograph, can still be seen in those coastal environs. Photograph by Rupert Decker, 1929. Rupert Decker Collection, Photography Collection, Mystic Seaport Museum, #1994/62/69, © Mystic Seaport Museum.

crumbled, pigmentation ceased to shape political action. Moya Pons, reflecting on the use in early nineteenth-century Santo Domingo of the term *blancos de la tierra* (whites of the land) by colored people to describe themselves, notes that paradoxically "while their skin gradually became darker, the mentality of Dominicans turned increasingly whiter." But the context of this paradox is an earlier historical process, whereby social position had come to supersede skin color in the articulation of identity for people of African descent. Blacks and mulattos who approximated the level of their former masters through either their own social ascent or the white colonists' descent were, indeed, the equivalent of former *blancos*. They lacked a material frame of reference in which to construct a concept of identity based on racial self-differentiation, that is, on affirmation of their blackness.

While the death of the plantation economy and indiscriminate poverty in seventeenth-century Santo Domingo contributed to the decline of slavery and the rise of people of African descent as a preponderant social force, they also eroded the bases for a sense of solidarity with blacks in general. As a result, we find, for instance, the mulatto Juan Baron (?–1805) collaborating with the invading French forces against the black troops of Toussaint-Louverture in 1802, despite the fact the year before the Haitian leader had abolished slavery and encouraged racial equality in Santo Domingo. Similarly, the black Dominican warrior Juan Suero (1808–1864), popularly known as the Black Cid, fought vigorously against black Haitians during the independence war in 1844 and did not hesitate to side with Spain's invading white soldiers when Dominicans were struggling to recover their national sovereignty during the annexation. One could argue that for Dominicans of African descent, history had conspired against their development of a racial consciousness that would inform their building of alliances along ethnic lines. At the same time, their deracialized consciousness precluded the development of a discourse of black affirmation that would serve to counterbalance intellectual negrophobia. . . .

We must remember that turn-of-the-century Dominican intellectuals pursued their education preferably in Europe at a time when Western thinkers were advancing blatantly racist theories of culture and human society. . . . Concomitant with the unquestioned superiority of Caucasians was the notion of racial mixture as an oddity that resulted in mental degeneracy. Thus, in about 1916, the otherwise estimable novelist and essayist Federico García Godoy (1857–1924), recognizing that interracial marital relations in the Dominican past had led "to a specific and differentiated human type during the colony," convinced himself that precisely in that "hybridity of our ethnic origin lie the corrosive germs that" have impeded "the development of an effective and prolific civilization" in the country. . . .

The openness of the concept lent itself to the malevolent manipulation of the Trujillo regime, whose propagandists exploited its flexibility for their own ends. They recognized the historical identification of the Dominican population with the indigenous Taíno inhabitants of Hispaniola, who had endured oppression and extermination at the hands of the Spanish conquerors at the outset of the colonial experience. Ethnically, the Indians represented a category typified by nonwhiteness as well as nonblackness, which could easily accommodate the racial in-betweenness of the Dominican mulatto. Thus, the regime gave currency to the term *indio* (Indian) to describe the complexion of people of mixed ancestry. . . . While in the minds of most Dominicans who use it, the term merely describes a color gradation somewhere between the polar extremes of whiteness and blackness much in the same way that the term *mulato* does, the cultural commissars of the Trujillo regime preferred it primarily because it was devoid of any semantic allusion to the African heritage and would therefore accord with their negrophobic definition of Dominicanness.

Origins of Merengue and Musical Instruments of the Republic

J. M. Coopersmith

Dominican music is unique and has deep roots. Today, it is most often associated with the merengue dance, although there are contending schools of thought on where merengue originated. This selection includes the explanation of the American scholar Jacob Maurice Coopersmith (1903–1968), who was an accomplished organist, songwriter, professor, and musicologist. In 1943 he surveyed the musical forms of the Dominican Republic while on an extended stay there during which he traveled around the country recording and interviewing musicians and singers. In his resulting book, Music and Musicians of the Dominican Republic, *published in a bilingual edition by the Pan-American Union, he presented an overview of the basic components of a typical Dominican musical ensemble. Like so many aspects of the culture of the Dominican Republic, popular musical instruments and songs there demonstrate influences from Africa, Europe, and the native Indian population, combined to create a unique hybrid. The instruments described here can still be found in merengue típico bands, and call-and-response styles of vocalization and lyrical improvisation continue to be heard.*

Coopersmith subsequently received the Order of San Pablo from the Dominican government in recognition of his work; his original recordings are now preserved in the Library of Congress. He may have had his Dominican sojourn in mind when composing one of his own more successful songs, "Tropical Serenade."

The *tumba dominicana* disappeared from the Dominican Republic about 1850, when the *merengue* came into vogue. Known to have existed since the first years of the Republic, the *merengue* has become the national dance. The origin and derivation of its name are still under discussion. It has been suggested by Flérida de Nolasco that the dance took its name from the confection made from sugar and the whites of eggs—i.e., from the light and frothy character of the dance, or from its short, precise rhythms, suggesting the whipping of the whites of eggs.

Rafael Vidal, discussing the origin of the *merengue*, writes that it was danced in early 1844 for the first time at a camp of Dominican soldiers during the Battle of Talanquera. When the Dominican troops had reached the pass at Macabón, they were obliged to retreat because of the pressure of the Haitian army. A Dominican mulatto, Tomás Torres, had abandoned his station during the battle; later that day the Dominicans counterattacked and were victorious. During the night, round their campfires, the soldiers sang and danced a new melody, which satirized the conduct of the fugitive standard-bearer, Torres, as follows:

> Tomás fled with the flag,
> Tomás fled from Talanquera;
> Were it I, I should not have fled,
> Tomás fled with the flag.

. . . In 1855, a fierce reaction to the *merengue* appeared in the literature of the Republic, of which the following *estrofa de una sextina* by an anonymous poet is a good example:

> "Complaint of the *Tumba* Against the *Merengue*"
> The *tumba*, exiled today
> By the despicable and foul *merengue*,
> Lies forgotten in obscurity
> Crying in cruel and horrible exile.
> But now, at last, aroused by anger,
> In this fashion expresses her sorrow:
> Impure child of the impure Avernus [the Underworld],
> Born of the Devil and a Fury,
> *Merengue*, when but a tender babe
> You were rocked in the arms of lust.
> You villain, who mock chastity,
> Vile usurper, give me my scepter.

Another anonymous poet of the same period wrote:

> The *merengue*, a great corvette
> With gaffsail and fore-topsail,
> Has all her papers ready
> And is sailing away.
>
> We advise the public
> And all who dance the *merengue*
> That from the port of Tripero
> She will weigh anchor tomorrow.

Merengue fever resulted in crowded ballrooms such as this one. Photographer unknown, undated black-and-white photograph. Social Activities Series (8), Archivo General de la Nación, Santo Domingo.

Many different ensembles performed merengue at the height of its popularity, including the Tropical Ambience Orchestra. "Orquesta Ambiente," photograph by Kurt Schnitzer, an Austrian photographer who used the professional name "Conrado" and lived in the Dominican Republic from 1939 to 1943. Conrado Collection (8), Archivo General de la Nación, Santo Domingo.

Despite this disapproval, the *merengue* has continued to gain favor as the popular dance of the Dominican Republic, where it is now accepted and enjoyed as the national dance. . . .

The *palitos* . . . are two round sticks of hardwood, usually *lignum-vitae*, which are beaten together. One is held loosely in the palm of the left hand, the right hand beating out the rhythms with the other. . . .

Common to all the regions of the Antilles, the *maracas* are made from the dried and hollowed-out fruit of the *higüera* tree, and filled with seeds or pebbles. . . .

Probably of Indian origin, the *güiro* is made from the fruit of the *higüero* tree. The fruit, also known as *calabazo*, is hollowed-out and dried. Horizontal serrations are cut half way around the front side; on the back, a sound-slit and a thumb-hole are cut. The serrated edges of the *güiro* are scraped with a *púa* which is constructed from two pieces of metal wire attached to a wooden handle and held in the right hand. Played in the same manner as the *guayo*, a metal variation of the *güiro* is made from tin-plate.

The origin of the *marimba dominicana* can be traced to the "thumb-piano" found throughout the West Coast of Africa. The Dominican instrument is made from a wooden packing-box, about 18" wide, 10" deep, and 12" high. From 3–6 metal prongs are attached to one side of the box with iron bolts; directly above the prongs, a sound-hole is cut. The player taps out the rhythms on the left side of the box with his palm and fingers; using a leather thong held in his right hand, he plucks the metal bars from the bottom up. The *marimba dominicana* is used as a bass percussion-instrument in the *merengue* and other native lively dances. . . .

The *acordeón*, according to several elderly informants, was introduced to the Dominican Republic at Santiago de los Caballeros about 65 years ago [c. 1885], by two Spanish merchants, Bernabé Morales and Joaquín Beltrán. Used throughout the Republic, its limited harmonic possibilities—tonic and harmonies—have unfortunately tended to retard the natural evolution of the earlier folk-music. . . .

The *tambora* is the national percussion instrument of the Republic. Of the many types observed, the most authentic is constructed from the chiselled-out trunk-section of the *lana* tree which has a soft pith. The drum-heads, which are prepared goatskins, are mounted on hoops and held in place by a second set of hoops which is fastened to the body by means of sisal-cord. A male goatskin is used for the top head, and a female, for the bottom. The main rhythms are played with the palm and fingers of the left hand; the secondary rhythms, with a *palito* [small stick] held in the right hand. . . .

Dominican Music on the World Stage: Eduardo Brito

Arístides Incháustegui

*Eduardo Brito (1905–1946) was one of the pioneers of the Dominican recording indus-
try and the first internationally known performer from the Dominican Republic.
He found success in New York City from 1930 to 1932, singing at the Empire Room of
the Waldorf Astoria Hotel and the Paramount Theater on Broadway, among other
places, with set-lists that ranged from Dominican folk tunes to famous opera arias.
Brito went on to become an even bigger hit in Madrid in the years before the Spanish
Civil War cut short his period of stardom there. After he left New York, the "merengue ambassador," Rafael Petión Guzmán (1894–1983) took up where he left off,
forming the first Dominican orchestra in the city and playing the Stork Club, the Co-
pacabana, and Radio City Music Hall. Brito returned to the Dominican Republic in
1941, having performed across Latin America, but he suffered a mental breakdown
and died in a mental hospital at the age of forty. Patrons of the Dominican National
Theater are reminded of him at every event in the main performance space there,
which is named Eduardo Brito Hall. This selection from a discography of Dominican popular music gives a brief summary of his life and work.*

The Dominican baritone Eduardo Brito was the illegitimate son of Julián
Álvarez Brito and Liboria Aragonés. While he was still a very young boy, in
the city of Puerto Plata, he helped his mother as an "order boy" in the Venus
restaurant, owned by the Cuban Amancio Martínez.

With time he would be an apprentice to a blacksmith and to a shoemaker,
a tobacco packer, a furniture mover, a boxing referee, and a shoe-shine boy,
nonetheless always demonstrating in each one of those humble jobs his exceptional vocal talent and undeniable artistic calling.

He took the step from shoe-shine boy to professional singer in Santiago,
primarily from the assistance of the most popular troubadours, such that
his artistic career would develop within a very special ambience, permitting

The cover of this album of the international recording star Eduardo Brito's greatest hits, produced three years after his death in 1946, had a patriotic theme featuring the handsome singer against the Dominican flag. *Eduardo Brito: El Gran Baritono Dominicano*, OTOAO Records International for Luraber Productions and Colony Records, ORC 1012, 1949, 33⅓ rpm. Courtesy of the Roorda/Doyle Collection.

him to sing everything from merengues to creoles, love songs, boleros, *son* music, tangos, romantic ballads, *zarzuelas*, all the way to bits of opera.

Some people still remember how at the very beginning of the decade of the 1920s, still very young, Brito sang in the capital in Pulo Padrón's nightclub, accompanied on the guitar by Antonio Vásquez, and returned again to Santiago, where once more he resumed his double identity as shoe-shine boy and singer.

During those years he sang frequently in one restaurant or another in the city, and occasionally performed in the Apollo Theater in that city, along with Julio Alberto Hernández or Juan Francisco García.

Luis Rivera gave him the opportunity to sing in the Ideal Theater, also in Santiago; the quartet from the opera *Rigoletto*, by Verdi . . . and from then on his talented amateur performances would leave the others behind.

In Santo Domingo, the high society of the capital discovered him when they heard him sing in 1927 at a banquet offered by the press . . . , prompting the poet Juan Bautista Lamarche to write the first important review in the artistic life of Eduardo Brito: "We were unaware that a singer of his abilities existed in Santo Domingo. It was a veritable revelation."

In the year 1928 Brito sang into the microphones of HIX, the official station that was created on April 18 of that same year, and participated together with other Dominican artists on the first recordings made in the country, the proofs of which would be pressed by Victor Records in New York.

Then in December of that year his 78 rpm record of "To See If You Have a Heart," by Piro Valerio, and "Never Cry," by Julio Albert Hernández.

During that time he met Rosa Elena Bobadilla, and a few weeks later they were married.

He traveled with the group "The Internationals" to Haiti and Curacao, where he joined the Company of Cuban Burlesque of Margot Rodríguez, with whom he debuted in Puerto Rico. At that point the career of Rosa Elena Bobadilla as a singer and dancer began, and she joined her husband to form the [group] Quisqueya Duet, which became the Brito Trio with the addition of Edelmira Bobadilla (Kiki).

The Quisqueya Duet returned to the country after finishing its tour and again Juan Bautista Lamarche offered them his warmest welcome from the pages of *Listín Diario* by proudly affirming in one of his columns: "We have homegrown artists!"

In 1929 the Grupo Dominicano was formed, who went to New York to record creole songs for Victor Records . . . with Eduardo Brito as lead vocal and percussion.

In eight sessions, this artistic ambassador recorded fifty songs by Dominican composers, putting on his first disc the creole *Lucía*, by Max Guzmán, with words by Dr. Joaquín Balaguer, and *La Mulatona* [the mulatto-looking woman] by Piro Valerio.

To the present day, this series of recordings of Dominican music represents the most important legacy of the popular national songbook [that was] produced by Dominican artists with an international label of the stature of Victor Records.

After that, Dominican music became known to North and South America and the Caribbean. . . .

The artistic career of Eduardo Brito, who rose from the humblest layers of the people to the summit of international art, becoming one of the few Latin American singers to triumph completely in Spain, will serve as a guide and example to the new generations of Dominican artists.

Translated by Eric Paul Roorda.

"The People Call All of It Merengue"

Johnny Ventura

The often-repeated tale of merengue originating at an 1844 battle, which did not appear in print until 1927, is probably a myth. What merengue's actual beginnings were is impossible to say with certainty, although that has not prevented music scholars from adamantly staking out contradictory claims on the question. These range from the insistence that merengue is entirely Spanish in origin, which was the party line during the Trujillo regime, to opposite contentions made in the 1970s that the dance can be traced to African rhythms alone. It seems likely that merengue is a blend of Spanish ballroom dances such as the danza *with the Haitian* mareng, *itself a combination of dances such as the* chica *that African slaves brought, and the French* contre-danse. *But in the absence of solid facts, the amount of influence exerted by each of the different musical traditions will always be unclear.*

In this address, delivered to a national conference on merengue in 1978, the merengue star Johnny Ventura weighed in on its history and its identification with the Dominican people. Ventura, born in Santo Domingo in 1940, began his musical career at the age of eighteen, when he also began to get involved in the Dominican Revolutionary Party. His musical and political careers rose in tandem, and by the time of the national merengue conference he had twenty years of experience as a performer and politician. But even bigger things were in store for "El Caballo Negro," as he became known—literally "The Black Horse," "horse" having a macho connotation like that of a tiger, though a caballo *is more respectable. Ventura was elected mayor of Santo Domingo and served from 1998 until 2002, in the midst of a twenty-year period during which he released an average of two albums annually.*

Merengue in the Present

The history of our merengue, perhaps a little more so than Dominican history in general, is lost in memories, anecdotes, and appreciations. The very few people who have been dedicated to those sources have not gotten much help in their work.

Couples dance in a dark bar in this photograph by the Austrian photographer
Kurt Schitzer ("Conrado"). Conrado Collection (57), Archivo General de la
Nación, Santo Domingo.

A very short while ago, I heard an authority on merengue say, and demonstrate with a dance company, that four compositions and interpretations
distinctly different from one another were all merengues. When this authority[1] was asked about that statement by an interviewer, he denied the
statement was his and attributed it to the people: "The people," he said, "call
all of it merengue."

And because the people are the authority today, I say, even though they
don't attend the university or take part in these very important events such
as congresses, seminars, and conferences, we must admit that all of it is
merengue. And if one contemplates the past, if one goes back to the origins
of Dominican society, to the development of merengue from those origins,
there is no recourse but to admit that that is merengue and merengue is,
also, that which is played today.

Johnny Ventura led the revival of merengue in the 1960s and 1970s, becoming personally identified with the rhythm, as his 1983 album title captured it: "I Am Merengue." *Yo Soy El Merengue*, Combo Records, RSCD 2016, 1983, 33⅓ rpm. Used by permission of Johnny Ventura. Courtesy of the Roorda/Doyle Collection.

As all of you know, they could not call on me to speak about the history of merengue. I am not a historian, only a *merenguero* to whom the public has given its favor for more than twenty years. They have given me the honor, which is also a personal satisfaction, to choose what I am going to say very much in my own way and very much in my understanding of what Merengue is in the Present. . . .

What I want to say, without beating around the bush, is that the merengue the people like today, the merengue the people ask for today, the merengue the people dance to today is nothing more than the result of the trajectory that our traditional music has followed, enriching itself with those antecedents of the popular arts that had been embraced in the developed countries.

In 1961, when the dictator Trujillo died, many people will remember that we had a more or less traditional merengue, this smooth and monotonous merengue that was already being left behind by a people who moved quickly toward their liberty and their progress, [as] more than ever through the opening of our country's frontiers came all of the modern currents of politics, of thought, of high art and of popular art.

It must be recalled, equally, that between the last years of the 1950s and the first years of the 1970s, there arose in the United States, and arrived in our country, a musical movement that departed completely from the traditional tunes of popular North American music. The compositions of Cole Porter and the interpretive style of Frank Sinatra had been replaced in the taste of that same society by the nervousness and clatter of "rock and roll" music and by the interpretations of Elvis Presley, Bill Halley, and so on.

This music and this interpretation, without doubt, was more in keeping with what had begun to be the North American society of those years and with that which came to be, in the end, all of the societies of all the nations dependent on the United States. From then on, "rock" set the pace of modern music, which right from the start was much more rapid than the traditional.

During those years, soon after Trujillo died, it was evident that traditional merengue was identified with the tyranny and had been pushed aside by the enormous enthusiasm that "rock and roll" had awakened in the Dominican youth.

Because during that epoch I also was an adolescent, and after many, many gyrations to the rhythms of "rock" and later the twist, there arose in me the spirit and the vocation of the merenguero. It was merengue I loved the most, and I remember that I was very mortified when I came to recognize that merengue could disappear. . . .

While original merengue remained the interpretive responsibility of our folklore groups, and of the museums of history and popular art, the merengue of the modern orchestras and bands has to march shoulder to shoulder with the progress of popular music worldwide.

We have traveled abroad, as we continue to travel—and when I say we travel I do not refer only to my group—in the capacity of Dominican musical representation, but of a Dominican music that is the daughter of a historic process of growth and improvement, such that Dominican music has a place today with the most modern and most innovative currents of composition, instrumentation, and interpretation in the whole world.

Translated by Eric Paul Roorda.

Note

1. Probably Fradique Lizardo (1930–1997), author of several books on music and dance, choreographer, and founder of the Dominican Folkloric Ballet.

A *Bachata* Party

Julio Arzeno

The word bachata *used to mean a party in the countryside. These all-night, alcohol-fueled affairs, typically starting on Saturday evening and concluding at dawn on Sunday, invariably included guitar music for dancing. When legions of rural Do-minicans moved to Santo Domingo in the 1960s, the word* bachata *came to refer to that music, but it remained one of many guitar-based genres, lacking any particular acclaim in the Dominican Republic, and it was virtually unknown beyond the nation's borders.*

Bachata music was a marginalized music, considered lower class and vulgar by Dominican society, until it was brought to a wider world by the international merengue superstar Juan Luis Guerra, who has sold more than 30 million albums worldwide in his career. One of Guerra's most successful recordings was Bachata Rosa, *released in December 1990, which went Platinum in the United States and won the Grammy Award for Latin American/Tropical Performance of the Year. The record also sold more than 100,000 copies in Brazil and was a hit in Japan and the Netherlands, among other places. But as Deborah Pacini Hernández has pointed out in* Bachata: A Social History of a Dominican Popular Music *(1995), the ver-sion of bachata popularized by Guerra, while delightful in its own right, is a far cry from its musical antecedents from the campo.*

While merengue is still the most internationally recognized Dominican musical genre, bachata music has steadily risen in popularity since the 1990s. Nowadays it is more popular than ever and is increasingly played at dance clubs where only salsa and merengue dominated in the past, especially in places with large Dominican populations such as New York City. The Bronx-based pop bachata group Aventura, with a sound that fuses bachata with R & B *influences, sold out Madison Square Garden in 2007. Luny Tunes, the* regguetón *production duo of Dominican origin, has also raised the profile of bachata music by infusing regguetón songs with ba-chata instrumentation, as did the Dominican producer Edward Bella Pou, aka El Cata, when he arranged Shakira's album, including her version of his song "Soy loca con mi tíguere." Whereas bachata purists argue that such fusions are denigrating the genre, the sounds of bachata have become increasingly popular throughout the world.*

The best description of an original bachata party (which usually ended with a sunrise breakfast of sancocho, *the quintessential Dominican stew) is this one left by Julio Arzeno (1892–1932), a popular band leader who is regarded as the first Dominican folklorist.*

On the arrival of Saturday, or the last day of the week, when night falls, all that is needed is our popular troubadour, a guitar, a tambourine, and the indispensable maracas to have a good time with the dance and impromptu party called bachata, where the commentator [singer] on everything that happens is king and master, employing for it the improvised bolero; and not only for the simple pleasure of singing about a momentary passion or easy romantic conquest or otherwise any incident or event of the day, but to plunge into the mute poetry of expressive beauty: the dance that he loves with frenzy, with devout worship, and poetic love.

[The musicians] practice this art in an empirical manner, without knowing theory; they learn the various pieces that are in fashion by memory, in that way building their repertoire, but they also improvise lovely songs like the following:

> Because I have to sing to you, Springtime,
> if you are the mother of tenderness,
> if you adorn all, enchanting, sublime,
> with your inspired gifts of loveliness;
> May the influence of your life revive
> the pretty fronds below, above
> the birds sing, the flowers thrive,
> and the women dream, they dream of love.

The jocular tone adds liveliness and wit to these healthy and popular parties, because the improvisation makes fun of everything. The important thing for them is to rhyme while keeping the beat of the dancing, although somewhat childishly:

> Ay, my aunt died
> on the highway,
> her life ended
> from dysentery.

There were colors associated with the insignias of all the political parties in our region during that era: red was the historical color of the Baecista Party; blue was for that of Luperón, green, of González; it was logical, therefore, that they sang also of political colors:

The red ribbon,
the favorite,
is not as pretty
as the blue;
For this reason Juana
I like to see you,
always wearing
your blue outfit;
Nothing is more beautiful
than your hair,
if it is embellished
by the blue ribbon.

When [the musicians] did not know the bolero, or the *guaracha* [another musical style] of our [the Dominican] region, they sang and danced music of a rough and romantic flavor, although of tranquil grace, whose lyrics always alluded to some anecdote or familiar current event, repeating at length and insistently their insubstantial and incongruous couplets that for being pure and simple hardly approach the epigrammatic:

Silly María
wants to get married,
to a young man
from the capital.

And in that style, thousands of unnamed couplets, which, although insignificant in terms of lyric, were always in rhythm with the music that they underlined.

Translated by Eric Paul Roorda.

The Tiger

Rafael Damirón

In 1895 Rafael Damirón (1882–1956) wrote this essay about the tigre *(often written as* tíguere *following its popular pronunciation), which originated during the Haitian occupation as a social label for street children who begged and picked pockets. During the late nineteenth-century economic growth that fueled urbanization,* tíguere *became established as referring to a quintessentially urban male social type, who perturbed elites because he was a stranger able to dissimulate, even pass for someone he was not, in a way that was not yet common in the face-to-face context of rural small-town life.* Tíguere *today is one of the most widely used terms in the Dominican vocabulary. While it has a negative tinge and thus can mean "delinquent" in rural settings, among male peers over a beer it can also connote respect for someone who "gets away with murder" by acquiring wealth, a woman, or a position he does not necessarily deserve. As a cultural stereotype, the* tíguere *conveys the myth of upward mobility, which is a common feature of a mestizo or mixed-race society that, like the Dominican one, lacks the hard racial boundaries of biracial plural societies and allows people to move in the social hierarchy. The Dominican* tíguere *has been characterized by Christian Krohn-Hansen as a trickster or hustler, a survivor in his environment; he is thus the modern* montero *who finds a way to get ahead without the trappings of credentials or a formal occupation, often through illicit means. This figure is a byproduct of the culture of informality one finds in many postemancipation societies in which former slaves fled from harsh labor forms such as sugar plantations to become masters of their own destiny as peasants (even if in the Caribbean most did not necessarily own their own land) or, in the Dominican case,* monteros *or pirates. In this selection we hear the mistrust of the Dominican elite toward the* tíguere, *casting him as an outsider who is unknowable and untrustworthy due to his lack of social location and readability, one who frequents public locales such as the theater and the hotel. Damirón underscores the illegitimate and possibly criminal forms of work and the aggressive masculinity characteristic of the underclass* tíguere.

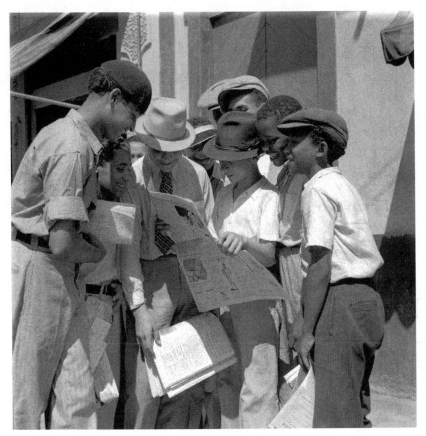

The urban population supported a rich tradition of journalism. These boys, potential *tígueres*, hawked newspapers in the street. Photograph by Kurt Schnitzer ("Conrado"). Conrado Collection (18), Archivo General de la Nación, Santo Domingo.

Today we are going to have a truce, leaving behind the poets and troubadours that formerly garnered our attention to speak to our readers about the new type of fellow that can be found in the capital, which has emerged for the sake of pestering and even tormenting those who despise the rotten side of society.

The subject of discussion is not a mystery. Indeed, its newfound ubiquity makes it a familiar topic of discussion for all.

Where does he come from?

Who is his father?

Who is his mother?

His sister?

His grandmother?

His closest relative?

Who knows!

He sleeps in the ruins or in the open air, whatever the circumstances permit.

What does he eat?

When does he eat?

No one knows! He eats sometimes, is always sleeping, and dresses in a pathetic way, but he does not parade around naked.

He hovers around the doors of hotels and theaters where decent people convene. His face blackened by the sun, his hands and feet covered in grime, almost always toothless, and with long hair and hungry eyes.

In times of harvest, he freeloads mangoes and *cajuiles* (cashew fruit), limoncillo (Spanish lime) and crabs, at his ease like a lord of the manor.

A thief at times by necessity and most often by vice, this character is well known to the courts and especially the police. He gambles with coins, losing all the money he has stolen or begged for. In this irresponsible hustle, his soul prepares itself for crime, pain, and treachery.

In his small world, love is not a matter of honor, but an issue of exaggerated manly pride emboldened by the hunger for personal domination that shields him from the sentimental missteps of his more cowardly friends.

He shuns school, and he hates books and the good manners associated with decent people.

He prays because he learned how to from someone in his childhood who did so to bribe the gods with promises of piety; he beseeches God to protect himself from the spells he fears from the bottom rungs of society.

He is the natural product of the rapid growth of a city, where he has created his small domain that he has conquered, at the expense of all others and by any means necessary.

Without a legal residence, or a permanent address, he has maliciously avoided all civil formalities that could serve to track him down when he makes a mockery of the law and disobeys the police.

He has not learned to cry, and for this reason his sadness lives hidden beneath cynicism.

When he approaches old age he is plagued by degeneracy and vices that without fail have placed him outside the margins of the right path.

The jail, the brothel, the card table, his treatment of women, and all that is vile and rude render him the definitive gigolo, unworthy of compassion.

You will see him the same at dawn as you will at midnight, as you will in the afternoon; he will be circulating through one neighborhood, and then another, because in his childhood his mother left him unsupervised while she worked all day for an abject salary until nightfall, and many times the little bread that she carried was not sufficient to share between him and his numerous siblings, who were already preparing to take the path of those pilgrims of suffering whom life corrupts and whose souls, chests, thoughts, and ambitions fate scars.

He was born as rats are born: without anything in a cave. Upon opening his eyes and being born into this world, nothing around him was his.

And alone, under the cold cruelty that allows these populations to expand, he prepares for ceaseless wandering that will without fail transform him into the new persona that has garnered our attention today: *El tigre.*

Translated by Lauren Derby and Alex Huezo.

La Montería: The Hunt for
Wild Pigs and Goats

Martha Ellen Davis

Just as the buccaneers did centuries earlier, Dominican peasants continued to hunt wild pigs, goats, and cattle and to preserve their meat into the twentieth century. The traditional process is detailed in this testimony, which was collected by Martha Ellen Davis as part of a Dominican National Archives project to gather the oral history of subsistence farmers.

Peasants eighty years old and older remember a time of great fertility of the soil and an abundance of harvests and wildlife. Subsistence farmers chopped down forest to make their conucos *(personal garden plots), employing the tropical technique of "slash and burn," working in* juntas *or* convites *(work brigades) and singing* coros, plenas, *and* salves *(work songs). They deforested the island to the rhythm of the axe. The breeding of domestic animals and the hunting and fishing of wild animals supplemented the sowing of the fields.*

The animals that complemented the farmers' diet were not all domesticated but were also feral: pigs, goats, and cattle. The hunting of these feral animals, called montería, *is an integral part of the history of the island.*

Don Baldemiro Féliz, raised in La Lajita in the Bahoruco Mountain Range between lowland Cabral and the mountain town of Polo in Barahona province, told Davis and her colleagues about hunting wild pigs and goats from his youth in the 1930s to the 1950s.

I hunted these wild animals a great deal. Our parents taught us this when we were little. The people who worked their conucos did not buy meat because there was more than enough wild pig and wild goat. This hunting was not illegal, because if the animal was not branded, there was no owner; animals with an owner were marked on the ear.

There were two types of male wild pigs: the one called a "boar" [*barraco*], which was a large pig, and the other one called "little boar" [*barraquete*]. The large pig grows long tusks [*cuchillas*, "knives"], and the small boar grows

446

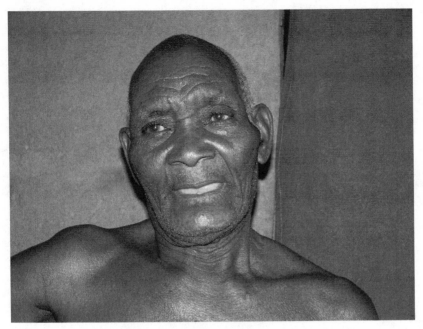

Former montero Baldemiro Féliz ("Baldé"). Tierra Blanca, Cabral, Barahona. Photograph by Martha Ellen Davis, 2006. Used by permission.

little tusks [*media navajas*, "small knives"]. When those tusks grow, they curl back. The female pigs grow a smaller type of tusk [*colmillo*, "eye tooth"].

Before today's firearms there was a shotgun they called an "assault shotgun." And what they loaded it with was ammunition and powder and they used cartridge caps called *extranjeros* [foreigners] in that barrel. That's what we used to kill pigs, to kill goats, and all kinds of birds in the Laguna [Laguna del Rincón, the largest freshwater lake in the country] and in the mountains. We also killed bothersome animals like the mountain cat [*gato montero*] that ate chickens. But we never killed people, because that gun was only for hunting. The guns made today are for killing people, something we never saw.

My father had some hunting dogs bred especially for hunting, one called Rojito ["Little Red"] and the other called Creo en Díos ["I Believe in God"]. There were two types of dogs: the "bay dog" [*perro de meneo*] and the "catch dog" [*perro de coger*]. We would go with them to the woods, one with a halter and the other one loose. And when that bay dog signaled that he had found a bunch of pigs or goats, we would come and release the other dog. The one dog would work in front, barking, what they call "holding it" [*aguantándolo*]. And when he was holding the pig or goat, we would let the catch dog loose,

La Loma de la Hoz (Sickle Mountain), Bahoruco Mountain Range. Photograph by Martha Ellen Davis, 2006. Used by permission.

and pow! That dog would grab the animal from behind, by the testicles, or the belly if it was female. And when he grabbed it by the testicles or the belly, he would pull it down, no matter how big. Because in that position the pig could not fight with the dog, but from the front he could fight with those tusks. So one of us would come and pow! Slit its throat!

And right there we would skin it, and then feed the dogs, because they were used to that. To skin the animal, we would bring fire with us, and sometimes water. We would sprinkle it, rotate it, sprinkle it. Then we would take a palm leaf, whether it was coconut palm or *cacheo* [similar to a palm tree], and we would light it and fan the animal. Then we would take a knife and scrape off the hair. We would make the skin very, very white. And afterward, we would turn it upside down, we would slit it open, and we would take out the guts—what they call tripe, the entrails, and all that stuff. And what was left were two clean strips of pork—what they called a *tasajera*.

We would bring home these fresh strips of meat and would chop them up and sprinkle salt, sour orange juice, and lime juice on them. Then we would put them on a stick to dry, rotating them. They could take three or four days to dry. After that meat had dried, we would put it in a can, and we would eat from it to feed ourselves. And we would never be in need of meat, never.

And it would not go bad. Do you know why? Because that process got rid of the water; and having put it out in the sun and gotten rid of the water and applied a lot of salt, lime juice, and sour orange juice, it didn't spoil.

That's what we call *montear*, and people don't do that anymore.

Translated by Alex Huezo and Martha Ellen Davis.

Everyday Life in a Poor Barrio

Tahira Vargas

After the death of Trujillo, many Dominicans began to move from rural areas to the capital, a phenomenon that accelerated as the economy, restructured with free trade, shifted from traditional agroexports such as sugar and tobacco to manufacturing and assembly jobs expanded. Tahira Vargas has studied the poor neighborhood of La Altagracia de Herrera, which started out a rural hamlet and has over time become part of the extended periphery of Santo Domingo. The place originated in the 1500s as a settlement of enslaved people who labored on a nearby sugar ingenio or plantation. In the twentieth century land struggles occurred there; some found their land expropriated under the Trujillo regime and, later, some by the state. Vargas's fine-grained ethnography challenges many of the assumptions that sociologists of the "culture of poverty" school held in the 1950s. She discovered a community whose earners have considerably less income than is necessary to support a family (the average income is only US$214 per month). Yet this community is highly organized and entrepreneurial and has organized crucial services such as child care and the sharing of domestic tools—from coffeepots to hair dryers—and innovated lotteries and credit associations largely through family networks. While most conjugal unions are not formalized by either church or state (as is the norm in the Dominican Republic), family networks are extraordinarily strong. Indeed, kinship provides the organizational principle of the community: 75 percent of those living on the street she surveyed were members of two extended family clans. She also found that the barrio is young; more than 83 percent are under age thirty-nine, and only about 50 percent had had some elementary school. Most were employed in the informal sector: as the street vendors called chiriperos; *as self-employed motorcycle* taxistas; *in family-based microenterprises—repairing shoes, styling hair, selling meat, clothes, or accessories, or preparing street food. With most families having resided in the neighborhood over several generations, the stability of this barrio confounds the image of underclass urban shantytowns in Latin America, since most of the houses are made of concrete block rather than recycled detritus, and most people reside and work in the barrio, which has knitted these communities together very tightly. And while most women do not engage in formal employment, women play a central role*

because the family is matrifocal, defined by women and their offspring, and as a
result, the clan matriarchs are held in high esteem. In this selection Vargas reports
on the everyday lives of men and women in el barrio through an analysis of the pro-
totypical male rural pastime of the game of dominoes, which is usually played in the
street and accompanied by the drinking of beer, and a discussion of the female rela-
tions of exchange and how these provide key forms of support for poor women. We
also see in the style of domino playing described here the role of backstage habilidad,
skill, or rule stretching—traces of the tíguere *hustling lifestyle that is so patently a*
part of Dominican popular culture.

One of the most common activities in the street and in the neighborhood is
the game of dominoes. . . . Dominoes is basically played by men. In it, relations of power articulated through gender are expressed and legitimized.
Women are excluded from the game. Their exclusion is not explicit but
rather implicit. The rules of the game of dominoes do not prohibit the presence of women. This element I identified after observing many games. In
none of the games I observed did a woman appear. All of the players were
men. In interviewing the players, this fact was implicit; they never said it.
All of them said that women don't play the game, or said they didn't know
why women did not play it, or they assumed that they did not play.

In dialogue with some of the men [who were] interviewed about dominoes, one of them proposed that "a few women play dominoes," but at
home, because in public women cannot be seen mixing with so many men.
"Imagine if during the game the men tell stories and make off-color jokes
and say curse words. The women are going to feel bad. Moreover, this is not
a space for a woman. They would feel disrespected." . . .

Winning the game involves blocking the opponent's game and the explicit demonstration of the "skill" (supposedly mixed with luck) of com-
municating among the players that one is breaking the rules and secretly
doing "tricks." The rules of the game operate contrary to skill in this sense,
since the more skillful the players, the more the rules are broken (everyone
knows that the rules are broken, but this is an open secret that is denied),
and the greater the possibility of tricks or cheating.

Those who play dominoes are family or neighbors. Others, either from
outside the family or the territory, are absent, and family and neighbor relations are strengthened through leisure with the game of dominoes. "My
father and I get along well; we play dominoes together."

The act of drinking beer is a ritual expression of leisure in the street. Beer
is associated with leisure and is not uniquely masculine; women also drink.
This association of leisure and beer drinking has made beer the principal

A couple in front of their home in Villa Mella, a municipality in the northern perimeter of Santo Domingo, chatting as they watch a *palo* (traditional drumming performance) (2002). Photograph by Giovanni Savino. "A Life Together," © Giovanni Savino Photography.

sales item in the barrio. "Here what is sold most is beer; I can stop buying food or milk at the *colmado* [corner grocery] but not beer, especially on the weekends."

Ninety percent of the men interviewed in the street, when asked what they did for entertainment, responded that they "drank a beer quietly at home with my neighbors." In the case of women it is less; 75 percent said they drank beer, although they added "with their husband."

These responses demonstrate the legitimacy of the cultural norm of privacy noted above. "At home" establishes a distinction from the act of drinking in public, in *colmadones* [larger corner groceries with music and tables for beer drinking]. But in practice, what happens is very different; beer is consumed in groups differentiated by gender, women on one side and men on the other, and generally on the sidewalk or in the colmados, with the difference that women don't drink inside the colmados in groups but they will on the sidewalk. . . .

The concept of the neighbor is mixed with family, and the family-neighbor becomes a unity through constant exchange. Exchange on the street has several aspects.

1. Availability of exchange without limits. The symbol of the neighbor is colored by the unlimited availability of domestic objects, the exchange of favors, services, and use of domestic space. This availability is expected to have no limits, because the presence of limits generates conflict. It is expected that the neighbor or family member is ready, for example, to have kids play in front of their house. This is very common in the street; kids play everywhere, in the patio, the house stoop, and inside everyone's house. The neighbors allow their neighbor's kids to play on their property without hindrance. I perceived some conflicts in street relations in which one neighbor was called *comparona* ["stuck up"] because she did not allow other kids to play on her stoop.

2. Availability for service and need solicitation. The sense of exchange that permeates neighborly relations in the street assumes that one's neighbor must always need a thing or a service. Just as one requests services or things, one receives services and things. To not need a service breaks with the dynamic of exchange and interaction in the street. "If a neighbor asks me for something, I like to be helpful. But there are neighbors on the street who never ask for anything; who never take advantage because one is not important to them." I heard this comment in different forms all the time. The neighbor who does not ask for help is seen as one who doesn't need others, thus is *comparon*, which is the clearest expression of lack of communication between neighbors.

3. Exchange implicitly implies exchange of information, hence social control. In this sense one must underscore that neighborly relations are permeated with gossip. Above all, women must be ready and willing to gossip and exchange information and moralizing opinions among themselves. Among neighbors one is permitted to provide advice [and] suggestions related to love relations and the management of family dramas, and even make decisions related to information provided by neighbors. "I punished my child because the neighbor

said that he was bothering him in the street." "Neighbor, check on that kid for me, and tell me if he does anything." This type of command implies that not only does one allow information collection from neighbors about one's child, but they are even entitled to discipline them.

To observe the daily life of the women in the street one can make a balance sheet of the time that women are immersed in networking with their neighbors, sisters, mothers, and aunts in everyday activities in which they socialize while they work. This ethos is very important for these women, for whom the streets and the stoop of their houses are shared spaces, since housing [in this place keeps people] physically very close together.

The frequency with which women get together in networks during the day [takes up] between 56–67 percent of the time. This figure demonstrates the daily schedule of these women during the week, and how this socializing intensifies during the weekend. Out of fifteen hours of daily activity, between eight or nine hours each day are permeated with constant and occasional networking, of meeting and mutual exchange, among women who live on the same street in the neighborhood, or with other women of the barrio. Domestic labor in the street is a constant, thus enabling support, reciprocity, and conflict among the female neighbors. All the women wash on the same day of the week. On the street, I observed that all the women of one block of ten houses washed on one day. Another block of seven houses washed on Saturday morning, and another block of thirteen houses washed on Fridays.

The domestic activities that are integrated into collective networks are: clothes washing, babysitting, food shopping, and assistance in case of scarcity of a service or item, such as water, gas or charcoal, soap, detergent, or food. The presence of a collective connotation of these domestic activities in the street is one of the ways we see the home extend into the street. A "domestic" activity, thus, is actually an extensive activity that incorporates several homes and family groups.

The women go out in front of their houses and put all of their dirty clothes together, and then they divide up the clothes equally to do the washing. The distribution is carried out as a form of unburdening the women who have the most clothes to wash so as to enable an equitable distribution of time and effort among the group. This activity is made into a weekly routine, and the collective character is evident in the distribution of tasks, from rinsing to hanging out to dry. Clothes washing is thus a symbol of collective interaction that gives shape to important elements of mutual help and exchange of services. Conflicts emerge in discussions among the women, but the conflict is aggravated, because they argue openly and shout insults at one another. The conflict is of such magnitude and in such close quarters that this dialogue becomes a constant element in the social network that both threatens and dynamizes the collectivity.

Translated by Lauren Derby.

The Name Is the Same as the Person

José Labourt

The spectrum of popular Dominican beliefs is broad and diverse, but much of it seeks to improve one's chances for good luck. This can be seen in Sana, Sana, Culito de Rana, the veritable catalogue of cultural practices that José Labourt published in 1979. The title refers to the ditty people sing to distract children when they have a small injury: "Heal! Heal, frog's little butt! Five words. . . . If you don't heal today, heal tomorrow!" Also called "the boo-boo song," it originated as a spell; many of the following contemporary examples go far back in Dominican history.

The belief that a name is part of the essence of a person has meant that many Dominican peasants will keep their legal names a secret. A *vendegente*, or person thought to have the task of supplying human bodies to the Devil or to other beings associated with supernatural activities, can accomplish this task with the knowledge of one's complete name. It is also believed that if you divulge your legal name you may become the victim of witchcraft. *Guanguás* or *guangás* [magical packets prepared by sorcerers], which cause fatal spells, are made using the recitation of people's names. It is difficult for strangers to acquire the complete names of many peasants. And it is said that the full names of many of these people are not even known to members of their immediate family.

Peasants prefer to give their children long names. Many times these names are chosen from the *Bristol Almanac*, an annual publication in the countryside. On certain occasions they have selected up to four names of saints mentioned in the almanac for the specific day their child was born. Pedro Muñoz, in reality, was not named so at birth. His complete name was Pedro Jacinto y Tiburcio López Muñoz. He was born the ninth of September.

One time the news arrived in a rural community that Clemente Columbano Abad Rosario Pérez, a person native to the community, had died. Nobody recognized that name. A relative, after quite some time, said that they thought that was the real name of Songo el de Pedro. And actually, it was

Songo el de Pedro, whose other name in the town was Clemente Pérez. The name Songo el de Pedro was given to him because his father's first name was Pedro. Songo el de Pedro was the equivalent of saying "Songo the son of Pedro." Songo was nothing more than a term of endearment.

María, because she was Julio's woman, was called María la de Julio (Julio's María) by her neighbors. And with time her name became María Julio. María Julio is a different person from María Manuel, the woman of a peasant named Manuel. And so, if one of these two women had done something worthy of commentary and someone, in close proximity to both of them had simply said María, surely they would have responded, "María? Which María?" And that person would have responded, "María Manuel."

This phenomenon of María Julio, María Manuel, and Songo el de Pedro no longer derives from a desire to keep one's name secret. It comes from the fact that in the countryside people are not interested in last names, when the occasion is not a formal one. Besides, it is easier to say María Manuel than it is to say María Carmen López Sánchez, if the complete name was ever known.

Just as a woman is identified with the name of her husband, the man is also identified with his woman's name. Andres Julian, that is, Andres the son of Julian, married Juliana Carmen, that is, with Juliana the daughter of Carmen. Now his name is Andres Juliana, and his wife is known as Juliana Andres.

Peasants are inclined to nickname their sons. Manfeo (Ugly Man), Negrito (Blackie), La Negra (Black Woman), and Mecho (Candlestick) are some of the nicknames chosen by parents. None of these nicknames is derived from real names, as you can see. Yet a peasant would be quick to kill if somebody [else] nicknamed their offspring.

There is the case of the family whose children died shortly after birth. A witch was consulted and she advised the family to name family members after animals. Now this family has little girls named La Rana (Frog), La Ratona (Mouse), and La Mariposa (Butterfly). Not even their grandparents or aunts and uncles know their real names.

In this case the belief in one's name being the self, or the name being part of the essence of a person, has been revived.

Many of the peasant nicknames are products of their parents' affections. And they are stuck with those names. Some of these nicknames are very strong. So strong that it is better not to write some of them. Every Dominican reader, surely, knows of at least one nickname like this. . . .

Desperate to reach the Unites States, many Dominicans try to obtain a US visa by turning to sorcery. They also turn to the sorcerer to obtain work, to win the national lottery, to improve the fortune of their business, and for "good luck."

The majority of sorcerers do the visa work for 13 pesos and 13 centavos. This work is dedicated to Saint Santiago [Saint James], who in some parts is known as "Saint Santiago of Travels," and "Saint Santiago of Visas." The sorcerer knows that his client would like the visa rituals performed when the client greets him the following way. The interested client says his good morning to the "old man" and, with his forehead, bumps into the sorcerer's forehead, at the same time that his arms are maintained in the shape of a cross.

The *papa-bocó* [Santería practitioner] takes his client's left hand and lifting it up and toward the backside, makes the client do two turns, "a reverse turn and turn to the front." After entering negotiations, the sorcerer drinks water and later, with the liquid, forms a cross on the floor. He lights a cigarette, lights a candle "backward," and puts on his sorcery table a transparent white vase, next to [which] he places the passport. Where the passport is sitting, he smears a drop of ink.

"You will not obtain a visa on your first visit, but on your second," he says to the client while he blows smoke in his face.

He says goodbye to the client and puts together the "service." He makes a mixture with holy water, oil, sweet spices, rum, five little leaves of mint, and cologne. He empties the contents into the vase on the table and, with a wick [in it to serve as a candle], he places it in a predetermined location for twenty-one days, "in the names of the consuls of the United States."

On his second visit to the sorcerer, the client receives a flask with contents that should be used on the hands and around the neck, when the person goes to visit the consulate. The ingredients of this mix are, in some cases, seven different perfumes "obtained from people who are using the fragrance," white sugar, divine water, good luck water, patchouli water, and holy water.

"In the name of the five senses of the consuls," the believer proclaims when applying the mixture. . . .

When he gets to the consulate, the client, from what I am told, has succeeded in learning the name of the public official who will meet with them, although, it has been established, the magical practice of providing the name is not obligatory, "but helps with the effectiveness," said one "recipient." The name, written [on a piece of paper] inside the footwear, is stomped heavily.

Some sorcerers, when their work "fails," attribute the failure to the fact that the client was unable to write the American name of the consulate official, "because it is necessary that the name is written with all of the letters, completely."

A sorceress from Mao, now a resident of the capital, does the visa ritual differently from her colleagues. She gets a handkerchief and knots it at the corners. She hangs it from the ritual table and places on top of it a piece of nutmeg. She perfumes the cloth with ingredients that she will not reveal to her clients and recommends that the client keep the cloth in a Bible on a Tuesday night. The client puts the Bible in his house, with five lit candles.

Although the visa magic is dedicated to Saint Santiago of the Visas, when writing the name of the consul in the shoes, [the client] should utter, in a soft voice, a prayer to Saint Michael.

During the fact-finding [for this book], someone told the author an anecdote about a woman from Cibao who said the consul's name while she was stomping her feet. It was hilarious, according to the storyteller, to hear that woman pronounce the North American official's name with a heavy accent from Cibao.

The sorcerers appeal to Saint Pancras to be the protector of the unemployed. It should be noted that the Catholic saints who are used in Dominican sorcery represent a *lúa* [Santería god] or "being" and in other cases have been converted into multiple beings. "I will find you work in one month," says the sorcerer, and he dedicates his rituals to Saint Pancras for the next nine days. The magic costs 21 pesos and 21 centavos. Grab a green lemon, split it into a cross shape, throw the pieces into a mixture of sweet spices, *agua de Florida* [bottled shaman water from Peru], a small branch of mint, and green oil. Also add into the magical mix the names of the executives of the businesses where you have solicited a job. It is also recommended that the client take *anís* baths, Vini-Vini, Agua de Florida and other colognes, holy water, and black sugar. The ingredients for those baths, according to the fact-finding, should be bought in stores where there is "a lot of movement." This is, a well-stocked store that is always full of clients.

There are sorcerers who prepare flasks with "good luck" water, which the believers douse on their lottery tickets, with the purpose of winning the lottery. Some people, when they receive change in the form of winning lottery tickets, have the custom of smelling the tickets. If they find that they are fragrant already, they reject the tickets. This is because they believe that the ticket won through "dirty magic."

In the country there are people so obsessed with sorcery that they go to the sorcerers just to be prescribed "good luck baths."

There are people who in order to maintain their jobs, through the recommendations of sorcerers or people who "know," bring to their workplaces, written on a piece of paper in their shoes, the name of their boss. When for some reason they are called to the boss's office and they think they are "doing badly," before entering the office, in a place out of sight, they stomp three times, really hard.

"That way, you always have the boss pressed into your feet," said a young typist employed in a Santo Domingo bank.

Translated by Eric Paul Roorda.

"I Hope It Rains . . .": Juan Luis Guerra

Eric Paul Roorda

The international recording sensation Juan Luis Guerra may be the best known Dominican on the planet. He first became popular in his native country in the late 1980s as the leader of the quartet "4:40." By that time, he had studied an eclectic range of subjects at the Autonomous University and the National Conservatory of Music, both located in his hometown of Santo Domingo, where he was born in 1957, and at Berklee Academy of Music in Boston, where he received a degree in jazz composition in 1982. These intellectual and musical influences came through in the music of 4:40, who had their first hit in the Latin American market in 1989 with Ojalá que Llueva Café (I Hope It Rains Coffee). The following year's landmark album, Bachata Rosa, served both to elevate "Juan Luis Guerra y 4:40" to international fame and to resurrect the musical style of bachata, turning it into a global phenomenon. In 1992, the five-hundredth anniversary of Columbus's "discovery" of the Taíno people, Guerra released the controversial Areito, filled with songs about historic and contemporary injustices, including "The Cost of Living," his first number one Latin American hit. He turned to traditional rural musical forms, in particular the proto-merengue style perico ripiao, for Fogaraté (1994). The first of his albums to win Latin Grammy Awards was No es lo mismo ni es igual (Neither the Same nor Equal), which won three in 1998. After a six-year hiatus, he added fuel to the evangelical revival sweeping the Dominican Republic with Para tí, an album inspired by his own religious conversion, which won Billboard awards in the categories of both gospel and tropical. His biggest success to date came in 2007, when his partly bilingual album La llave de mi corazón (The Key to My Heart) won five Latin Grammy Awards. He won two more in 2012, one for a duet he recorded with Milly Quezada.

Guerra captured the contemporary embodiment of the tíguere in Dominican culture in this composition, "El Primo," which was a hit in 1998. The lyrics describe a multitalented cousin whose list of abilities—even superpowers—lengthens as the song goes on.

I have a cousin, Baldemiro, who is an expert at the craps table.
But I have a cousin, Baldemiro, who's a lawyer, has a Ph.D.,

is a surgeon and a good actor, a journalist on salary,
everything he wants and more.

I have a cousin, Baldemiro, who knows Michael Jordan and is an actor,
who breathes underwater and is a painter, who's a sociologist and airplane
pilot.

It must be noted that most Dominicans seem to have a cousin with exceptional talents, which suggests the ubiquity of the tíguere figure to the present day.

Guerra and 4:40 have performed all over the world, with the drawing power to sell out Madison Square Garden in Manhattan in minutes, but he chose the Olympic Center in Santo Domingo as the venue for a live album in June 2012. With tickets on sale for as little as 100 Dominican pesos, about US$3.00, the event attracted fans across the social spectrum, who filled the old stadium, built in 1974 for the Central American and Caribbean Games, on a night that promised rain. When the concert and the downpour began in tandem, the crowd did not disperse but instead became wildly enthusiastic and stayed that way, even during an unplanned intermission to remove the dangerous buildup of water on the cover of the enormous, temporary stage. Guerra said, "This rain is a blessing! Don't worry."

Guerra's set list from that Woodstock-like gathering, which he released as a recording and video in May 2013, featured many of the most popular in his repertoire of songs, which range from meltingly romantic ballads to biting political commentaries and across many musical styles.

Set List of Juan Luis Guerra Concert, Centro Olímpico, June 16, 2012

"Turn It Off and Let's Go," from *A son de Guerra* (2010), which features the dance music called *son*. His world tour that included the Santo Domingo concert was entitled "A son de Guerra."

Oh, oh, my Darling! Turn it off and let's go, because it's the same.
What do we do with the deafness and cynicism?
The same bolero, the same cassette, the shredded meat, and the same
   puré.
The same hope, the same check stub; with memories of Achilles, we
   dance a *son*.

"Bilirubin," from *Bachata Rosa* (1990). Before launching into this upbeat hit, Guerra greeted the crowd. "Good evening, Santo Domingo! It's a pleasure to be here with you! Long live the Dominican Republic!"

The international recording superstar Juan Luis Guerra, whose work includes music in the styles of merengue, *bachata, son,* and *perico ripiao,* displayed a Dominican flag during a performance in Viña del Mar, Chile, on Dominican Independence Day, February 27, 2012. Photograph by Jorge Saenz/AP, 120228168536 © The Associated Press. Used by permission.

Listen, I ran a fever the other day because of your love. . . .
My bilirubin levels go up when I look at you and you don't look at me,
    and aspirin doesn't help, not even a serum of penicillin.
It's a love that contaminates, bilirubin overwhelms me.
Oh, look Negra, find me an IV and inject me with your love like insulin,
    I have a yellow face. . . .

"The Journey," from *La Llave de mi Corazón* (2007).

I've never met another woman like you on Earth, my Life.
I have searched in Namibia, in the Alps and on the Champs d'Elysee.
I've crossed the seas and climbed the Eiffel Tower, walked through
    Manhattan and reached the Empire State Building.
But there's no one like you in this life, not in China, nor in Siberia; my
    search is in vain!

"The Key to My Heart," the title track from *La Llave de mi Corazón* (2007); a mambo.

> I was listening the other day, a radio broadcast, a psychiatrist, Dr. Louise was giving marriage advice.
> "Hey Doc, I'm calling about a friend I met on a website, I ask you to give me a solution, because she has the key to my heart;
> I'm from New York and she is from San Pedro de Macorís, you know, land of baseball players, where Sammy Sosa lives." . . .
> "Make a point, you're on the air."
> "What do you want me to do, do I have to learn Spanish and dance on one foot until she gives me her love?"

"My Blessing," from *A son de Guerra.* Guerra introduced the song this way, to cheers: "Allow me to dedicate the next song to my wife Nora. Today is our twenty-eighth wedding anniversary! Nora, this one's for you. You have been, you are, and you will be the love of my life!"

> They say that the flowers did not stop singing your name, your dear name.
> That the waves on the seas made you a shawl of seaspray, and clouds and water-lilies. . . .
> To have you, to kiss you, to walk hand in hand with you, my Sky, to look at you, to talk to you and listen to you, what a blessing!

"The Street," written and recorded in 2010 with the Colombian performing star Juanes, who appeared to perform the duet live.

> You told me that the lie used contact lenses and a Valentino shoe proclaims itself to be cheap,
> That a tariff fell in love with the tax system of the Free Trade Zone,
> That the anesthesia went to London for a congress on tourism.
> Oh! The street is hard.

"Niagara Falls by Bicycle," from *No Es Lo Mismo Ni Es Egual* (1999), tells the true story of the time Guerra "fainted and fell, flopped like a soursop on the sewer grate," and was taken by passersby to an understaffed, undersupplied public hospital in Santo Domingo. He compares the difficulty of getting care under such circumstances with trying to cross Niagara Falls on a bicycle.

> Don't tell me that the doctors have left; don't tell me that there is no anesthesia.

Don't tell me that they drank the alcohol, and that the suturing thread
    was embroidered in a tablecloth.
Don't tell me that the tweezers have been lost, that the stethoscope is at
    a party,
That the X-ray machine is broken, and that the serum was already used
    to sweeten coffee.

"Visa for a Dream," released on Guerra's *Greatest Hits* (2010), a song
inspired by the news of a shipwreck of Dominicans trying to reach Puerto
Rico in a small boat.

It was five in the morning, a worker and a seminarian with a thousand
    papers to prove solvency, if not sincerity.
It was seven in the morning, and one by one to the slaughter, because
    everyone has their price, seeking a visa for a dream.
It was nine in the morning, Santo Domingo, eighth of January, with
    patience running out, and no visa for a dream. . . .
It makes me so mad, seeking a visa for a dream, to sink in a shipwreck,
    meat for the sea, seeking a visa of no return. . . .

"Chilly, Chilly," from *Areito* (1992), performed with the bachata superstar
Romeo, the artist formerly known as Antony Santos, who began his career
fronting the best-selling bilingual boy band Aventura in New York City.

Chilly, chilly like the water of the river
or hot like the water of the hotspring.
Warm, warm like the kiss that quiets
and enflames, if it comes from someone you love.

"The Wasps" from his religiously inspired album *Para Ti* (2004).

I have an admirable God in Heaven and the love of the Holy Spirit.
Through His grace I am a new man and my song is filled with joy. . . .
Jesus told me to laugh if the enemy tempts me along the way,
and He also told me, "Don't torture yourself, because I will send the
    wasps to sting them."

"Bachata in Fukuoka," from *A son de Guerra*, a love song set in Japan, where
Guerra is very popular.

"The Bus," from *A son de Guerra*, comments on the government. Guerra
introduced it this way: "We're so happy to be here, with the best audience
that exists on Earth!"

You promised me a *guaracha* to liven up my party. . . .
Where's the party? The Cuban music?
All your promises go in the oil can; pull the gear shift and get it right!
Because the bus is going in reverse, listen, the bus is going backward.

"In Heaven There Are No Hospitals," from *Colección Cristiana* (Christian Collection; 2012), is a kind of reply to "Niagara Falls by Bicycle." It has a boisterous chorus that says everyone in Heaven is so healthy, they all "dance on one foot." The music video for this hit features Guerra and his two very portly percussionists energetically doing just that.

ENCORES
"Medley of Bachatas," two songs from *Bachata Rosa*.

"Little Stars and Elves"

I will live on in your memory as a simple rain shower
Of little stars and elves.
I will wander to your belly,
Biting every illusion.

"Bubbles of Love"

I would like to be a fish, to touch my nose against your fishbowl,
To make bubbles of love everywhere,
To stay awake all night
Soaked in you.

"Asking for Her Hand," from *Bachata Rosa*; a lively song in rural dialect about a young man coming to pop the question to his beloved in a neighboring village.

"I Hope It Rains Coffee," Guerra's first big hit, was the last encore. From *Ojalá Que Llueva Café* (1989), it features the sound of a heavy rainstorm.

I hope it rains coffee in the countryside, that there's a downpour of yucca,
That a drizzle of melted white cheese falls from the sky, and to the South, a mountain of watercress and honey.
So that there isn't so much suffering in the countryside, in the *conuco*, oh man,
I hope it rains coffee.

Transcribed and translated by Eric Paul Roorda.

XI

The Dominican Diaspora

Emigration from the Dominican Republic has taken place periodically, going back to the exodus of colonists to Mexico in the wake of Cortes, and including mass departures after Haitian incursions and the periodic flight of exiles from repressive governments. The current surge of emigrant activity, the largest by far, is of fairly recent vintage, having begun in the 1960s after the death of Trujillo, who restricted the outward flow of his subjects during the latter stages of his long rule. Unemployment, inflation, electrical blackouts, and crime have combined in the decades since then to make life difficult for millions in the Dominican Republic and to make the move to the United States more attractive. New York, or *Nueba Yol* in Dominican dialect, has been the most common destination for Dominicans, and the neighborhood around Washington Heights, Manhattan, has the highest concentration of Dominican inhabitants, earning it the nickname "Quisqueya Heights." Perhaps three-quarters of a million Dominicans and Dominican Americans reside in the boroughs of New York City, and a great many more live in Massachusetts, Rhode Island, and other US states. Recognizing the strength and importance of this transnational community of Dominicans in the United States and elsewhere around the world, including Canada, Dominican electoral law now extends the vote to citizens living abroad.

The First Immigrant to Manhattan, 1613:
Jan Rodrigues

Crew Members of the Jonge Tobias and Fortuyn

The first non-Indian to live independently on Manhattan Island was Juan Rodríguez, a Dominican man. He was called Jan Rodrigues aboard the Jonge Tobias, the Dutch ship that took him there in the spring of 1613 and that may have been smuggling on the Hispaniola coast with his aid. When the ship prepared to leave Manhattan for Holland after a season of trading for beaver pelts, the Santo Domingo native refused to go. He preferred to stay with the local people, whom he seems to have befriended. Captain Thijs Mossel of the Jonge Tobias, who apparently had found Rodríguez a disruptive presence aboard his ship, allowed him to have his way and provided him with an assortment of supplies as payment for his wages. Prior to Mossel's arrival, the Dutch explorer Adriaen Block (best known for the New England resort island named after him) had been trading in the area of Manhattan in his ship Fortuyn. He objected to Mossel's competition as unfair trading and on his return to Amsterdam filed litigation over the matter in a civil court. The following year the Fortuyn, returning to Manhattan under a new captain, found Rodríguez still living there, and the Dutch skipper hired him to assist in trading. Mossel showed up again, and trouble ensued. We know of Juan Rodríguez from this testimony given in Amsterdam in 1613 and 1614, but then he disappears from the historical record. Centuries later, hundreds of thousands of his compatriots would follow his example.

1613, August 20, Declarations of Some Members of the Crew of Adriaen Block's and Thijs Volckertsz. Mossel's Ships

The said Mossel's ship arrived in the river of New Virginia [the Hudson River] about seven weeks later than the said plaintiff's [Adriaen Block's] ship arrived there. They [the crew members] know . . . that the aforementioned Thijs Mossel and [Hans Jorisz. Hontom], the supercargo [supervisor of cargo], arrived there for the first time in Virginia and that they had not been there before and that this was the plaintiff's third voyage.

They also truly know that the aforementioned Thijs Mossel and his supercargo sought and tried to spoil the trade of the said plaintiff there. They made him suspicious partly because they gave or supplied twice as many goods of the same quality and quantity for a beaver as the plaintiff gave before they arrived there, namely three pieces, where the plaintiff gave only one.

Finally [they declare] that when the said Mossel sailed away from the river with his ship, a mulatto born in St. Domingo, who had arrived there with the ship of the said Mossel, stayed ashore at the same place. They had given this mulatto eighty hatchets, some knives, a musket, and a sword. The said Thijs Mossel and his supercargo themselves declared that this Spaniard had run away from the ship and gone ashore against their intent and will and that they had given him the said goods in payment of his wages and therefore had nothing more to do with him. Moreover they testified that the crew of the plaintiff ought to have killed him [perhaps to prevent further competition], seeing that he had declared that he would not come to this country [Holland] and that he would have jumped overboard if they [Mossel's crew] had not allowed him to depart. The deponents declare also to have knowledge that nobody of the said Mossel's crew stayed ashore in the said Virginia other than the said Spaniard.

1614, July 23: Declarations of Crew Members of the Ship Fortuyn, Master Hendrick Christiaensen

[The crewmen] declare that when they were lying in the river Montanges [the Hudson River] a certain Jean Rodrigues came on board their ship who said that he was a free man and requested of his own accord to serve the producer [the captain, Christiaensen] and his partners and stay on their ship, giving them to understand that he had nothing to do with and had no business with either [Hontom] or Thijs Mossel, and that he was not bound to them. Since the producer was not on board the ship then, [Rodrigues] came aboard their ship a second time. In the presence of the witnesses the producer then asked the said Jan Rodrigues if he was free. The same replied as before and gave answer that he was a free man and that he had nothing to do with anybody. . . .

[The crewmen] declare it to be true that [some days later] Jan Rodrigues, who was [now] in the producer's service and who was on shore with certain trading-goods for trade, fired a shot. Thereafter they, the witnesses, jumped into the boat with five men and went ashore unarmed without thought of the difficulty or danger. As soon as they came ashore they saw that many members of Mossel's crew, of whom [Hontom] himself was the leader, also immediately followed in their boat, leaving the mess, armed with muskets, and burning matches. They [Mossel's crew members] also went ashore, where four . . . [of them] immediately attacked Jan Rodrigues. They took away his musket, drove him in the water, and arrested him by force. Then they said Jan Rodrigues took the sword away from one of the crew of [Hontom] who held him.

When they, the witnesses, saw this, they did their best to rescue him. They jumped in the water to get him, and they took the said Jan Rodrigues, who was injured, into their boat and rowed to their ship. And when one of the witnesses then asked [Hontom] why they [he and Mossel's crewmen] should arrest and injure Jan Rodrigues, the said [Hontom] answered that "that black rascal," referring to the said Jan Rodrigues, [missing words] in order to get the money due us.

Player to Be Named Later:

Osvaldo/Ossie/Ozzie Virgil,

First Dominican Major Leaguer

Enrique Rojas

Some of the best known Dominicans in the United States are major league baseball players, and Dominicans are now a dominant force in the organization. Dominican participation in the American big leagues began with Osvaldo Virgil (1932–). A versatile player and later a coach, Virgil began playing infield positions, then moved to the outfield, and then finished his playing career as a catcher, spending almost a decade with six different teams. Because fans in the United States pronounced his nickname "Ossie" like "Ozzie," he changed the spelling to match how they said it. He was a teammate of the great Dominican pitcher Juan Marichal on a San Francisco Giants roster that included two of the three Alou brothers, also among the pioneer Dominican players in major league baseball in the late 1950s and early 1960s. Virgil's son, "Ozzie Jr.," also played in the major leagues for a decade. By the fiftieth anniversary of Virgil's 1956 debut in New York City, however, the first Dominican in the majors had been virtually forgotten, as reflected in this selection from an ESPN report on the occasion.

No fanfare, announcements, or big expectations. Almost silently. That's how Osvaldo Virgil made his major league debut on Sept[ember] 23, 1956, for the New York Giants at the Polo Grounds.

The 50th anniversary of the arrival of the first Dominican ballplayer in the majors also will happen without a major celebration. Although Virgil's arrival changed baseball radically, it will barely be mentioned in either the US or the Dominican Republic. But Virgil hasn't forgotten.

Fifty years later, Ozzie Virgil clearly remembers his first game as a major leaguer.

"I can still remember my blood streaming furiously through my veins and adrenaline almost choking me on my first day in the majors. . . . It was

Estadio Trujillo
Ciudad Trujillo, R. D.

Baseball exploded in popularity with the formation of semiprofessional teams and an organized league during the Trujillo regime. The dictatorship also built the first large stadium in 1955, Santo Domingo's Estadio Trujillo, now Quisqueya Stadium, to be the nation's premier sports venue. Photographer unknown, black-and-white photograph, c. 1950s, Archivo General de la Nación, Santo Domingo.

very hot, and we were playing the last game of a series of three against Philadelphia. I was placed on third base and went 0-for-4, but I felt as if I'd finished 4-for-4," Virgil said. "I had been upgraded from the minors two or three days before, and I knew I would be the first of my small country to arrive in the best baseball league in the world. But what I never suspected was that in time, it would become something ordinary. I have always felt grateful and fortunate to have been chosen by God to open the doors of major league baseball for my countrymen, considering that hundreds with more talent than me hadn't been given the chance."

In nine seasons with New York, Detroit, Kansas City, Baltimore, Pittsburgh, and San Francisco, Virgil played every position but pitcher and hit .231 with 14 home runs and 73 RBI.

In 1958, he became the first black ballplayer for the Detroit Tigers, who were among the last teams to break the racial barrier. In his Tigers' debut, he was 5-for-5.

But it is not his athletic talent that makes him important to the Dominican Republic. Virgil was the pioneer for a country that has become the strongest international force in the world's best baseball league.

That seemingly insignificant event 50 years ago was the root of an extraordinary phenomenon that has greatly improved America's national pastime. Since Virgil's debut, another 446 Dominicans have played major league baseball, including 28 who arrived during the 2006 season. The list includes third baseman Alex Rodríguez, outfielder Moises Alou, and second baseman Ron Belliard, born in the United States of Dominican parents.

Virgil played for the Tigers for three years.

"Virgil should be for my country as important as [Jackie] Robinson [is] to the African-American," Boston Red Sox slugger David Ortíz said. "I'd place his legacy up there with that of those who established our republic. . . . If I weren't playing baseball, I would most likely be working in my country. I thank God every day for opening the doors to the big leagues for me."

A report issued by the commissioner's office indicates that major league baseball has contributed almost $80 million to the fragile Dominican economy and helped create about 2,000 jobs, directly or indirectly, on the island.

Virgil was 14 years old when his family moved to New York in 1947. He was signed for a $300 bonus by the Giants in 1953 and never earned more than $18,000 in a season during his career. . . .

Virgil is rarely mentioned by the Dominican sports media, and available sources to spread the news about this historic event are practically nonexistent.

"It is a shame that in the Dominican Republic there isn't even a [park] with my name. But there are no facilities with the name of Marichal or Felipe Alou either, only to name some examples," said Virgil. . . .

The Dominican Dandy: Juan Marichal

Rob Ruck

After Osvaldo "Ossie" Virgil, Juan Marichal was the second Dominican to play in baseball's major leagues. Moreover, he was one of the best players in the history of the sport; he was inducted into the Baseball Hall of Fame in 1983. His career statistics rank among the most impressive ever compiled by a pitcher. He spent his most prolific years with the San Francisco Giants, playing alongside the great Willie Mays, from his major league debut in 1960 (a complete-game one-hitter, with twelve strikeouts) to 1973. Marichal and the Dominican brothers Felipe and Matty Alou helped the Giants reach the World Series in 1962. He averaged an astounding twenty-three wins per season from 1963 to 1966, and won a career high of twenty-six games in 1968, on his way to a lifetime record of 243 wins and 142 losses. His career earned run average was 2.89, and he struck out more than 2,300 batters, with a no-hitter in 1963. A National League All-Star nine times, he won the All-Star Game Most Valuable Player Award in 1965. Not only was Marichal an incredibly productive pitcher, he was also among the most flamboyant baseball players of all time, becoming famous for his acrobatic, high-kicking throwing style. A Time *cover story in 1966 dubbed Marichal "the Dandy Dominican."*

Juan Marichal had to contend with lingering prejudice against players of color, particularly those from Latin America. His own manager stated his opinion that "we have trouble, atrocious mistakes, because we have so many Spanish-speaking and Negro players on the team. . . . You can't make most Negro and Spanish players have the pride in their team that you get from the white players. And they just aren't as sharp mentally."

Marichal had uncanny accuracy, and was not afraid to pitch the ball inside, but accusations that he intentionally threw at batters' heads led to trouble for him. A series of such perceived "brush backs" led to a notorious fight that took place between him and the Los Angeles Dodger Johnny Roseboro on August 22, 1965, that marred his brilliant career and made him the target of abuse from fans at many venues around the United States. On that occasion, Roseboro was catching when Marichal came up to bat, and an altercation took place at home plate. Marichal thought Roseboro was going to punch him, so he clubbed him on the head with the bat he was holding, opening up a bloody gash on Roseboro's face, and then brandished the bat to ward off the rest of the Dodger team during the ensuing melee. The league commissioner suspended Marichal for nine games after the incident, and the Giants ended up losing the pennant race without him.

The Marichal-Roseboro dispute was the first of many controversial moments involving Dominican major leaguers through the years, which have contributed to some of them gaining the reputation of being headstrong, confrontational players. One of the most famous (some fans would say infamous) among them in recent years has been Pedro Martínez, who idolized Marichal growing up. One of the dominant pitchers of recent years, Martínez emulated his hero by sometimes throwing inside pitches to intimidate opponents, a practice that sparked a memorable brawl between the New York Yankees and Martínez's Boston Red Sox in the 2003 playoffs. Five years later, Marichal and Martínez both received criticism from US animal rights activists after they were filmed attending a cockfight together in Santo Domingo. Martínez responded with a statement defending the sport of cockfighting as a legal part of Dominican culture and calling Marichal his idol.

After his retirement in 1975, Marichal worked in broadcasting, announcing the 1990 World Series when his son-in-law José Rijos, who played for the Cincinnati Reds, won the Most Valuable Player award. He then became minister of sports in the first government of President Leonel Fernández, a position he resumed when Leonel returned to power.

Marichal's story was encapsulated in Rob Ruck's book The Tropic of Baseball (1991), based on Ruck's interviews with the great ace. The book tells how the Trujillo regime transformed baseball in the Dominican Republic from an informal network of amateur and semiprofessional teams into a professional circuit subsidiary to the major leagues of the United States. That trend has continued, with the Dominican Winter League and summer instructional leagues serving as training grounds for major league baseball. In this selection from Ruck's book Marichal lovingly describes his impoverished rural youth in Laguna Verde, near Monte Cristi.

"We had a farm," the tall, still sturdily built Marichal resumes. "We called it a *parcela*, a parcel of land, a few kilometers outside Laguna Verde, when I was growing up. It was small, something like 60 acres, and we grew mostly rice, *platanos*, and beans. Now it's bigger, because when I started making a little money, we started buying more land and I bought a tractor for it. It's over a thousand acres now."

Juan's father died when he was three, but Doña Natividad held the family together with the help of relatives. "I don't think my father played baseball, but I know he used to live for the *gallos*, for cockfighting. I think that's why I've got that in my blood. I love roosters. I'm a member of a club that has

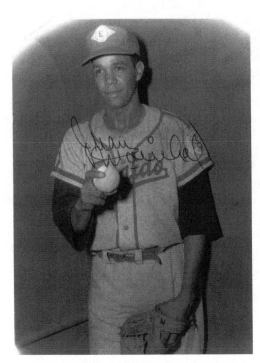

Juan Marichal was a slender unknown playing for the Santo Domingo team Leones del Escogido (The Lions of the Chosen One) sometime in the late 1950s, when this photograph was taken. He went on to become the first famous Dominican major leaguer and a Hall of Fame pitcher. Photographer unknown, black-and-white photograph, c. 1958. Courtesy of the Roorda/Doyle Collection.

an arena for *peleas de gallos*, cockfighting. In the Dominican Republic, *gallos* come right after baseball."

Laguna Verde numbered about four hundred residents then and is only up to two or three thousand 50 years later. While the *casa de Marichal* was comfortable by peasant standards, with indoor plumbing and a tank of water that could be filled by hand for bathing, like the other homes in Laguna Verde, it lacked electricity. "We had propane gas for cooking, just like most people still do. And we had a battery-powered radio on which I listened to the ball games. There was a player then from Laguna Verde, "Gallo" Martínez, and when he did something in a game, his father would shout '*Ese es mi gallo!*' (That's my rooster!) I would tell my mother that some day she would listen to the radio and shout '*Ese es mi* Juan!'"

During the morning, Juan worked the *parcela*, before walking eight kilometers to school in El Duro each afternoon. "We didn't have any money but we had a lot of food. Almost everything that we needed to eat we had right there. My mother had a herd of goats and one of my brothers and I used to take care of them. I grew up on goat milk." (Could that be the source of Marichal's incredibly high leg kick?) "Later on, I used to send my mother five hundred dollars every 15 days and when I got back here I see she has been buying cattle and more goats with it."

As Marichal recounts the saga of his youth, he misses little on the field. When a player slides at home and misses the plate, Marichal is on his feet, shouting "He missed the plate!" to the catcher. The umpire, who had not yet made his call, waits until the catcher follows the runner into the dugout and tags him to signal him out.

"In 1947, when I was nine years old, I almost died," Marichal continues. "We had been working on the farm, doing what we called *en junta*. That is when you invite all the families around you to help when you are doing something that needs lots of hands. You would feed them for their efforts and go to their farm when they needed help. We were harvesting and cleaning rice. After the work was done, my mother fed all the children first so that they would go away and not bother the adults while they ate.

"We started swimming in the canal right away after eating and I got cramps. The next thing I know it was a week later. When the doctor looked at me after they fished me out of the canal, I'm told he said 'I don't see too much chance. But be sure to give him lots of baths with very hot water.' They sent me to the house of one of my uncles where they gave me lots of baths but nothing happened. On the seventh day of my coma, the doctor looked at me and told my mother that if I did not come out of it by midnight, I was not coming back. At fifteen minutes to midnight, I awoke. . . .

"It seems like all I did as a boy was work on the farm, go to school a little, and play ball. We swam in canals, and hunted and fished some, but mostly it was baseball.

"All the boys in my town played baseball. I used to love baseball and dream of playing it. And I will tell you, I feel very proud that, coming from that little community, I went all the way to Cooperstown. . . .

"All we wanted to do was play ball. We made our own bats from branches that we cut from the *guásima* tree and dried in the sun. For gloves, we would take a piece of canvas, the kind of stuff they used to cover trucks, and fold it around a piece of cardboard and then sew up the sides. And for balls, we would get some golf balls from the golf course at Manzanillo and wrap nylon stocking or tape around them, then take them to the shoemaker who would sew a leather cover around them. Then we would play!"

The Queen of Merengue

Milly Quezada

*Milagros Borbón Quezada, better known as Milly Quezada, the Queen of Meren-
gue, was born in Santo Domingo and moved to New York as a child. She became the
lead singer of Milly y Los Vecinos [The Neighbors], a neighborhood group formed
with her brothers and sister in Washington Heights during the 1970s. In 2003, she
became the first female Dominican artist to win a Grammy, and a "Milly Quezada
Day" was declared in New York City. She released her thirtieth album in 2011, and
her duet with Juan Luis Guerra, "Toma Mi Vida" [Take My Life], became a hit song.*

What did your parents and grandparents do to earn a living?

My grandparents are from a town called Esperanza in the Cibao region.
My parents told me that they had very humble earnings, my grandmother used to be a seamstress. She became a widow in her early thirties. My grandmother moved with her three children to Santiago. My
mother married my father in Santiago and then they moved to Santo
Domingo where they had me, my brother Rafael, my sister Jocelyn, and
my brother Martín. My father used to work as a presser at a dry cleaner
and my mother worked as a salesperson in a department store. Their
income was very limited. As we were growing up the economic situation became precarious, and my grandmother suggested that the family
move to New York to give us better opportunities in life.

I was very talented at a young age and so was my brother Rafaelito,
who is my musical director. As children we had no means of acquiring
expensive toys, so we had to be very creative. We would use our imagination in the backyard to create toys and entertain ourselves. We would
put a big sheet over the clothesline and make a show and we would perform for each other and the other kids in the neighborhood. Someone
would climb into a tree and pretend to be an airplane . . . things that
demonstrated our creativity. And it would always end up being musical,
we would always end up playing instruments, whether it was paint cans

or taking two sticks and making rhythms. The singing just came natural. I guess our precarious economic situation was helpful in developing our talents that would eventually become the talent we would use in the streets of Washington Heights.

We left in the middle of the Trujillo crisis. Trujillo had already been killed in 1961, and in 1965, after the first democratic election, there was a coup and the United States had to intervene. Right in the midst of it, specifically April 25, 1965, we had to leave, as we had already been arranging our papers to leave the country.

Were there any obstacles to you becoming a musician in the DR [Dominican Republic]?

I tend to think that our opportunities were greater in New York versus what they could have been in the DR. First and foremost, our family was extremely poor. As we emigrated to New York we became part of the system; we learned the English language, we received a good education . . . public school in New York, but a superior education than what was possible for us in the DR. We took advantage of the opportunities available to us living in New York and we were part of a growing community of Dominicans doing the same.

We naturally turned to music as a way of fulfilling our nostalgia for the DR. It was not planned—it was a natural development of circumstances that led to us becoming more and more artistic and creating what would eventually become Milly Jocelyn y Los Vecinos. We would perform in the community, wherever there was a summer festival. We had the instruments in the apartment that we lived in. If there was a get-together we would bring the instruments and we would be the kids in the neighborhood that had the music. We provided the music for the local church . . . when the mass became musical we would be there with the instruments to perform.

So it was a natural progression that led us to play music in the US. It was not planned for us to come here for better opportunities in music. It was a very cultural experience and one thing led to another and eventually the music became our livelihood. In the process of developing our musical talent it was just a matter of getting together, of having a good time, of remembering the homeland, and giving our neighbors the music that they needed to be entertained. It was born out of a need to keep connected with our roots.

A lot of Dominicans, my husband and myself included, always thought that we would one day come back to the country where we were born. The first generation of Dominicans in New York is full of stories and dreams of one day coming back to the DR. But you spend ten, fifteen, thirty years in the US without realizing that you are becoming more and more American. Of course there is the preservation of a traditional and conservative way of life and that, in itself, became a conflict for us kids as we were growing up. In the school system the American way was one thing and we came home and there was the Dominican way. We had to respect our parents' rules and regulations that in no way reflected the American lifestyle. My husband, Rafael Vásquez, and I always used to think that we would come back to the DR to live one day. And the more and more we traveled to the DR we became more aware that we were Americans. We attempted to buy a house in the DR. The system, the customs, and the lifestyle did not reflect what we had already become. It never materialized, not for our parents or for ourselves. I have friends that have moved back, bought houses, and started businesses and they moved back after a short while because they realized that they were no longer that essential Dominican that left the homeland ten or twenty years before. They came back to the United States and they became American citizens, as we did. I became an American citizen a good ten years ago.

It is funny because the nostalgia idealizes the country but you become a mixture, just as my kids have become. My kids were born in New York and they have become American Dominicans, not Dominican Americans.

What challenges did you face as a female performer?

At the time the group became popular there was a sense of women's liberation sparking up in the music industry. The idea of a female lead singer in an industry dominated by men took the male performers by surprise. Johnny Ventura and Wilfrido Vargas have said time and again that when they heard me sing on the radio they said, "Oh, what is this woman looking for in trying to sing what we sing?" Just by that expression I knew that I had hit a sensitive chord in that male chauvinistic mentality. We realized that our popularity was based on that element of surprise. We continued the role of singing to that male chauvinist and uncovering their ways. We were reminding men that changes were coming along and that there was no longer a need for women to shut up and take it. They could speak up and say, "Listen. If you are going to be a male chauvinist you have no place in my life." Women as well as men considered the music joyful, but also a message in and of itself.

I consider myself a female merengue singer. It was difficult, not because I was a female, but because it is difficult to get doors opened in the industry when you are not well known. It took well over five years for the group to become recognized, between 1970 and 1975. After 1975, when we became known as a group, we started recording one album per year. With each album we would become a tradition in the Christmas season to come to the DR and do parties. In Barranquilla, Colombia, we became a Carnival tradition in February. In Puerto Rico in the seventies we became a tradition in the months of May, June, and July, when there were lots of graduations and other events we were hired for.

We were very lucky as a group to coincide with not only the growth of the Dominican community in the US but also the popularity of merengue at the international level. We would come to the DR for Christmas at the same time that 15,000 Dominicans would come to celebrate the holidays with their families. When those people would go back to the States to their jobs they would take back the Dominican rum, the Dominican candies, and the Dominican song that was in style at the time. And every Christmas they would take back a popular song from our recording efforts.

It was all very much meant to be. It was two decades of absolute beauty in the sense of popularity, touring, being recognized not only as merengue singers but as women . . . it was all a very beautiful experience.

Interview conducted and translated by Alex Huezo.

Dominican Hip-Hop in Spain

Arianna Puello

Arianna Puello is a hip-hop artist of Dominican descent. Her family moved from the Dominican Republic to Spain when she was eight years old. Puello was heavily influenced by the local hip-hop scene and has become one of Spain's most prolific rappers, with five solo albums and a number of collaborative recordings under her belt. In this interview, which took place on the day in 2011 when her album Kombate o Muere (Fight or Die) *was released in Spain, Arianna was asked to comment about her identity and upbringing as a Dominican woman of color in Spain.*

When did you come to Spain from the Dominican Republic and for what reason?

I came in 1986 when I was eight years old. My mother had married and established her life in Spain.

We had the hopes of any immigrants—to be able to succeed, study, and gain a livelihood. Unfortunately there are a lot of problems with the educational system in the Dominican Republic. Here in Spain there were better opportunities to cultivate my mind—through schooling and the culture. Although I do not have a career in the traditional sense, I could obtain one with my education.

How did the locals react to a Dominican family and how did this affect you?

The Spanish are considerably racist by nature. Of course there are many Spaniards that are not. There are many Spanish very dear to me, that are not racists, but by and large it is a racist society, one that I think is changing slowly with the passage of time. Here they use the phrase "I am not racist but I do not acknowledge *moros* [Moors or dark-skinned people from Africa]." I have lived racism in Spain. If there is something I have had to fight for, it was that, to defend my race, to defend my culture, and to show the ignorant people in Spain that they have to accept other types of people because we are equals as human beings, with different cultures, but at the end of the day, we are all the same.

María Montez was probably the most famous Dominican in the world in the 1940s, when she was one of the "Latin bombshell" actresses who starred in escapist wartime Hollywood movies. Her roles included Scheherazade and "The Cobra Woman." Photographer unknown; private movie star scrapbook, c. 1940. Courtesy of the Roorda/Doyle Collection.

Columbus went to colonize America, and in the majority of Latin American cultures and customs there are many elements of Spanish culture because Columbus inculcated that, right? So let's see, the Spanish are discriminating against us Latin Americans when it was they that imposed the laws, religion, et cetera. And now they are discriminating against Latin Americans who have come to Spain to earn a living. They did not exactly come to the Americas to earn a living. They came to massacre. Spaniards discriminate against Latin Americans, while the majority that come to Spain, come to work, and they are treated badly. I take issue with that. Columbus was a swine to Latin Americans and now we are able to come to Europe, to work in Spain.

One thing that people often criticize me about, the frustrated nitpickers of the Internet, is that I speak with two accents. When I am with Dominicans I speak Dominican. I speak Dominican with my mother in my house and with my husband, who is Dominican. When I am in the street I speak with a Spanish accent, but not because people are going to discriminate against me for being a *sudaca* [a derogatory term for Latin Americans in Spain]. I was raised in Spain—that is just how I speak. It is as if it were two different languages, like English and French. I speak Dominican with other Dominicans and Spanish with the Spanish. They criticize me for changing my accent, but I am from the two places and no one can deny me that. The only thing I can do is take the best elements from each culture, spend time with my family, and be a better person. It makes no difference if they criticize me for changing my accent.

At times Dominicans, much like other Caribbean people, are criticized for denying their African roots.

I also used to identify myself as *taína* [a woman of Taíno ancestry] until I learned what it meant, and I never identified that way again. It clearly is a racial identity specific to the Dominican Republic, but when I learned it signified discrimination [toward] the African roots of Dominicans, I said enough! If there is something clear to me about my identity it is that I have African blood. It is not something we can deny. I consider myself Dominican, Spanish, and African as well. I think it is an error on the part of Dominican society to deny those African veins that we have.

Is there a difference between being a Dominican woman versus a Dominican man in Spain?

Yes, of course. I don't want people to be enraged by my telling the truth, because it is the truth. Regrettably, the majority of Dominican women immigrate to Spain for prostitution. The truth is that it is unfortunate, but yes, it is reality. I believe that little by little this is changing, just as the woman's role in society is changing as well.

I am constantly mistaken for a prostitute when I am in the streets. Mind you, I am not dressed provocatively, I do not wear a miniskirt, but yes, I have found myself harassed many times by men who want me to go with them. That makes my blood boil! Every day I experience the same thing, every day the same thing. One time I had to throw rocks at this guy who was in his car.

Interview conducted and translated by Alex Huezo.

Black Women Are Confusing,

but the Hair Lets You Know

Ginetta Candelario

A New York City hair salon became a research laboratory for Ginetta Candelario when she was gathering information for her book Black behind the Ears: Dominican Racial Identity from Museums to Beauty Shops. *This selection is an excerpt from that insightful monograph.*

The transformation of Dominican women's hair into racially acceptable signs hinges their sense of being Dominican on certain norms and models. For Dominicans, hair is the principal bodily signifier of race, followed by facial features, skin color and last, ancestry. Harry Hoetink discerned the connection between identity and race in his coining of the term "somatic norm image" to improve on "race" as an explanatory concept in the Caribbean. He defined somatic norm image as "the complex of physical (somatic) characteristics that are accepted by a group as its norm and ideal." . . .

Hoetink convincingly argued that the somatic norm image of whiteness in the Hispanic Caribbean is distinctive from the somatic norm image of whiteness in the United States. . . .

Hoetink goes on to argue that, although throughout the Americas features identified with black somatic norms are universally construed as ugly and undesirable, and features identified with white physical norms are considered beautiful and desirable, "the physical norm image of Latin American whites is 'darker' than that of the North-West European American." Because of this, the "somatic distance" between Latin American whites and mulattos/mestizos is much shorter than it is between North American whites and blacks (who because of the U.S. hypo-descent rule include those who would be considered mulattos in Latin America). . . .

The core research questions guiding the elicitation were: Who do Dominican women consider beautiful? Is the physical norm closer to or further from whiteness or blackness? How are "Hispanic looks" conceptualized?

What is the relationship between aesthetic preferences and social status? While a sample of eighteen respondents is not a statistically valid one, the results resonate with larger, historical indications of Dominican race ideologies, as well as with my ethnographic findings in the beauty shop. . . .

Of the thirteen hairstyle books referred to by customers at Salon Lamadas when selecting a hairstyle, ten were labeled as displaying white models and hairstyles. Three of the books feature black or dark-skinned women. All of the books available at the salon had been purchased by Chucha. One afternoon I approached her with one of the three books of African American hairstyles and asked her about the styles it contained.

CHUCHA: I just bought that book. I bought it because my clients have to locate themselves in the hair they have.

GINETTA: How so?

CHUCHA: Why, Dominican women don't want to see that book. They ask for the white women's book; they want their manes long and soft like yours.

GINETTA: Why?

CHUCHA: It's because of racism. It's just that we don't even know what race we are. That if we're white, that if we're black, *Indio*, or what . . . I don't want to know about blacks so I don't have to be fucking around with kinks. Look, I came out like one of my aunts and there was suffering in my house in order to lower my kinks. The Dominican woman wants her soft mane, long hair. They don't want to see that book. They ask for the white women's book, the one for good hair like yours. Look, I have a client who brings me a three-year-old girl so I can blow dry her hair. You know what that is? Three years old. And in the end, when she gets home and starts playing, her hair stands on end again. (Laughs) The latest was that she wanted her to have her hair set. That little girl sat under the dryer better than some grownups, reading her magazine. Do you think that's right? That's suffering. It's not fair. I tell her, "Leave her with her curly hair. Put a ribbon in it and leave it!" But no, they want their soft manes.

That Chucha's purchase was recent and geared toward pointing her clients out to themselves, and given that the book featured women of the African diaspora, the selves Chucha was pointing Dominican women to were black. But it was an image rejected by her clients. . . . As she indicated by tracing her own *grenas* [kinks] to her aunts, blackness is errant and betrays girls and women. It leads to "suffering."

Interestingly, Chucha depersonalized her own suffering and hairstyle, referring instead to "Dominican women," to her clients' and to her family's suffering. The ambiguity Chucha expressed as a woman whose own hair was treated as a cause of sorrow in her childhood and as a stylist who actively participated in the very system she condemned typifies the paradox of Dominican beauty culture. She was critical of her clients' choosing the white book, subjecting their three-year-olds to "suffering" under the dryer, and preferring "long manes." She relished the resiliency and unruliness of a child's kinky hair and refusals to relax. Yet she was an active agent of the very system she criticized. Further, she was subjected to it herself, even as an adult.

The texture of Chucha's hair was variously described as *pelo macho* [macho hair], *pelo durito* [slightly hard hair], and *pelo fuerte* [strong hair] by her staff and as *grenas* and *pasas que hay que bajarlas* [kinks that have to be tamed] by herself. . . . Salon Lamada's staff politely overlooked and worked to fit Chucha's hair texture to her high status, both through their grooming of her hair and through their softened descriptions of it. Chucha herself was open about her hair's secret, as the following selection from my field notes indicates:

Chucha and Leticia attended a Sebastian hair-product seminar in New Jersey today. The topic was how to use a new color product. Chucha sat down and recounted the details of her experience to María: "They don't work on bad heads there. It's all for good hair, like hers [pointing to me] and yours [María]." I asked why not and whether they had ever asked for a different kind of hair on their dummies. Again Chucha responded: "There it is! Our job is to adapt straight hair, good hair products, to ours. I was dying laughing, thinking about the surprise they'd experience if my hair got wet!" she laughed. "If my hair got wet!"

The "they" Chucha referred to were the white producers, marketers, and the beauty culturalists at Sebastian. Chucha's laughter and pleasure in relating the story indicated to me awareness on her part of her corporate host's ignorance. Water would return her hair to its natural, tightly curled state. Her looks, she recognized with relish, were deceiving; she too, was a "bad head." So it seemed that Chucha was well aware that she was transforming herself racially when she did her hair. The question is: What is she transforming into? I argue that it was not a desire for whiteness that guided Dominican women like Chucha. Instead, it was an ideal notion of what it means to "look Hispanic," an intermediate between white and black "types" grounded in the Iberian somatic norm image.

When asked for their opinions of the appearance of women depicted in an African American braiding book, Salon Lamada's staff members were vehemently derogatory in their commentary. At one point, a debate ensued over whether the woman depicted in one of the hairstyle books, and who Chucha had previously described as having *una cara de arroz con habichuelas* [a rice-and-bean face], was Latina or African American. Nilda, María, and Flor felt that she was Hispanic; Nene, Alma, and Leonora disagreed, particularly Nene, who felt that she was definitely black.

NENE: Her features are rough, ordinary black muzzle, big mouth, fat nose.

NILDA: Blacks are dirty and they smell. Hispanics are easy to spot! [Turning to me] You have something Hispanic.

GINETTA: What?

NILDA: Your nose. Fannie is white with good hair, but her features are rough black ones.

LENORA: It's just that black shows.

NILDA: Black is not the color of the skin. Really pretty, really fine. The person has black behind the ears.

Los Dominicanyorks

Luis Guarnizo

The Trujillo regime severely restricted the mobility of Dominican people, preventing all but a relative few of them from traveling or taking up residence abroad. At the end of that period, fewer than 12,000 Dominicans were living in the United States. A decade later there were five times as many, many of them sent into exile unwillingly by the government in order to remove political opposition. Dominicans continued to come to the United States during the 1980s, topping a half million in the early 1990s, and gaining even greater momentum in the twenty-first century. The 2010 US census counted more than 1,600,000 Dominicans and probably missed a good many others. Dominican communities have sprouted in many cities, from Miami to New England, but the salient feature of the Dominican diaspora is their enormous community in New York City. The Upper West Side of Manhattan at 141st Street is the heart of a sprawling Dominican neighborhood that has taken shape there in just the last few decades, and one that is using its buying power to transform their homeland overseas. The sociologist Luis Guarnizo studied the uniquely transnational nature of that community in the early 1990s and produced this portrait of it. The dual citizenship measure he describes was passed by the legislature in 1997 and went into effect in 2004.

Continuous mobility between the two countries by long-term emigrants residing abroad as well as by short-term migrants is typical of the complex interconnections migrants build over the years. Such mobility, among other things, has deeply affected family formation and generated the emergence of new domestic units. These units are characterized by the spatial dispersion of their members across the two countries in what we can call multinuclear households—that is, nuclear families living in more than one household, whereas similar domestic units in nonmigration circumstances would live in one.

Furthermore, Dominicans residing in New York travel often to the island for social reasons—such as to visit friends and relatives, to join in traditional festivities, to see family doctors or buy cheaper medicine—or for economic reasons, such as to buy real estate, to invest in a new business, or to tend to an already existing business. According to the Dominican Secretariat of Tourism, Dominicans living abroad accounted for one-fifth of the total number of international visitors to the country and contributed almost one-third of the total revenues from tourism in 1985. Since the tourist industry is officially recognized as the principal source of foreign exchange, the contribution of emigrant visitors makes these figures more relevant. Similarly, returned migrants—those who return to the island with the idea of remaining there—often travel back to the United States for social and familial reasons, to oversee their own businesses, to work for a salary for short stints, or just to comply with legal requirements in order to keep their US visas from expiring. Finally, others travel constantly between the two countries as informal, small international merchants to supply demands from both sides, or as brokers of Dominican economic interests in either country—such as Dominican Republic–based developers in search of buyers and investors abroad looking for market niches in their country of origin.

In addition to people and money, migration-driven nonmonetary resources such as ideas, cultural values, fashion, and so on move daily between the two countries: Dominican newspapers are distributed in the United States on their day of publication, popular Dominican television series are simultaneously aired in New York and on the island, and Dominican media—print and electronic—regularly cover Dominicans abroad. Similarly, exclusive and not so exclusive boutiques on the island offer the latest fashions imported from New York by small, informal traders, while Dominican stores in New York retail foodstuffs and other Dominican-made products. New York–based merengue bands frequently tour the island, while songs about Dominican migration are hits in Latin discos and radio stations in the United States, on the island, and even in Latin America. . . .

Already by 1988, the Dominican Central Bank estimated that migrants' remittances were the country's second most important source of foreign exchange, trailing tourism but surpassing earnings from sugar and other traditional export commodities. If migrants' participation in the tourist and housing industries and their investments in other sectors are taken together with family remittances, migrants become not only the primary sources of hard currency—well above revenues from tourism and Export Processing Zones, the flagships of the country's economic restructuring—but also the single most important social group contributing to the national economy.

The significance of their economic presence is underscored by the fact that nowadays some traditional activities and some new ones are labeled as activities for or of migrants. This labeling signifies that the migrants are the principal consumers of these activities, are the most noticeable operators of them, or have themselves introduced them to the Dominican Republic. Specifically, different industries on the island are targeting migrants as their preferred clients. There are housing projects built exclusively *para ausentes* and *para retornados* (for absent and returned migrants), entertainment establishments—such as discos—catering mainly to them, and educational institutions—such as English-only schools and boarding schools—that have been started to serve solely their children. By 1986, according to the Dominican Chamber of Construction, already some 60 percent of the formal housing industry on the island had been purchased by Dominicans residing abroad. At the dawn of the 1990s, I was told by major urban developers in the two largest Dominican cities that Dominican migrants represented between 80 percent and 90 percent of their clientele.

Similarly, early successful incursions of migrant entrepreneurs into certain types of businesses have encouraged fellow migrants to follow suit. An ensuing overrepresentation of migrants in these activities—and even a redundancy of their establishments—has resulted in their being labeled as *negocios de retornados* or *negocios de dominicans* (migrant businesses). The most visible business niches so labeled are real estate agencies, *financieras* (financial and commercial institutions extremely popular among migrant investors, especially until the late 1980s, when the state regulated them), *remesadoras* (remittance-transferring houses), small supermarkets and corner grocery stores, laundry and dry cleaning stores, car-wash services, car dealers and car rentals, and discos—all of them closely mimicking the physical appearance of Dominican-owned businesses in the United States.

Regardless of their unsophisticated economic and technological makeup, these activities form an economy associated with a social group thus far perceived as different from mainstream Dominican society. In the same way that Dominican ventures overseas have a tinge of Dominicanness, migrant businesses on the island have a streak of Americanness. Whereas businesses in New York are typically named after traditional establishments or locations on the island, in the Dominican Republic, migrant-owned firms are easily identifiable by signs celebrating their owners' endeavors abroad. For example, some of the firms are identified in English, especially using the names of North American cities and neighborhoods where Dominicans concentrate, or are decorated and furnished à la Americana.

Migrants' Double Visage: Dominican Immigrants and Dominicanyorks

In the United States, Dominicans may well be considered a non-assimilationist, persistently ethnic group. Certainly, significant features of immigrants' Dominicanness are reproduced in their everyday social interactions and are imprinted on the urban space. The colorfulness, blaring music, and liveliness of Dominican neighborhoods in New York City, for example, are a replica of life on the island. Yet by Dominican standards, immigrants' Dominicanness is utterly exaggerated. As one informant, who used to live in Washington Heights while pursuing her graduate studies, put it, "Dominicans in New York want to be more Dominican than the Dominicans themselves." Partly due to their subordinate social position in the city, partly because of their nostalgia for their homeland, partly because of their sheer numbers, their high concentration, and their physical appearance (which may lead to their being misidentified as either African Americans or Puerto Ricans), Dominican immigrants reaffirm and re-create their origins to a degree rarely seen among other Latin American groups. . . .

In stark contrast to their sociocultural reaffirmation while overseas, migrants in the Dominican Republic are perceived as Americanized Dominicans, whose behavior, for the most part, is seen by nonmigrants as an affront to authentic Dominican culture. Migrants' style of living, their tastes, and their manners, especially those of youngsters and the most prosperous (particularly excruciating in the case of those seen as drug traffickers), are judged as tasteless and revolting especially by the upper classes. The epithets minted to refer to migrants, such as *Dominicanyork* (seen as the opposite of an authentic Dominican), *cadenú* (gold necklace user; the wearing of a gold necklace is associated with drug kingpins and drug peddlers), and *Joe* (an anonymous American-like migrant youngster) are some of the sociolinguistic expressions of such sentiments. . . .

The words of some informants effectively illustrate the opinion of the Dominican elite. A Dominican national business and political leader and owner of one of the most important commodity export houses in the country asserted, "Those who emigrate are the cancer of our society; for that reason, their departure is not that negative for the country. When they return, they bring the vice of drugs; their ostentatious wealth induces others to emigrate too." Another businessman expressed his dismay about the harmful impact of migrants on the discipline of the Dominican workforce, with its disastrous effects on the functioning of the national economy: "Migrants exercise a very damaging influence on workers. Nowadays, employees rebel more easily against employers because, they say, if fired they can always go to New York."

Dominican political participation in New York City is rapidly escalating. Dominicans' struggle to improve their children's school conditions led them to confront and overcome the political forces controlling the educational system. . . . One of the first victories of Dominicans was gaining some positions on the school board [of Washington Heights (School District 6), where the majority of the student population were Dominican], followed by their entry into the city's broader political arena. These early political triumphs, as well as subsequent ones, were the result not only of the presence of a critical mass of Dominicans in the city but also of an intelligentsia formed by immigrant professionals, former political activists back on the island, and some business leaders.

In the Dominican Republic, on the other hand, migrants' political participation has changed from being followers to becoming activists and leaders. Migrant organizations, especially business organizations, have actively lobbied for legislation favoring migrants. Some migrants have already gained public office, especially in small migration towns, while maintaining their connections with their townspeople overseas. The most important political effort of migrants has been their push for the approval of a unilateral dual citizenship for Dominicans. Under this arrangement, while residing as citizens in the United States, migrants would preserve their Dominican nationality as inactive. Upon return, their Dominican political rights would be reactivated as their US citizenship became inactive. In this sense, they would enjoy the right to live and work in either country, without losing the right to do the same in either. This measure would formalize their current informal access to the two countries' opportunities. . . .

The *Yola*

Milagros Ricourt

The most treacherous route for Dominican emigrants to take to reach the United States is crossing the stormy Mona Passage to Puerto Rico in small boats called yolas. Predatory criminals control this human traffic, which began in the 1970s and has killed untold thousands of desperate people.

The great merengue artist Wilfrido Vargas wrote the hit song "La Yola" in 1983, when economic hardships were causing an increasing number of Dominicans to attempt the passage. Its lyrics catalogue the dangers of the crossing:

> Don't climb aboard that yola because they'll treat you wickedly.
> Don't climb aboard that yola because they'll throw you in the sea.
> Stay in your homeland, with your friends and family
> and not on the high seas without knowing if you are going to arrive.
> Listen to this advice, my brother.
> things are as bad over there as in our country.
>
> Puerto Rico is close but get on a plane.
> And if you get a visa, immigration's no pain.
> But don't fool yourself and get on a boat with those easy marks
> because in the Mona Passage you'll be eaten by sharks.

As a native of the coastal city of Puerto Plata, Vargas may have drawn from his personal familiarity with the sea in singing about its perils. Despite the popularity of the song, with its denunciation of the dangerous system and its advice to stay put or take an airplane, Dominicans kept setting out in yolas. Today the death toll continues to mount; the worst disaster in years took place in February 2012, when more than forty people drowned when their yola sank.

The following selection, based on interviews with several women who survived "la AA . . . agua alante y agua atrás [water ahead, water behind]" details the deadly risks involved in a voyage in a yola.

It was dark, and the small boat fought against the fury of the Caribbean Sea. In the middle of nowhere, without food or water, twenty-eight women and men lost their hope of reaching the promised land in Puerto Rico. They were miraculously alive. They did not perish because they took turns bailing water from the boat, [they] sucked milk out of one of the women's breasts in the boat, and the Divine Providence impeded the waves from swallowing the boat. When rescued by the authorities after more than twenty days of misery, the woman who fed her companions was interviewed by news crews. She was asked: "Why did you risk your life?" She answered: "I was in search of life, there was no life here." She added she would do it again.

Hundreds of undocumented boats exit the eastern coasts of the Dominican Republic every year with thousands of people in search of life. Many encounter only death in the journey. Others are returned. Others reach their goal. The question still remains, why do people risk their lives? In the search for life Dominicans engage in a suicidal attempt to remedy their misery in the homeland. In their attempt to cross the Mona Strait in fragile *yolas*, they have also created one of the saddest tragedies in the history of the Caribbean. . . .

The Dominican Republic is a good example of massive international migration. During the 1980s, hundreds of thousands of Dominicans—mostly women—abandoned their homeland seeking a life abroad. The Dominican Republic was the leading nation sending immigrants to New York City during the 1980s and 1990s. From 1989 to 1991 more than 20,000 Dominicans migrated to Spain, and a similar number migrated to other European nations. The Dominican population in Puerto Rico has grown from 1,812 people to 61,455 in 2000.

The restructuring of the Dominican economy plays a significant role in this development in a number of ways. For example, the Dominican Republic's economic growth is higher than any other country in Latin America and the Caribbean, showing success in global economic developments and free trade. Women represent more than 80 percent of workers in La Zona [Free Trade Zones] and tourism, the two pillars of the new Dominican economy. But economic growth does not translate into the improvement of people's quality of life. Paradoxically, the poverty rate has increased dramatically, affecting negatively the quality of life of Dominicans in terms of education, health, and income. An average of more than 50 percent of Dominican households live in poverty. Alarmingly, the majority of Dominicans live on less than a dollar a day. Further, the educational system fails to provide adequate instruction to Dominicans. For example, 50 percent of students enrolled in first grade only reach fourth grade, 22 percent complete eight years of education, and only 8 percent finish high school. In terms of health, the Dominican Republic has more than triple the percentage of infant mortality that it should have according to international standards. Employment is reduced, and social security is almost nonexistent. . . .

Apparently the movement of labor that began during the 1980s was composed of factory and informal sector workers with low pay, long working hours, and limited access to the market. These workers moved to Puerto Rico's needy informal labor sector. There, though they are still exploited, they are better paid and there are less limitations in accessing the market. They have generated new patterns of migration capable of altering significantly the previous theoretical explanations of the international movement of Dominicans. . . .

To fulfill their dreams, many women choose to engage in the danger of crossing the Mona Strait. Undocumented migration to Puerto Rico is an easier choice for poor women for two main reasons. Poor women do not have access to financial resources to obtain a United States visa and travel by airplanes. Undocumented migration to other destinations in the United States, such as New York or Miami, requires greater financial resources. The only cheap choice many immigrants have is to embark on a journey of crossing the Mona Strait. In some occasions, undocumented migration to Puerto Rico is also a way to travel to the mainland. Traveling from Puerto Rico to the United States does not require immigration screenings. These are domestic flights, making it easier for illegal Dominican immigrants to evade immigration authorities. . . .

In order to escape the misery of poverty, women go through a complicated process of making connections, saving, and arranging who will take care of their children. The first step in this process is contacting the relative or friend waiting for you in Puerto Rico. Karina had a sister in Puerto Rico, who sent money to pay for the trip and was expecting her in Puerto Rico. Second, it is necessary to approach an organizer or recruiter, as Karina did. Third, one must get the money to pay for the trip. Not all undocumented migrants are as fortunate as Karina. Mayra, for example, had to mortgage her house and her husband's business, losing all in her unsuccessful attempt to migrate. Marta kept a *san* (credit-rotating association) for three years to get the money. A friend lent her money that she paid after she began working in Puerto Rico. Other women in the sample told me that the organizer/ recruiter stole their money. Juana, for example, was robbed three times before she finally made it to Puerto Rico. She said to me: "They told me I had to give them $2,000 pesos up front, and then they divided us in three groups. I counted 60 people all together. We were left behind in the wilderness, and we saw the boat, but the captain left with our money." For her final, successful attempt she gave her television set to the captain of the boat.

More important than having a contact in Puerto Rico is having an honest recruiter in the Dominican Republic and the money to pay for the journey; also, family arrangements loom large in migration plans. Women in my sample had small children, and before they engaged in the journey, arrangements were made to find a reliable person who would care for the children. In many cases the woman's mother or sister took on the responsibility. The plan also included arranging their situation so that their children could be brought to Puerto Rico. For example, Aurelia told me that she left her three-year-old daughter with her mother, and the day she left she did not tell her daughter in order not to scare her, but when she finally made it to Puerto Rico, she called her and promised her she would soon be with her. . . .

Amparo from San Francisco de Macorís said: "I arrived with twenty people to a place near the beach. There we met El Capitán, and he told us he had too many people, and he did not know if everybody would fit in the boat. He told us to stay right there and to meet at 7 P.M. on the beach. At 7 o'clock there were 65 people and among them like twelve women. The captain told us to jump into the boat, and after we left we had to return because the boat was going to shipwreck and the police came, we ran into the wilderness, but the police attacked the captain and broke his head. We stayed hidden until next morning. I did not go this time, but six months later I tried again. This time the contact took me to Boca Chica, and we left almost at 2 A.M. and stopped in the island of Catalina (near La Romana). The boat we took in the island of Catalina had two engines, and before we left, the captain jumped out of the boat and sent us with another guy who he said knew the directions. The second day at sea, two men started a knife fight and they spoiled the compass. We got lost and I don't remember how many days we wandered in the middle of big waves, we cried every time dolphins jumped out of the water, believing they were sharks. Women had to pour the water out of the boat, but we didn't have strength and we were very thirsty. I lost consciousness and I dreamed of my daughter Jacqueline and I asked her for water and she gave me a cup of water. I woke up and saw the people praying in loud voices, and then we saw a big boat and started to follow it and it was dark, but God illuminated us with a full moon and continued until we reached El Desecheo (an island near Aguadilla in Puerto Rico). [We left on] Thursday and we arrived in El Desecheo on Tuesday of the next week. Or was it the following week? It was 9 P.M." . . .

"Other people can rob your money and even kill you. Women are raped." Juana told me that men want to have sex with the women, that they will not take them on the trip if they do not comply. She said she was spared from being raped because her brother was with her. . . .

The number of Dominicans killed in the journey is unknown, but it might be as many as hundreds every year. The tragedy of the lost boats, and drowned and shark-eaten corpses is a daily experience in the Dominican Republic.

The Dominican Who Won
the Kentucky Derby

Joel Rosario

The Dominican Republic has one horseracing track. And yet it has produced the top jockey in North America, Joel (joe-EL) Rosario, who vaulted to fame by winning the Kentucky Derby on a horse named Orb in May 2013. That triumph came on the heels of his victory in the richest horse race in the world, the $10 million Dubai World Cup, five weeks before. Given the global popularity of horse racing, Rosario may be the most famous Dominican in history, in terms of the sheer number of people who have heard his name.

According to the statistics and the experts alike, Rosario is something special in the equine world. Born in San Francisco de Macorís in the Cibao, he began riding at the age of thirteen. He went professional in 2003, when he was eighteen, riding a grand total of five horses for earnings of less than $5,000. But he rose rapidly to be the best among Dominican jockeys. In 2006 he migrated to California, where he quickly found success. The next year his earnings exceeded $3 million, and since 2010 he has topped $15 million annually.

This selection is from an interview with Rosario conducted six weeks after his victory in the 2013 Kentucky Derby. Around the same time Kenneth Ramsey, the winningest owner in thoroughbred racing, and Michael Maker, a leading trainer, also offered their views to the interviewer. Ramsey said he prefers Rosario to any jockey in the game and will fly him to Louisville for important races. Maker added that for Rosario "the sky's the limit. When you win the World Cup, the Derby, coast-to-coast, what can you say? He's seen all he can all by himself." Asked if Rosario has a special way with a horse, Maker said, "He definitely does. Any kind of horse he gets, he gets the run out of them. He has a natural talent."

The interview took place when Rosario returned to Churchill Downs, drawn to Louisville from his new base in New York to compete in a rich slate of races on a Saturday night in June, beneath a half moon and before a large crowd dressed in accordance with an event billed as "The White Party." After winning two big races, the Fleur de Lis Handicap, and the Regret Stakes (aboard a Ramsey horse) and coming

The leading jockey Joel Rosario posed with the Dominican flag at Churchill Downs in Louisville, Kentucky, on a successful night of riding in June 2013, six weeks after winning the Kentucky Derby there. Photograph by A. E. Doyle. Used by permission of A. E. Doyle and Joel Rosario.

in second on a long shot in the featured race, the half-million-dollar Stephen Foster Handicap, Rosario took a few minutes to reflect on his experience in this interview. Then he went back out on the track at 11 P.M. to win the last race of the night on a horse named Magical Moon. The next day he flew back to New York to race at Belmont, and the day after that he flew to England to race in Royal Ascot, which is a long way from San Francisco de Macorís.

I was born in the Dominican Republic, and I'm very proud to be Dominican.

I grew up in San Francisco, Castillo San Francisco de Macorís. Right now we live in Santo Domingo, with my family, we don't live there any more. For me, more than anything, the memories I have of growing up in the Dominican Republic are of my mother and my father, my stepdad, the guy who really was my real dad, I grew up with him. I remember they were really poor, we were a really poor family, you know.

And I have a chance now, you know, to really do what I want to be doing. To be here in the US, it's something really very special to me, and for my family, so I'm really proud to be here.

I've been riding for fourteen years, half the time here and half in the Dominican Republic. You know, I came to the US, people really gave me an opportunity here, and I really appreciate that. Some people helped me when I came here for the first time, when I was in California, it was something really special to me, and I feel there's a lot of nice people here, and I'll be happier where I am now.

I meet a lot of Dominicans, especially in New York, yeah. I'm always looking for them, and when I have a chance it's like "Oh, you're Dominican!" "Yeah!" It's something special to me and I'm really happy when I see people like that. They're from my country, so I feel good.

There's a little bit of difference between Dominicans in the US and Dominicans at home. But also, every country you go to, it's a little bit different. You know, [for instance] you go to Panama, they speak a little bit different, they have a little bit different way that they go about things.

So I'm really happy to be here, I'll say it one more time, and to be from my country. To be Dominican is something really important to me, it's something great to be in New York and see other Dominicans, because I was born in the Dominican Republic, it's a point of pride for me.

When I won the Kentucky Derby, I remember I was at the last 1/16 [mile] pole, and I said, "Wow, I'm in front!" And I thought I had a good chance to win the race. I could not believe how I felt, you know, it's like, I had this feeling, I don't know, I felt really special and just so happy to be there. It was something that really went to my heart, so I appreciated it.

Yeah, I've heard them say I'm the most famous Dominican, and I'm proud of that. It's a Dominican pride [*un orgullo dominicano*]. I'm representing my country, and that's really special to me.

Interview conducted and translated by Eric Paul Roorda.

You Know You're Dominican . . .

Anonymous

*Various versions of this list have been circulating since electronic mail was young
and now can be found on the Internet in media ranging from blogs to YouTube
postings to Facebook profiles. This selection is an amalgam of items from all these
sources.*

You Know You're Dominican . . . if people tell you to stop screaming
when you're really talking.

If you grew up afraid of something called "El Cuco" [a Dominican
variant on the bogeyman].

If you clap your hands while laughing.

If you have many *Primos* and *Primas* [cousins], and you talk about at
least one that is famous or rich.

If you're able to dance without any music.

If you learned how to dance merengue and *bachata* before you could
walk.

If you point things out with your nose and mouth.

If you've ever gone outside in *rolos* and *chancletas* [hair curlers and flip
flops].

If you consider plantains one of the major food groups.

If while in your country you hear people on the block yelling, "Se fue la
luz!" ["The light went out!," meaning the electricity, a very common
occurrence in the Dominican Republic due to frequent rolling
blackouts]; then you also hear "Llegó la luz" ["The light's back on"].

If your house has an oil lamp in every room.

If you told scary stories and funny jokes while there was no electricity.

If you intentionally pour a little bit of liquor on the floor when you
open a bottle, and say "Eso e pa lo muerto!" ["That's for the dead!"].

If you like *el concón* [the blackened layer of rice at the bottom of the pot]
and *habichuelas con dulce* [sweet creamed beans].

If you've ever gotten whipped by a *diablo cojuelo* or *lechon* [people

costumed as devils or boars for Carnival, when those on parade stage
attacks on spectators].

If your grandma has a saint picture in her living room.

If you ate rice, beans, and some type of meat for dinner yesterday,
today, and probably will tomorrow. Also for breakfast and lunch. . . .

If you ride in a four-passenger car, you have seven people in it,
and someone is yelling, "Caben ma'!" ["We can take another
passenger!"].

If you use an old t-shirt, towel, or anything as a mop, and use your feet
to mop.

If you've ever let someone throw Agua Florida on you for good luck.
[Literally "flower water," spiritualist cologne sold in botánicas—
religious supply stores.]

If your house has pieces of broken glass [embedded in concrete along
the tops of the walls and on the rooftop] to keep away robbers.

If you refer to every cat as "Mishu." [Dominicans say "Mishu" to call
cats, the way other people might say "Psspsspss" or other sounds
meant to attract the attention of domestic animals.]

If you call all kinds of breakfast cereal *cornflé* [cornflakes].

If your childhood games were called *El Escondido* [hide-and-seek], *Pollito
Pleibi* [a variation of patty-cake played with hands or feet], *Apara y
Batea* [played by bouncing a ball off city walls and trying to hit it on
the return], *El Gallo* [another hand-clapping game like patty-cake,
played to variations of this song:

> Se, se, se, se, ve, re, ve, re, ve, re
> The rooster, the hen, and the horse
> The Principle is a simple dance
> A, a, a, Little Mary already left
> I, i, i, Little Mary isn't here
> O, o, o, Little Mary took off
> U, u, u, Little Mary's in the club
> Drinking Country Club soda
> Clup, Clup, Clup, Clup]

If your parents dressed you up for Halloween as a cowboy, peasant,
gypsy, or hula dancer.

If your sofas are covered in plastic.

If you have at least three porcelain figurines in your living room.

If your local bodega does *fiao* [shortened form of *financiado* or layaway
plans and buying on credit].

If you think bananas and plantains are a source of power and call it
  "Banana Power."

If since you were little Balaguer has been dying.

If to you a frosted beer is *vestida da novia* [wedding dress] or *una fria* [a
  cold one].

If some of your favorite expressions consist of

  "El diache" ["Damn!"]

  "La creta" ["Damn!"]

  "Dimelo" ["What's up?"]

  "Qué lo Qué?" ["What's happening?"]

  "Ta' To" [shortened form of *Está todo bien*, meaning everything is
    fine, or "It's all good"]

  "A Po Ta Bien" [shortened form of *Ah pues todo bien*, meaning "Ah,
    well, everything is fine," same as "Ta' To."]

  "Que Vaína" ["What a pain"; original meaning of *vaína* is a sheath for
    a sword, a noun that had a sexual connotation]

  "Y es facil" ["And that's easy," or "You think that's easy," said with
    sarcasm about something that is difficult]

  "Anda el diablo" ["It's gone to hell"]

  "Qué Tripeo" [literally "What a trip," as in a stumble, but it means
    "What a funny practical joke"]

  "Qué Bufeo" [literally "What buffoonery," meaning the same as
    "Qué Tripeo"]

  "Montro" ["dude"]

  "Qué Loquera" ["What a crazy, fun time"]

  "Tá Cool" ["That's cool"]

  "Tá Jevi" ["That's heavy," meaning "That's cool"]

  "Tú tá pasa" [shortened form of *Tú está pasado*, "You're done," or in
    Dominican slang "You're rotten," but in this case meaning "You're
    crazy."]

  "Tranquilo" [literally "calm," means "Take it easy"]

  "Cójelo suave" ["Take it easy"]

  "Cójelo" ["Take that!"]

  "Manso" [an easygoing person; *tranquilo* can also mean a laid-back
    person]

  "Malvá" [a mean-spirited person]

  "Degrasia" ["lowlife" or "deadbeat" or "scum"]

  "Barbarazo/a" [someone who wears bizarre outfits and/or makes
    bizarre statements]

"Pariguayo" [perhaps shortened from English "party watcher"; a
shallow, nerdy person]

"Chulo" [for men: cocky, handsome], "chula" [for women: sassy, cute]

"Chulería" [for men: bravado, insolence; for women: style, grace]

If you're proud to be Dominican, and you pass these jokes on to all your
Dominican friends!

Translated by Eric Paul Roorda.

Suggestions for Further Reading

General

Atkins, G. Pope, and Larman Wilson. *The Dominican Republic and the United States: From Imperialism to Transnationalism.* Athens: University of Georgia Press, 1998.

Bell, Ian. *The Dominican Republic.* Boulder, CO: Westview, 1981.

Betances, Emelio. *State and Society in the Dominican Republic.* Boulder, CO: Westview, 1995.

Betances, Emelio, and Hobart Spalding. *Dominican Republic Today: Realities and Perspectives.* New York: Bilder Center for Western Hemisphere Studies, 1996.

Cassá, Roberto. *Historia social y economica de la República Dominicana.* Santo Domingo: Alfa y Omega, 1991.

Fernández, Eladio. *Hispaniola: A Photographic Journey through Island Biodiversity.* Cambridge, MA: Harvard University Press, 2007.

Moré, Gustavo, et al. *Historias para la construcción de la Arquitectura Dominicana, 1492–2008.* Santo Domingo: Grupo Leon Jiménez, 2008.

Moya Pons, Frank. *The Dominican Republic: A National History.* 3rd ed. Princeton, NJ: Markus Wiener, 2010.

Moya Pons, Frank, ed. *El siglo XX dominicano: Economía, política, pensamiento y literatura.* Santo Domingo: CODETEL, 2002.

Moya Pons, Frank, ed. *Historia de la República Dominicana.* Madrid: Consejo Superior de Investigaciones Científicas, 2010.

San Miguel, Pedro L. *The Imagined Island: History, Identity and Utopia in Hispaniola.* Chapel Hill: University of North Carolina Press, 2009.

Valdez, Juan R. *Tracing Dominican Identity: The Writings of Pedro Henríquez Ureña.* New York: Palgrave Macmillan, 2011.

Vega, Bernardo. *Imágenes de ayer.* Santo Domingo: Fundación Cultural Dominicana, 1981.

Vega, Bernardo. *Más imágenes de ayer.* Santo Domingo: Fundación Cultural Dominicana, 1988.

Part I. European Encounters

Arroyo, Antonio Stevens. *Cave of the Jagua: The Mythological World of the Taínos.* Scranton, PA: University of Scranton Press, 2006.

Bercht, Fatima, et al., eds. *Taíno: Pre-Columbian Art and Culture from the Caribbean*. New York: Monacelli, 1997.

Las Casas, Bartolomé de. *The Devastation of the Indies*. Translated by Herma Briffault. Baltimore: Johns Hopkins University Press, 1992.

Mann, Charles C. *1493: Uncovering the New World Columbus Created*. New York: Knopf, 2011.

Rouse, Irving. *The Tainos: Rise and Decline of the People Who Greeted Columbus*. New Haven, CT: Yale University Press, 1993.

Sale, Kirkpatrick. *The Conquest of Paradise: Christopher Columbus and the Columbian Legacy*. New York: Plume, 1995.

Wilson, Samuel M. *The Archaeology of the Caribbean*. Cambridge: Cambridge University Press, 2007.

Wilson, Samuel M. *Hispaniola: Caribbean Chiefdoms in the Age of Columbus*. Tuscaloosa: University of Alabama Press, 1990.

Part II. Pirates, Governors, and Slaves

Deive Esteban, Carlos. *La esclavitud del negro en Santo Domingo, 1492–1844*. Vols. 1 and 2. Santo Domingo: Museo del Hombre Dominicano, 1980.

Deive Esteban, Carlos. *Los cimarrones del Maniel de Neiba: Historia e etnografía*. Santo Domingo: Banco Central, 1985.

Exquemelin, Alexander O. *The Buccaneers of America*. Mineola, NY: Dover, 2000.

Fraginals, Moreno Manuel, Frank Moya Pons, and Stanley Engerman. *Between Slavery and Free Labor: The Spanish-Speaking Caribbean in the Nineteenth Century*. Baltimore: Johns Hopkins University Press, 1985.

González, Raymundo. *De esclavos a campesinos: Vida rural en el Santo Domingo colonial*. Santo Domingo: Archivo General de la Nación, 2011.

Kelsey, Harry. *Sir Francis Drake: The Queen's Pirate*. New Haven, CT: Yale University Press, 2000.

Lane, Kris. *Pillaging the Empire: Piracy in the Americas, 1500–1750*. Armonk, NY: M. E. Sharpe, 1998.

Moya Pons, Frank. *Cinco siglos de iglesia dominicana*. Santo Domingo: Editora Amigo del Hogar, 1987.

Moya Pons, Frank, ed. *La vida escandalosa en Santo Domingo en los siglos XVII y XVIII*. Santiago: Universidad Católico Madre y Maestra, 1976.

Price, Richard. *Maroon Societies: Rebel Slave Communities in the Americas*. 3rd ed. Baltimore: Johns Hopkins University Press, 1996.

Thomas, Hugh. *The Slave Trade, 1440–1870*. New York: Simon and Schuster, 1999.

Part III. Revolutions

Cruz Sánchez, Filiberto. *Mella: Biografía política*. Santo Domingo: Ediciones El Nuevo Diario, 1996.

Duarte, Juan Pablo. *Escritos*. Santo Domingo: Instituto Duartiano, 1997.

Dubois, Laurent. *Avengers of the New World: The Story of the Haitian Revolution*. Cambridge, MA: Harvard University Press, 2005.

Fick, Carolyn. *The Making of Haiti: The Saint Domingue Revolution from Below*. Knoxville: University of Tennessee Press, 1990.

Fischer, Sibylle. *Modernity Disavowed: Haiti and Cultures of Slavery in the Age of Revolution*. Durham, NC: Duke University Press, 2004.

Geggus, David Patrick, and Norman Fiering. *The World of the Haitian Revolution*. Bloomington: Indiana University Press, 2009.

Geggus, David Patrick, and David Barry Gaspar. *A Turbulent Time: The French Revolution and the Greater Caribbean*. Bloomington: Indiana University Press, 1997.

Inoa, Orlanda. *Biografía de Juan Pablo Duarte*. Santo Domingo: Editorial Letra Gráfica, 2008.

James, C. L. R. *The Black Jacobins: Toussaint L'Ouverture and the San Domingo Revolution*. New York: Vintage, 1963.

Michel, Emilio Cordero. *La revolución haitiana y Santo Domingo*. Santo Domingo: Editora Nacional, 1968.

Ott, Thomas O. *The Haitian Revolution, 1789–1804*. Knoxville: University of Tennessee Press, 1987.

Picó, Fernando. *One Frenchman, Four Revolutions: General Ferrand and the Peoples of the Caribbean*. Princeton, NJ: Markus Wiener, 2011.

Part IV. Caudillos and Empires

Álvarez-López, Luis. *The Dominican Republic and the Beginning of a Revolutionary Cycle in the Spanish Caribbean: 1861–1898*. Lanham, MD: University Press of America, 2009.

Hernández Flores, Ismael. *Pedro Santana, totalmente negativo*. Santo Domingo: Alfa y Omega, 1984.

Martínez-Fernández, Luis. *Torn between Empires: Economy, Society and Patterns of Political Thought in the Hispanic Caribbean, 1840–1878*. Athens: University of Georgia Press, 1994.

Nelson, W. J. *Almost a Territory: America's Attempt to Annex the Dominican Republic*. Newark: University of Delaware Press, 1991.

Sang, Mu-Kien Adriana. *Buenaventura Báez, el Caudillo Del Sur*. Santo Domingo: INTEC, 1991.

Part V. The Idea of the Nation: Order and Progress

Alvarez, Julia. *In the Name of Salomé*. Chapel Hill, NC: Algonquin Books, 2000.

Baud, Michiel. *Peasants and Tobacco in the Dominican Republic, 1870–1930*. Knoxville: University of Tennessee Press, 1995.

Franks, Julie Cheryl. *Transformando la propiedad: La tenencia de tierras y los derechos políticos en la región azucarera dominicana, 1880–1930*. Santo Domingo: Academia Dominicana de Historia, 2013.

González, Raymundo. *Pedro Francisco Bonó, el intelectual de los pobres*. Santo Domingo: Tobogan, 2003.

Hoetink, Harry. *The Dominican People, 1850–1900*. Baltimore: Johns Hopkins University Press, 1982.

Martínez Vergne, Teresita. *Nation and Citizen in the Dominican Republic, 1880–1916*. Chapel Hill: University of North Carolina Press, 2009.

Peguero, Valentina. *The Militarization of Culture in the Dominican Republic, from the Captains General to General Trujillo*. Lincoln: University of Nebraska Press, 2004.

Sang, Mu-Kien. *Ulises Heureaux: Biografía de un dictador*. Santo Domingo: Instituto Tecnológico de Santo Domingo, 1987.

San Miguel, Pedro. *La Guerra silenciosa: Las luchas sociales en la ruralia dominicana*. Mexico City: Instituto de Investigaciones Dr. José María Luis Mora, 2004.

San Miguel, Pedro. *Los desvarios de ti noel: Ensayos sobre la producción del saber en el Caribe*. San Juan: Ediciones Vértigo, 2001.

Sommer, Doris. *Foundational Fictions: The National Romances of Latin America*. Berkeley: University of California Press, 1991.

Sommer, Doris. *One Master for Another: Populism as Patriarchal Rhetoric in Dominican Novels*. Lanham, MD: University Press of America, 1983.

Zeller, Neici. *Discursos y espacios demeninos en República Dominicana, 1880–1961*. Santo Domingo: Editorial Letra Gráfica, 2012.

Part VI. Dollars, Gunboats, and Bullets

Calder, Bruce. *The Impact of Intervention: The Dominican Republic during the U.S. Occupation of 1916–1924*. Princeton, NJ: Markus Wiener, 2006.

González Canalda, María Filomena. *Los gavilleros, 1904–1916*. Santo Domingo: Archivo General de la Nación, 2008.

Veeser, Cyrus. *A World Safe for Capitalism: Dollar Diplomacy and America's Rise to Global Power*. New York: Columbia University Press, 2007.

Welles, Sumner. *Naboth's Vineyard: The Dominican Republic, 1844–1924*. New York: Arno, 1972.

Part VII. The Era of Trujillo

Alvarez, Julia. *In the Time of the Butterflies*. Chapel Hill, NC: Algonquin Books, 2010.

Cassá, Roberto. *Los orígenes del movimiento 14 de Julio*. Santo Domingo: Editora Universitaria. 1999.

Cassá, Roberto. *Minerva Mirabal: La revolucionaria*. Santo Domingo: Tobogan, 2000.

Crassweller, Robert D. *Trujillo: The Life and Times of a Caribbean Dictator*. New York: MacMillan, 1966.

Derby, Lauren H. *The Dictator's Seduction: Politics and Popular Imagination in the Era of Trujillo*. Durham, NC: Duke University Press, 2009.

Diederich, Bernard. *Trujillo: The Death of the Dictator*. Princeton, NJ: Markus Wiener, 2000.

García, Juan Manuel. *La matanza de los haitianos: Genocidio de Trujillo, 1937*. Santo Domingo: Editora Alfa y Omega, 1983.

Roorda, Eric Paul. *The Dictator Next Door: The Good Neighbor Policy and the Trujillo Regime in the Dominican Republic, 1930–1945*. Durham, NC: Duke University Press, 1998.

Turits, Richard Lee. *Foundations of Despotism: Peasants, the Trujillo Regime, and Modernity in Dominican History*. Palo Alto, CA: Stanford University Press, 2004.

Vargas Llosa, Mario. *The Feast of the Goat*. New York: Farrar, Strauss and Giroux, 2001.

Vega, Bernardo, ed. *Control y represión en la dictadura trujillista*. Santo Domingo: Fundación Cultural Dominicana, 1986.

Part VIII. The Long Transition to Democracy

Bosch, Brian J. *Balaguer and the Dominican Military: Presidential Control of the Factional Officer Corps in the 1960s and 1970s*. Jefferson, NC: McFarland, 2007.

Brea, Ramonina. *Estado de situación de la democracia dominicana (1978–1992)*. Santiago: PUCAMAIMA, 1995.

Brea, Ramonina, and Isis Duarte. *Entre la calle y la casa: Las mujeres dominicanas y la cultura política a finales del siglo XX*. Santo Domingo: Profamilia, 1999.

Brea, Ramonina, Rosario Espinal, and Fernando Valerio-Holguín, eds. *La República Dominicana en el umbral del siglo XXI: Cultura, política y cambio social*. Santiago: PUCAMAIMA, 1999.

Cassá, Roberto. *Los Doce Años: Contrarevolución y Desarrollismo*. Santo Domingo: Alfa y Omega, 1986.

Cassá, Roberto. *Mauricio Báez: Líder del proletariado*. Santo Domingo: Tobogan, 2003.

Chester, Eric Thomas. *Rag-Tags, Scum and Commies: U.S. Intervention in the Dominican Republic, 1965–1966*. New York: Monthly Review Press, 2001.

Espinal, Rosario. *Autoritarismo y democracia en la política dominicana*. San José, Costa Rica: Centro Interamericano de asesoría y promoción estatal, Instituto Interamericano de derechos humanos, 1987.

Ferguson, James. *Beyond the Lighthouse*. New York: Monthly Review Press, 1992.

Gleijesis, Piero. *The Dominican Crisis: The 1965 Constitutionalist Revolt and American Intervention*. Baltimore: Johns Hopkins University Press, 1978.

Hartlyn, Jonathan. *The Struggle for Democratic Politics in the Dominican Republic*. Chapel Hill: University of North Carolina Press, 1998.

Krohn-Hansen, Christian. *Political Authoritarianism in the Dominican Republic*. New York: Palgrave Macmillan, 2009.

Lowenthal, Abraham F. *The Dominican Intervention*. Baltimore: Johns Hopkins University Press, 1994.

Lozano, Wilfredo. *El reformismo dependiente*. Santo Domingo: Editora Taller, 1985.

McPherson, Alan L. *Yankee No! Anti-Americanism in U.S.-Latin American Relations*. Cambridge, MA: Harvard University Press, 2006.

Part IX. Religious Practices

Andujar, Carlos. *Identidad cultural y religiosidad popular*. Santo Domingo: Editora Cole, 1999.

Betances, Emelio. *The Catholic Church and Power Politics in Latin America: The Dominican Case in Comparative Perspective*. Lanham, MD: Rowman and Littlefield, 2007.

Davis, Martha Ellen. *La otra ciencia: El vodú como religión y medicina popular*. Santo Domingo: Editora Universitaria, 1987.

Davis, Martha Ellen. *Ruta hacia Liborio: Mesianismo en el sur profundo dominicano*. Santo Domingo: UNESCO, 2004.

Deive, Carlos Esteban. *Vodú y magia en Santo Domingo*. Santo Domingo: Museo del Hombre Dominicano, 1979.

Hernández Soto, Carlos. *Kalunga Eh! Los Congos de Villa Mella*. Santo Domingo: Editorial Letra Gráfica, 2004.

Hernández Soto, Carlos. *Morir en Villa Mella: Ritos funerarios dominicanos*. Santo Domingo: CIASCA, 1996.

Lundius, Jan, and Mats Lundahl. *Peasants and Religion: A Socioeconomic Study of Dios Olivorio and the Palma Sola Movement in the Dominican Republic*. New York: Routledge, 2000.

Martínez, Lusitania. *Palma Sola: Opresión y esperanza (su geografía mítica y social)*. Santo Domingo: Ediciones CEDEE, 1991.

Ripley, George. *Imágenes de possesion: Vodú dominicano*. Santo Domingo: Cocolo Editorial, 2002.

Savino, Giovanni. *La comarca fija de Liborio*. Makonda, IL: Earthcds.

Savino, Giovanni. *Misterios*. Makonda, IL: Earthcds.

Part X. Popular Culture

Austerlitz, Paul. *Merengue: Dominican Music and Dominican Identity*. Philadelphia: Temple University Press, 1997.

Brennan, Denise. *What's Love Got to Do with It? Transnational Desires and Sex Tourism in the Dominican Republic*. Durham, NC: Duke University Press, 2004.

Cabezas, Amalia. *Economies of Desire: Sex and Tourism in Cuba and the Dominican Republic*. Philadelphia: Temple University Press, 2009.

Carruyo, Light. *Producing Knowledge, Protecting Forests: Rural Encounters with Gender, Ecotourism and International Aid in the Dominican Republic*. University Park: Pennsylvania State University Press, 2008.

Castillo, José del, and Manuel A. García Arévalo. *Anthology of the Merengue*. Santo Domingo: Banco Antillano, 1989.

Collado, Lipe. *El tíguere dominicano*. Santo Domingo: El Mundo, 1992.

Davis, Martha Ellen. *Aspectos de la influencia africana en la música tradicional dominicana*. Santo Domingo: Museo del Hombre Dominicano, 1980.

Davis, Martha Ellen. *Voces del purgatorio: Estudio del salve dominicana*. Santo Domingo: Museo del Hombre Dominicano, 1981.

Duarte, Isis. *Los hogares dominicanos: El mito de la "familia ideal" y los tipos de jefaturas del hogar.* Santo Domingo: Instituto de Estudios de Población y Desarrollo, 1995.

González, Clara. *Aunt Clara's Dominican Cookbook.* New York: Lunch Club Press, 2007.

Klein, Allan M. *Sugarball: The American Game, the Dominican Dream.* New Haven, CT: Yale University Press, 1991.

Lizardo, Fradique. *Cultura Africana en Santo Domingo.* Santo Domingo: Editora Taller, 1979.

Lizardo, Fradique. *Danzas y bailes folklóricos dominicanos.* Santo Domingo: Fundación García Arévalo, 1975.

Maggiolo, Marcio Veloz, Pedro Delgado Malagón, and José del Castillo. *Bolero: Visiones y perfiles de una pasión dominicana.* Santo Domingo: CODETEL, 2009.

Pacini-Hernández, Deborah. *Bachata: A Social History of Dominican Popular Culture.* Philadelphia: Temple University Press, 1995.

Padilla, Mark. *Caribbean Pleasure Industry: Tourism, Sexuality and AIDS in the Dominican Republic.* Chicago: University of Chicago Press, 2007.

Poupeye, Veerle. *Caribbean Art.* London: Thames and Hudson, 1998.

Ruck, Rob. *The Tropic of Baseball: Baseball in the Dominican Republic.* Lincoln, NE: Bison Books, 1991.

Saez, José L. *Historia de un sueño importado: Ensayos sobre el cine en Santo Domingo.* Santo Domingo: Ediciones Siboney, 1983.

Savino, Giovanni. *Bachata: Music of the People.* New York: Cinemaguild, 2003.

Savino, Giovanni. *Culture of Palo: Palo Music and Oral Traditions from the Dominican Republic.* Makonda, IL: Earthcds.

Tejeda Ortíz, Juan Dagoberto. *Atlas folklórico de la República Dominicana.* Santo Domingo: Editorial Santillana, 2003.

Tejeda Ortíz, Juan Dagoberto. *El carnaval dominicano: Antecedentes, tendencias y perspectivas.* República Dominicana: Instituto Panamericano de Geografía e Historia, Sección Nacional de Dominicana, 2008.

Vargas, Tahira. *De la casa a la calle: Estudio de la familia y vecindad en un barrio de Santo Domingo.* Santo Domingo: Editora Búho, 1998.

Vega, Bernardo, ed. *Dominican Cultures: The Making of a Caribbean Society.* Princeton, NJ: Marcus Wiener, 2007.

Part XI. The Dominican Diaspora

Alvarez, Julia. *How the García Girls Lost Their Accents.* Chapel Hill, NC: Algonquin Books, 2010.

Breton, Marcos, and José Luis Villegas. *Away Games: The Life and Times of a Latin Baseball Player.* Albuquerque: University of New Mexico Press, 1999.

Candelario, Ginetta. *Black behind the Ears: Dominican Racial Identity from Museums to Beauty Shops.* Durham, NC: Duke University Press, 2007.

Díaz, Junot. *The Brief, Wondrous Life of Oscar Wao.* New York: Riverhead Books, 2007.

Díaz, Junot. *Drown.* New York: Riverhead Books, 1996.

Fischkin, Barbara. *Muddy Cup: A Dominican Family Comes of Age in a New America.* New York: Scribner, 1997.

Gregory, Steven. *The Devil behind the Mirror: Globalization and Politics in the Dominican Republic.* Berkeley: University of California Press, 2006.

Hoffnung-Garskof, Jesse. *A Tale of Two Cities: Santo Domingo and New York after 1950.* Princeton, NJ: Princeton University Press, 2007.

Hudes, Quiaria Alegria, and Lin-Manuel Miranda. *In the Heights: The Complete Book and Lyrics of the Broadway Musical.* New York: Applause Theater and Cinema Books, 2013.

Levitt, Peggy. *The Transnational Villagers.* Berkeley: University of California Press, 2001.

Marichal, Juan, and Lew Freedman. *Juan Marichal: My Journey from the Dominican Republic to Cooperstown.* Minneapolis: MVP Books, 2011.

Méndez, Danny. *Narratives of Migration and Displacement in Dominican Literature.* London: Routledge, 2012.

Pessar, Patricia, and Sherri Grasmuck. *Between Two Islands: Dominican International Migration.* Berkeley: University of California Press, 1991.

Safa, Helen. *The Myth of the Male Breadwinner: Women and Industrialization in the Caribbean.* Boulder, CO: Westview, 1999.

Acknowledgment of Copyrights and Sources

Part I. European Encounters

"The People Who Greeted Columbus," by Irving Rouse, from *The Tainos: Rise and Decline of the People Who Greeted Columbus* (New Haven, CT: Yale University Press, 1992), 9–17, 161–164. Used by permission of Yale University Press.

"Religion of the Taíno People," by Ramón Pané, from "Relación de Fray Ramón acerca de las antigüedades de los indios" in *La Historia del Almirante Don Cristobal Colón* (Madrid: Tomás Minuesa, 1892), vol. 1, 282–297; vol. 2, 3–8.

"First Descriptions of the Land, First Violence against Its People," by Christopher Columbus, from *The Journal of Christopher Columbus (During His First Voyage, 1492–93)*, translated by Clements R. Markham (London: Hakluyt Society, 1893), 101–161.

"Death of the Spanish at Navidad," by Diego Álvarez Chanca, from "The Letter of Dr. Diego Álvarez Chanca, Dated 1494, Relating to the Second Voyage of Columbus to America," translated by A. M. Fernández de Ybarra, *Smithsonian Miscellaneous Collections* 48, no. 3 (July 1905), 428–458.

"The First Christian Converts—and Martyrs—in the New World," by Ramón Pané, from "Relación de Fray Ramón acerca de las antigüedades de los indios" in *La Historia del Almirante Don Cristobal Colón* (Madrid: Tomás Minuesa, 1892), vol. 2, 12–20.

"Founding Santo Domingo," by Antonio de Herrera y Tordesillas, from *Historia general de los hechos de los Castellanos en las islas i tierra-firme del mar océano* (Madrid: Imprenta Real, 1601), bk. 3, 71.

"The Indian Monarchs," by Luis Joseph Peguero, from *Historia de la Conquista, de la Isla España de Santo Domingo trasumptada el Año de 1762: Traducida de la Historia general de las Indias escrita por Antonio de Herrera cronista mayor de Su Magestad, y de las Indias, y de Castilla, y de otros autores que han escrito sobre el particular*, edited by Eduardo J. Santiago (Santo Domingo: Publicaciones del Museo De Las Casas Reales, 1975), vol. 1, 91–93, 141–143, 148–149, 187–188.

"Criminals as Kings," by Bartolomé de Las Casas, from *New Iberian World: A Documentary History of the Discovery and Settlement of Latin America to the Early Seventeenth Century*, edited and translated by John H. Parry and Robert G. Keith (New York: Times Books, 1984), vol. 1, 251.

"A Voice in the Wilderness: Brother Antonio Montesino," by Bartolomé de Las Casas, from *New Iberian World: A Documentary History of the Discovery and Settlement of Latin America to the Early Seventeenth Century*, edited and translated by John H. Parry and Robert G. Keith (New York: Times Books, 1984), vol. 1, 308–312.

"The Royal Response," by King Ferdinand I, from *New Iberian World: A Documentary History of the Discovery and Settlement of Latin America to the Early Seventeenth Century*, edited and translated by John H. Parry and Robert G. Keith (New York: Times Books, 1984), vol. 1, 312–313.

Part II. Pirates, Governors, and Slaves

"Las Casas Blamed for the African Slave Trade," by Augustus Francis MacNutt, from *Bartholomew de Las Casas: His Life, Apostolate, and Writings* (Cleveland: Arthur H. Clark, 1909), 97–100.

"The Slave Problem in Santo Domingo," by Álvaro de Castro, quoted in unpublished court documents c. 1540, excerpted from "Maroons and Slave Rebellions in the Spanish Territories," by José L. Franco, in *Maroon Societies: Rebel Slave Communities in the Americas*, edited and translated by Richard Price, 3rd ed. (Baltimore: Johns Hopkins University Press, 1996), 38–39. Used by permission of Richard Price.

"Lemba and the Maroons of Hispaniola," by Alonso López de Cerrato, quoted in unpublished court documents c. 1540, excerpted from "Maroons and Slave Rebellions in the Spanish Territories," by José L. Franco, in *Maroon Societies: Rebel Slave Communities in the Americas*, edited and translated by Richard Price, 3rd ed. (Baltimore: Johns Hopkins University Press, 1996), 39–41. Used by permission of Richard Price.

"Francis Drake's Sacking of Santo Domingo," by Walter Bigges, from *A Summarie and True Discourse of Sir Frances Drakes West Indian Voyage* (London: Richard Field, 1589), 15–19.

"Colonial Delinquency," by Carlos Esteban Deive, from *La Mala Vida: Delincuencia y Picaresca en la Colonia Española de Santo Domingo* (Santo Domingo: Fundación Cultural Dominicana, 1988), 50–51, 69. Used by permission of the author.

"The Bulls," by Flérida de Nolasco, from *Días de la Colonia* (Santo Domingo: Editora del Caribe, 1974), 86–87. Used by permission of Ruth Nolasco.

"The Buccaneers of Hispaniola," by Alexander O. Exquemelin, from *History of the Bucaniers of America*, 5th ed. (London: T. Evans and Richardson & Urquhart, 1771), 41–50.

"Business Deals with the Buccaneers," by Jean-Baptiste Labat, from *The Memoirs of Père Labat, 1693–1705*, edited and translated by John Eaden (London: Frank Cass, 1970 [1931]), 170–178.

"The Idea of Value on Hispaniola," by Antonio Sánchez Valverde, from *Idea del Valor de la Isla Española* (Madrid: Imprenta Don Pedro Marín, 1785), 110–112, 185–187.

Part III. Revolutions

"The Monteros and the Guerreros," by Manuel Vicente Hernández González, from *El sur dominicano (1680–1795): Cambios sociales y transformaciones económicas* (Santo Domingo: Archivo General de la Nación, 2008), 99–101, 106. Used by permission of the author.

"The Border Maroons of Le Maniel," by Médéric Louis Élie Moreau de Saint-Méry, from "Description topographique, physique, civile, politique et historique de la partie française de l'isle Saint-Domingue," originally published in 1797, in *Maroon Societies: Rebel Slave Communities in the Americas*, edited and translated by Richard Price, 3rd ed. (Baltimore: Johns Hopkins University Press, 1996), 135–141. Used by permission of Richard Price.

"The 'People-Eater,'" by Raymundo González, from *De esclavos a campesinos: Vida rural en el Santo Domingo colonial* (Santo Domingo: Archivo General de la Nación, 2011), 141–149.

"The Boca Nigua Revolt," by David Patrick Geggus, from "Slave Resistance in the Spanish Caribbean in the Mid-1790s" in *A Turbulent Time: The French Revolution and the Greater Caribbean*, edited by David Patrick Geggus and David Barry Gaspar (Bloomington: Indiana University Press, 1997), 139–149. © 1997, Indiana University Press. Used by permission of Indiana University Press.

"Hayti and San Domingo," by James Franklin, from *The Present State of Hayti (Saint Domingo): With Remarks on Its Agriculture, Commerce, Laws, Religion, Finances, and Population, Etc. Etc.* (London: John Murray, 1828), 24–36.

"Toussaint's Conquest," by Jonathan Brown, from *The History and Present Condition of St. Domingo* (Philadelphia: Wm. Marshall and Co., 1837), 30–37.

"After the War, *Tertulias*," by William Walton Jr., from *The Present State of the Spanish Colonies including a Particular Report of Hispañola or the Spanish Part of Santo Domingo* (London: Longman, Hurst, Rees, Ore, and Brown, 1810), 38–39, 72, 133–136, 142–149.

"Stupid Spain," by Carlos Urrutia de Montoya, from "Bando del Buen Gobierno," unpublished edict from 1814, quoted in Maria Ugarte, *Estampas Coloniales* (Santo Domingo: Editora Amigo del Hogar, 1998), 307–313.

"The Dominican Bolívar," by José Núñez de Cáceres, from "El Conejo, Los Corderos y El Pastor," originally published in *El Duende*, c. 1821, reprinted in *Dos Siglos de Literatura Dominicana: Poesía I*, edited by Manuel Rueda (Santo Domingo: Editora Corripio, 1996), vol. 10, 52–54.

"Arrogant Bell Bottoms," by César Nicolás Penson, from "¡Profanación!" in *Cosas añejas: Tradiciones y episodios de Santo Domingo* (Santo Domingo: Imprenta Quisqueya, 1891), 75–85.

"Dominicans Unite!," by La Trinitaria, from "Manifestación de los Pueblos de la parte del Este de la Isla antes Española Haitiana o de Santo Domingo, sobre las causas de la separación de la República Haitiana," written January 16, 1844, reprinted in *Las Actas de Independencia de America*, edited by Javier Malagón Barceló, 2nd ed. (Washington, DC: Organization of American States, 1973), 126–128.

Part IV. Caudillos and Empires

"Pedro Santana," by Miguel Ángel Monclús, from *El Caudillismo en la República Dominicana* (Santo Domingo: Editora Montalvo, 1946), 15–17.

"The Caudillo of the South," by Buenaventura Báez, (1) "A Question," originally published as "Una Pregunta," *La Acusación*, November 20, 1856; (2) "Message to the President of the Republic," originally published as "Mensaje del 9 de marzo de 1866," *La Acusación*, March 9, 1866; (3) "To His Fellow Citizens," originally published as "A sus conciudadanos," *Gaceta de Santo Domingo*, December 16, 1876. Courtesy of El Archivo General de la Nación, Santo Domingo.

"In the Army Camp at Bermejo," by Pedro Francisco Bonó, from "En el Cantón de Bermejo," written in 1863, published in *Diarios de la guerra dominico-española de 1863–1865*, edited by Emilio Rodríguez Demorizi (Santo Domingo: Editora del Caribe, 1963), 119–123.

"The War of the Restoration," by Carlos Vargas, from "Private Dispatch to the Minister of War in Madrid from Carlos Vargas, Captain General of Santo Domingo, Dated February 29, 1864," in *Highlights in the Debates in the Spanish Chamber of Deputies Relative to the Abandonment of Santo Domingo*, edited and translated by David G. Yuengling (Washington, DC: Murray and Heister, 1941), 142–143.

"Spanish Recolonization: A Postmortem," by US Commission of Inquiry to Santo Domingo, from *Dominican Republic: Report of the Commission of Inquiry to Santo Domingo*, by B. F. Wade, A. D. White, and S. G. Howe (Washington, DC: Government Printing Office, 1871), 10–11.

"Making the Case for US Annexation," by Ulysses S. Grant, from "Second Annual Message to Congress," December 5, 1870. Available at http://www.presidency.ucsb.edu/ws/?pid=29511. Accessed May 23, 2013.

"Dominican Support for Annexation," by US Commission of Inquiry to Santo Domingo, from *Dominican Republic: Report of the Commission of Inquiry to Santo Domingo*, by B. F. Wade, A. D. White, and S. G. Howe (Washington, DC: Government Printing Office, 1871), 11–14.

"Opposition to US Annexation," by Justin S. Morrill, from *Annexation of Santo Domingo. Speech of Hon. Justin S. Morrill of Vermont, delivered in the Senate of the United States, 7 April 1871* (Washington, DC: F. & J. Rives & G. A. Bailey, 1871). Reprinted version available at http://name.umdl.umich.edu/ADH0563.0001.001. Accessed May 23, 2013.

"Dominican Nationalism versus Annexation," by Gregorio Luperón, from "Agitaciones contra la Anexación a los Estados Unidos," quoted in *Gregorio Luperón e Historia de la Restaúracion* by Manuel Rodríguez Objío (Santiago, Dominican Republic: Editorial el Diario, 1939), 315–317.

"A Lesson in 'Quiet Good-Breeding,'" by Samuel Hazard, from *Santo Domingo Past and Present with a Glance at Hayti* (New York: Harper and Brothers, 1873), 175–176, 180–181, 184–187, 229–233, 301–302, 323–325, 365–368, 375.

"Martí's Travel Notes," by José Martí, from "De Montecristi a La Vega" and "De La Vega a Montecristi" in *Apuntes de un viaje*, prologue and notes by Manuel Isidro Méndez (Havana: Dirección de cultura, 1938), 30–33, 50–51.

"Ulises 'Lilís' Heureaux," by Américo Lugo, from "Prologue" in *Cosas de Lilís*, Victor M. de Castro (Santo Domingo: Cuna de América, 1919), 7–9.

"Your Friend, Ulises," by Ulises Heureaux, (1) unpublished letter to D. Elias Pereira, Dominican Consul, Port-au-Prince, November 6, 1893, Heureaux Papers, folios 190–195, Archivo General de la Nación, Santo Domingo, quoted in Juan Daniel Balcácer, *Lilís: Cartas y Comunicaciónes* (Santo Domingo: Editora Cosmos, 1977); (2) unpublished letter to Charles I. Well[e]s, Paris, October 7, 1896, Heureaux Papers, bk. 55, 105, Archivo General de la Nación, Santo Domingo.

Part V. The Idea of the Nation: Order and Progress

"Street People and Godparents," by Luis Emilio Gómez Alfau, from *Ayer o El Santo Domingo de Hace 50 Años* (Santo Domingo: Pol Hermanos, 1944), 131–133.

"From Paris to Santo Domingo," by Francisco Moscoso Puello, from *Cartas a Evelina* (Santo Domingo: Editora Cosmas, 1974), 84–90, 97–98.

"Public Enemies: The Revolutionary and the Pig," by Emiliano Tejera, from "Memoria que al ciudadano Presidente de la República presenta al Secretario de Estado de Relaciones Exteriores," *Gaceta Oficial*, March 17, 1906. Reprinted in *Escritos Diversos*, edited by Andrés Blanco Díaz (Santo Domingo: Archivo General de la Nación, 2010), 173–174.

"The 'Master of Décimas,'" by Juan Antonio Alix, from "Negro tras la Oreja" and "Los Mangos Bajitos" in *Décimas de Juan Antonio Alix* (Santo Domingo: J. R. vda. García, sucesores, 1927).

"Barriers to Progress: Revolutions, Diseases, Holidays, and Cockfights," by Pedro Francisco Bonó, from "Cuestión Hacienda," *El Amante de la Luz*, no. 8, July 6, 1876.

"Food, Race, and Nation," by Lauren H. Derby, from "Gringo Chickens with Worms" in *Close Encounters of Empire: Writing the Cultural History of United States-Latin American Relations*, edited by Gilbert M. Joseph, Catherine LeGrand, and Ricardo D. Salvatore (Durham, NC: Duke University Press, 1998), 468–470.

"Tobacco to the Rescue," by Pedro Francisco Bonó, from "Apuntes sobre las clases trabajadoras dominicanas," *La Voz de Santiago*, no. 83, October 23, 1881.

"Patrons, Peasants, and Tobacco," by Michiel Baud, from "The Transformation of Rural Society: Peasants and Landowners in the Villa González Region" in *Peasants and Tobacco in the Dominican Republic, 1870–1930* (Knoxville: University of Tennessee Press, 1995), 96–124. Used by permission of University of Tennessee Press.

"Salomé," by Salomé Ureña de Henríquez, from "27 de Febrero" and "Diez y seis de Agosto" in *Poesías de Salomé Ureña de Henríquez* (Santo Domingo: Imprenta García Hermanos, 1880).

"The Case for Commerce, 1907," by Dominican Department of Promotion and Public Works, from *The Dominican Republic* (Washington, DC: B. S. Adams, 1907), 12.

Part VI. Dollars, Gunboats, and Bullets

"Uneasiness about the US Government," by Emiliano Tejera, from "Memoria que al Ciudadano Presidente de la República presenta el Secretario de Estado de Relaciones Exteriores, Año de 1907," *Gaceta Oficial*, 9 March 1907. Reprinted in *Escritos Diversos*, edited by Andrés Blanco Díaz (Santo Domingo: Archivo General de la Nación, 2010), 190–191.

"In the Midst of Revolution," by US Receivership of Dominican Customs, from *Seventh Annual Report: Dominican Customs Receivership under the American-Dominican Convention of 1907, August 1, 1913 to July 31, 1914* (Santo Domingo: Office of the General Receiver of Dominican Customs, October 1, 1914), 3–5, 13–19.

"Gavilleros," by *Listín Diario*. (1) "Untitled," *Listín Diario*, September 16, 1916; (2) "Gavilleros azotan campesinos," *Listín Diario*, October 19, 1916. Reprinted in *Los gavilleros,*

1904–1916, by María Filomena González Canalda (Santo Domingo: Archivo General de la Nación, 2008), 151.

"A Resignation and a Machine Gun," by Frederic Wise and Meigs O. Frost, *A Marine Tells It to You* (New York: J. H. Sears, 1930), 138–149.

"The 'Water Torture' and Other Abuses," from "Inquiry into Occupation and Administration of Haiti and Santo Domingo" in *Hearings before a Select Committee on Haiti and Santo Domingo*, 67th Congress, 1st and 2nd sessions, Records of the U.S. Senate, vol. 2 (Washington, DC: Government Printing Office, 1922), 1117–1118, 1120–1123, 1141–1144.

"The Land of Bullet-Holes," by Harry Franck, from "The Land of Bullet-Holes" and "Santo Domingo under American Rule" in *Roaming through the West Indies* (New York: Century, 1920), 190–191, 194–196, 233–235.

"American Sugar Kingdom," by César J. Ayala, from "Vertical Integration in the Colonies" in *American Sugar Kingdom: The Plantation Economy of the Spanish Caribbean, 1898–1934* (Chapel Hill: University of North Carolina Press), 101–107. Copyright © 1999 by the University of North Carolina Press. Used by permission of the publisher.

"The Universal Negro Improvement Association in San Pedro de Macorís," by Officers and Members of the Association, unpublished letter to Rear Admiral Samuel S. Robison, San Pedro de Macorís, September 5, 1921, recipient's copy, file M-201-M-202, Records of the Office of the Chief of Naval Operations, 1975–1989, Record Group 38, National Archives, Washington, DC. Available online from Marcus Garvey Papers Project, UCLA African Studies Center, http://www.international.ucla.edu/africa/mgpp/sample11.asp. Accessed May 25, 2013.

"The Crime of Wilson," by Fabio Fiallo, from *The Crime of Wilson in Santo Domingo* (Havana: Arellano y Cia., 1940), 25–31, 64–78.

Part VII. The Era of Trujillo

"The Haitian Massacre," by eyewitnesses. These accounts appeared in Lauren Derby and Richard Turits, "TemwayajKoutKouto, 1937: Eyewitness to the Genocide" in *Revolutionary Freedoms: A History of Survival, Strength and Imagination in Haiti* (Coconut Creek, FL: Caribbean Studies Press, 2006). © 2006 Caribbean Studies Press, an imprint of Educa Vision, Inc. Reprinted with permission.

"Message to Dominican Women," by Dr. Darío Contreras, Secretary of State of Public Health and Beneficence, from "Inspirado en los ideales del benefactor de la patria: Mensaje a la mujer," presented to the Sección Femenina del Partido Trujillista, Santo Domingo, September 1942.

"The Sugar Strike of 1946," by Roberto Cassá, from *Movimiento obrero y lucha socialista en La República Dominicana (desde los orígenes hasta 1960)* (Santo Domingo: Fundación Cultural Dominicana, 1990), 445–452.

"Informal Resistance on a Dominican Sugar Plantation," by Catherine C. LeGrand, from "Informal Resistance on a Dominican Sugar Plantation during the Trujillo Dictatorship," *Hispanic American Historical Review* 75 (November 1995), 555–596. Used by permission of Duke University Press.

"Biography of a Great Leader," by Abelardo Nanita, from *Trujillo: The Biography of a Great Leader* (New York: Vantage, 1957), 31–36, 48, 96–97, 99.

"A Diplomat's Diagnosis of the Dictator," by Richard A. Johnson, from (1) "The Personality and Current Policies of Generalísimo Trujillo," 27 January 1953, file 739.11/1-2753, General Records of the State Department, Record Group 59, National Archives, College Park, MD; (2) "A Review of Political and Economic Developments in the Dominican Republic," January 8, 1954, file 739.11/1-854, General Records of the State Department, Record Group 59, National Archives, College Park, Maryland.

"A British View of the Dictatorship," by W. W. McVittie, letter to the Foreign Office, May 30, 1958, file 132044, Political Departments: General Correspondence from 1906 to 1966, FO 371, National Archives, Kew, England.

"Exile Invasions," by anonymous, from "El pueblo, no los soldados, aplastó la invasión de los barbones de Fidel Castro Ruz," *Revista de las Fuerzas Armadas*, August 1959, 30–31.

"I Am Minerva!," by Mu-Kien Adriana Sang, from *Yo soy Minerva! Confesiones más allá de la vida y de la muerte* (Santo Domingo: Amigo del Hogar, 2003). Used by permission of the author.

Part VIII. The Long Transition to Democracy

"'Basta Ya!': A Peasant Woman Speaks Out," by Aurora Rosado, from *La Era de Trujillo: Décimas, Relatos y Testimonios Campesinos* (Santo Domingo: Taller Mujeres en Desarrollo, 1989), 161–165.

"Without Begging God," by Joaquín Balaguer, previously published as "Yo" in *Tebaída Lírica: Poesías* (Santiago: F. Hermanos & Co., 1924), 7. Used by permission of La Fundación Balaguer.

"The Masters," by Juan Bosch, from "Los Amos" in *Cuentos Escritos en el exilio* (Santo Domingo: Edición Especial, 1974), 171–173. Translation by Melissa Madera.

"The Rise and Demise of Democracy," CIA Reports, 1961–1963, from "Central Intelligence Agency Weekly Summary," October 20, 1961, to September 27, 1963, Declassified CIA Files, CIA-RDP79-00927A003400010001-5 to CIA-RDP79-00927A004900010001-9, National Archives and Records Administration II, College Park, Maryland.

"Ni Mató, Ni Robó," by Juan Bosch, from interview with Juan Bosch by Lloyd N. Cutler, June 9, 1964, transcript, John F. Kennedy Library Oral History Program, John F. Kennedy Presidential Library, Boston. Available at http://www.jfklibrary .org/Asset-Viewer/Archives/JFKOH-JUB-01.aspx. Accessed May 23, 2012.

"Fashion Police," by Elías Wessin y Wessin, from the testimony of Brigadier General Elías Wessin y Wessin, in "Communist Threat to the United States Through the Caribbean," *Hearings before the Subcommittee to Investigate the Administration of the Internal Security Act and Other Internal Security Laws of the Committee on the Judiciary*, 89th Congress, 1st session. Records of the U.S. Senate (Washington, DC: Government Printing Office, 1965), 117–118.

"The Revolution of the Magi," by José Francisco Peña Gómez, from the broadcast by

José Francisco Peña Gómez during the program *Tribuna Democrática*, 1:30 P.M., January 7, 1965, in "Communist Threat to the United States through the Caribbean," *Hearings before the Subcommittee to Investigate the Administration of the Internal Security Act and Other Internal Security Laws of the Committee on the Judiciary, 89th Congress*, 89th Congress, 1st session. Records of the U.S. Senate (Washington, DC: Government Printing Office, 1965), 191.

"United States Intervention in the Revolution of 1965," by William Bennett, from telegram to Secretary of State Dean Rusk, April 28, 1965, F760007-0861, folder POL 23-9, box 2125, Central Files, General Records of the State Department, Record Group 59, National Archives and Records Administration II, College Park, Maryland.

"The President of the United States Chooses the Next President of the Dominican Republic," by Lyndon Johnson, from telephone conversation with Thomas Mann, 9:35 A.M., April 26, 1965, Recording 7362a, Lyndon Baines Johnson Presidential Library, Austin, Texas. Transcribed by Eric Paul Roorda.

"Operation Power Pack," by Lawrence A. Yates, from *Power Pack: U.S. Intervention in the Dominican Republic, 1965–1966* (Ft. Leavenworth, KS: Combat Studies Institute, U.S. Army Command and General Staff College, 1988), 121–140. Used by permission of the author.

"The Twelve Years," CIA Special Report, from "Weekly Summary Special Report: The Dominican Republic under President Joaquín Balaguer" (June 9, 1971), Declassified CIA Files, CIA-RDP85T00875R001500030024-2, National Archives and Records Administration II, College Park, Maryland.

"Why Not, Dr. Balaguer?," by Orlando Martínez, from *Microscopio* (Santo Domingo: Taller, 1980), 219–220. Originally printed in *El Nacional*, February 25, 1975.

"Dominican, Cut the Cane!," by the State Sugar Council, from an advertisement for the Consejo Estatal del Azúcar placed weekly in *Ahora!* between April and June 1973.

"The Blind Caudillo," by anonymous, from blog entry on www.joaquínbalaguer.com. Retrieved from http://www.joaquinbalaguer.com.do/Sus%20obras.htm. Accessed May 31, 2010.

"The 'Eat Alones' of the Liberation Party," by Andrés L. Mateo, from "Los Come Solos: Una Lectura" in *Las palabras perdidas* (Santo Domingo: Editora Cole, 2000), 167–172. Used by permission of the author.

"The Election of 2000," by Dominican Central Election Commission, text of a full-page advertisement published by La Junta Central Electoral de la República Dominicana in *Listín Diario, Hoy*, and other newspapers, May 15, 2000.

"The Sour Taste of US-Dominican Sugar Policy," by Matt Peterson, from "American Sugar Policy Leaves a Sour Taste," *Policy Innovations*, July 8, 2009. Available at http://www.policyinnovations.org/ideas/commentary/data/000136. Accessed January 23, 2010.

"Leonel, Fidel, and Barack," (1) by Fidel Castro, originally published as "Mi encuentro con Leonel Fernández, Presidente de la República Dominicana," *Juventud Rebelde*, March 4, 2009. Available at http://www.juventudrebelde.cu/especiales/fidel-castro/reflexiones/2009-03-05/mi-encuentro-con-leonel-fernandez-presidente-de-larepublica-dominicana/, accessed November 10, 2013; (2) "Obama Holds Joint Media Availability with Leonel Fernández of the Dominican Republic," www.whitehouse .gov video. Posted July 12, 2010, http://www.whitehouse.gov/blog/2010/07/12/president-obama-president-fernandez-meet-trade-drug-trafficking-and-haiti, accessed November 10, 2013. Transcribed by Eric Paul Roorda.

Part IX. Religious Practices

"Mercedes," by Flérida de Nolasco, from "Devociones tradicionales" and "El Santuario del Santo Cerro" in *Días de la Colonia*, by Flérida de Nolasco (Santo Domingo: Editora del Caribe, 1974), 65–67. Used by permission of Ruth Nolasco.

"Altagracia," anonymous prayer, from "Prayer to Our Lady of Altagracia, Patroness of the Dominican People," prayer card, Imprenta Librería De La Rosa, n.d., reprinted in José Labourt, *Sana, sana, culito de rana* (Santo Domingo: Taller, 1979), 36.

"The Catholic Bishops Say No to the Dictator," by the five bishops of the Dominican Republic, letter to President Dr. Joaquín Balaguer, from "Carta al Dr. Joaquín Balaguer, Presidente de la República y a los Miembros de Gabinete, contestando que no es posible dar el título de benefactor de la iglesia a Trujillo," February 6, 1961, in *Documentos de la Conferencia del Episcopado Dominicano 1955–1990*, edited by La Conferencia del Episcopado Dominicano (Santo Domingo: Comisión Dominicana Permanente para la Celebración del Quinto Centenario del Descubrimiento y Evangelización de América, 1990), 63–65. Found in the Biblioteca Digital Dominicana, Archivo General de la Nación, Santo Domingo. Used by permission of the Patronato de la Ciudad Colonial de Santo Domingo.

"Liberation Theology," by Octavio A. Beras, from "Declaración sobre la situación campesina," in *Documentos de la Conferencia del Episcopado Dominicano 1955–1990*, edited by La Conferencia del Episcopado Dominicano (Santo Domingo: Comisión Dominicana Permanente para la Celebración del Quinto Centenario del Descubrimiento y Evangelización de América, 1990), 159–160. Found in the Biblioteca Digital Dominicana, Archivo General de la Nación, Santo Domingo. Used by permission of the Patronato de la Ciudad Colonial de Santo Domingo.

"To Die in Villa Mella," by Carlos Hernández Soto, from *Morir en Villa Mella: Ritos funerarios afrodominicanos* (Santo Domingo: Centro para la Investigación y Acción Social en el Caribe, 1996), 31, 34, 40, 43, 44, 66, 71, 81, 98, 99, 100–101, 111, 113, 114, 117. Used by permission of the author.

"A Tire Blowout Gives Entry into the World of Spiritism," by Martha Ellen Davis, from "Goma explotada da entrada al mundo espiritual," *El Caribe*, June 18, 1977, 2–3. Used by permission of the author.

"Díos Olivorio Mateo: The Living God," interview with Irio Leonel Ramírez López by Lauren Derby, July 21, 2010, San Juan de la Maguana.

"Jesus Is Calling You," by Frances Jane "Fanny" Crosby, from the hymn "Jesus Is Tenderly Calling You Home" (1854).

Part X. Popular Culture

"Carnival and Holy Week," by Luis Emilio Gómez Alfau, from "Carnival" and
   "Semana Santa" in *Ayer o El Santo Domingo de Hace 50 Años* (Santo Domingo: Pol
   Hermanos, 1944), 134–135, 137–139.

"Tribulations of Dominican Racial Identity," by Silvio Torres-Saillant, from "Tribulations of Blackness: Stages in Dominican Racial Identity," *Latin American Perspectives*
   25, no. 3 (May 1998), 1–8. © 1998 by SAGE Publications. Reprinted by permission of
   SAGE Publications.

"Origins of Merengue and Musical Instruments of the Republic," by J. M. Coopersmith, from *Music and Musicians of the Dominican Republic* (Washington, DC: Pan
   American Union, 1949), 19–22.

"Dominican Music on the World Stage: Eduardo Brito," by Arístides Incháustegui,
   from "Eduardo Brito" in *El Disco en la República Dominicana* (Santo Domingo:
   Amigo del Hogar, 1988), 31–39. Used by permission of the author.

" 'The People Call All of It Merengue,' " by Johnny Ventura, from *"El Merengue en el
   Presente,"* message in the printed program of the conference *Encuentro con el Meren-
   gue* (Santo Domingo: n.p., n.d.), 21–25. Contained in the Roorda/Doyle Collection.
   Used by permission of the author.

"A *Bachata* Party," by Julio Arzeno, from *Del folklore musical dominicano* (Santo Domingo: Imprenta la Cuna de Amèrica, 1927), 102–104.

"The Tiger," by Rafael Damirón, from *De Soslayo* (Santo Domingo: Luis Sánchez
   Andujar, 1948), 104–106.

"La Montería: The Hunt for Wild Pigs and Goats," by Martha Ellen Davis, from "La
   montería, o cacería de puercos y chivos cimarrones," *Memorias de Quisqueya*, no. 2,
   January–March, 2010, 3–4. Used by permission of the author.

"Everyday Life in a Poor Barrio," by Tahira Vargas, from *De la Casa a la calle: Estudio
   de la familia y la vecindad, en un barrio de Santo Domingo* (Santo Domingo: Editora
   Búho, 1998), 93, 96, 101–106, 108–110. Used by permission of the author.

"The Name Is the Same as the Person," by José Labourt, from "El nombre es la persona misma," and "Brujos, vini-vini, pachulí y visa gringa" in *Sana, sana, culito de
   rana* (Santo Domingo: Taller, 1979), 19–21, 191–194.

" 'I Hope It Rains . . . ': Juan Luis Guerra," Juan Luis Guerra concert set list, Centro
   Olímpico, Santo Domingo. Transcribed by Eric Paul Roorda.

Part XI. The Dominican Diaspora

"The First Immigrant to Manhattan, 1613: Jan Rodrigues," by Crew Members of the
   Jonge Tobias and *Fortuyn*, from "Declarations of some members of the crew of Adriaen Block's and Thijs Volckertsz. Mossel's ships," August 20, 1613, Notarial Archives
   197, pp. 614v–615, and "Declarations of crew members of the ship the *'Fortuyn,'*
   master Hendrick Christiaensen," July 23, 1614, Notarial Archives 198, pp. 97, 97v,
   98, both recorded by Notary Jan Fransz. Bruyninch, City Archives of Amsterdam,
   published in *The Prehistory of the New Netherland Company*, compiled by Simon Hart

and translated by Rosalie L. Colie (Amsterdam: City of Amsterdam Press, 1959), 75, 80. Used by permission of the City of Amsterdam.

"Player to Be Named Later: Osvaldo/Ossie/Ozzie Virgil, First Dominican Major Leaguer," by Enrique Rojas, from "50 Years Ago, Ozzie Virgil Made Baseball History," *ESPNdeportes.com*, September 22, 2006. Reprinted by permission of ESPN. Available at http://www.sports.espn.go.com/espn/hispanichistory/news/story?id=2598606. Accessed November 7, 2010.

"The Dominican Dandy: Juan Marichal," by Rob L. Ruck, reprinted from "The Dominican Dandy" in *The Tropic of Baseball: Baseball in the Dominican Republic* by Rob L. Ruck, by permission of the University of Nebraska Press. Copyright 1991 by Meckler Publications. Afterword Copyright 1998 by the University of Nebraska Press.

"The Queen of Merengue," interview with Milly Quezada by Alex Huezo, Los Angeles, March 2011.

"Dominican Hip-Hop in Spain," interview with Arianna Puello by Alex Huezo, Los Angeles, January 2011.

"Black Women Are Confusing, but the Hair Lets You Know," by Ginetta Candelario, from "Black Women Are Confusing but the Hair Lets You Know": Perceiving the Boundaries of Dominicanidad" in *Black behind the Ears: Dominican Racial Identity from Museums to Beauty Shops* (Durham, NC: Duke University Press, 2007), 223–255.

"*Los Dominicanyorks*," by Luis Guarnizo, from "*Los Dominicanyorks*: The Making of a Binational Society," *Annals of the American Academy of Political and Social Science* 533 (May 1994), 70–86. © 1998 by SAGE Publications. Reprinted by permission of SAGE Publications.

"The *Yola*," by Milagros Ricourt, from "Reaching the Promised Land: Undocumented Dominican Migration to Puerto Rico," *Centro Journal* 19, no. 2 (fall 2007), 226–238.

"The Dominican Who Won the Kentucky Derby," from interviews conducted with Joel Rosario, Kenneth Ramsey, and Michael Maker by Eric Paul Roorda, Louisville, Kentucky, June 15 and 16, 2013.

"You Know You're Dominican . . . ," by anonymous, from a collection of "dominican-ismos" based on an ongoing Internet meme, compiled by Eric Paul Roorda.

Every reasonable effort has been made to obtain permission. We invite copyright holders to inform us of any oversights.

Index